W9-DEJ-669

The Gods
and Symbols
of Ancient Mexico
and the Maya

MARY MILLER AND KARL TAUBE

The Gods
and Symbols
of Ancient Mexico
and the Maya

An Illustrated Dictionary of
Mesoamerican Religion

260 illustrations

THAMES AND HUDSON

For Michael D. Coe

Frontispiece:
The Aztec Calendar Stone found beneath the
central plaza of Mexico City. The monument is
not a fully functioning calendar, but
commemorates the five mythical world-creations
(the Five Suns).

First published in the United States in 1993 by
Thames and Hudson Inc., 500 Fifth Avenue,
New York, New York 10110

Library of Congress Catalog Card Number
92–80338

Printed and bound in Singapore

Contents

Reader's Guide

The Gods and Symbols of Ancient Mexico and the Maya offers the reader at any level an introduction to Mesoamerica and its religious principles. The dictionary entries are organized alphabetically and include both discursive commentary and encapsulated identifications, ranging from concepts and ideas, ritual practices and participants, to particular deities, objects, symbols, flora and fauna, natural phenomena, and sacred places. Through topical investigations, the reader can review conceptual questions, while dozens of line drawings and brief texts provide quick guides to identifying Mesoamerican gods and their symbols. Cross-references appear in text in SMALL CAPITALS. A Subject Index following the Introduction guides the reader to entries of particular interest and groups information otherwise scattered alphabetically, such as "Maya deities."

We offer the reader two introductory essays, one a cultural history of Mesoamerica and the other a conceptual overview of Mesoamerican religion. In general, we have made direct citations in this book only from 16th c. sources, and we have tried to attribute important post-1950 discoveries to those responsible. We provide a bibliographic essay (Guide to Sources) as well as a bibliography, not only to document the sources for this book but also to explain the complicated history of the sources themselves.

Mesoamericans today speak many languages (not "dialects," as they are often called erroneously), as did their Precolumbian predecessors. Although no single set of rules can govern all pronunciation, we offer some guidelines. Most standard transcriptions were devised by Spanish speakers, so without other indications, all vowels and most consonants should be pronounced as they are in Spanish. *U* before another vowel has the sound of *w*, and the entry title UAY is pronounced roughly like the English word *why*. In 16th c. Spain, *x* had the sound of English *sh*, and so it should be pronounced in most native words in this book. Most *c*'s, regardless of the following vowel, are hard.

In Nahuatl, the language of Central Mexico, the stress usually falls on the penultimate syllable, as it does the Tenoch*tit*lan, while Mayan words generally take a final stress. The final *l* in many Nahuatl words is very soft and often vanishes when words are borrowed by European languages. The Nahuatl *tomatl*, for example, has become the Spanish *tomate* and the English *tomato*.

Maya*n* is used to refer to language; otherwise, the adjective or noun Maya is used. Mayan languages include both glottalized and unglottalized consonants, an unfamiliar concept to English speakers but present in the speech of those who swallow the double *t*'s of *little*, for example. The difference between glottalized and non-glottalized consonants in Mayan languages distinguishes altogether different words. In the orthography that we use, the glottalized consonants are as follows:

non-glottalized	*glottalized*
c	k
ch	ch'
tz	dz
p	p'
t	t'

Because plurals are formed in different manners in the various Mesoamerican languages, we have followed the English practice of adding *s* to form them, except when we are dealing with a deity name. A single member of the *tzitzimime*, dreaded Central Mexican star demons, for example, would be a *tzitzimimitl*.

Acknowledgments

When we began this project, we chose to write on separate topics, ranging throughout the alphabet. As we have written the book we have learned a great deal from each other, and we hope that the resulting text reviews not only agreed-upon points of view but opens up some new questions for Mesoamerica. We thank our colleagues who have generously shared their photographs and drawings with us. We add a special acknowledgment of Mary Miller's daughter Alice, born with the writing of SERPENT, before Mary could finish the alphabet.

Masonry ballcourts are one of the defining features of Mesoamerican civilization. (*Above*) A ballcourt at the Classic Maya site of Copán in Honduras. (*Below*) A Classic period Zapotec ballcourt at Monte Albán, Oaxaca.

Introduction

Mesoamerican Culture and Chronology

Archaeologists, anthropologists, and art historians use the term Mesoamerica to describe the known world of the Aztecs in 1519. It encompasses much of modern Mexico – as far north as the old Aztec frontier with the Chichimecs or "barbarians," where non-agricultural, nomadic peoples lived – and the Maya realm in eastern Mexico, Guatemala, Belize, and the western strip of Honduras and El Salvador, and on down through Nicaragua, incorporating the Nicoya Peninsula of Costa Rica. Sharing a constellation of beliefs and practices, highly developed civilizations among different cultures and ethnic groups first rose in Mesoamerica around 1000 BC and then thrived off and on for 3000 years. What makes them all part of a Mesoamerican tradition are such things as use of the unusual 260-day calendar, a rubber ballgame played in an alley defined by two parallel structures, and use of cement made by burning limestone or shells, as well as many more subtle patterns of life and belief. Mesoamericans never saw themselves as a unity, and indeed, no single dominant culture ever imposed unity on them, but they were interested in each other, in their various pasts, and even, in some cases, in leaving a record for the future.

Early Settlement

The early peopling and settlement of the Americas remains obscure. Certainly by 15,000 years ago, waves of people had crossed the Bering Strait during times of low water, and by 10,000 years ago people were living within the bounds of Mesoamerica. The first widespread reliable evidence for humans in the Western Hemisphere comes around 12,000 years ago, with the makers of flint and other stone fluted points called Clovis. For some 3,000 years, nomadic hunters migrated into Mesoamerica, perhaps in search of megafauna, and archaeologists have found human remains with those of the long-extinct mammoth. Generations later, humans would domesticate small animals, including the dog and turkey, but no large mammals would be available for domestication.

Around 7000 BC, the New World began to dry out. At this point, during what is called the Archaic, people in Mesoamerica slowly shifted their way of life, as many animal species vanished from the planet and humans adapted to the warmer, drier environment. The domestication of major foodstuffs in Mesoamerica accompanied and fueled the impulse to settled life, eventually supporting the development and growth of civilization. A primitive but domesticated maize can be documented by 3500 BC. Waves of migration continued after the onset of sedentary life. The Nahuatl-speaking peoples of Central Mexico may have been among the latest arrivals. When they migrated south, they left their linguistic cousins among the Uto-Aztecan language group behind, largely within the borders of the United States and Canada. The Aztecs spoke Nahuatl, as did their predecessors, the Toltecs, and although

		CENTRAL MEXICO	OAXACA	GULF COAST	WEST MEXICO	MAYA HIGHLANDS/ PACIFIC COAST	LOWLAND MAYA South	LOWLAND MAYA North
1519	LATE POSTCLASSIC	*Tenochtitlan* *Tlaxcala* (Aztecs)	Mixtec independent kingdom	Aztecs	Tarascans	Maya independent city-states *Mixco Viejo, Iximché, Utatlán*	*Tayasal* (Itzá)	*Tulum* *Sta Rita*
1200		*Tula* (Toltecs)						*Mayapán*
	EARLY POSTCLASSIC		*Mitla* *Yagul*	Huastecs				*Chichen Itzá* (Toltec Maya)
900	TERMINAL CLASSIC	*Xochicalco*				*Cotzumalhuapa*		
		Cacaxtla	Monte Albán IIIb	Classic Veracruz			*Palenque, Tikal, Yaxchilán*	Puuc and Central Yucatán
600	LATE CLASSIC			*Remojadas* (El Tajín)				
	EARLY CLASSIC	*Teotihuacan Phases I–IV*	Monte Albán IIIa	*Cerro de las Mesas*	*Ixtlán del Rio*	*Kaminaljuyú* *Escuintla*	*Tikal, Uaxactún, Río Azul*	*Izamal Dzibilchaltún*
300								
	PROTO-CLASSIC		Monte Albán II		*Chupícuaro*	*Izapa, Kaminaljuyú,*	*Cerros*	
AD								
BC			*Tres Zapotes*		*Colima*	*Abaj Takalik*		
		Cuicuilco						
300	LATE FORMATIVE							
			Dainzú Monte Albán I	*La Venta*			*El Mirador Nakbé*	
600	MIDDLE FORMATIVE	*Tlatilco*		(Olmecs)				
900				*San Lorenzo*				
	EARLY FORMATIVE				*Xochipala* *Capacha*	*Ocos*		
1500								
	ARCHAIC							

Chronological chart for Mesoamerica.

linguists disagree about the language of Teotihuacan – the single largest city in Mesoamerica during the first millennium AD – it may well have been the first important Nahuatl civilization.

Timescales

Archaeologists and anthropologists have divided the chronology of Mesoamerica and assigned terminology to the various periods. During the Archaic (7000–2000 BC) people gradually domesticated plants, especially the important foodstuffs maize, beans, squash, chili peppers, and avocados, as well as animals, particularly the turkeys and dogs already mentioned, although others were hunted to extinction as village life took root. The Formative period – also known as the Preclassic – is defined as beginning with the introduction of pottery and settled life *c.* 2000 BC. (Early pottery manufacture is known in Colombia and Ecuador, and even earlier reports have now been offered from the Amazon; pottery technology may have been slowly diffused from South America.) The Formative era ushers in the first high civilizations in Mesoamerica – the Olmec and Zapotec – and ends around 100 BC.

During the Protoclassic, roughly 100 BC–AD 300, the patterns for the great Classic cultures began to be established. The Classic, AD 300–900, roughly coincides with the flourishing of Teotihuacan in highland Mexico and the Maya cities in lowland Yucatán, Guatemala, and Belize, although by AD 300, Teotihuacan was a fully blossoming culture, while the Maya were still nascent. Scholars introduced the term Classic to describe the Maya at Tikal, Palenque, Copán and elsewhere, peoples who were falsely believed to have dwelt in a peaceful realm under an idyllic theocracy. Investigators also called contemporary states at Monte Albán and Teotihuacan theocracies; the term "Classic" itself initially carried a value judgment that equated these civilizations with the achievements of the Classical Greeks. We use it in this book without prejudice to describe the time period AD 300–900 and note that it – and other periodizations – inaccurately suggest a cultural lockstep throughout Mesoamerica. The term Terminal Classic is used here to refer to the last century of the Classic era, when Teotihuacan had already fallen into decline and many Maya cities faltered. New stars rose and fell quickly during the Terminal Classic, including such significant developments as those at Cacaxtla and Xochicalco. During the Early Postclassic, AD 900–1200, the Toltecs dominated the Mesoamerican picture. Although the Aztecs are the featured players of Mesoamerica during the Late Postclassic (1200 to the Spanish Conquest), the Maya, Totonacs, Huastecs, Mixtecs, and Tarascans all remained important.

Topography and Trade

Rugged, high mountain chains run north to south along the eastern and western sides of Mesoamerica and then cut across its middle, cinching it like a belt studded with volcanoes, from the Valley of Mexico to the Isthmus of Tehuantepec. Mesoamerica offers every possible ecological niche of the tropics, from hot, dry or wet, to cooler, drier highlands, including in between the rare cloud forest, where tropical vegetation flourishes at 3000–4000 feet (900–1200 meters) of altitude, offering the ideal environment for the quetzal, a bird known throughout Mesoamerica and held precious for its brilliant blue-green plumage. Although no quetzal ever flew near the cool and high (7500 feet, 2300 meters) capital of the Aztecs at Tenochtitlan, quetzal feathers formed their most prized headdresses. Some Maya kings were known as *kuk*, the Maya word for quetzal, and on the eve of the Spanish Conquest, Quetzalcoatl, one of the greatest and oldest gods in Mesoamerica, was known throughout the region. His very name suggests the opposition of air and earth (*quetzal* = bird, *coatl* = snake), the duality that characterized Mesoamerican life and religion.

Few Mesoamerican civilizations integrated the sharply varying environments of the region, and the differing resources offered keen opportunities for trade. The

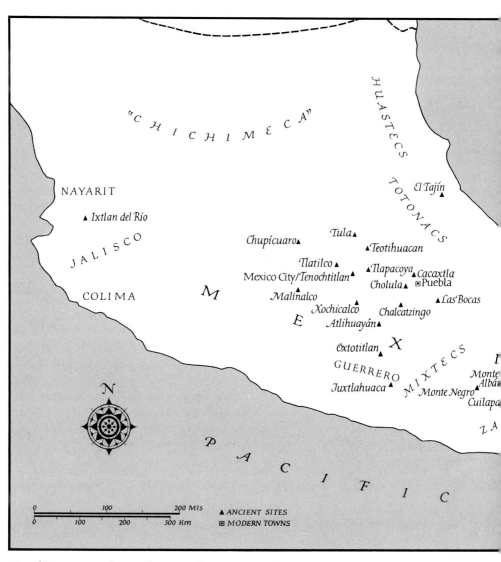

Map of Mesoamerica showing the principal sites mentioned in the text.

Aztecs lived too high for cotton to grow, and so the cotton mantle functioned as a
standard of exchange in their dominion. On his last voyage to the New World,
Christopher Columbus encountered Maya traders plying the waters off Honduras
in ocean-going canoes piled high with woven cottons, part of the vast web of
Mesoamerican trade and tribute about which relatively little is known. Throughout
Mesoamerica, highland obsidian from volcanic flows commanded high values, since
all households sought blades from this "steel" of the native New World. And
wherever volcanoes erupted, they renewed and enriched the soil. Today coffee
plantations have generally replaced tracts of cacao trees and vanilla orchids that
once flourished along the Pacific Coast of Guatemala and Chiapas and in Veracruz,

but cacao beans once functioned as a near-currency throughout Mesoamerica. How tempting to imagine such edible money!

Technology

By the time of the Spanish Conquest, Mesoamerican technology had progressed to what archaeologists call "New Stone Age," in that some metals were worked but played little practical role as tools. Copper axes were a relatively recent phenomenon; stone axes and flint knives, along with diverse obsidian blades, were the main tools with which generations of people had quarried stone, cut flesh and hide, and brought down the forest. The gold and silver that so astonished the European invaders formed religious works or jewelry; the Europeans were equally astonished by the greater value Mesoamericans attributed to jade. Blue-green, like the most precious things of the Mesoamerican world (quetzal feathers or maize foliage or water), jade symbolized preciousness. The hardest stone commonly known in Mesoamerica, jade also signified permanence, and when Maya nobles died, they carried such a bead in their mouth to enter the Underworld.

Throughout the world, the wheel often played a role in religious imagery, but in Mesoamerica (as in the rest of the New World), no wheel was ever developed for mundane purposes – although graves in Veracruz have yielded wheeled toy-like objects – perhaps because of the absence of draft animals. Today, as in Prehispanic times, in many regions men and women are the beasts of burden, and Mesoamerican people carry heavy loads on their backs with tumplines stretched across their foreheads.

Defining Mesoamerican Civilization

What distinguishes civilization from what has gone before it? Is it exploitation of new resources, or competition to control them? Is civilization initiated by new ideological concepts or only heightened by them? Are newly expanded populations a requirement for civilization, or its by-product? In a world so technologically simple as Mesoamerica, does technology play a role in its "take-off"?

Anthropologists offer no single answer – although they would check yes to a number of the queries offered above – nor do they agree on its causes. Despite their differences, they usually agree that complex culture in Mesoamerica began to take shape during the Formative period, in both the Olmec region and in Oaxaca, with the development of what are usually called chiefdoms. What marks the rise of complex culture in Mesoamerica is the emergence of recognizable shared practices and principles at several locations and the subsequent subscription to them by others at yet more distant locations. Through long-distance trade, early Mesoamericans began to recognize the extent of their world. Through surpluses amassed (probably through trade or warfare), some families began to have what we call wealth, that is, the wherewithal to devote themselves to activities outside food production, and the first surviving works of art give evidence of that leisure time. Through shared religious practices, the efficacy of the gods became manifest. Through both ancestor worship and a desire to leave a record for posterity, they began to record linear time. Once they sought permanence in the materials they transformed, they left a record that modern people can consider evidence of a complex society, or, in ordinary language, civilization.

At the end of the Formative period, early states developed, with special hierarchies among administrative centers, towns, and hamlets. States gather a surplus from tribute or tax, and they use force to back up their sanctions against reluctant contributors. They also develop systems of notation. A surplus can support full-time specialists who give up agricultural endeavors and devote themselves to the arts or religion. Although anthropologists agree that state-level political organization characterizes civilization, the charismatic complex culture of the Olmecs is more baffling, partly because we know so little about their political organization. They made small cities, but we do not know whether they functioned as city-states, like those of the later Maya. They traveled long distances, presumably to seek precious trade goods, but did they use force?

The Olmec Enigma

The Olmecs emerged about 1200 BC along the slow-moving rivers of lowland Veracruz and Tabasco, when people first began to make a permanent record of gods and rulers, with a standardized means of codification, in the ceremonial precincts of their settlements. The ethnic identity of these early people now dubbed the Olmecs remains unknown (although some have speculated that they may have spoken a Mixe-Zoquean or Mayan language), and in the absence of archaeological data, the size and extent of their cities or sites is also a blank. Earlier Mesoamerican peoples must surely have worshipped a complex range of gods, but it was not until the time of the Olmecs that schematic representations came to portray specific gods and god-complexes. Incised flame eyebrows on a small pot might cue the observer to a powerful sky-dragon, and the symbol could reach beyond both local time and geography. What distinguishes the Olmec civilization is its making of a permanent record of religion and ritual that can be recognized today. The nature of Olmec civilization remains obscured by time and lack of preservation, but it clearly offered unifying religious principles and a model for emulation by peoples all across Mesoamerica.

For a thousand years or so and across a broad and varied geography the Olmecs communicated using a standard notation for symbols and gods, most of which has so far proved impenetrable. The complexity itself suggests the rise of priests and shamans, specialists who manipulated and interpreted the system and who could make manifest religious experience and share it with a broader populace. One imagines that the Olmecs had developed a systematic cosmology to explain creation, the origins of humankind, and the movement of heavenly bodies, and they seem to have used the human body as a metaphor of the cosmos. Living in the tropical rain forest, the Olmecs identified with the powerful animals that, like humans, occupied the top of the food chain – felines, eagles, caimans, and snakes – and recognized that they shared with them the consumption of flesh. And they first gave permanence to practices and preoccupations that endured in Mesoamerica – human sacrifice, bloodletting, pilgrimages, quadripartite division of the world, cave rituals, the offering of caches, and a fascination with mirrors among them – until the Spanish Conquest, and in some cases long afterward.

Three major Olmec sites are known for the Gulf Coast lowlands: San Lorenzo, La Venta, and Laguna de los Cerros. San Lorenzo thrived first, probably by 1200 BC, and suffered what seems to have been brutal destruction c. 900 BC, about the time La Venta began to flourish. No certain data are available for Laguna de los Cerros, as yet unexcavated. All three sites share layouts based on bilateral symmetry, a preoccupation of Olmec art and symbolism as well, in which mirror images fall along a central axis. La Venta features the first pyramidal form of Mesoamerican architecture, what is perhaps a radial pyramid but which has also been interpreted as a volcano effigy. At La Venta the Olmecs buried pavements and caches following a pattern along the central axis; at San Lorenzo, basalt sculptures were interred along the edges of a vast ceremonial platform. The Olmecs carved huge thrones (dubbed "altars" by early scholars) from which lords presumably ruled; the Olmecs commemorated their powerful lords with portraits in colossal heads. Olmec stone sculpture achieved a high, naturalistic plasticity, yet it has no surviving prototypes, as if this powerful ability to represent both nature and abstract concepts was a native invention of this early civilization.

Early in the first millennium BC, the Olmecs forged connections across Mesoamerica, from Central America to western Mexico, perhaps in search of scarce highland resources, particularly jade, from which they carved precious objects. By 900 BC, the nascent Maya civilization at Copán made imitations of Olmec ceramics and jade. In western Mexico, the Olmecs encountered a sophisticated culture at Xochipala, where naturalistic human figures had been made after 1500 BC. Later, coeval with La Venta, the Olmecs covered the giant rock outcropping at Chalcatzingo, Morelos, with depictions of their lords and gods. Olmec-style petroglyphs also mark the cliffs of highland Guatemala and Chiapas, further suggesting Olmec contacts in the Maya region. They established a highland center at Teopantecuanitlan, Guerrero; Olmec artists also made paintings celebrating cave rituals at Cacahuazqui, Juxtlahuaca, and Oxtotitlan. In Central Mexico, the Olmecs encountered communities with well-developed traditions of figurine manufacture at Tlatilco and elsewhere. These places subsequently adopted Olmec forms and imagery and in modern times have yielded the finest Olmec ceramic sculpture, particularly large hollow "babies."

The Early Zapotecs and Their Contemporaries

By 600 BC, if not earlier, civilization also rose in Oaxaca among the Zapotecs, who began to reshape the hillside acropolis of Monte Albán into their capital. The Zapotecs early on dominated the region and commemorated their victories by recording dates in the 260-day calendar and depicting captives with what are probably their names and places of origin on buildings such as the so-called Temple of the Danzantes ("Dancers") at Monte Albán. The Zapotecs probably invented Mesoamerican writing, and they may also have devised the first systems for recording time. At the end of the Formative era, the Zapotecs constructed Mound J at Monte

Mound J at Monte Albán, Oaxaca. Possibly an observatory, the structure features walls covered with more than 50 carved slabs describing the conquests of the early Zapotecs.

Albán (and at least one other similar building at Caballito Blanco), an unusual pointer-shaped building, possibly an observatory oriented toward the rise of the star Capella on the night of the first zenith passage. These buildings probably confirm knowledge of a large body of star lore.

Toward the end of the Formative era, from 100 BC to AD 300 or what is also termed the Protoclassic, many of the principles and beliefs common to Classic-period civilization appear to have come together, particularly along the axis of the Isthmus of Tehuantepec and ranging from Atlantic to Pacific Coasts, at places as far-flung as Monte Albán, Dainzú, Tres Zapotes, La Mojarra, Chiapa de Corzo, Izapa, and Kaminaljuyú. Across the region, the Principal Bird Deity – probably the same as Vucub Caquix of the *Popol Vuh* (the native epic of the Quiché Maya transcribed into the Roman alphabet at the time of the Conquest) – gained prominence; the *Popol Vuh* account of origins, humanity's relationship to chaos, and the Hero Twins' harrowing of the Underworld, may have been widely subscribed to.

Tres Zapotes in the Olmec Gulf Coast heartland may have flourished about the time of La Venta, and also exhibits some late Olmec colossal heads, but the site experienced continued occupation into the Protoclassic, and old Olmec concepts underlay the foundation of new Mesoamerican ones shared from Oaxaca to Honduras. Working at Tres Zapotes in the 1930s, Matthew Stirling found part of what seemed to him to be a date written in the place-notational calendar generally called the Long Count and most prevalent among the later Maya. Although Tres Zapotes Stela C lacked its first number glyph, Stirling correlated the date to 32 BC, and subsequent discovery of the upper fragment confirmed his reading. Other early Long Count dates occur at Chiapa de Corzo, on the Tuxtla Statuette, and on La Mojarra Stela 1, which bears two dates in the second century AD and which depicts a standing lord wearing the Principal Bird Deity headdress and adorned in regalia like that of later Maya kings. Together, these and other examples give evidence of the development of a new eastern Mesoamerican tradition that emphasized dynastic rule and a method of recording time and space permanently using calendrics and phonetic writing. In this way, linear time as well as cyclical time gained prominence. Phonetic writing was refined and elaborated by the Maya, but even in its earliest appearance, it probably allowed the rough replication of speech.

The Protoclassic Maya

It is the special characteristic of their writing that sets the Maya apart from all other Mesoamerican peoples. It is probably the technology of writing itself that enabled them to be what they were. Had the Maya flourished at a single center, say, at Tikal – as Teotihuacan civilization had done at Teotihuacan or Zapotec civilization at Monte Albán – they would not seem so extraordinary to us. But it was their ability to communicate across distance and through time, to remember a particular history and to write for posterity, that allowed dozens of cities and towns to subscribe to a single reigning belief system.

At Protoclassic Izapa, the Maya broadcast their religious ideology on stelae and on pairs of altars and stelae, presenting the first public confirmation of certain gods – Chac, for example – and the rich narrative of the *Popol Vuh*, as well as of certain concepts, such as the World Tree. At Abaj Takalik, stelae depict single and paired lords adorned with the regalia of rulership and accompanying texts, of which only dates can be read. Kaminaljuyú lords commissioned their portraits in the costume of the Principal Bird Deity and received rich offerings when subsequently interred.

A single Kaminaljuyú slab depicts a sequence of enthroned lords and kneeling captives suggestive of a genealogy. Giant toad sculptures there may indicate the incorporation of the toad in religious ritual. Perhaps aided by the new technology of writing, Maya speakers in disparate locations all began to recognize shared religious imagery and the cult of the ruler.

At sites all across the Maya lowlands in the Protoclassic, but especially as known from archaeology at El Mirador, Nakbé, Uaxactún, and Cerros, the Maya began to build huge pyramidal structures and cover their main façades with stucco ornament shaped to represent the heads of various deities. These configurations fall into no uniform cosmogram but vary from place to place. Jaguars, probably representing the night sun, often occur on the lowest level, with the Principal Bird Deity on top; at Uaxactún, at least one early pyramid is configured as a sacred mountain, or Uitz, from which maize issues. At the end of the Protoclassic, some Maya sites, including El Mirador and Cerros, suffered near-abandonment.

Although most known West Mexican art derives from looted tombs in the states of Jalisco, Colima, and Nayarit (which have given their names to related but distinct styles of ceramic forms), a few careful excavations place the height of ceremonial activity and use of the shaft tombs during the Protoclassic. Recent excavation and survey at Ixtlán del Río, Nayarit, and highland Jalisco indicate that West Mexico participated in Mesoamerican ceremonialism during the period, particularly in the construction of vast platforms and round structures.

The Rise of Teotihuacan

During the Protoclassic, two large centers emerged in Central Mexico, Cuicuilco and Teotihuacan, but the latter gained prominence after volcanic eruptions buried Cuicuilco and its massive round platform by AD 100. Teotihuacan thrived, and by AD 250, many of its most famous buildings, including the Pyramids of the Sun, Moon, and Quetzalcoatl, rose from the high, arid city, following a rigid grid. Paintings of supernatural beings and religious practices covered the walls of shrines, temples, and dwellings. Archaeologists have supposed that Teotihuacan may have held some 200,000 souls at its peak in the Classic era, many of whom lived within the closed apartment compounds that filled the interstices of the grid. Although the presence of "foreigners" – in particular, an enclave of Zapotecs – can be discerned in the archaeological record of Teotihuacan, the ethnic identity of the Teotihuacanos remains unknown, although various Nahua speakers, Totonacs, and Otomis have all been named as candidates.

The tradition of Teotihuacan is what we can call western Mesoamerican, and it emphasizes community over dynastic rule, cyclical time over linear, and offers a separate religious pantheon from that of the Maya and other peoples in eastern Mesoamerica. In fact, an explosion of new iconography and beliefs characterizes early Teotihuacan, developing essentially *ex nihilo*. During the Early Classic, the Maya and Teotihuacanos became keenly aware of one another and their separate religious practices. The Maya adopted many Teotihuacan practices, particularly the cult of war, its patrons and regalia, while ignoring others, such as its many female deities. The Teotihuacanos surely knew of and recognized the flexibility of the Maya writing system, but they chose not to adapt it to their own needs: in fact, they may have banished it from their city, and the recently documented paintings from Techinantitla that feature isolated glyphs, probably names of people and places, may only prove the point by demonstrating how different Teotihuacan writing is.

Aerial view of the great city of Teotihuacan, with the Pyramid of the Moon in the foreground, and the Pyramid of the Sun in the center.

Although the ceremonial precinct of Teotihuacan was ravaged by fires c. AD 725, the city was still occupied for many generations, and even after its abandonment it held a place in the religious imagery of all subsequent Central Mexican civilizations. The Aztecs conceived of it as the setting of cosmogonic events, and Motecuhzoma II made pilgrimages there.

The Classic Zapotecs and Classic Veracruz
All Mesoamerica flourished during the Classic era. Monte Albán grew in both scale and population: temples ringed the ceremonial precinct and a powerful nobility inhabited adjoining palaces. Particularly important persons received interment in underground tombs that sometimes bore elaborate paintings. Ceramic urns featuring the Zapotec pantheon accompanied the dead, as did abundant vessels for food and drink. Stone stelae at Monte Albán show what may be Zapotec rulers and some examples depict Teotihuacan visitors, characterized by distinct costume. Although never completely abandoned, Monte Albán fell into disrepair during the Postclassic,

and the Mixtecs emptied out old Zapotec tombs and reused them for their own noble dead.

No single city dominated the Gulf Coast during the Classic era, nor did competing centers display a unity of belief and ritual, although modern understanding of the region has been hampered by rampant looting and insufficient archaeology. In much of southern Veracruz, at places like Las Remojadas, thousands of "smiling" figurines have been exhumed; other sites have yielded life-size hollow ceramic tomb sculptures. Dramatic paintings of bloodletting have been uncovered at Las Higueras.

To the north, El Tajín dominated the region, particularly during the Late Classic, under the Huastecs, who spoke a Mayan language. Acres of temples and palaces survive. The Pyramid of the Niches at El Tajín features 365 empty niches, perhaps a calendrical reference, although other buildings use varied niche configurations. Ballcourts and ballgame paraphernalia abound, and architectural sculpture illustrates the playing of the game and human sacrifice.

The Classic Maya

In the 3rd c. AD, the Maya cities in the tropical lowlands continued to thrive under dynastic kings. As demonstrated archaeologically at Tikal, the portraits of individual rulers were carved on stone monuments with accompanying texts that glorified their reign, and competing Maya dynasties emerged at Uaxactún, Xultún, Río Azul, and elsewhere in the Petén; by AD 500, Caracol, Copán, Yaxchilán, Piedras Negras, Bonampak, Calakmul and other cities emerged as the centers of small but ambitious polities. Tikal may well have been the first dynasty to exploit the ideology and technology of warfare promulgated by Teotihuacan when it took hold of power at Uaxactún. Maya rulers began to record their victories, parentage, and the passage of time itself on their monuments. Archaeologists had long used the 6th c. lapse in hieroglyphic inscriptions at Tikal to divide Early from Late Classic; that lapse has now been explained by the ignominious defeat of Tikal by Caracol in a six-year war, an event proudly recorded by Caracol upon its culmination in 562. Although Tikal recovered its economic well-being by the 8th c., its ruling family was apparently rent by the defeat, and, after establishing themselves in the Petexbatún, one competing branch caused Tikal plenty of trouble.

During the 8th c., the Maya nobility experienced both unparalleled wealth and unprecedented problems. All across the region, polity fought with polity, kings fell captive and suffered sacrifice. Populations grew rapidly and degraded the environment in desperate attempts to cultivate sufficient food. At the end of the 8th c. and over the course of the 9th c., ceremonial precincts fell into disrepair and abandonment in what has been called the Classic Maya collapse; populations shrank, although the entire region was still populated at the time of the Conquest. During the 9th c., Maya kings at Uxmal and elsewhere in the Puuc hills commissioned elaborate buildings before these, too, suffered abandonment.

To modern viewers, Maya cities often seem a baffling web of rambling structures punctuated by tall pyramids, all laid out randomly across the tropical landscape. Maya cities lack streets and later buildings overlie earlier ones, further complicating the picture. But these buildings bear fundamental meanings and many had specific uses. Most tall pyramidal buildings house tombs underneath them (the Temple of Inscriptions at Palenque and Temple I at Tikal are the best-known examples), enshrining ancestors and revealing the Maya cult of ancestor worship, which in practice may have been the primary form of religious devotion. And, particularly

(*Top* and *above*) The Temple of
the Inscriptions at Palenque
contained the tomb of the Late
Classic Maya king, Pacal. The
cutaway view illustrates the
stairway leading down to the
tomb. (*Left*) Temple I at Tikal in
Guatemala also housed a major
tomb, in this case of the Late
Classic Ruler A. Here, however,
as was the case with most Maya
tombs, the burial chamber lacked
a stairway.

Late Classic polychrome mural from Cacaxtla, Tlaxcala. Standing on a Feathered Serpent, the figure is clad in a bird costume and carries a ceremonial bar.

as revealed by painted ceramics of the Late Classic period and in the Bonampak murals, a burgeoning Maya elite lived rich and abundant lives within their palaces where they engaged in courtly arts, including writing and painting.

The Terminal Classic
The decline of both Teotihuacan and the Maya cities left a power vacuum in Mesoamerica by the 9th c. Regional cultures flourished at Xochicalco, Cholula, and Cacaxtla in the Mexican highlands; profoundly affected by foreign influence, the Maya city of Seibal underwent a renewal; although El Tajín, too, went into decline along the Gulf Coast, the Huastecs flourished, as did Zapotecs south of Monte Albán, at Mitla and Yagul. The period seems to have been a time of great interregional interchange, and both Maya iconography and formal concepts became part of a new Mesoamerican synthesis that may have been possible only with the demise of Teotihuacan. By 900, however, a new force had appeared on the scene: the Toltecs.

The Early Postclassic: Tula and Chichen Itzá
From their high, arid, cool capital of Tula (or Tollan), the Toltecs took on aspects of the Teotihuacan heritage that served their purposes. They adopted many of their

gods, left little evidence of public writing, and like the Teotihuacanos, lived in palace compounds. Of all Mesoamerican traders, the Toltecs are perhaps the most legendary: they forayed into the far north, to what is now the American Southwest, to trade for turquoise, but they established their most profound contacts with the Maya at Chichen Itzá in northern Yucatán and capitalized on the integration of Mesoamerica.

Around the year 900, Chichen Itzá rose to new prominence and may well have been the largest city in Mesoamerica. Its Sacred Cenote was one of the most important pilgrimage destinations of the ancient Mesoamerican world. Whether through voluntary alliance or through domination by one culture of the other, the Toltecs and Maya developed new forms of architecture and sculpture – including *chacmools* (stone sculptures of reclining human forms that received human sacrifices) and serpent columns – that flourished at both cities. Whereas the old Maya order invested its power in the individual ruler and his or her cult, at Chichen and Tula it is the position and power of the warrior-king, rather than his lineage and portrait, that holds sway. As a result, ruler portraits vanished from Chichen, to be replaced by carved thrones, on which any suitable candidate might sit. Mayan hieroglyphic texts nevertheless record the names of those who ruled in the period. At Tula, perhaps initially a major receptor for Maya ideology, ruler portraits on stone slabs were tried before the practice was abandoned. Although heart sacrifice was known to the earlier Maya, at Chichen Itzá it took on new ritual force after its introduction in the Toltec era.

Like all centers of Mesoamerican civilizations, Chichen and Tula eventually both fell into decline, and by no later than the 12th c., Mesoamerica entered a period when no major city or culture exerted much influence beyond its local region. At Mayapan, Maya lords built a walled city and reigned for almost two centuries. In

Reconstruction drawing of the Early Postclassic site of Chichen Itzá, Yucatán. The Sacred Cenote, from which the site took its name, is depicted in the foreground.

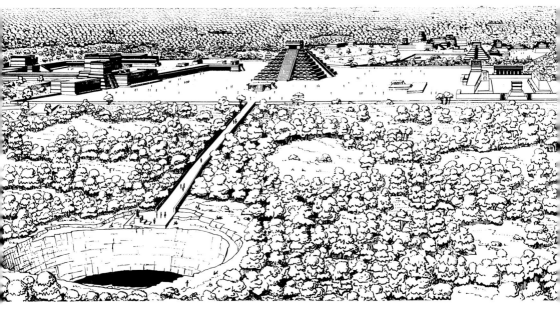

the final centuries before the Spanish Conquest, the Yucatec Maya had organized themselves into balkanized, quarreling states, using different styles and media to record their gods and their rituals at Santa Rita, Tulum, and elsewhere, and in the four surviving Maya codices. In the Guatemalan highlands, Maya lords ruled from hilltop acropolises. In 1524, the Spanish allied with the Cakchiquel at Iximché to defeat the Quiché Maya at Utatlan. After the Conquest, a Quiché nobleman used the European alphabet to transcribe his people's sacred book, the *Popol Vuh*. Other important religious texts, including the Books of Chilam Balam, were transcribed through the late 1700s.

The Postclassic Mixtecs and Aztecs

In Oaxaca, the Mixtecs rose to power during the Postclassic. They took over some of the ancient places sacred to the Zapotecs, and they began to inter their noble dead in the old Zapotec tombs at Monte Albán. At the time of the Spanish Conquest, they kept genealogies documenting both continuity and internecine strife over generations. The Aztecs referred to great artisans as *tolteca*, but the greatest resident craft specialists in Tenochtitlan at the time of the Conquest were the Mixtecs, known for their skills in metalwork and mosaics. Alfonso Caso's discovery of a royal Mixtec tomb at Monte Albán in 1932 offered the 20th c. the closest comparisons we may ever have to what Aztec gold may have looked like, since so little gold from Tenochtitlan survived the Spanish invasion.

After years of nomadic wandering, a warlike group of Nahuatl speakers founded their capital on an island in Lake Texcoco in 1345. They called themselves the Mexica and their city Mexico-Tenochtitlan, or Tenochtitlan. Since the 19th c., the Mexica have usually been grouped with other Nahuatl-speakers in the Valley of Mexico under the name Aztecs, the name we also use, but they gave the name of their city, Mexico-Tenochtitlan, to the 16th c. capital of New Spain that grew up on top of it and subsequently to the new republic of Mexico in 1810.

Inheritors of the rich and complex Mesoamerican past, the Aztecs shared many gods with the civilizations that had gone before, but they honored Huitzilopochtli, their own solar cult god, above all. In their ceremonial precinct, they built a dual pyramid, the Hueteocalli or *Templo Mayor*, and dedicated its southern shrine to Huitzilopochtli and the northern one to Tlaloc, a god that had come to symbolize antiquity and legitimacy as well as rain, earth, and fertility. After they defeated the neighboring Tepanecs in 1428, the Aztecs embarked on a campaign to exact both trade and tribute, first, from near neighbors, and later, from places as far flung as Guatemala and the Veracruz coast. The *pochteca*, or long-distance traders, were the key to both economic and military success, for their preliminary missions often led the way to Aztec imperialism. The Aztecs adopted new gods – Xipe Totec, for example, had flourished along the Gulf and in Oaxaca before gaining a major role among the Aztecs – and elevated old ones, while some others they humiliated by placing their idols in a dark temple designed to be their prison. After a brutal conquest, the Aztecs often insisted that a subject town take on Huitzilopochtli as its god, but he was usually an unwelcome addition, for his worship required regular human sacrifice.

The Aztecs turned their swampy island into a city whose beauty and complexity dazzled the Spanish conquerors, who also marveled at the cuisine, the gardens, the exotic animals kept in a zoo, and the fastidiousness of the populace. Like Venice, Tenochtitlan was laid out along canals, and boatmen poled canoes instead of gondolas

The ceremonial precinct of the Aztec capital city, Tenochtitlan, depicted in a reconstruction painting by Ignacio Marquina. In front of the massive Templo Mayor one can discern the circular wind temple of Ehecatl-Quetzalcoatl and the platform supporting the *temalacatl* disk of gladiatorial sacrifice.

along its axes. Aqueducts brought fresh water to the city from Chapultepec, a region of hilly springs to the west, and causeways connected the island to the mainland. At Tlatelolco on the north side of the island, Cortés described a market teeming with goods and traders, with what he believed to be some 60,000 souls in attendance. The Aztec ruler Motecuhzoma II and his retinue lived in a grand palace to the west of the *Templo Mayor*. Ordinary folk, or *macehuallis*, lived in clan groupings called *calpulli*, the essential administrative component of the city. Foreigners, including Mixtec craftsmen, lived in their own barrios.

For years, the Aztecs had engaged in what they called *xochiyaoyotl* or "flowery war." In these contests, the Aztecs fought neighboring cities in order to garner sacrificial victims but not to win outright victory. Young Aztec soldiers became seasoned fighters, and the demanding Huitzilopochtli received his due, but the Aztecs earned a hatred more relentless from their enemies, particularly in Tlaxcala, than if they had subjected them to a clear-cut defeat and death on the battlefield. When the Spanish invaded Mesoamerica, this sort of warfare baffled them, for the Aztecs sought to capture their new Spanish foes for subsequent sacrifice. The Spanish cut a swath of destruction, slaughtering their Aztec enemies. And where the Aztecs might have anticipated that a negative outcome would lead to an unfavorable tribute arrangement, they could never have guessed that the Spanish would seek to bring their world to an absolute end.

In 1519, Cortés received Doña Marina (often known as La Malinche, but Cortés is also called Malinche in some accounts), a young multilingual noblewoman, as a gift, after her skills as a translator had been demonstrated to him. She, along with

Jerónimo de Aguilar, a Spanish priest stranded for years among the Maya, could translate for Cortés, so that he could begin to understand the world around him. No such informed interlocutors interpreted the Spanish world-view for the Aztecs, or for any of the peoples of Mesoamerica, although they quickly found out what the future had in store for them. Demographers have estimated that some 20 to 25 million people lived within the boundaries of what is now Mexico in 1519. The Spanish surveyed the population late in the 16th c. and found a scant million souls, the survivors of an invasion that wreaked death and destruction.

In 1521, once Cortés and his men reigned triumphant in Tenochtitlan, the Spanish Crown and the Catholic church began to devise plans for both the administrative control and religious conversion of the vast entity soon known as New Spain. Disparate native groups found themselves lumped together under a new name, Indians, an awkward term with which we still labor. Native lords often served the new masters, keeping much administrative control in native hands in the early Colonial period.

Artists went to work for the new regime, copying Aztec tribute lists, making maps of the conquered world, and, from time to time, copying or transcribing a religious document that managed to escape the torch. Some new hybrid types of books were devised that used native artists and ideas to warn missionaries of the "idolatry" they were fighting, while at the same time, some traditional forms of writing and record-keeping went on. Mixtec lords, for example, continued to keep detailed pictorial genealogies, and some of these manuscripts later served as evidence in civil suits over rights to land.

Independence from Spain removed native peoples from protection that had been offered by the Spanish Crown and in some cases led to more brutal exploitation. In recent times, despite both oppression and the lure of urban life, many native peoples and cultures have survived, and some have thrived.

The Conceptual Framework of Mesoamerican Religion

At the time of first contact in the 16th c., Europeans were both intrigued and horrified by Mesoamerican religion. Certain ritual practices, such as human sacrifice and cannibalism, suggested unholy pacts with the forces of Satan. Other aspects of native religion, such as baptism, penance, the use of incense, and the concept of a primordial flood, were perhaps as disturbing, since they offered resonant parallels with Christian ritual and belief. The early Spanish chroniclers noted the striking similarity of the Aztec word for god, *teo* or *teotl*, with the Spanish *dios*. Nonetheless, although it is possible to find correspondences between Mesoamerican religion and those of the Old World, these similarities are the result of independent development rather than diffusion. Aside from the distant origins of New World peoples from Asia, there is no evidence of any European, Asian, or African influence upon Prehispanic peoples of Mesoamerica. The wonderful sophistication and complexity of Mesoamerican religion derives from millennia of gradual independent development.

Early Beliefs and Rituals
Virtually nothing is known of the religious concepts of the earliest Paleoindian inhabitants of Mesoamerica. Certain later Mesoamerican beliefs, such as a multi-layered heaven and earth, shamanic transformation, the moon as a rabbit, and the

A possible Archaic period ballcourt at Gheo-Shih in Oaxaca, 5th millennium BC.

importance of world directions and trees, suggest a distant and ancient relation to Asia. Nonetheless, however profound or early these links may be, they are not reflected in the scant archaeological remains of the earliest peoples. It is not until the Archaic period (7000–2000 BC), in the arid highlands of southern Mexico, that concrete evidence of complex religious activity appears. Excavations in the Tehuacan Valley of Puebla have uncovered two groups of human burials dating to approximately the 6th millennium BC. Wrapped in blankets and nets, the bodies were also accompanied by baskets. Some of these individuals were burned and partly dismembered, perhaps as an early form of ceremonial cannibalism. Although the actual significance of this ritual mutilation remains to be established, these Tehuacan burials clearly demonstrate an early concern and belief in the afterlife.

The site of Gheo Shih, situated in the Tlacolula Valley of highland Oaxaca, reveals other tantalizing evidence of ceremonialism during the Archaic period. Gheo Shih roughly dates to 5000–4000 BC, and seems to have been a seasonal site where bands of people would gather together to collect certain wild plant foods. Archaeologists uncovered an ancient surface flanked by lines of stones on the two longer sides. Some 65 feet (20 meters) long and 23 feet (7 meters) wide, the floor area seemed to have been swept and was virtually devoid of debris. Although the lines of stones may have delineated a dance floor, it is also possible that they marked the sides of an early, simple ballcourt alley. The ancient Oaxacans may have imported rubber balls for the ballgame, but it is far more likely that they were fashioned of locally available leather, wood or stone. Ritualized competitive games may have been an important form of social interaction during seasonal gatherings in the Archaic period.

The Early Formative period saw major changes that were important for the later development of Mesoamerica: the introduction of farming, the growth of populations thanks to settled village life, and the production of pottery. With the appearance of sedentary villages containing relatively large populations, greater evidence of complex religious activities and beliefs survives. During the mid 2nd millennium BC, Formative villages appear widely in the southern coastal region of Chiapas, Mexico. Known as Ocos, this Early Formative culture already displays a number of important elements observed in later Mesoamerican religious systems. In certain Ocos burials, mourners placed mica mirrors with the dead: obsidian, pyrite, and other stone mirrors continued to be revered objects of ornament and ritual until the Spanish Conquest in the 16th c. With the appearance of pottery, ceramic figurines become common at Ocos and other Formative sites. The function of these Formative figurines is unknown; many examples portray youthful, full-bodied women, as if they reflect a concern with human or agricultural fertility. Often beautifully worked, Ocos figurines frequently represent curious blendings of human and zoomorphic traits that have no obvious counterparts in the natural world. At times, these strange figures are seated upon thrones. According to archaeologist John Clark, these throne figures may portray shamanic chiefs wearing animal masks of their spirit companions.

The Olmecs and the Natural World

In contrast to Ocos, the Olmecs after 1200 BC constructed huge earthworks and carved magnificent stone sculptures. Massive thrones, stelae, and colossal heads all testify to both the virtuosity of Olmec artisans and the power of the early rulers who commissioned such works. Monuments from San Lorenzo, La Venta, and other Olmec sites frequently portray actual Olmec kings, and thus clearly these sculptures are at least partly historical in nature. However, the power of these early kings was by no means simply secular; instead, they carefully portrayed themselves in relation to gods and other supernatural forces. Moreover, there are strong indications that the Olmecs had complex concepts regarding shamanic transformation. As among later Mesoamerican peoples, particularly powerful individuals were believed to be able to transform themselves into jaguars.

Among the Olmecs and later peoples of Mesoamerica, certain places were considered especially sacred. Quite often, these locations corresponded to critical junctions between the planes of sky, earth, and Underworld. The Olmecs regarded caves, or entrances to the netherworld, as powerful and magical places. Similarly, at the junction of sky and earth, mountains were also considered to be particularly sacred places, and it is probable that like later Mesoamerican peoples the Olmecs considered pyramids to be replications of mountains. Mountains that contained springs or caves were particularly revered, since they offered simultaneous access to all three planes: sky, earth, and Underworld. Certain Olmec mountain sites, such as El Manatí, Chalcatzingo, and Oxtotitlan, may have served as important oracles, a means of communicating with the powers of the heavens, earth and Underworld.

Like their successors, the Olmecs exhibited a fascination with creatures and forces of the natural world. In their early art one can discern representations of jaguars, harpy eagles, sharks, caimans, and other denizens of their lowland environment. But there are also strange mergings of animal species, as if the Olmecs were attempting to amalgamate the sky, earth, and sea into a dynamic and coherent whole. Although little is known of the Olmec pantheon, it appears that like later peoples they had gods of particular phenomena, such as rain, the earth, and maize.

A Middle Formative Olmec representation of a figure seated inside a cave. From Chalcatzingo, Morelos.

In the better known religious systems of Classic and Postclassic Mesoamerica, allusions to such gods abound. Even to this day in rural Mexico and Guatemala, rituals are performed to gods of earth, wind, water, lightning and other natural forces.

From Formative times to the present, agriculture has been a major focus of Mesoamerican religion. Many of the forces of nature worshipped and evoked in Mesoamerican mythology and ritual concern farming and maize, the primary agricultural product. So ingrained is the importance of corn that in a number of regions maize is explicitly or implicitly said to be the substance of human flesh. References to maize are widespread in the iconography of the Formative Olmecs. Moreover, the importance of forces of water and earth in Olmec and later Mesoamerican religions is clearly related to agricultural fertility. It is thus not surprising that some of the oldest continuously worshipped gods, such as Tlaloc, Cocijo, and Chac, are deities of lightning and rain. Despite centuries of European domination, many of these rain and fertility gods survive to this day.

Although certain aspects of ancient Mesoamerican religion may appear bizarre to the modern viewer, a great deal of native ritual and belief is based on preeminently practical concerns. Much of the ceremonialism is focused not on the afterlife, but on this world and such matters as health, fertility, prosperity, and the prediction and averting of natural disasters. A central concern – today as in antiquity – is that of balance and harmony. This may be expressed in terms of the individual, the community, or the surrounding world. Imbalance and discord can lead to sickness, death, social discord, famine, and even world destruction. In ancient Mesoamerica, there were even gods who personified excess. In Postclassic Central Mexico, the Ahuiateteo simultaneously portrayed particular vices and their consequent punishment. Through particular forms of religious observance, the peoples of Mesoamerica have sought to ensure harmony both with themselves and with the greater cosmos.

Sacrifice and Replication

Among the best-known religious practices of ancient Mesoamerica is human sacrifice. Lurid images of sacrificed maidens and virile warriors have fascinated European imaginations since the Spanish Conquest. But for Mesoamericans human sacrifice was a fundamental means to maintain world harmony and balance. According to the Quiché Maya *Popol Vuh*, the gods fashioned the present human race, the people of maize, to supply nourishment in the form of prayer and sacrifice. The offering of nourishing human substance could be in the form of penitential bloodletting, or more dramatically, the sacrifice of individuals. In both cases, the act signified the offering of the self, either by individual voluntary bloodletting, or collectively with a human victim. The concept of retribution was closely tied to the act of sacrifice. In exchange for life, humans needed to acknowledge and even reimburse the forces that made life possible. The Aztecs viewed human sacrifice partly as retribution for cosmic theft. According to Aztec belief, Ehecatl-Quetzalcoatl stole the bones out of which people were created from the Underworld death god. Similarly, in the *Popol Vuh*, the pregnant Xquic escapes from the Underworld to give birth to the Hero Twins on the surface of the earth. In ancient Mesoamerican thought, humans survive on not merely borrowed but stolen time.

One of the underlying organizational principles of Mesoamerican religion is replication, in which essential patterns of everyday life and the surrounding world are copied and incorporated as models of religious thought and action. Basic features of the social world are often repeated on an increasingly larger scale to encompass the world and the workings of the universe. For example, in the Maya region, the house with its four walls and corner posts could stand for a maize field, the community, and the structure of the cosmos. Grand and abstract concepts are placed in human terms, and conversely, the ordered structure of the universe serves to sanctify and validate human social conventions. Quite frequently, such series of structural associations are expressed in ritual, with similar rites being performed for the individual, the community, or the cosmos. Thus personal penitential bloodletting could be repeated on a larger and more elaborate public scale in the form of human sacrifice. The Aztec New Fire ceremony provides another example. In Aztec rites of personal purification, straws or sticks used in bloodletting were bound in bundles with a paper strip. The large bound stick bundles in the great New Fire ceremony held once every 52 years were probably but glorified versions of the small bundles used in personal bloodletting. Like the penitential bloodletting event, the rite was also for purification, but in terms of the world rather than simply the individual.

Just as basic features can be replicated from the small to the large, the reverse is also true. Objects or concepts of cosmic distance or size are copied into a human scale. The sacred centers of Mesoamerican sites often copy cosmic geography. The Aztec *Templo Mayor* dual pyramid, situated in the center of Tenochtitlan,

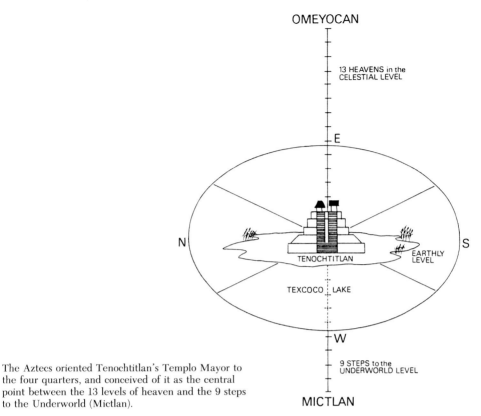

OMEYOCAN

13 HEAVENS in the
CELESTIAL LEVEL

E

N   S

TENOCHTITLAN   EARTHLY
                                LEVEL

TEXCOCO LAKE

W

9 STEPS to the
UNDERWORLD LEVEL

MICTLAN

The Aztecs oriented Tenochtitlan's Templo Mayor to
the four quarters, and conceived of it as the central
point between the 13 levels of heaven and the 9 steps
to the Underworld (Mictlan).

represented two sacred mountains, Coatepec and Tonacatepetl. Recent epigraphic
research by David Stuart has revealed that the Classic Maya conceived of the
monumental art and architecture of their sites as a living landscape of sacred
mountains and trees.

Religious Metaphors in Art and Writing

In Mesoamerica, metaphor is an essential means of describing abstract religious
concepts. Thus, for example, Mesoamerican peoples often consider humans to be
like maize or flowers that are planted on the surface of the earth, born to die, but
containing the seed of regeneration. Through metaphor, particular subjects are given
a vivid range of associations and meanings. At times, the similarities shared between
a subject and its metaphoric comparison reflect a real and special bond. Quite
frequently, these relationships are expressed through ritual. The magical efficacy of
particular agricultural sacrifices, for example, depended on the fact that the victim
not only reflected processes of nature but actually embodied them during the ritual
act. However, the metaphoric substitutions should not be taken too literally or
exclusively. And the metaphors may vary according to what qualities are being
expressed. Thus among the ancient Maya, the earth was thought of in a variety of
ways, as a rectangular house or maize field, as a great caiman, or as the rounded
circular back of a great tortoise.

Prehispanic Mesoamerican art richly expresses these ancient metaphors. Few
regions of the ancient world used visual art so intensively to express complex
religious concepts. Fully present by the Early Formative Olmec, complex systems

of Mesoamerican iconography antedate actual writing. Moreover, writing never replaced iconography. In the Classic Maya area, the complexity of the hieroglyphic inscriptions is entirely matched by the attendant iconography, the texts and the pictorial images conveying different qualities of information. Unlike the specificity of writing, the power of Mesoamerican iconography lies in its subtle ambiguity and ability simultaneously to express different levels of meaning. In a single scene, a richly costumed king can be regarded as a deity impersonator, an actual god, or both. In terms of metaphoric expression, the iconography comes alive. Lightning can appear as a burning serpent, blood as writhing snakes or gouts sprouting sweet flowers, and a mature maize ear as a human head awaiting decapitation from the stalk.

There is considerable debate concerning the extent of literacy in ancient Mesoamerica. Although writing may have been widely used to record mundane daily transactions, it also had a strongly religious component. Priests, commonly culled from the elite, often performed as scribes in Postclassic Mesoamerica. Certain gods were divine patrons of writing. Among the Postclassic Maya, writing was identified with Kinich Ahau Itzamna, an aspect of the aged creator god, and scenes in Classic Maya art also suggest that Itzamna was a god of writing. When we see the detailed historical texts on Maya monuments, it should be borne in mind that we are observing not simply historical but sacred writing. The phrases recorded by this writing are not everyday talk but ritual speech, much like sacred narratives of contemporary Mesoamerica.

The Mesoamerican Calendar and Astronomy

Calendrics served as an essential means by which Mesoamericans organized and conceived of their world. Through wonderfully intricate calendrical cycles, they sought to foresee particular events that could have major influence upon their lives. Although these could include such relatively mundane occurrences as business ventures or curing, they could also concern famine, political instability, or world annihilation. The 260-day calendar had an especially important role in Mesoamerican religion. In Postclassic Central Mexico, patron gods reigned over specific day names and the 20 13-day divisions of the 260-day calendar. From at least Classic times, each of the 20 day names was associated with a particular direction, passing in a continual counterclockwise motion from one day to the next. Considering the central importance of the 260-day calendar, it is entirely fitting that the earliest known example of writing concerns a calendrical notation, found on a Zapotec monument dating to approximately 600 BC. By the Protoclassic period (100 BC–AD 300), abundant evidence of the 260-day calendar survives in many parts of Mesoamerica; together with the vague solar year of 365 days, the 260-day calendar serves as one of the essential defining traits of Mesoamerican culture.

In ancient and contemporary Mesoamerica, time is essentially cyclical. Even the famous Maya Long Count, filled with allusions to historical events and the distant mythical events of gods, is cyclical in nature. The great Long Count Baktun cycle, in which the Classic Maya lived and in which we continue to dwell, began in 3114 BC and will soon end on 23 December AD 2012. In ancient Mesoamerica, temporal cycles ran in increasingly larger units. The Maya Long Count, for example, consists of units marking days, 20 days, 360 days, 20 × 360 days, and 400 × 360 days, and still larger units encompassing millions of years. Similarly, in Late Postclassic Central Mexico, there were the 365-day vague year, the 52-vague-year cycle, and a still greater cycle of 104 years. Of crucial importance in Mesoamerican ritual and thought are period endings, during which a unit of time is terminated and another begins. For the Postclassic Maya of Yucatán, the end of the 365-day year was a major concern, whereas for the Aztecs, it was the completion of the 52-year cycle. The completion of major Long Count cycles must have been of momentous significance to the Classic Maya. There have even been suggestions, albeit unlikely, that the completion of the tenth Baktun (10.0.0.0.0) of the Maya Long Count in AD 830 was a major reason for the Classic Maya collapse.

The ending and renewal of calendrical periods were commonly expressed through concepts of world creation and destruction. In fact, the New Year rites of the Yucatec and the New Fire ceremony of the Aztecs concerned the reassertion of the ordered world from the forces of chaos and darkness. In both regions, it was believed that such period endings could mark the end of the present world. In Mesoamerican thought, creation, as well as calendrics, is also cyclical. The Maya *Popol Vuh*, Aztec accounts, and contemporary mythology share common and explicit references to multiple creations and destructions. Just as the series of previous worlds were destroyed, it was believed that this world in which we live would also end.

One of the basic concerns of Mesoamerican calendrics was the recording and prediction of astronomical events. The sun, moon, planets and constellations exerted powerful influences upon people and the world. Two astronomical events that were of supreme importance were solar eclipses and the first appearance of Venus as Morning Star. The ancient Maya, with the most developed form of astronomical notation known for Mesoamerica, had elaborate tables recording and predicting eclipses and the cycle of Venus. It was widely believed that the world could be destroyed by demons of darkness during solar eclipses. Moreover, the rays of the Morning Star at heliacal rising were considered to be particularly dangerous, and threatened specific people and things of the natural world. It is now known that the Classic Maya frequently scheduled battles to coincide with the movements of Venus, especially the first rising of Venus as evening star.

The apparent movements of the planets and constellations were considered to be the reenactments of cosmic mythical events. To the Aztecs, the movement of Ursa Major into the sea may have represented Tezcatlipoca losing his foot during the cosmic battle with the great earth monster. Recent investigations by Linda Schele and David Freidel suggest that the Classic Maya also observed mythological events in the movement of the stars, probably based on an ancestral form of the *Popol Vuh* creation epic.

Religion and Statecraft

The religious worlds of all classes of society were closely integrated in ancient Mesoamerica. Agricultural fertility was a major concern of all, and through replication, ritual acts of commoner and elite were linked. Nonetheless, the sophistication and complexity of Mesoamerican writing, calendrics and astronomy all point to the existence of full-time specialists, even though the office of priest has not yet been documented in Classic period writing or art. Priestly offices are well known for the Postclassic period. Classic-period kings and other individuals of high office were also religious experts, and the rituals and beliefs surrounding rulers were extremely complex. Ancestor worship was a major concern of elite dynasties in ancient Mesoamerica, and Classic Maya art is filled with scenes of rulers and their kin offering blood and other sacrifices to the honored dead.

Many peoples of ancient Mesoamerica lived in highly stratified state-level societies. In such societies, mythology and ritual frequently served as divine charter for state policies. The use of ideology in statecraft is best documented for the Aztecs. It is known, for example, that the Aztec emperor Itzcoatl destroyed historical accounts in order to rewrite the legendary past of his people. A number of Aztec myths describe the necessity of political expansion and human sacrifice. The myth of the birth of Huitzilopochtli at Coatepec is also a description of the political ascendancy of the Aztecs and their defeat of other city states. Both this mythical event and the creation of the fifth sun at Teotihuacan stress the importance of human sacrifice for world balance and survival.

Following the fall of Tenochtitlan to the Spanish in 1521, Mesoamerican religion was rapidly transformed. Many of the more elaborate manifestations associated with the elite, such as hieroglyphic writing and iconography, virtually ceased to exist by the end of the 16th c. Native temples, sculptures, and books were systematically destroyed. The Spanish conquerors vigorously suppressed native religious ceremonies, particularly those involving human sacrifice. The rituals, mythology, and gods

This scene from the Yanhuitlan Codex depicts two
Mixtec nobles standing behind a Dominican priest.

pertaining to rulership and other high offices were likewise suppressed, not only because of their challenge to Christian doctrine but also because of their essentially political nature, which could serve as catalysts for rebellion. However, the eradication of native Mesoamerican customs was by no means total. Many of the more profound and lasting religious beliefs continue to the present day. Rich oral traditions encompassing ritual speech, songs, and mythology are contained in Nahuatl, Mayan, Mixtec, and other modern native languages. Forms of the 260-day and vague 365-day calendar are still used in southeastern Mesoamerica. Ceremonies to ensure agricultural fertility are widely performed in Mesoamerica, and *copal* incense, flowers, and prepared foods are among the offerings still presented to the gods and ancestors. Although this volume specifically concerns Preconquest Mesoamerican religion, it should be remembered that we are describing but the ancient origins and history of a still living and vibrant culture.

Subject Index

A

accession Accession is the English word generally given to the process by which a ruler was installed formally in office. Accession rituals among the Mixtecs, Aztecs, and Maya are known to have been elaborate events, frequently lasting for days. Probably most Mesoamerican cultures engaged in this procedure by which a mere mortal became a leader often perceived by the world around him (and occasionally her) to be divine.

Among the Aztecs, the ruler, known as the TLATOANI (literally "he who speaks") acceded to power over a series of days, even weeks, beginning with his selection after the death of the previous ruler. Ranking nobles chose from a pool of candidates, sometimes numbering in the hundreds, of younger men, the sons, nephews, grandsons and great-grandsons of former rulers. The candidate would then prove himself in battle and proudly lead CAPTIVES, living trophies of his prowess, back to the Aztec capital.

Official accession celebrations began with the ordering of new robes for all nobles to be in attendance, and invitations were sent far and wide, even including traditional enemies, who were to be impressed (and perhaps cowed) by the display of Aztec power. Once the ceremonies had begun, four or five days of feasting and dancing culminated in a royal procession to five sites within the sacred precinct and environs of Tenochtitlan, at each of which the candidate offered INCENSE, quail, and his own BLOOD. To the Aztecs, the *tlatoani* transcended mere mortality and was recognized as divine. With such status, the Aztec king Motecuhzoma II, for example, was neither touched nor gazed upon by his subjects, and according to the accounts written by the Spanish at the time of the Conquest, the *tlatoani* repelled efforts by Cortés to shake his hand or meet his gaze.

A key feature of the Mixtec accession ceremony was the official insertion of a nose plug; the Mixtec lord 8 Deer may have journeyed to a PILGRIMAGE site to receive the nose plug from a PRIEST. The notion of travel in order to receive sanction for accession was common in ancient Mesoamerica. At the time of the Spanish Conquest, for example, Maya kings of the Quiché and Cakchiquel peoples in highland Guatemala described a time deep in the past when their rulers had gone to TOLLAN where legitimacy was conferred upon them.

Classic Maya hieroglyphic texts usually state simply the accession verb, roughly, "to be seated as *ch'ul ahau*," that is, seated as the sacred lord, but the range of associated depictions offers clues to the various components of accession rituals, which, like the Aztec ones, may have required that sacrificial victims had previously been taken, and which probably followed a familiar sequence. Monuments commemorating accession at Piedras Negras, for example, feature newly seated lords on cushions within niches, high above sacrificial victims who rest at the base of cloth-draped latticed scaffolding, their probable place of SACRIFICE. Bloody footprints spot the cloth, marking the steps of the new ruler from the sacrifice site to the THRONE. Some monuments include visitors, implying that – like their Aztec counterparts – Maya accession rituals may have drawn the attendance of nobility throughout the region. Although succession among the Maya could follow from one brother to another, primogeniture was a general rule.

In no Mesoamerican civilization is there any evidence of retirement or abdication from rulership. Once a king acceded to office, he apparently served until DEATH, and no successor acceded until proper arrangements could be made, a process that generally took anywhere from a few weeks to a year. The ten-year interregnum (AD 742–52) between the reigns of Maya kings Shield Jaguar and Bird Jaguar the Great at Yaxchilán is anomalous.

acrobats In 16th c. Mesoamerica, acrobats and contortionists formed an important class of ritual entertainers. In his triumphal return to Spain in 1528, Hernan Cortés included native acrobats in his entourage. In that year, Christopher Weiditz illustrated one of these acrobats, juggling a beam of wood with his feet. Similar acrobats are known for both the Late Postclassic Mixtecs as well as Aztecs.

Contorted acrobats also appear in Classic Maya art, frequently with their legs arching over their heads. At times they are supplied with snake markings, as if alluding to the almost miraculous, sinuous contortions of the SERPENT. This fascination with acrobatic contortionists appears as early as the Olmecs. A fine representation of a contortionist grasping his feet appears on a late Olmec relief reportedly from the south coast of Guatemala.

afterlife Mesoamerican beliefs of afterlife varied with region and time, but for few people was there any sense that human morality affected the afterlife. For the Aztecs, the key to one's afterlife was the manner of DEATH itself; for the Maya, one was tested after death by the gods of the UNDERWORLD.

Although no texts survive from the Formative era, rich offerings placed in TOMBS reveal belief in an afterlife. At La Venta, JADE treasures accompanied deceased Olmec nobles laid to rest in basalt sarcophagi. In West Mexico, ancient residents of the states of Jalisco, Nayarit, and Colima dug shaft tombs deep into the earth and offered burnished ceramics. Both real and ceramic DOGS frequently accompanied the dead, suggesting that an animal companion may have been necessary for a journey in the afterlife.

The Maya conceived the afterlife to be a journey, a harrowing that one might successfully overcome. Burial rituals included the interment of useful goods for the deceased's journey, and noble tombs held the richest offerings: pots of a chocolate beverage, human attendants, even dogs, and frequently great piles of jade, CLOTH, and rope. But even a commoner would be buried with a jade bead in his mouth, a bit of currency he might need in the afterlife. The best record of the journey itself is recorded in the 16th c. Quiché epic, the POPOL VUH, but the Maya had probably believed in a similar quest after death for about two millennia, if not longer.

The entry into the Maya Underworld began with passage through still WATER, sometimes rendered in Classic Maya art as a passage by CANOE. Subsequently, the afterlife journey led through various levels of the Underworld (known in Quiché as Xibalba, or place of fright), many of which were hot and steamy sites of decomposition and decay and inhabited by foul-smelling gods of death. A Maya overcame death by outwitting these old gods, as the Hero Twins do in the *Popol Vuh*. Once the repellent beings were defeated, the victors rose in the night SKY as heavenly bodies. The Maya likened the cycle of death and regeneration to the life cycle of MAIZE.

For the Aztecs, the world of the afterlife was stratified, with 13 layers of heavens and

A noble figure is surrounded by a contorted **acrobat**, Shook Panel, Late Formative period, Guatemala.

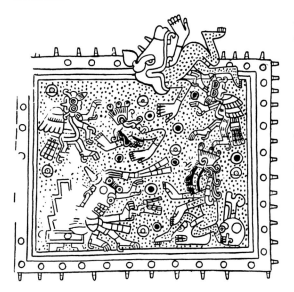

This scene describes the **afterlife** journey of a sacrificial victim. At the upper right, he is first swallowed by the caiman earth. The center of the scene depicts the victim being greeted by Mictlantecuhtli in the dark interior of the earth Codex Borgia, p. 42, Late Postclassic period.

nine of the Underworld. The means of death determined one's fate after death, and most of those who went to heaven died violent deaths. Suicides, for example, dwelt in a single stratum. One layer of the heavens was reserved for sacrificial victims, those who died in combat, and for women who died in childbirth (who were recognized as warriors who fell to the battling infant); another heavenly layer, dedicated to the RAIN and EARTH god TLALOC, received those struck by LIGHTNING, or who drowned, or who fell prey to the DISEASES dispatched by the rain gods. But most Aztec souls, and all those who died ordinary deaths, entered Mictlan, the Underworld, where they, like their Maya counterparts, faced a series of trials during their journey.

Ahuiateteo Among the Postclassic peoples of Central Mexico, many forms of pleasure, when in excess, were considered to be causes of DISEASE and misfortune. A series of five gods, the Ahuiateteo, embodied the dangers and punishments of excessive drinking, gambling, sex, and other pleasures. Each of these five gods bore a calendrical name with the coefficient of 5, *macuil*, a number alluding to excess. Thus according to the Aztecs, the fifth cup of PULQUE denoted drunkenness and loss of control. The five gods were named Macuil-cuetzpalin (5 Lizard), Macuilcozcacuauhtli (5 Vulture), Macuiltochtli (5 Rabbit), MACUIL-XOCHITL (5 Flower) and Macuilmalinalli (5 Grass). These gods were clearly associated with the DIRECTION south: their five day names constitute the five days of the south and derive from the five southern TRECENAS of 1 Xochitl, 1 Malinalli, 1 Cuetzpalin, 1 Cozca-cuauhtli and 1 Tochtli.

The Vaticanus B and Borgia codices contain passages representing the five Ahuiateteo and their accompanying *trecena* dates. Although the two passages differ, in both cases the figures display characteristics of TEZCATLIPOCA. Moreover, in both codices, the Ahuiateteo can be rendered with a human hand across the mouth, clearly a reference to the five digits, and by extension, the number five. In the Borgia and Vaticanus B passages, the Ahuiateteo pair with the five female CIHUAT-ETEO, the demon goddesses of the west. The Prehispanic Fons Mexicains 20 contains the most ambitious pairing of the Cihuateteo with the Ahuiateteo. In this single scene, the five Ahuiateteo and Cihuateteo are placed

according to specific Mixtec place names. *See also* DEFORMITY.

alcohol *see* PULQUE

altar Typically, in Mesoamerica an altar is a large stone, with a flat surface suitable for the making, offering, or burning of SACRIFICES. Many carved ancient stones of Mexico and Guatemala, however, were included in this category long before their function had been determined. Some large so-called table-top altars of the Olmecs were probably THRONES. At many Maya cities, commemorative stelae pair with altars in what has often been termed the stelae "cult": in fact the practice was not a cult but rather a pattern of commemorating ruler portraits on stelae and offerings (sometimes sacrificial victims) on altars. Among the later Maya, Toltecs, and Aztecs, CHACMOOLS frequently functioned as receptacles for sacrifices. Some Aztec altars for HUMAN SACRIFICE were simply plain stones.

amaranth A family of plants rich in both protein and starch, various amaranths (*Amaranthus* spp.) were cultivated in Mesoamerica before the Conquest. The Aztecs called this plant family *huatli*, and identified some 11 specific varieties. Like many other foodstuffs, amaranth was treated with reverence, but it was especially important for the seeds were mixed with human BLOOD, forming a dough called *tzoalli*, and then shaped into figures and worshipped. During the month of Panquetzaliztli, such dough figures were set high atop the *xocolli*, a ritual tree, and then subsequently consumed by participants in a ritual that the Spanish likened to Christian Communion.

At the time of the Conquest, the Aztecs collected some 200,000 bushels of amaranth annually in tribute, only slightly less than they took in of MAIZE and beans. But because of its close association with ritual, amaranth consumption was driven underground by the Spanish, and the nutritious foodstuff ceased to be a significant part of the native diet. Today amaranth is mixed with a honey paste and sold as a snack called "alegria," or joy, on the street corners of Mexico.

ancestral couple Native creation accounts frequently refer to the mythical first human couple, who, because of their origin in remote antiquity, are often portrayed to be of great age. As was the case with many aged people of ancient Mesoamerica, this pair possessed powers of DIVINATION and CURING. Because of the importance of the 260-day CALENDAR in divination, the primordial couple can also be identified with the origin of the calendar. Although known as Oxomoco and Cipactonal among the Nahuatl-speaking peoples of Central Mexico, there is no certainty as to which of the two figures these names refer to. The term Cipactonal is surely a reference to the day name Cipactli in the 260-day *tonalpohualli* calendar. In Central Mexican thought, the day name Cipactli, meaning "CAIMAN," is frequently associated with beginnings and creation episodes.

In their identification with the powerful, sacred arts of curing and divination, the aged ancestral couple merges into the original pair of male and female creator gods. The Quiché Maya POPOL VUH mentions a similar pair of aged diviners who, although not described as the first humans, are referred to as grandparents. This aged pair, Xpiyacoc and his consort, Xmucane, play an active role in the creation of people. By divining with cast *tzite* seeds, this couple instruct the creator gods how to fashion humankind. Xmucane grinds the corn from which the first true people are made. *See also* CREATION ACCOUNTS; DIVINATION.

atl-tlachinolli A widespread characteristic in ancient Aztec thought is the use of paired terms to refer metaphorically to a single concept. One of the best known examples of this is the Nahuatl term *atl-tlachinolli*. Composed of the terms for WATER (*atl*) and FIRE (*tlachinolli*), this phrase refers to war, and the words for fire and water themselves are a pair of battling oppositions. In Aztec WRITING and art, this phrase is usually rendered as a pair of intertwined bands, one delineating fire, the other, water. The use of fire and water to describe war also appears in manuscripts of non-Aztec origin, such as the Codex Borgia. The use of water and fire to allude to war may be as old as Early Classic TEOTIHUACAN. In Teotihuacan art, symbols of water and fire often appear together in contexts of war. During the Postclassic period, the use of water and fire to delineate war appears to be especially strong among the Nahuatl-speaking peoples of Central Mexico. The fire-and-water motif does not appear in the Prehispanic manuscripts of the Postclassic Mixtecs or Maya.

Macuilcuetzpalin, one of the five **Ahuiateteo** gods, Codex Borgia, p. 47.

The aged **ancestral couple**, Cipactonal and Oxomoco, portrayed as priests letting blood and casting lots, detail of Codex Borbonicus, p. 21, 16th c. Aztec.

Fire and water, or **atl-tlachinolli**, the Aztec sign for war, detail of wooden drum from Malinalco.

autosacrifice Literally the sacrificing of one-self, autosacrifice in the form of BLOODLETTING played a role in ancient ritual from at least Olmec times until the Spanish Conquest. The very act of such self-sacrifice was recorded widely in Mesoamerican art, and quantities of ritual paraphernalia survive that were designed specifically for sacrifice on the part of the nobility.

According to Aztec accounts, the gods gathered at TAMOANCHAN following previous destructions of the EARTH. They drew BLOOD from their own bodies to generate a new race of humans; QUETZALCOATL, in particular, sprinkled blood from his penis on ancient bones he stole from the UNDERWORLD. Then, in an act of autosacrifice at TEOTIHUACAN, the god Nanahuatzin immolated himself on a bonfire to create the SUN, and Tecuciztecatl followed suit, becoming the MOON. The story of such divine sacrifice survives only from the Aztec tradition, but probably all ancient Mesoamerican peoples were held in the thrall of this "blood debt," in which humans end-lessly owed gods human blood and flesh. In the Maya epic, the POPOL VUH, the gods destroy successive generations of living beings until a race of humans learns to praise their makers and nourish them through prayer and blood SACRIFICE.

Aztec lords drew blood from their ears, elbows, and shins with sharp MAGUEY spines or filed bones. A twisted grass ball held the spines when not in use, and the emblem of the ball and spines was carved on dozens of major Aztec sculptures to signify the responsi-bilities of Aztec nobility.

Of all Mesoamerican deities, Quetzalcoatl most embodied the burden of sacrifice. On a Huastec relief, Quetzalcoatl pierces his tongue with a huge perforator, and STARS and other precious elements stream from the wound, as if given birth from his offering.

Both Maya men and women performed bloodletting as autosacrifice. Men character-istically drew blood from the penis. The act is graphically recorded on a number of Classic Maya painted pots, but even in the years after the Spanish Conquest, Bishop Diego de Landa saw such autosacrifice performed in Yucatán, and a Madrid Codex illustration shows several gods linked together by a rope that runs through all their penises. Women drew blood from the tongue or ear, as men also did upon occasion, and both collected the blood offerings on PAPER, which was then burned. In the smoke from the burned offer-ings, Maya nobility communicated with their ancestors, as was recorded at Yaxchilán.

Although no explicit depictions of Olmec autosacrifice survive, sharp JADE perforators and stingray spines indicate such a practice at an early date, as do terracotta sculptures from West Mexico that vividly depict cheek perforation.

axis mundi *see* WORLD TREE

Aztlan "Place of whiteness" or "place of herons," Aztlan was the mythical point of departure for the Mexica (Aztecs). The myth-ical Aztlan was an island in a lake whose replica the Mexica sought in Tenochtitlan, their final home in Central Mexico, also an island in a lake. Scholars have attempted to identify Aztlan anywhere from the American Southwest to points just north of the Valley of Mexico, but such efforts have been in vain. Although Aztlan may have been a mythic location, further inquiry into islands in Lake Patzcuaro and Mexcaltitán in a lagoon along the Pacific coast of Nayarit may prove useful. According to Aztec traditions, their ancestors departed Aztlan and went to CHICOMOZTOC, the "seven caves," at the beginning of their long peregrination.

The word Aztec means "people of Aztlan," although they rarely called themselves by such a term. They were usually known among themselves and their neighbors as the Mexica, or sometimes the Culhua-Mexica, to emphas-ize their connection to the old Toltec lineages established at Culhuacan. However, William Prescott's *Conquest of Mexico*, published in 1843, popularized the term Aztec (introduced by Alexander von Humboldt earlier in the 19th c.) as a catch-all reference to all Nahuatl-speakers in Central Mexico at the time of the Conquest.

B

ballgame All over Prehispanic Mexico and Central America, for some three millennia, games were played with a RUBBER ball, and in parts of northwestern Mexico an indigenous ballgame is still played. Ballgames may have developed along the Gulf Coast, where the resilient properties of latex were probably first observed. Typically, the best-known games were played in a "ballcourt," usually an alley formed by two parallel structures, sometimes with clearly defined end zones that gave the entire area the shape of a capital letter I. Points were scored by striking a solid rubber ball, aiming it toward a ring or markers set along the alley or in end zones. The rules varied, but the game was played between two teams composed of two or three team members each, giving a total of four or six players. In the most widespread version of the game, the ballplayers controlled the ball by hitting it with the upper arm and thigh; touching it with the hands was forbidden, except to put the ball into play.

Another ballgame was played with instruments resembling field hockey sticks and a small ball. In that game, found mainly in Central Mexico and depicted in paintings at TEOTIHUACAN, goals and courts were defined by freestanding markers of round disks atop posts.

Such sport was reserved for men and gods. Only at the Maya site of Yaxchilán are women depicted in association with the game; there, they sit beside a staircase on which a ball bounces. In the Codex Borbonicus, in the TRECENA 1 Eagle, the Aztec goddess XOCHIQUETZAL presides over games in general, including the ballgame and PATOLLI.

The ballgame had many levels of meaning, and could be played for many reasons, from sandlot sport to court ritual. At the time of the Spanish Conquest, amateurs and professionals alike engaged in the game, and heavy gambling frequently accompanied the competition. Spectators wagered their finely woven mantles, leaving a trail of garments behind them when they lost.

Many Mesoamerican peoples saw in the ballgame a metaphor for the movements of heavenly bodies, particularly the SUN, MOON, and VENUS; the ball itself may have been understood as the sun journeying in and out of the UNDERWORLD, seen as the narrow alley of the ballcourt. Round ballcourt markers in alleys of Maya courts frequently bear a quatrefoil cartouche, indicating an opening to the Underworld. In the POPOL VUH, the Hero Twins descend to the Underworld to play ball against Underworld gods; the game becomes the metaphor of life, DEATH, and regeneration, and they resurrect their father, the MAIZE GOD, from the court of death.

The ballgame also served as public reenactment of warfare and incorporated HUMAN

The departure from **Aztlan** in the year 1 Flint, detail of Codex Boturini, 16th c. Aztec.

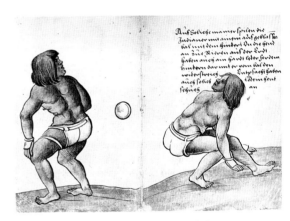

The **ballgame**: (*above*) ballplayers, sketch by Karl Weiditz, 1528; (*below*) Aztec ballcourt, Codex Magliabechiano.

SACRIFICE. In some instances, victorious ball-players decapitated the defeated ones; skullracks for the trophies often adjoin ballcourts (*see* TZOMPANTLI). Among the Classic Maya, a ritual paralleled the ballgame in which defeated players, usually CAPTIVES of war, were bound and trussed in order to be used as the ball itself. In this final act of the game, the captive-as-ball was bounced down a flight of stairs.

The equipment for the ballgame varied through time and space, but generally consisted of a rubber ball and, for the players, heavy padding. Solid rubber balls are heavy and dense: modern-day ballgames in northern Mexico use balls that are 10 cm or 4 inches in diameter and weigh 500 g or 1 lb. Some very large balls are depicted in Maya and West Mexico art; a solid ball 30 cm or 12 inches in diameter would weigh 3.5 kg or 7.5 lb and could have maimed or killed an off-balance player. At Chichen Itzá, carvings of the ballgame show a skull on the surface of the large ball, and skulls – perhaps of previously defeated ballplayers – may have been imbedded in such balls to create a hollow center.

Vast quantities of ballgame paraphernalia survive, mostly from the Gulf Coast of Mexico and the Pacific Coast of Guatemala. Carved from hard stone, the YOKES, handstones, HACHAS, and PALMAS (both of which are known by their modern Spanish appellations) may have been made as commemorative trophies for successful players or for occasional ceremonial wear. Stone yokes, for example, can be worn snugly across an adult's hips, but weigh about 13.5 kg or 30 lb. For actual protection in the game, the equipment may have been made of wood, wicker, or cotton batting. *Hachas* and *palmas* fit into yokes and offer some protection for the chest; handstones may have been used to put the ball into play or to allow for use of the hands in competition. *Hachas* may also have adorned the court or marked locations for scoring. Stone ballgame trophies were prized funerary offerings and may have been required by the interred in order to face the Underworld gods.

baptism When the first Spanish priests arrived in New Spain, they were surprised to find native forms of baptism, in this case the ritual bathing of infants and children. In Yucatán, according to Diego de Landa, a native PRIEST sprinkled male and female chil-

dren of approximately three years of age with WATER from a serpent-tailed aspergillum. In addition, one of the principal citizens of the community anointed the children with water from a moistened bone. Landa notes that this rite cleansed and purified the children, an important function of baptism.

Book 6 of the Florentine Codex provides detailed descriptions of the ritual speech and rites associated with Aztec baptism. In contrast to the Yucatec ceremony, baptism took place soon after BIRTH. However, the Aztec rite was also associated with PURIFICATION, to remove any pollution acquired from the parents. During the ritual bathing, the infant was named and presented with the tools necessary for adult life.

This crucial episode of Aztec birth rites is illustrated in the 16th c. Codex Mendoza, where the midwife prepares to bathe the infant in a vessel of water placed on a reed MAT. Immediately above and below the mat appear the articles representing the occupations of men and women. Above, one can discern the masculine tools of the sculptor, featherworker, painter, and goldsmith, along with the all-important feather and shield of the warrior. Clearly, the lot of the female child is less enviable, as she is supplied only with the dreary tools for sweeping and spinning cotton.

bats As a nocturnal creature, the bat is commonly identified with the forces of death and darkness in Mesoamerican thought. The behavior of the vampire bat also contributed to the association of bats with DEATH and bloody SACRIFICE, and the Maya may well have been aware that the vampire bat does not suck the BLOOD of its victims but makes an incision and then laps the blood. However, the natural trait of bats snatching fruit from trees may have contributed to the widespread identification of bats with decapitation. Among the Classic and Postclassic Maya, bats were identified with death and sacrifice. In the Quiché POPOL VUH, the Underworld Camazotz, or "death bat," cuts off the head of the Hero Twin, Hunahpu. In Classic Maya vessel scenes, bats are commonly rendered with death markings, such as extruded eyeballs and crossed bones.

In Postclassic Central Mexico, bats were similarly associated with death and sacrifice. In a number of scenes, the bat carries a severed human head to identify it as a beast

of decapitation. In addition, FLINT blades –
probably denoting sacrifice – can appear on
the snout or wings of the creature.

The bat plays a prominent role in the
art of the Classic Zapotecs, and commonly
appears on ceramic funerary urns. Like the
later examples of Postclassic Central Mexico,
the Zapotec bat is often depicted with chipped
stone blades, probably an allusion to sacrifice.
Supplied with large claws, round ears, and a
toothy muzzle, the Zapotec bat figure
resembles the JAGUAR save for one curious
convention: a large crest projecting from
the top of the forehead. A fine JADE mosaic
example of a bat head was discovered during
excavations at the Zapotec site of Monte
Albán. Dating to approximately the beginning
of the Christian era, this figure displays the
forehead crest as well as the rounded ears
and fanged snout. The three pendant CELT-
like stones identify this remarkable mask as
a pectoral or belt piece. In ancient Mesoamerica, such masks seem to have been modeled
on TROPHY HEADS, again suggesting the association with decapitation.

Bicephalic Monster Literally, a two-headed
monster, of which there are a number in
Maya art, and specifically, the two-headed
monster also known as the Celestial Monster
or Cosmic Monster.

This particular supernatural creature usually has either a crocodilian or SKY BAND body,
but in at least one example, cloud scrolls form
the body. The front head generally bears
either a VENUS sign or crossed bands in the
eye, DEER hooves or deer ears and is fully
fleshed while the rear head is characteristically skeletal and rendered upside down.
The front head also functions as the head
variant for the day sign Lamat and as the
patron of the month Yax. The rear head bears
on its forehead a quadripartite sign: a stingray
spine, spondylus shell, and crossed bands
inside a cache vessel. Both heads may spew
BLOOD scrolls. The CELESTIAL BIRD may be represented at the center of the monster's body.

Most commonly, the Bicephalic Monster
frames scenes of ACCESSION or rulership for the
Maya, but its intrinsic meaning may be to
represent the arc of the heavens, the front
head being identified with Venus, pulling
behind it the fleshless head of the SUN in the
UNDERWORLD.

birth The creation of life by human birth

The **baptism** of Aztec
infants, tools for males
above and females
below the central bowl of water;
detail from Codex
Mendoza.

Jade mosaic **bat** image,
Protoclassic Zapotec,
Monte Albán. This object
was probably worn as a
pectoral.

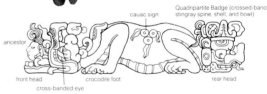

Bicephalic Monster, Copán
Altar 41, Late Classic
Maya.

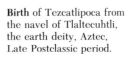

Birth of Tezcatlipoca from
the navel of Tlaltecuhtli,
the earth deity, Aztec,
Late Postclassic period.

was a source of great fascination in ancient Mesoamerica. Not only was birth an important event of great concern in everyday life, but it also played a major role in the CREATION ACCOUNTS of the gods. It was common for an infant at the time of birth to be ritually introduced into some of the most essential truths of human existence, such as the origins, nature, and fate of mankind.

The mysteries of gestation and birth were the domain of a particular class of curers, the midwives, who tended to be aged, post-menopausal women well-versed in plants, DIVINATION, and other esoteric lore. The most famous supernatural patron of midwives, the Yucatec Maya IXCHEL, was honored at a major PILGRIMAGE shrine on the island of Cozumel, situated off the northern coast of Quintana Roo, Mexico. Although Ixchel is often ident-ified as the youthful Goddess I of the Maya codices, she is almost certainly the aged Goddess O, who is named epigraphically *chac chel* in the ancient Maya books (*see* SCHELLHAS GODS).

In the art of Late Postclassic Central Mex-ico, goddesses are frequently shown in the posture of birth known as *hocker*, from the German word signifying a squatting position. *Hocker* figures typically have their arms upraised, as if mirroring the crouching squat of the lower limbs. But although these figures squat in the birth posture, rarely do they give birth from the loins. Instead, in a number of instances, individuals emerge from a JADE placed on the navel, representing the center of conception and gestation.

blood Most Mesoamerican peoples identified blood with other substances, particularly MAIZE, JADE, FLOWERS, and the sap of trees. According to some Maya accounts, the gods offered their own blood on ground maize, yielding a doughy paste from which humans could be formed. Native maize was red, blue, and yellow in color; likewise human blood appears blue in the veins when seen through the yellowish tones of skin, but when cut is red (*see* COLORS).

Blood was understood in Mesoamerica to mean kinship, or bloodlines, as well as the actual substance that courses through veins and arteries.

In Mixtec and Aztec manuscripts, human blood is sometimes rendered as a jagged red stream tipped with jade beads; in the art of Classic Veracruz and Chichen Itzá, blood-streams – particularly when spurting from fresh wounds – are often configured as live SERPENTS. The Classic Maya frequently show blood as a series of droplets, particularly in scenes of scattering or sprinkling, in which kings hold their hands near the groin and shower the ground with their blood. Blood-streams can be rendered as streams of flowing precious things or their symbols edged with beads or dots. Blood may also appear as a series of lazy S-scrolls, although such imagery more commonly refers to clouds.

bloodletting The act of drawing BLOOD from the human body was practiced routinely throughout Mesoamerica for ritual purposes. Because the GODS had shed their own blood to create humanity, human blood was the single most important offering that could be made in return. In this state of blood "debt," CAPTIVES of battle were taken alive, their blood shed later in TEMPLES and shrines to honor the pact with the gods. The nobles, and perhaps all people, performed AUTOSACRIFICE.

Jade versions of the sharp spines from the stingray survive from Olmec times, indicating that during the first millennium BC Mesoamerican peoples were familiar with the serrated bony spine that arms the tail of this SEA creature. Because of the acute angle of the serrations, once a stingray spine has pierced the skin it cannot be removed without causing painful damage: it is easier in fact to pull the spine completely through a perfor-ation. The Maya buried their noble male dead with stingray spines – perhaps in pouches long decayed – over the groin, and these spines were the perforators used to draw blood from the penis.

The Maya also pierced their flesh with OBSIDIAN bloodletters and carved bones. They collected the dripping blood on strips of PAPER which they then placed in broad, flat-bottomed bowls and set afire. The implements, as well as the bowls, were fre-quently prized funerary offerings; nobles wrapped bloodletting equipment in their sacred BUNDLES. Yaxchilán women often wore headdresses like those of warriors when undergoing autosacrifice and it was not uncommon for men to adopt the mutilated, shredded attire of captives, as if identifying their own bloodletting with that of sacrificial victims. Captives themselves may have been forced to perform autosacrifice; some bear the necessary spines and paper in ancient depictions. In other cases, victors forcibly drew the blood of captives, as shown in the Bonampak murals, where warriors pull out the fingernails of their prisoners.

Maya bloodletters and other things associated with bloodletting often bear the triple "bow tie," probably a representation of knotted paper. The motif turns up at Tula (*see* TOLLAN) and Tenochtitlan, where it is featured on the body of the XIUHCOATL, linking it to blood and sacrifice.

Most Central Mexican peoples used the spines of the MAGUEY plant to draw blood, and to keep these spines sharp and at hand they stored them in a ball of twisted grass, much as a seamstress keeps her needles and pins in a cushion. The grass ball with spines became an important symbol of Aztec nobility, indicating both their privilege and their responsibility to let blood. In Aztec representations of bloodletting, lords and gods draw blood from the ear, shin, knee, and elbow. *See also* HUMAN SACRIFICE.

bundle Sacred bundles were an important part of Mesoamerican history and ritual. In contrast to MERCHANT bundles, which are oblong and wrapped with rope and matting, sacred bundles are usually round with prominent, large knots. Clear examples occur in the art of the Classic Maya as well as of the Postclassic Aztecs and Mixtecs.

Sacred bundles often play an important role in the journey and migrations of a people to their chosen place. In the POPOL VUH account of the legendary migrations of the Quiché Maya, the Pizom Gagal bundle represents the deceased ancestor Balam Quitze. In its account of the Aztec journey from Aztlan, the Codex Boturini carefully represents four bundle-bearers. The most important of these bundles belonged to HUITZILOPOCHTLI, the patron god of the Aztecs. As late as 1539, 18 years after the fall of Tenochtitlan, Spanish officials accused an individual named Don Miguel of caring for Aztec god bundles, including that of Huitzilopochtli.

According to one 16th c. account from the Valley of Mexico, the first god bundles were fashioned from the remains of gods sacrificed after the creation of the SUN at TEOTIHUACAN. Masked deity bundles resembling funerary bundles occur in Maya iconography as early as the 4th c. AD. On Tikal Stela 4, the ruler Curl Snout holds a masked TLALOC bundle rendered in the fashion of Teotihuacan. Aside

Blood serpents emanating from the neck of a decapitated ballplayer, El Aparicio, Veracruz, Late Classic period.

Figure engaged in **bloodletting** from his penis, detail of Huastec conch shell pendant, Postclassic period.

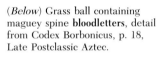

(*Below*) Grass ball containing maguey spine **bloodletters**, detail from Codex Borbonicus, p. 18, Late Postclassic Aztec.

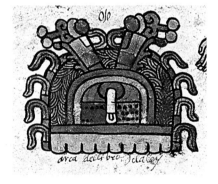

(*Below*) Sacred **bundles**: (left to right) bundle with *icatz* glyph, Yaxchilán Lintel 1, Late Classic Maya; smoking bundle, Codex Borgia, p. 35, Late Postclassic; bundle with flint blade of 9 Wind, Codex Nuttall, p. 15, Late Postclassic Mixtec.

from masked god bundles, round, knotted bundles commonly appear in Classic Maya scenes. In a number of instances, they are epigraphically labeled *icatz*, meaning "bundle" or "burden" in several highland Mayan languages. *See also* MORTUARY BUNDLES.

butterfly Although relatively rare in ancient Maya art, butterflies commonly appear in the iconography of highland Mexico, particularly at the great center of TEOTIHUACAN, where they often display wings, antennae, feathered proboscises and feather-rimmed eyes. In addition, they may be depicted with the toothy maw of the JAGUAR. The butterfly-jaguar also appears among the Classic period Zapotecs and Maya, frequently in contexts of war. In Late Postclassic Central Mexico, butterflies symbolized both FIRE and the souls of dead warriors. Seen in the light of the militaristic butterfly-jaguar and the widespread appearance of butterflies on Teotihuacan INCENSE burners, the Teotihuacan butterfly can also be identified with FIRE and war.

cacao Whether consumed as an esteemed drink or exchanged as money, cacao (*Theobroma cacao*) was one of the most important plant products of ancient Mesoamerica. The seeds derived from the pod of the cacao tree were widely used as currency and John Lloyd Stephens reported the use of cacao currency as late as the mid-19th c. in Yucatán. When ground into powder, the seeds were mixed with water and flavoring agents to create a frothy beverage greatly favored by the native elite. Recent epigraphic research has established that the word *cacao* was fully present among the Classic Maya – in fact, many of the fine Classic Maya polychrome vases are glyphically labeled as cacao drinking vessels.

caiman One of the most venerated carnivores of Mesoamerica was the caiman (*Caiman crocodilus*). Because of its aquatic habitat, great size, and spiny back, the caiman was a common metaphor for the mountainous EARTH floating upon the SEA. Explicit portrayals of the caiman appear as early as the Formative Olmec, where it is rendered both in portable art and monumental sculpture. In the art of Late Preclassic Izapa, caimans are depicted

as the trunks of trees, presumably to represent the *axis mundi*, generally considered as the CEIBA (*Ceiba* spp.). With its thorny, swelling trunk, the ceiba does indeed bear some resemblance to the rough back of the caiman. In Nahuatl, the term for caiman is *cipactli*, meaning "spiny one."

Both the Maya and Central Mexicans identified the caiman with aged creator gods. In Central Mexico, the aged TONACATECUHTLI, or Lord of Our Sustenance, presided over the first of the 20 day names, Cipactli, or Caiman, as well as the 13-day TRECENA of 1 Cipactli (*see* CALENDAR). Among the Maya, this aged creator god was known as ITZAMNA, quite possibly the paramount god of the Maya pantheon. In a number of instances, Itzamna is portrayed within the body of the caiman, probably Itzamna as Itzam Cab Ain, meaning Itzam Earth Caiman.

calendar Mesoamerican calendars tracked the solar year, lunar year, Venus cycle, and other perceivable phenomena as well as supernatural and ritual cycles whose fundamental bases remain unknown. The calendar was essential to the arts of prediction and DIVINATION as well as to the celebration of religious festivals. The most sophisticated calendrical observations in ancient Mexico and Guatemala were made by the Classic Maya, AD 300–900, but written evidence for use of a calendar goes back to the 6th c. BC.

260-day almanac
Common to all Mesoamerica, the 260-day cycle, the oldest and most important calendar, remains in use among a few groups of highland Maya in Guatemala and among some Oaxacan peoples. (Some highland Maya still keep a 365-day calendar as well.) In this calendar, a repeating cycle of 20 day names pairs with 13 day numbers, yielding a count of 260 days, a number that bears no relation either to astronomical or to agricultural phenomena. It was probably devised by midwives to calculate birthdates, working from first missed menstrual period to BIRTH, approximating the 9-month human gestation period. In many parts of Mexico, humans and gods took their names from their date of birth in this calendar, and were regarded as having completed one 260-day cycle at birth.

This calendar took a special name in every native language, although many of the names are now lost, and archaeologists have some-

(*Left*) **Butterfly** warrior with shield and spearthrower, Xelhá, Quintana Roo, Early Classic period. Although found in the Maya area, this mural painting is in typical Teotihuacan style.

Maya glyph to be read **cacao**, from cacao vessel excavated at Río Azul, Guatemala, Early Classic period.

Caiman tree, detail of Izapa Stela 25, Protoclassic Maya. This tree probably refers to the great ceiba, which has a green spiny trunk reminiscent of the caiman.

times invented terms like the pseudo-Yucatec Maya *tzolkin* to refer to the count of 260 days. The Aztecs called it the *tonalpohualli*, and the book in which it was recorded the *tonalamatl*. No other book in Mesoamerica was so important to the diviner, for the 260-day almanac was the fundamental guide to the future, and every day and number offered clues for interpretation. Gifts and short-comings were bestowed by one's date of birth, and those born on troublesome days were often renamed on more auspicious ones.

Each one of the 20 day names had a specific association with a supernatural patron, and many had associations with natural phenomena. The Maya and Aztec associations are as follows:

	Maya, Yucatec name	Aztec name	meaning, association
1	Imix (waterlily)	Cipactli (caiman)	surface of the earth
2	Ik (wind)	Ehecatl (wind)	wind
3	Akbal (darkness)	Calli (house)	night, darkness, jaguar
4	Kan (maize)	Cuetzpallin (lizard)	maize, abundance
5	Chicchan (celestial snake)	Coatl (snake)	snake
6	Cimi (death)	Miquiztli (death)	death
7	Manik (deer)	Mazatl (deer)	deer
8	Lamat (Venus)	Tochtli (rabbit)	Venus, rabbit
9	Muluc (jade, water)	Atl (water)	water
10	Oc (dog)	Itzcuintli (dog)	dog
11	Chuen (monkey)	Ozomatli (monkey)	monkey
12	Eb (evil rain?)	Malinalli (grass)	
13	Ben (green maize)	Acatl (reed)	
14	Ix (jaguar)	Ocelotl (jaguar)	jaguar
15	Men (eagle)	Cuauhtli (eagle)	eagle
16	Cib (wax)	Cozcacuauhtli (king vulture)	
17	Caban (earth)	Ollin (movement)	earth, earthquake
18	Edznab (flint)	Tecpatl (flint)	flint
19	Cauac (storm)	Quiahuitl (rain)	rain, storm
20	Ahau (lord)	Xochitl (flower)	sun

The trecena

In the *tonalamatl*, the period of 260 days was divided into TRECENAS (the Nahuatl word is no longer known, and Mesoamericanists use the Spanish term), or periods of 13 days, counted 1–13, with each new *trecena* beginning with the numeral 1. The first day of the *trecena* and its auguries reigned over the entire 13-day period, as did one or two gods. According to the Codex Borbonicus, for example, those born in the *trecena* 1 Atl would be impoverished, and the entire 13-day period begun on that particular day was in general a bad one.

The solar year

In conjunction with the 260-day almanac a 365-day calendar was used. Corresponding roughly to the solar year but lacking the leap days necessary for long-term accuracy of the true tropical year, this calendar was divided into 18 periods of 20 days each, plus 5 "nameless" and unlucky days at the end of the year. In Central Mexico, each 20-day period was called a VEINTENA, literally a "unit of twenty" in Spanish. Each group of 20 days had its own "month" name and was linked with a number from 1 to 20 or 0 to 19, depending on the region. Among the Classic Maya, each of the months had a supernatural patron; the Water Lily Jaguar, for example, oversaw the first month, Pop.

Each Aztec year bore the name of the 260-day almanac that occurred on the last day of the 18th month. This works out to be one of four possible day names (with its number). The Maya and most other peoples named their years for the first day of the new year in the 260-day almanac. These days were called YEARBEARERS and historical dates from the Aztec reign are generally known by the yearbearer name. The Spanish, for example, began their march to the Aztec capital in the year 1 Acatl (1 Reed). Without leap days, the calendar slowly wandered through the seasons, requiring movable feasts or periodic reconfiguration of agricultural festivals. Archaeologists call this year the "Vague Year," and, in the Maya region, refer to it as the *haab*.

The veintena

Less important than the *trecena* to the Aztecs was the VEINTENA, the 20-day period, or "month." The 18 Aztec *veintenas* were succeeded by the *nemontemi*, or nameless days, after Tititl, before the beginning of a new 365-day year. Among some groups, the five nameless days were thought to be particularly dangerous, and it was considered ill fortune for a child to be born at that time.

The calendar round, or 52-year cycle

When the 260-day calendar and 365-day calendar were set in motion with one another, it took exactly 52 years of 365 days, a total of 18,980 days, for a given date to repeat. This period is called a calendar round, and any human completing a calendar round would have been old indeed. The Aztecs represented the calendar round as the *xiuhmolpilli*, or "year bundle," and carved sculptures of 52 sticks bound together to symbolize it.

Among the Aztecs, the completion of 52 years – and the beginning of a new calendar round – commanded widespread preparation. To initiate a new calendar round, the Aztecs celebrated the ritual of New Fire. The last New Fire ceremony was celebrated during the month of Panquetzaliztli, a few months after the new year of 2 Acatl (2 Reed) had begun in AD 1507. *See also* FIRE.

The Long Count and Initial Series

Charting longer periods of time required a different kind of calendar. Toward the end of the Late Preclassic, in all likelihood somewhere along the Isthmus of Tehuantepec, what is known as the Long Count was introduced, to be perfected by the Maya in Classic times. Long Count dates record the total number of days elapsed since a mythological zero date that can be correlated to 2 August 3114 BC in European notation. Like all Mesoamerican counts, the Long Count used the vigesimal (i.e. based on the number 20), rather than decimal, system. The most fundamental unit was the day, or *kin*, to follow the Yucatec Maya terminology from the time of the Conquest. Periods of time were counted by days, periods of 20 days (the *uinal*), years – sometimes called "computing years" by archaeologists – of 360 days (the *tun*), 20-year periods of 360 days each (the *katun*), and 400-year periods (the *baktun*). Even larger periods of time were calibrated, and at the time of the Conquest, words were still known for 8000 *tuns* (the *pictun*) and 160,000 *tuns* (the *calabtun*). Long Count dates were inscribed in place notation, beginning with the largest unit, usually the *baktun*, and moving in order to the smallest one, the *kin*, in a pattern that has also come to be called

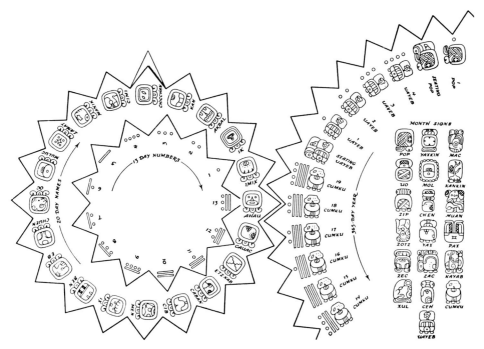

All Mesoamerica observed the *calendar round or 52-year cycle*, created by the intermeshing of the 260-day calendar (left) and the 365-day calendar (right). It is drawn here as a system of interlocking cog wheels and follows standard Maya notation, although the days and months had different names and symbols in each culture.

The 260-day calendar is composed of 20 day names (outer wheel) and 13 day numbers (inner wheel), both of which rotate endlessly. It takes 260 days for all the combinations to occur.

The 365-day calendar comprises 18 months, each of which has only 20 days, numbered 0–19 or 1–20 depending on the region, and the 5 unlucky days. In this larger wheel, the end of the month of Cumku and the 5 unlucky days are shown – other month glyphs are at the right.

Here, 13 Ahau (left) and 18 Cumku interlock. It will take 52 × 365 days (or 52 years) before the cycles will all reach this point again.

(Below) Calendar wheel representing the 52 years of the yearbearer cycle, Manuscrit Tovar, 16th c. Central Mexico.

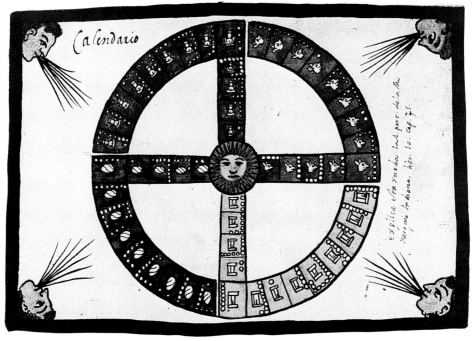

the Initial Series. This calendar bore no relation to the solar year and was usually used in conjunction with dates in both the 365-day calendar and the 260-day almanac.

Long Count or Initial Series dates can be easily recognized: they usually begin Maya inscriptions and are indicated by large introductory glyphs called "Initial Series Introducing Glyphs." The coefficients to the glyphs referring to the periods of time are frequently recorded in bar-and-dot numeration in which five dots equal one bar.

To hold open filled places, this calendar requires a null cipher, a placeholder similar to our zero, although in the Maya conception the place is full, or completed, rather than empty. The intellectual development of the idea of zero took place only twice in history – once in ancient India, among the Hindus, and once in Mesoamerica. The Postclassic Maya represented the symbol for completion as a SHELL, probably because they used such shells in working out their arithmetic. The Classic Maya used an abstract cruciform symbol somewhat resembling the European Maltese cross, possibly a schema derived from an outstretched human body, the 20 digits of fingers and toes indicating a full vigesimal place. The head variant of the completion sign is the head of a death god.

The Maya celebrated period-ending dates, that is, dates of completion of periods of time, frequently *katuns* or half-*katuns*. The completion of 13 *katuns* in the tenth *baktun* (that is, after the completion of the ninth and while the tenth was ongoing) was much celebrated by the Maya and would be transcribed in Arabic numbers as 9.13.0.0.0.

The tropical year
Despite the fact that Mesoamerican calendars included no mechanisms for tracking true tropical years and the leap days they require, the pattern of anniversaries celebrated at some Maya cities and recorded in the Long Count indicates that those who counted the solar years were well aware of the problem. At Piedras Negras, true tropical year anniversaries were calculated over periods of at least 200 years.

The lunar calendar and solar eclipses
Although lunar calendars may well have been kept across Mesoamerica, the only recorded ones survive in Maya inscriptions, appended to the Initial Series as part of what has been called the Supplementary Series, and in the series of lunations counted in the Postclassic Dresden Codex. In the Supplementary Series, ages of lunations on a given date are generally reckoned from the first appearance of the new MOON, counted by their position in the six-month lunar half-year, and tallied for total days, either 29 or 30. Eventually, the Maya came to recognize that 149 lunations = 4,400 days, or 29.53020 days per month in decimal terms, a number very close to the 29.53059 used by modern astronomers.

In and of itself, a lunar calendar may have been of intrinsic interest, but careful lunar calculations were also necessary in order to produce ECLIPSE warning dates. Eclipses were believed to threaten disaster for Mesoamerican people, so their prediction would have been of great use. Solar eclipses take place only during the dark of the moon, and within 18 days of when the moon's path crosses the apparent path of the SUN. The lunar tables of the Dresden Codex calibrated such coincidences in order to generate eclipse warning dates. Late in the 8th c., a total eclipse did occur during the dry season in the Maya lowlands, and the phenomenon was recorded in the Supplementary Series of a stela at Santa Elena Poco Uinic.

Supplementary Series
The calendrical data that follow the Initial Series in Maya inscriptions are known as the Supplementary Series, or Lunar Series, because most of the information carried there deals with the moon. The glyphs have been given alphabet labels by modern scholars and run in reverse order, starting with the letter G and continuing on through A. Glyph G comprises the nine various Maya Lords of the Night (see below). Glyph F refers to Glyph G and probably signifies its seating. Glyphs E and D record the age of the current moon. Glyph C records the number of moons completed in the current lunar half-year, and so it usually bears a coefficient. After the letters had already been designated, scholars noticed that a glyph following C varied depending on the coefficient of Glyph C, and it was labeled X, with variants X1-X6. Glyph B features a rodent head; it links Glyphs X and A indicating only that X names A. Glyph A confirms that the current lunar month is of 29 or 30 days. Glyphs Y and Z occasionally appear between Glyphs F and E; their meaning is obscure.

819-day count

The Maya held the numbers 7, 9, and 13 to be sacred. Multiplied, they yield 819, the number of days counted in a never-ending cycle that occasionally exists as a separate clause inserted in the Supplementary Series following an Initial Series. (Only 13 examples are known.) No beginning date is known for the cycle, but days are always counted backward from the Initial Series in order to reach the last date on which the cycle was completed. These 819-day references have four different stations, each associated with one of the four cardinal DIRECTIONS and its associated COLOR.

Lords of the Night

Most Mesoamerican calendars included a separate count of the Nine Lords of the Night, who ruled over the nighttime hours. The Maya Nine Lords are known as the "G" series of the Supplementary Series. Some of the Maya Nine Lords have been identified with specific gods: G7, for example, may well be the jaguar-pawed patron of the month Pax; G9 is a PAUAHTUN. The Maya Lords of the Night ran continuously through the Long Count. Since the 360 days of the Maya *tun* are perfectly divisible by nine, every period ending date of the Long Count of a *tun* or larger included G9.

The Aztec Lords of the Night were inscribed in the divinatory *tonalamatl* section of many of the Conquest-era manuscripts that survive – sometimes with notations in European script, which facilitate their identification. Although there was some variation depending on time and region, many of the Nine Lords were standard, and the cycle generally ran: XIUHTECUHTLI, Itztli or Tecpatl, Piltzintecuhtli, CINTEOTL, MICTLANTECUHTLI, CHALCHIUHTLICUE, TLAZOLTEOTL, Tepeyollotl, and TLALOC. Each one of these nine gods probably held an association with one of the nine levels of the UNDERWORLD. Unlike the Maya series, the Aztec series did not always run continuously and sometimes began anew with each *trecena*.

Birds of the Day

Associated with the 13 levels of the heavens, 13 birds served as patrons of the daytime hours. They repeat in order, following the day numbers of the *trecena*, or 13-day "week" of the Aztecs. Jonathan Kendall has recently revised Alfonso Caso's identifications.

A *Long Count* date from Burial 48 at the Maya site of Tikal, Guatemala. The date given – reading from top to bottom – is 9.1.1.10.10 4 Oc, or 9 baktuns, 1 katun, 1 tun, 10 uinals and 10 kins, with the day name 4 Oc at the bottom. In modern terms this is 19 March AD 457.

Glyph G of the Supplementary Series, referring to the nine *Lords of the Night*, Late Classic Maya.

Although often referred to as Birds of the Day, these creatures are more appropriately called "volatiles," since one is specifically a BUTTERFLY. Most are creatures of the daytime, but at least two OWLS occur in the series. They can be identifed as the following, in English and Nahuatl, with possible zoological identifications:

1. Hummingbird, probably xiuhuitzilin
2. Hummingbird, probably quetzalhuitzilin, *Calypte costae*
3. Dove, cocotli, *Scardafella inca*
4. Quail, tecuzolin, *Cyrtonyx montezumae*
5. Raven or Black Hawk-eagle, possibly itztlhotli
6. Owl, chicuatli, *Tyto alba*
7. Butterfly, papalotl
8. Eagle, cuauhtli, *Aquila chrysaëtos*
9. Turkey, totolin, *Melealgris gallopavo*
10. Great Horned Owl, tecolotl, *Bubo virginianus*
11. Scarlet Macaw, chiconcuetzali, *Ara macao*
12. Quetzal, quetzaltototl, *Pharomachrus mocinno*
13. Parrot, toznene, *Amazona oratrix*

Lords of the Day
Thirteen Lords of the Day accompanied each day of the *trecena*, repeating anew and in order for each *trecena*. According to most Aztec sources, these gods ran as follows:

1. Xiuhtecuhtli
2. Tlaltecuhtli
3. Chalchiuhtlicue
4. Tonatiuh
5. Tlazolteotl
6. Mictlantecuhtli
7. Cinteotl
8. Tlaloc
9. Quetzalcoatl
10. Tezcatlipoca
11. Chalmecatecuhtli, a god of sacrifice
12. Tlahuizcalpantecuhtli
13. Citlalincue, goddess of the heavens

Venus cycle
Throughout Mesoamerica, VENUS was the most keenly observed planet, and its cycle of 584 days was carefully charted and inscribed alongside other calendrical reckonings. Although the synodic period of the planet varies from 580 to 587 days, any five cycles average out to 584 days for a total of 2920 days, also the multiple of 8×365. When considered in terms of two 52-year cycles, or

what the Aztecs considered a "great cycle," the Venus, 260-day, and 365-day cycles all lined up. Such numerical coincidences of interlocking cycles appealed to Mesoamerican calendar keepers and facilitated calculations.

In both Mexican and Maya records, Venus was recorded to appear for 236 days as the morning star, then to disappear for 90 days during Superior Conjunction, reappear as the evening star for 250 days, then briefly vanish into Inferior Conjunction for 8 days before reappearing as the morning star. For reasons impossible to reconstruct, these calculations ignore the pattern of Venus that can be observed by the naked eye: roughly equal periods of 263 days for both morning and evening star, divided by disappearances of 50 and 8 days.

Because of the extreme malevolence associated with Venus, its dramatic movements often assured baleful events, particularly warfare. In the Venus calendar, special attention was given to the risings of the morning and evening star immediately following conjunction, as well as to points of maximum brightness, maximum elongation, and to stationary points.

Camaxtli *see* MIXCOATL

cannibalism In recent years, the subject of Mesoamerican cannibalism has been hotly debated. Some scholars have suggested that cannibalism did not occur; others have argued that human flesh formed an essential component of the Aztec diet. It is unlikely that either assertion is true. Reports of cannibalism are not simply a product of European bias or propaganda for there is abundant evidence of cannibalism in early Colonial native documents. However, the eating of human flesh was neither common nor casual; it was a religious act imbued with sacred significance.

Probably of considerable antiquity in Mesoamerica, cannibalism is suggested by fractured human bone in Early Formative household refuse deposits at the Olmec site of San Lorenzo. However, the best documentation of cannibalism pertains to the Late Postclassic period. Among the Tarascans of Michoacán, the bodies of human victims were divided among the chief PRIESTS, who, after offering the flesh to the gods, would consume the remains. According to Diego de Landa and other Colonial sources, the Yucatec Maya also considered the flesh of HUMAN SACRIFICE to be sacred food. The holy quality of human flesh is most fully documented for the Aztecs. They commonly offered – as food for the gods – human HEARTS, flesh, and BLOOD. Thus, believing the Spanish to be gods, the Aztecs initially presented them with food soaked in human blood. But although human flesh was used to sustain the gods, it also served as a vehicle for consuming divinity, that is, as a form of communion. Thus DEITY IMPERSONATION was a frequent component of Aztec sacrificial rites. When the victim embodied the deity, then one partook of the divine being through the consumption of human flesh.

Cannibalism: the cooking and consumption of human flesh, Florentine Codex, Book 4, 16th c. Central Mexico.

canoe The dugout canoe was the most common form of boat in ancient Mesoamerica and was used by long-distance seafarers as well as by more conventional travelers on lakes and rivers. Neither sails nor oarlocks were known in the Precolumbian world; skilled paddlers propelled the craft. Christopher Columbus, on his fourth and final voyage in 1502, encountered a huge Maya canoe off the coast of Honduras, "as long as a galley and eight feet wide," manned by at least two dozen crew, a captain, and assorted women and children, and with some sort of cabin amidships. A trading vessel, this canoe carried cotton mantles, weapons, metalwork, pottery, and CACAO. Mesoamerican canoes are usually shown, however, as much smaller craft, with gunwhales near the water. In art and WRITING, Maya canoes sometimes bear the glyph for wood, to indicate what material they were made of.

A rain god (Chac) paddling a **canoe** containing the headdress and merchant bundle of God L, Dresden Codex, p. 43, Postclassic Maya.

In Maya iconography, canoes carry the dead through the precarious passage from the world of the living to the world of the dead. Like their human counterparts, gods also travel by canoe. The CHACS (rain gods) fish from canoes, and the PADDLER GODS escort characters into the UNDERWORLD. In the Mixtec codices, Mixtec kings frequently journey by canoe. Given the broad, slow-moving waterways that cut across the Olmec region of the Gulf Coast, canoes were probably of great significance to that early civilization, and a number of miniature canoes carved of translucent blue-green JADE have been recovered from Olmec finds.

captives In Mesoamerican combat, warriors sought not to kill opponents but to take captives alive on the field for subsequent

Bas-relief of a **captive** ("Danzante") at Monte Albán, Oaxaca, Middle Formative period.

SACRIFICE or slavery. Although many captives were slain shortly after capture, others may have been kept for years. A captive king – of which there were many among the Maya – would have made an ideal hostage and could have ensured large tribute payments. Among the Aztecs, and perhaps among their predecessors, captives were sometimes engaged to play gladiatorial games, in which they played with handicaps in order to be defeated (see TEMALACATL).

Prior to ACCESSION, kings needed to take captives to demonstrate their prowess in battle, and some captives would be slain at the inauguration itself. According to Durán, captives were offered and slain at every major festival of the agricultural cycle.

The Olmecs made the earliest depictions of captives and they are shown bound by ropes on the sides of altars or thrones at La Venta. At Monte Albán, Zapotec lords proclaimed their victories in the first millennium BC with a series of carved slabs which are misnamed "Danzantes," or "dancers" (see DANCE), but which actually depict humiliated captives, some with their genitalia cut away.

Captives appear trodden under the feet on some of the earliest Maya monuments, a tradition that continued during the Late Classic, when they are also frequently represented on both treads and risers of stairs, where their depictions would be repeatedly stepped on. Maya captives usually display signs of humiliation; they are often naked, sometimes with exposed and exaggerated genitalia, and they bear name glyphs on their bodies. Captives, as well as lords performing AUTOSACRIFICE, donned strips of PAPER or shredded and punched cloth. As recorded in art, they make gestures of abject obeisance, touching broken parasols to the earth, placing hands on the forehead or in the mouth, or crossing one arm across the body to the opposite shoulder.

Among the Aztecs and Mixtecs, captives in preparation for sacrifice bear paper banners; others wear tufts of down on their heads. The Aztecs painted other captives in the red candy-cane striping of the god MIXCOATL.

cardinal points *see* DIRECTIONS

cargo In many regions of contemporary Mesoamerica, a ritual system known as the cargo defines the means of participating in the civil and religious responsibilities of the community. Quite often, the individual provides both economic support and community service in the form of work tasks and ritual observances, in positions of rotating authority frequently held one year at a time.

Although the native and Spanish origins of modern Mesoamerican cargo systems are still a source of some debate, the concept of public office as a burden or "cargo" is of great antiquity in Mesoamerica. Among the Tarascans of Michoacán, one type of native priest, the Curitiecha, was said to carry the burden of the people upon his back. In the ritual address at the ACCESSION of the Aztec king, or *huey* TLATOANI, the office of rulership was described as a burden to be passed from one king to another. This idea of rulership as a burden may be also seen in both Olmec and Maya representations of atlantean figures supporting thrones. Among the Late Postclassic Yucatec Maya the concept of public office as a burden was definitely present. Here it was known as *cuch*, the Yucatec Mayan word for burden. In Late Postclassic Yucatán, wealthy commoners, rather than nobles, served in the office of *ah cuch cab*, or "bearer of the community." According to one 16th c. Spanish source, the *ah cuch cab* oversaw the payment of tribute and organized his town ward for war and public ceremonies.

Cauac Monster *see* MOUNTAINS

caves In traditional Mesoamerica, caves are generally regarded with a certain degree of ambivalence. Sources of fertility and riches, they also open into the UNDERWORLD and the dark, unwholesome world of the dead. In Late Postclassic Central Mexican art, open-mouthed SERPENTS represented caves, as if the convoluted passageways constituted the entrails of the snake.

Cave worship extends back to at least Olmec times. Olmec thrones commonly depict individuals emerging out of circular niches that probably represent caves. At Oxtotitlan, Juxtlahuaca, and other caves of highland Guerrero, paintings in pure Olmec style adorn entrances and walls deep within, strongly suggesting that these isolated caves were important PILGRIMAGE sites. The quatrefoil frequently symbolized the cave in Olmec art. Rock carvings at Chalcatzingo depict the quatrefoil in profile and *en face* as a monstrous face sprouting MAIZE foliage.

The ritual use of caves was common during the Classic period. Excavations in 1971 revealed that a quatrefoil cave lies directly underneath the massive Pyramid of the Sun at TEOTIHUACAN. Much like the later CHICOMOZTOC of Late Postclassic Central Mexico, this cave may have represented a place of emergence. Cave sites are widespread in the karstic terrain of the Maya lowlands. The cave of Naj Tunich, Guatemala, contains Late Classic paintings and hieroglyphic texts of exceptional refinement and beauty.

ceiba Sacred to the Maya, the ceiba tree was frequently recognized as a living axis mundi that penetrated the navel of the EARTH, reaching from the UNDERWORLD to the heavens. The Maya called the ceiba *yaxché*, meaning first or green tree. It is likely that one would have been found at the center of most pre-Conquest cities or villages, but ceibas may also have been found at the outskirts, one to mark each of the four cardinal DIRECTIONS.

Young ceiba trees are spiny, and some spiked Maya braziers may have been formed in their image. The fully grown ceiba shoots up tall and straight, with few or no branches until the level of rain forest canopy. There, the major branches may be limited to four, and thus the ceiba may also have served as the model for the cross motif in Classic Maya art. The four-petaled flower of the ceiba may play a role in Maya iconography.

At the time of the Conquest, the Yucatec Maya believed that the ceiba tree shaded the divine paradise, offering refuge to those fortunate enough to ascend there. According to some accounts, the ceiba was also the first tree of the world. At Izapa, in a depiction of what is probably a creation story, the ceiba arises from a CAIMAN.

As a member of the bombax (*Bombacacae*) family, ceiba tree pods hold kapok, or silk-cotton, a fiber with low specific gravity and complete water resistance that is now commonly used to fill life jackets.

celestial bird Celestial birds are associated with the cardinal points in Mesoamerican religion. On the first page of the Codex Féjerváry-Mayer, celestial birds perch atop each of the four trees associated with the four DIRECTIONS. The Aztecs also assigned 13 "volatiles," of which 12 are birds and 1 is a BUTTERFLY, to the 13 numbers of the calendrical TRECENA; because there are 13, they may bear

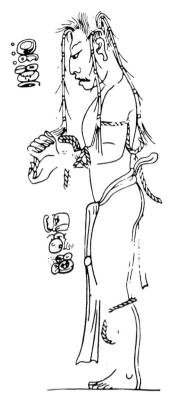

A **captive** incised on bone from Burial 116, Temple 1, Tikal, Late Classic Maya. According to the text, this individual was a captive from the site of Calakmul.

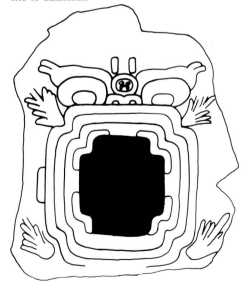

An Olmec representation of a **cave**, Middle Formative period. Probably from Chalcatzingo, Morelos, this relief possesses a quatrefoil mouth that may have served as an entrance to an actual cave in its original context.

association with the 13 levels of the heavens, giving them some celestial significance.

Among the Maya, VUCUB CAQUIX of the POPOL VUH is a celestial bird, for he rose as a false sun prior to the dawning of the era in which humans populated the earth. The Hero Twins shoot out his jaw with their blowguns, causing his demise. This Vucub Caquix of the Quiché Maya is the same celestial bird identified as the PRINCIPAL BIRD DEITY in Classic and Late Preclassic art. At Piedras Negras, the Principal Bird Deity presides over the niche scenes of royal inaugurations; at Palenque, it sits atop cruciform images. The Principal Bird Deity sometimes wears costume elements of ITZAMNA, and may therefore be an aspect of that god.

celt A celt is a ground stone axe head. During the Early and Middle Formative eras, when stone celts played an important role in Olmec ritual and belief, ground and polished celts of fine jadeite were frequently placed in caches. In many instances, these jadeite celts are incised with fine designs, and associated iconography suggests that they may have symbolized ears of MAIZE. Although this may be partly due to their form and verdant color, the association of celts with agriculture and maize may also derive from their use as axe blades. During the Formative period, the importance of maize and farming grew explosively, and farmers depended upon ground stone axes for clearing forests for planting. A similar situation prevailed in Neolithic Europe, where – during the initial period of farming and forest clearing – ground stone celts took on a significance far beyond that of simple tools. The many celt representations in Neolithic art together with actual examples in precious stone reveal that they also were held in great reverence.

The Olmecs deposited and buried vast pavements of celts at La Venta, part of a ritual whose meaning has never been determined. Images of Olmec deities, such as the WERE-JAGUAR of the Kunz Axe, were sometimes formed as celts themselves, and the Kunz Axe deity clasps a celt in his hands.

The Late Preclassic and Classic Zapotecs and Maya also made and used celts. Both Maya and Zapotec nobles wore head-and-celt assemblages, typically with three thin celts dangling from a large head ornament, and examples have been found in Maya and Zapotec tombs.

Contemporary Mesoamerican peoples regard Prehispanic celts discovered in fields as spent LIGHTNING. It is unknown whether such a belief was also present among the ancient Olmecs.

cenote Known by a word corrupted from the Yucatec Mayan *dzonot*, cenotes, or natural sinkholes, are the principal sources of water in the northern lowlands of Yucatán, where there are neither rivers nor lakes. Many cenotes served primarily as sources of fresh water, but others, most notably the Sacred Cenote at Chichen Itzá, were PILGRIMAGE destinations and places for offerings. Some cenotes occur deep within CAVES, such as Balankanché, where John Lloyd Stephens and Frederick Catherwood visited and documented an active practice of worship in the 1840s. Many cenotes that served as foci of worship were dedicated to the CHACS, the Maya RAIN gods.

The Sacred Cenote at Chichen Itzá may have been the single most important destination for pilgrims in pre-Conquest Yucatán. As Clemency Coggins has suggested, the great round surface of WATER may have been perceived as a giant MIRROR for DIVINATION and auguring. For generations, offerings were hurled into the water, including JADES, gold disks and humans. There is no evidence that virgins in particular were selected as cenote offerings, but much of the skeletal material recovered at the Chichen cenote was of pre-pubescent boys and girls. According to ethnohistorical accounts, some cenote victims apparently floated up from the well alive, with auguries garnered under water.

In 1536, during a period in which the Spanish withdrew from Yucatán, the ruler of the Xiu family, Ah Dzun Xiu, sought to appease the Maya gods by making a pilgrimage to the Sacred Cenote at Chichen Itzá. He and his entourage were guaranteed safe passage through Cocom territory, where they would need to pass en route to Chichen. Remembering old grievances, however, the Cocoms set upon their visitors at a celebratory banquet, slaughtering them all. No offerings were made to the cenote, civil war ensued, and the Spanish returned in 1540 to complete their conquest of Yucatán.

ceremonial bar Ceremonial bars are staffs held by Maya rulers, generally across the body in both arms. They were frequently used on the occasions of period endings (*see* CALENDAR). In its most conventional form, a ceremonial bar ends in two open SERPENT mouths, from which emerge deities, including God K (*see* SCHELLHAS GODS), CHAC, the Jaguar God of the Underworld (*see* JAGUAR GODS), and God N, among others. The body of the bar may be composed of crossed bands, the MAT motif, a SKY BAND, BLOODLETTING knots, or other motifs. The bar may well symbolize the SKY itself, as if to show that the ruler holds the sky in his arms. The ceremonial bar symbolizes the role the Maya ruler plays in supporting the cosmos and nurturing the gods.

Found on the earliest dated Maya stela with archaeological context – Tikal Stela 29 with a date of AD 292 – the ceremonial bar persists as an emblem of rulership and divine sanction until the end of Classic times. A black-painted Maya lord in a bird costume bears one in the Terminal Classic paintings at Cacaxtla, Tlaxcala. The ceremonial bar may have evolved from Olmec prototypes. Early Maya depictions of the ceremonial bar are sinewy and snake-like, perhaps because of the homophony between sky and snake in Mayan languages, while later ceremonial bars are depicted as rigid objects.

Chac The Maya god of RAIN and LIGHTNING, Chac is one of the longest continuously worshipped gods of ancient Mesoamerica. First known from the Protoclassic Maya sites, Chac continues to be worshipped among Maya peoples to this day. Izapa Stela 1 depicts Chac fishing with a net and carrying a creel upon his back; similar scenes of him fishing are known from the later Classic period. During the Classic period, he may be recognized by his catfish-like whiskers, blunt reptilian snout, and body scales. In addition, he frequently has a prominent bound shank of hair and a spondylus shell earpiece. The Postclassic form of Chac in Maya codices generally appears more human than his Classic antecedent. While this later Chac, designated God B by Paul Schellhas, lacks the serpentine body scales, his most striking trait is a long, pendulous nose which, although grotesque, appears more human than reptilian.

In Classic and Postclassic Maya scenes, Chac often wields his lightning weapons, sometimes a hafted stone axe or a SERPENT, a widespread metaphor for lightning in Mesoamerica and the American Southwest.

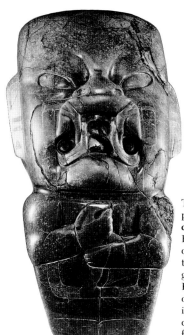

The Kunz Axe, a personified jadeite **celt**, Middle Formative Olmec, originally owned by the famed gemologist Frederick Kunz. Weighing over 15 lb (7 kg), it is among the largest carved jades known for Mesoamerica.

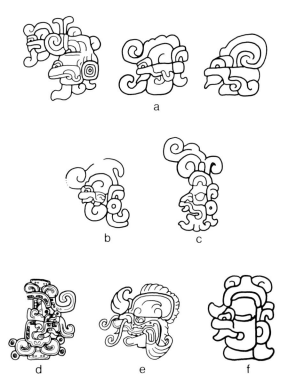

Protoclassic representations of **Chac**: *a*, Izapa Stela 1; *b*, Kaminaljuyú Stela 4; *c*, El Baúl Stela 1; *d*, carved stone vase; *e*, incised limestone disk; *f*, stucco sculpture, Uaxactún.

Flames or torches often allude to the fiery nature of Chac's lightning.

Because Chac presides over WATER and rain as well as lightning, he commonly appears in streams of falling water or water-filled CENOTES, and serves as a patron of agriculture. Colonial and contemporary Maya mythology credits Chac with breaking open a great rock containing the original life-giving MAIZE. Scenes in monumental art and pottery reveal that this myth was present among the Classic Maya over 1000 years ago. *See also* COCIJO; SCHELLHAS GODS; TLALOC.

chacmool A term coined by the 19th c. explorer Augustus Le Plongeon, *chacmool* literally means red or great jaguar paw in Yucatec Mayan, but Le Plongeon used the word to describe the three-dimensional, reclining figures found atop the TEMPLES at Chichen Itzá. Characteristically, the head of a *chacmool* is turned 90 degrees from the front of the body, and the figure supports himself on his elbows. The bowls or disks held on the chests of *chacmools* were receptacles for offerings; in one Aztec example, the vessel held by the reclining figure is specifically a CUAUHXICALLI, or receptacle for the HEARTS of sacrificial victims. *Chacmools* may symbolize fallen warriors who deliver offerings to the gods.

Known from Terminal Classic times on through the Spanish Conquest, *chacmools* have been found across Mesoamerica, from El Salvador to Michoacán, although most of the known examples come from Chichen Itzá or Tula. Many were set in association with THRONES or sacrificial stones.

Chalchiuhtlicue or She of the Jade Skirt is the Central Mexican goddess of lakes and streams. Patron of the day Serpent, she also presides over the TRECENA of 1 Reed. In the Nahuatl myth of the FIVE SUNS, she is the regent of Nahui Atl, or 4 Water, the previous world destroyed by flooding. The watery nature of the human womb thus ensures that Chalchiuhtlicue plays an important part in Central Mexican birth ceremonies, particularly BAPTISM. In codical representations of Chalchiuhtlicue, a pair of male and female infants may be seen in a stream issuing from the goddess. Quite clearly, these scenes illustrate Chalchiuhtlicue as a goddess of BIRTH. In the codices, Chalchiuhtlicue usually wears a JADE ornamented skirt. An especially

important attribute is the pair of one or two short black lines running vertically down her lower cheeks. *See also* WATER.

Chicomecoatl In highland Mexico, both gods and humans commonly took names derived from the 260-day CALENDAR. The name Chicomecoatl, or 7 Serpent, is an example of such a calendrical name. Chicomecoatl is an Aztec goddess of food and produce, especially MAIZE. In Aztec art, she appears with attributes of CHALCHIUHTLICUE, including the short, vertical facial lines and headdress. However, she can usually be distinguished by ears of maize carried either in her hands or on her back.

Chicomoztoc Literally "the seven caves," this was a legendary mountain perforated by a single cave or by seven caves, and was considered a sacred place by the Aztecs and most other Nahuatl-speaking people of Central Mexico at the time of the Conquest. For many groups, Chicomoztoc was the place of origin from which mankind emerged; the Aztecs believed that they had sojourned there some time after their initial departure from the legendary AZTLAN. In the mid-15th c., Motecuhzoma I sent 60 wise men to seek out Chicomoztoc, to learn more about Motecuhzoma's ancestors, and to find out if the mother of HUITZILOPOCHTLI was still alive.

At the time of the Conquest, most Maya peoples of highland Guatemala also recognized authority issued by a place that the Quiché called Tulan Zuyua, or "seven caves." In the POPOL VUH the tribal lineage heads journey to Tulan Zuyua to receive their gods; TOHIL, for example, was loaded into the pack of Balam Quitze to be carried back home.

In 1971, during excavations to install sound and lighting equipment at TEOTIHUACAN, a CAVE was found under the Pyramid of the Sun. The cave features several small chambers, almost in a clover-leaf arrangement, similar to the radiating caves depicted in the picture of Chicomoztoc in the *Historia Tolteca-Chichimeca*, and was used as a retreat for ritual. Caves have been found at other ancient sites, and a number may have been regarded at one time as a Chicomoztoc.

chocolate *see* CACAO

Cihuacoatl Literally "woman-snake," Cihuacoatl is one of a number of related mother and EARTH goddesses worshipped in Postclassic

Central Mexico. Cihuacoatl overlaps with Teteoinnan, TOCI, TLAZOLTEOTL, and perhaps most closely, ILAMATECUHTLI. She is one of the goddesses of midwifery, and through that association, of the SWEATBATH as well. She frequently has a warlike aspect and may bear spears and a shield. Midwives exhorted women to call out to her in childbirth and to be as warriors in the violent expelling of the child from the womb. Although frequently depicted as a skeletal hag, she can also overlap with XOCHIQUETZAL, a young and beautiful goddess.

In the addresses of midwives, Cihuacoatl is always paired with Quilaztli. According to the song of Cihuacoatl in Sahagún, she was the protector of the Chalmeca and the patron of Culhuacan.

Cihuacoatl was also the title borne by a secondary ruler in the Aztec capital of Tenochtitlan. Unlike the great TLATOANI, or speaker, the *cihuacoatl* handled internal affairs in the city. In the 15th c., Tlacaelel served as *cihuacoatl* under four sequential *tlatoanis*: Motecuhzoma the Elder, Axayacatl, Tizoc, and Ahuitzotl; he commanded the army, directed SACRIFICES, and served as senior counselor to the supreme ruler. In the title *cihuacoatl* we find embodied the very nature of duality that pervades the Aztec world-view: male versus female and internal versus external.

Cihuateteo The Aztecs believed that two groups of supernaturals accompanied the SUN on its passage from east to west. In the east, souls of warriors who died in combat exhorted and accompanied the sun as it rose to midday zenith. In the corresponding western sky (the place of solar descent) were the Cihuateteo, or Women Gods. The Cihuateteo were female warriors, the *mociuaquetzque*, women who died in childbirth. The Aztecs likened the act of BIRTH to that of obtaining a CAPTIVE in war, women who died in the attempt were valiant warriors slain in battle. Aztec warriors fought vigorously over the bodily remains of *mociuaquetzque*, which were kept as talismans to ensure bravery and success in battle. No benevolent mothers, the Cihuateteo wreaked havoc, and it was believed that they haunted CROSSROADS at NIGHT to steal children and to cause seizures and insanity. In addition, these night demons could seduce men and cause them to commit adultery and other sexual transgressions.

Chacmool, Tula, Early Postclassic period.

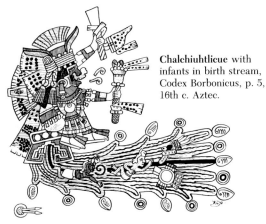

Chalchiuhtlicue with infants in birth stream, Codex Borbonicus, p. 5, 16th c. Aztec.

Chicomoztoc, the seven caves of emergence, Historia Tolteca-Chichimeca, 16th c. Central Mexico.

Probable forms of the Cihuateteo appear in the Borgia and Vaticanus B codices, corresponding to the days 1 Mazatl, 1 Quiahuitl, 1 Ozomatli, 1 Calli, and 1 Cuauhtli. As well as being the days on which the five western TRECENAS begin, these ominous days marked the descent of the Cihuateteo demons to the earth. A group of Aztec stone sculptures of kneeling women with skeletalized faces and taloned hands have also been identified as Cihuateteo. Like the women illustrated in the Borgia and Vaticanus B passages, these figures are also labeled with the days naming the five western *trecenas*.

cinnabar and hematite Cinnabar and hematite are naturally occurring mineral ores. They are both a brilliant, lasting red color and were applied to ritual objects throughout ancient Mesoamerica.

Hematite, or iron ore, occurs in diverse geological configurations of sedimentary rocks; its most desirable form was "specular," a sparkling, crystalline hematite formed by masses of compact platelets. It was often mixed with white stucco to make red stucco paint, with which, for example, the temples and palaces of Palenque were painted. Thin plates of crystalline hematite could also be assembled to form MIRRORS and mosaics.

Cinnabar, a red mercuric sulfide and the ore from which mercury (Hg) is extracted, is mined today in northern Mexico. In geological terms, however, it occurs in any volcanic environment, and so may have been available at a number of sites in Mexico and Guatemala. It is a soft red ore also known as "native vermilion," and sometimes yields mercury naturally. Generally, though, in order to produce mercury, the ore must be heated and the fumes then condensed. At Copán, Kaminaljuyú, and sites in Belize, liquid mercury has been recovered archaeologically. More typically, however, the ore itself was used. From Olmec times onward, cinnabar was rubbed into ritual objects. The skeletal remains of many Maya royal burials reveal that the bodies were liberally coated with cinnabar after DEATH.

Cinteotl Also known as Centeotl, this deity is the masculine Central Mexican god of MAIZE, *cintli* (*Zea mays*). According to the Florentine Codex, Cinteotl is the son of the aged earth goddess TOCI, Our Grandmother. In the codices, he is portrayed as a young man with yellow body coloration. Along with the frequent presence of maize in his headdress, one of his most characteristic traits is the jogged black line passing down the brow, across the cheek, and then down again to the base of the jaw. Precisely the same facial marking commonly appears with the Late Postclassic Maya MAIZE GOD.

cloth Cloth had intrinsic value in ancient Mesoamerica, and many aspects of its manufacture and use had particular religious associations. Among the Nahuatl-speaking peoples of Central Mexico, TLAZOLTEOTL and XOCHIQUETZAL were patrons of weavers, and in surviving depictions, Tlazolteotl frequently wears spools of spun cotton in her hair. In the VEINTENA of Ochpaniztli, the impersonator of TOCI was forced to weave as part of the ritual sacrifice.

In one Aztec hymn, Xochiquetzal is said to come from TAMOANCHAN, a legendary place that may lie in the rich tropical Gulf Coast or Maya region. One of Tlazolteotl's names is Ixcuina, a Huastec name from the Gulf Coast. Since much Prehispanic COTTON was cultivated along the Gulf Coast, these patrons of weaving may have been coastal goddesses before they were incorporated into the Aztec pantheon. Among the Maya, the old goddess named as Chac Chel in the Dresden Codex is also a patron of weavers.

Unspun cotton was made into thread by seated women who pulled down the fibers resting on their heads or held loose on their shoulders, giving them a twist with one hand and then pulling out the thread with the other. Once spun, cotton thread – or occasionally MAGUEY fiber – was woven on backstrap looms into long strips of cloth, frequently with elaborate designs, some of which can be seen in the Bonampak murals or the Codex Magliabechiano. Hand-loomed cloth was almost never cut, but in scenes of Maya SACRIFICE and in depictions of CAPTIVES, ripped, shredded, or punched-out cloth is sometimes depicted as a visual metaphor of the cutting and bleeding during sacrifice.

Because the native cotton plant (*Gossypium hirsutum*) of Mesoamerica will not grow at the high altitude of the Valley of Mexico, the Aztecs demanded cotton cloth from most of the 371 towns that paid them tribute; according to the Codex Mendoza, it was the single most important item of tribute. Cotton mantles functioned as a means of common exchange in a society without coinage. Sahagún said that one large mantle equaled the value of one canoe; 30 large cotton mantles equaled a slave, and 40 were worth a slave who could sing and dance! *See also* COSTUME.

Cloud Serpent *see* MIXCOATL

clowns Ritual clowns are widely known in both Colonial and contemporary Mesoamerica. Like the modern Pueblo clowns of the American Southwest, these performers provide both entertainment and biting social commentary. The following is a Spanish description of the early Colonial Yucatec clowns known as *baldzam*: "They are clever in their mottoes and jokes, that they say to their mayor and judges: if they are too rigorous, ambitious, or greedy, they portray the events that occurred and even what concerns the official's own duties, these are said in front of him, and at times with a single word."

But along with being amusing social commentators, the native ritual clowns tend to be endowed with considerable supernatural power. During their performances, the clowns are frequently believed to become particular gods, demons, and other supernatural entities. In addition, through role reversal and inversion, they often seem to embody the chaotic timeless powers from before creation. In Mesoamerica, sacred clowns commonly appear at critical junctures during rites of passage, such as ACCESSION to office, or new year celebrations and other calendrical events.

Ritual clowns are commonly depicted in Classic Maya art. Rather than appearing in monumental sculpture, they are usually rendered on small portable objects, such as figurines or vases. They tend to be aged and grotesquely ugly characters, often with animal attributes. In addition, they often appear dancing with FANS and rattles – signs of performers. Still earlier ritual clowns appear in the ceramic art of Colima. Dating to the Protoclassic period (100 BC–AD 300), these West Mexican sculptures portray rotund ithyphallic characters, animal-masked dancers, and other probable clowns. *See also* FAT GOD.

coatepantli The *coatepantli* was a common architectural feature of Late Postclassic Central Mexico. A wall of SERPENTS, the *coatepantli*

Cinteotl, the Central Mexican god of maize, Codex Borgia, p. 14, Late Postclassic period.

A Late Classic Maya **clown** with dancing fan and rattle, detail from a Maya vase.

was used to demarcate sacred enclosures within a ceremonial precinct. At Tenochtitlan, such a serpent wall framed part of the Templo Mayor, and some of the monumental XIUHCOATL serpent heads discovered there were probably parts of *coatepantli* walls. An intact *coatepantli* of Xiuhcoatl serpents can be seen surrounding a twin pyramid at the site of Tenayuca.

The *coatepantli* is not known at the Classic site of TEOTIHUACAN, and may have been first devised at the Early Postclassic site of Tula, Hidalgo (*see* TOLLAN), where a *coatepantli* flanks Pyramid B, one of the major structures. The wall of this *coatepantli* displays partly skeletalized human figures being devoured by rattlesnakes. The serpents have flames emanating from their bodies and it is probable that they are fire serpents, that is, forms of the Xiuhcoatl.

Coatepec or Serpent Mountain was one of the more important places of Aztec mythology. This sacred MOUNTAIN constituted the birthplace of HUITZILOPOCHTLI, and it was there that the newly born god defeated COYOLXAUHQUI and her 400 brothers, the Centzon Huitznahua. Although the actual Coatepec mountain is located close to the Toltec site of Tula, Hidalgo (*see* TOLLAN), this sacred place was replicated in the heart of the Aztec capital of Tenochtitlan, where it was long thought by archaeologists that the Huitzilopochtli side of the great dual Templo Mayor represented Mount Coatepec. Striking physical corroboration of this belief occurred in 1978 with the discovery of the dismembered Coyolxauhqui sculpture at the base of the Huitzilopochtli temple stairway. This sculpture corresponds perfectly to the Aztec myth which describes the severed remains of Coyolxauhqui tumbling to the base of Mount Coatepec.

Coatlicue According to Aztec belief, the mother of HUITZILOPOCHTLI was Coatlicue, She of the Serpent Skirt. In Aztec accounts, Coatlicue was miraculously impregnated with a ball of down while sweeping at COATEPEC. Her children, COYOLXAUHQUI and the Centzon Huitznahua, were furious at her condition and decided to kill her. At the moment of her DEATH, Coatlicue gave BIRTH to the fully armed Huitzilopochtli, who then defeated and slew Coyolxauhqui and the Centzon Huitznahua. According to a 16th c. account by Diego Durán, the Aztecs performed a festival in honor of Coatlicue at Coatepec.

Depictions of Coatlicue are fairly rare in Aztec art. The most famous representation, and one of the most powerful Aztec sculptures, is the colossal figure discovered in 1790 alongside the cathedral of Mexico. Standing on huge taloned feet, Coatlicue wears a dress of woven rattlesnakes. Her pendulous breasts are partially obscured behind a grisly necklace of severed HEARTS and hands. Writhing coral snakes appear in place of her head and hands, denoting gouts of BLOOD gushing from her severed throat and wrists. The two great snakes emerging from her neck face one another, creating a face of living blood. A monument of cosmic terror, Coatlicue stands violated and mutilated, her wounds mutely demanding revenge against her enemies. Although a stupendous monument, this Coatlicue sculpture is not unique; two very similar but poorly preserved examples have also been discovered in Mexico City.

Cocijo In Zapotec, the term *cocijo* signifies both LIGHTNING and the god of lightning and RAIN. The god Cocijo is commonly found on Zapotec ceramic urns from the Middle Formative period of Monte Albán I to the end of the Late Classic period. Like the Classic Maya CHAC, Cocijo usually has a zoomorphic face with a thick, blunt snout. One of his oldest and most consistent characteristics is his long bifurcated serpentine tongue. Although not occurring with the Maya rain god Chac, similar tongues are found with jaguar forms of the rain god TLALOC at Classic period TEOTIHUACAN.

Quite frequently, Cocijo appears with a particular sign – Zapotec Glyph C – in his headdress. In the Postclassic Mixtec codices, a similar glyph serves as a sign for the day name Water. It is probable, therefore, that Zapotec Glyph C represents the day name Water, an appropriate emblem for the god of rain and lightning.

The Postclassic Zapotecs termed the four 65-day divisions of the 260-day calendar "Cocijos," suggesting that there were four Cocijos oriented to the world DIRECTIONS. BLOODLETTING and other religious observations were performed to the Cocijos of the four calendrical periods. Passages in the Central Mexican Vaticanus B and Borgia codices also illustrate this four-fold division of the 260-day calendar. There, however, Tlaloc – rather than Cocijo – is portrayed in each of the four divisions.

codex The term codex generally refers to a rare manuscript. In Mesoamerican research, it is frequently used to denote native screenfold books formed of strips of pounded bark PAPER or DEER hide painted on both sides with a fine coating of white lime gesso. These strips were carefully folded into equal widths, with each fold creating two pages on opposite sides of the manuscript. Once folded, intricate scenes were first carefully outlined and then frequently filled in with brilliant colors. Both sides of the manuscript were usually painted, with the pages tending to run left to right across one side, and then returning left to right across the other.

Scenes on Classic Maya vases and the archaeological discovery of stucco remains of actual books reveal that screenfold codices were fully present among the Classic Maya. However, all the intact screenfolds that have survived date to the Postclassic and early Colonial periods. These contain a wealth of information about gods and rituals, mythology, history, flora, fauna, and even trade and tribute. Unfortunately, due to centuries of intolerance and neglect, only a small portion of these books survive to this day. Some 25 Postclassic and early Colonial screenfold codices are known, with 18 of these being in pure pre-Conquest style.

colors In Mesoamerican cosmology, colors are frequently associated with particular DIRECTIONS. The identification of colors with directions is most fully documented among the ancient Maya, who had specific glyphs for the colors red, white, black, yellow, and green. In the Yucatec Maya codices, these colors are associated with east, north, west, south and center, respectively. Monumental texts describing the 819-day cycle (*see* CALENDAR) reveal that the Classic Maya also identified red, white, black, and yellow with the same directions.

In Colonial accounts from Central Mexico, there is frequent mention of four basic colors. However, not only are the colors rarely oriented with regard to specific directions, but there is also considerable variation as to which are the four primary colors. According to one source, the directional colors were green, blue, red and yellow. However, other accounts suggest that the four cardinal colors

The serpent wall, or **coatepantli**, surrounding the Aztec Templo Mayor, Codex Durán, 16th c. Central Mexico.

Giant statue of **Coatlicue**, She of the Serpent Skirt, mother of Huitzilopochtli, Late Postclassic Aztec. Her head is composed of blood serpents pouring from her severed throat.

Cocijo, the Zapotec god of rain and lightning, ceramic urn, Classic period.

were the same as those of the Maya. Moreover, like the Maya, Central Mexicans appear
to have identified white with the north and
yellow with the south.

colossal heads After 1200 BC, the Olmecs
wrought colossal heads from huge boulders
of basalt from the Tuxtla Mountains that they
must have floated on balsa rafts along the
slow-moving rivers of the Gulf Coast. With
neither contemporary texts nor relevant
ethnohistory, the heads have been the subject
of speculation, and they have been identified
at one time or another as ballplayers, gods,
or humans. Most scholars now believe that
the heads commemorate actual rulers. The
majority of them suffered some ritual deface-
ment; at the very least dimpled depressions
were ground into them. Recent detective
work has proposed that some THRONES were
recarved into colossal heads. According to
such a theory, the place of seated power
would be extinguished and converted to a
more neutral human memorial.

At La Venta, four colossal heads were set
as if to guard the ceremonial core of the site,
three to the south and one to the north, all
with their backs to the architecture. With
their stern, solemn expressions, such heads
may have embodied living rulers, and they
would have been seen from a distance. After
the death of a ruler, the colossal heads may
have been the focus of ancestor worship.

completion sign *see* CALENDAR

confession Confession constituted an important form of ritual PURIFICATION. For the
Yucatec Maya, confession was performed
during the BAPTISM of children. Among the
Maya of Yucatán and Alta Verapaz, confession was common at times of grave illness
or approaching DEATH. According to Tomás
López Medel, Maya communities in Guatemala performed confession by selecting an
old woman as a scapegoat. Forced to hear
the confessions of all of the community, this
woman was then stoned. It was believed that
by her death, the whole town was purified.

For the Aztecs, TLAZOLTEOTL was the goddess of confessions. In the company of a
calendar priest, the individual would confess
in front of an image of Tlazolteotl. Along with
the confession, the penitent individual passed
pieces of grass through the tongue or phallus,
each piece corresponding to a particular

transgression. Fray Burgoa recorded that during the mid-17th c. the Zapotecs of Oaxaca
also performed BLOODLETTING in conjunction
with a confession to a native priest. The blood
was dripped upon strips of MAIZE husk which
were taken and presented by the priest to a
stone idol.

coronation *see* ACCESSION

costume Mesoamerican costume generally
encodes a wide variety of information in the
case of both human and divine protagonists.
Among the Aztecs, for example, costume and
facial representations differentiate closely
related deities from one another more effec-
tively than other physical characteristics.
Costume indicates the status and role of a
given individual; even today in Mexico and
Guatemala, costume is the key to ethnicity,
and village identity is reinforced through
common textile designs, styles of dress, and
headgear. At Mitla, the facades of Terminal
Classic palaces bear various geometric patterns and designs, perhaps references to uni-
fication of regional identity, both Zapotec and
Mixtec, through public display of costume
and cloth.

Men and women, both human and divine,
wore distinct garments. Some Aztec sculptures were meant to be dressed; now, without
their costumes, their identity as specific
deities is lost. Mesoamerican garments were
generally fashioned by draping CLOTH around
the body or sewing strips of fabric together
but rarely cutting and tailoring cloth. Basic
attire for men was the loincloth (the Nahuatl
maxtlatl); women wore skirts with draped
blouses (the Nahuatl *quechquemitl* and Maya
huipil). Warriors and priests donned sleeve-
less jackets (Nahuatl *xicolli*). Central Mexican
lords at the time of the Conquest wore the
tilmatli, a toga-like garment the wearing of
which was governed by strict sumptuary
laws. The most prestigious *tilmatlis* were the
longest ones with the most elaborate woven
designs; their wear was limited to the upper
classes and to men who had scarred their
bodies in battle. The importance of these
cloaks is emphasized by the pages devoted to
their motifs in the Codex Magliabechiano.
Commoners were generally restricted to
coarse *tilmatlis* woven of MAGUEY fiber. Fine
raiment rewarded victorious warriors, and
the more CAPTIVES they took, the fancier the
attire they wore.

The headdress is the most significant part of any costume. In depictions in the codices, Mixtec nobles and deities often wear their names in their headdresses, as do occasionally Maya nobility. It was not only humans and deities who bore insignia on their heads: the affiliations of TEMPLES were often presented by a billboard-like display on the roofcomb, or even by the shape of the roofcomb, resembling headgear. The temple to QUETZALCOATL in the sacred precinct of Tenochtitlan had a conical roof, akin to Quetzalcoatl's conical headdress. A number of Aztec goddesses wear a headdress that looks like a temple doorway, conflating the analogy between headdress, deity, and insignia.

Among the nobility, specific costumes were worn for particular rituals. Durán describes elaborate costumes distributed to all participants and observers of Aztec sacrificial rites, including crowns of feathers, gold arm sheathing, jaguar pelt sandals, fancy mantles and loincloths, and JADE nose plugs. In battle, Aztec warriors dressed as predatory animals: EAGLES, JAGUARS, pumas, and coyotes. The mantles of a bride and groom were tied together to symbolize their MARRIAGE. In all cultures, ballplayers donned thick padding at the waist, knee, and elbow. Once Cortés began his march to Tenochtitlan, Motecuhzoma II, according to some sources, sent four deity costumes to him to see if he would don one and reveal himself to be a god.

Among the Maya, a number of specific ritual costumes have been recognized. A beaded cape and skirt, worn with an open spondylus shell waist ornament that may symbolize the female womb, is a costume worn by noble women, but it also identifies the MAIZE GOD; men don the costume to embody the god and his fertility. In the depictions of ACCESSION to office at Piedras Negras, kings wear simple attire, with a headdress that sprouts MAIZE and maize foliage, as if to reinforce connections to community and agriculture; when those same kings conduct battles outside the immediate community, but against other Maya, they wear a costume based on foreign motifs from TEOTIHUACAN.

cotton Although the cotton used in ancient Mesoamerica was generally of a single species (*Gossypium hirsutum*), there were many varieties distinguished by growing cycles and fiber color. Woven cotton CLOTH not only functioned as clothing, but was also an

Maya directional **color** glyphs derived from the Dresden Codex.

Red (*chac*), east

White (*zac*), north

Black (*ek*), west

Yellow (*kan*), south

Green (*yax*), center

 Colossal head from La Venta, Tabasco, Middle Formative Olmec. These colossal heads constitute some of the earliest portraiture known for the New World.

Tribute sign referring to 400 bales of **cotton**, Matrícula de Tributos, 16th c. Aztec.

important article of tribute. It served too as religious offerings, as TEMPLE hangings or awnings, as vestments for god images, and as wrappings for sacred BUNDLES and MORTUARY BUNDLES.

Since the preparation and weaving of cotton was primarily a female task, goddesses are frequently portrayed as spinners and weavers. In the Yucatec Maya codices, both the youthful Goddess I and the aged Goddess O (see SCHELLHAS GODS) are portrayed as weavers. In Central Mexico, TLAZOLTEOTL is closely identified with weaving, and wears a headband of unspun cotton with a pair of cotton spindles as her headdress. One of her common epithets was Ixcuina, a Huastec term signifying Cotton Woman.

Coyolxauhqui The evil older sister of HUITZI-LOPOCHTLI and the Centzon Huitznahua, Coyolxauhqui was one of the major goddesses of Aztec mythology. Furious over the pregnancy of COATLICUE, Coyolxauhqui slew her mother with the aid of her 400 brothers, the Centzon Huitznahua. The dying Coatlicue gave birth to Huitzilopochtli, who, armed with his XIUHCOATL weapon, dismembered Coyolxauhqui and routed the Centzon Huitznahua at the hill of COATEPEC. According to the Florentine Codex account of this battle, the severed remains of Coyolxauhqui tumbled to the base of Coatepec.

In 1978, a massive representation of Coyolxauhqui was discovered at the base of the Huitzilopochtli side of the Templo Mayor in Tenochtitlan. As in the cited Aztec text, she is depicted with her head and limbs severed from her torso, as if tumbling down the hill of Coatepec. At least two other Coyolxauhqui monuments were found at the Templo Mayor. The stucco remains of an earlier nude and dismembered Coyolxauhqui lay directly under the stone sculpture. In addition to this stucco sculpture, fragments of another stone Coyolxauhqui disk were also discovered. Although similar in scale, style, and composition, this fragmentary sculpture does not appear to represent Coyolxauhqui with severed limbs. Nonetheless, it contains an especially important detail, for the tail and segmented body of the Xiuhcoatl can actually be seen penetrating the chest of Coyolxauhqui. This relief portrays the mythic charter for the ritual of heart sacrifice that was practiced on a massive scale at the Templo Mayor (see HEARTS). Each victim

thrown down the steps of the Huitzilopochtli temple replicated the battle at Coatepec.

Aside from the newly discovered reliefs from the Templo Mayor, another monumental Coyolxauhqui sculpture survives. In this case, she is represented as a lifeless severed head. As in the case of the intact disk from the Templo Mayor, she displays on her cheeks the metal *coyolli* bells for which she is named. In addition, she also wears the same metal year sign ear ornaments and circular elements of eagle down in her hair. Much of the costume and iconography of Coyolxauhqui seems to derive from Chantico, goddess of the hearth and patron of Xochimilco. Although it has been often stated that Coyolxauhqui represents the MOON, there is no explicit evidence for this identification. According to one recent study, Coyolxauhqui may actually be a goddess of the MILKY WAY.

creation accounts The origins of the gods, the world, and its inhabitants form the basis of Mesoamerican mythology. Unfortunately, our understanding of native creation mythology is only partial, and is best documented for Central Mexico and the Maya region. Nonetheless, common patterns can be discerned. Quite frequently, the act of creation begins in darkness with the primordial SEA. The Quiché Maya POPOL VUH contains a moving description of this original creative event. Surrounded by the still waters of the sea, the gods Tepeu and Gucumatz engage in dialogue and thus begin the act of creation. Through their speech, the EARTH and MOUNTAINS are raised out of the WATER.

Although the *Popol Vuh* creators place animals upon the earth, these creatures lack the voices and understanding to worship and nourish the gods. The GODS thus decide to create people. In their first attempt, they fashion people from mud; being soft and weak, however, the people are soon destroyed. In their second attempt, the gods consult the diviners Xpiyacoc and Xmucane, who suggest that men be fashioned from wood and women from rushes. Although this new race of people can speak and multiply, they still lack understanding of their world and their makers, so the gods send down a great flood and a rain of pitch to destroy them. Fierce demons, animals, and their own household utensils join in the attack. Those people that escape became the MONKEYS seen today.

Following the destruction of the wood and rush people, Tepeu and Gucumatz decide to fashion humans from MAIZE. Brought by four animals from the mountain of Paxil, this maize is ground into nine drinks from which the first four men are made. But although these people of maize worship and nourish the gods, they are too knowledgeable and wise, too like the gods who made them. For this reason, the gods cloud their eyes, limiting the vision of the present human race, the people of corn, to what is immediate and close. Following the creation of the first four men and their wives, the first dawning takes place and some animals and gods turn to stone.

In the *Popol Vuh*, the destruction of the wooden men and the creation of the people of corn is separated by a long and extremely important account describing the doings of two sets of twins. The older pair, HUN HUNAHPU and Vucub Hunahpu, are summoned to play ball with the lords of the UNDERWORLD, Xibalba, who then defeat and sacrifice the twins, placing the head of Hun Hunahpu in a gourd tree. This miraculous head impregnates an underworld maiden, Xquic, who escapes to the surface of the earth. Here she gives birth to the second pair of twins, the sons of Hun Hunahpu. Known as the Hero Twins, Hunahpu and Xbalanque are great monster-slayers and ballplayers. When they in turn are summoned to play ball in the Underworld, they eventually defeat the lords of Xibalba and retrieve the remains of their father and uncle.

The placement of the Hero Twins episode before the creation of the maize people is not fortuitous. The abundant Classic Maya scenes illustrating Hun Hunahpu and his sons Hunahpu and Xbalanque reveal that Hun Hunahpu is actually the god of corn. Thus the descent of Hunahpu and Xbalanque to rescue their father also signifies the search for corn, the material from which mankind is made. In a number of Late Classic Maya vessel scenes, Hun Hunahpu is flanked by his sons as he rises out of the earth as growing maize. This Classic episode of Hun Hunahpu, the ancestor of people, rising out of the earth constitutes a form of the emergence myth found widely over Mesoamerica and the American Southwest.

The concept of multiple creations is found among other contact period and contemporary Maya peoples. According to a 16th c.

Giant **Coyolxauhqui** stone, Aztec Templo Mayor, Tenochtitlan.

Maya **creation accounts**: Hun Hunahpu, the Tonsured Maize God, rising out of the tortoise earth; spotted Hunahpu at left, and Xbalanque with jaguar skin markings to the right. Scene from the interior of a Late Classic Maya bowl.

account from the Cakchiquel, neighbors of the Quiché, people were first fashioned of mud. Following their destruction, the present race of mankind was created from ground maize mixed with the blood of tapir and SERPENT. The flood myth is known for the Colonial Yucatec Maya, for in certain of the Books of Chilam Balam there is mention of a race of individuals destroyed in the flood. These accounts also describe the erection of WORLD TREES following the flood. Although the Colonial Yucatec sources provide only tangential references to previous creations, these are explicitly recorded in modern Yucatec texts, which describe three distinct worlds and races of people before the present creation.

Highly developed in Central Mexico, this notion of multiple creation reaches its highest complexity in the great cosmogonic myth of the FIVE SUNS. Although there is some variation in the known accounts, the basic pattern is quite similar to the Quiché *Popol Vuh*. With the first acts of creation, the creator couple prepared the way for the first of the four suns, or worlds, previous to the present creation. Named after the days on which they end, the four suns usually occur in the following order, Nahui Ocelotl (4 Jaguar), Nahui Ehecatl (4 Wind), Nahui Quiahuitl (4 Rain), and Nahui Atl (4 Water). Each sun is presided over by a deity and race of people who are either destroyed or transformed into a particular creature. TEZCATLIPOCA is the god of the first sun, Nahui Ocelotl. The people of this world are giants, and are devoured by JAGUARS. Presided over by the wind god EHECATL, the second sun of Nahui Ehecatl is destroyed by wind and its people become MONKEYS. The RAIN and LIGHTNING deity TLALOC is the god of Nahui Quiahuitl, which is consumed by fiery rain – possibly an allusion to volcanic eruption – while its people turn into BUTTERFLIES, DOGS, and turkeys. The water goddess CHALCHI-UHTLICUE presides over the fourth sun, Nahui Atl; the flood ending this sun transforms the human inhabitants into fish.

Following the flood ending the fourth sun, Tezcatlipoca and QUETZALCOATL raise the heavens by transforming themselves into two great trees. In several accounts, these two gods create the earth by slaying a huge earth monster described either as a CAIMAN or as the earth deity TLALTECUHTLI.

Although the earth is created at this point, no people inhabit its surface. In a journey

strongly resembling the *Popol Vuh* and Classic Maya mythology, Quetzalcoatl and XOLOTL descend to the UNDERWORLD to retrieve the remains of the people destroyed in the flood. In order to obtain the precious bones, they trick the wily god of death, MICTLANTE-CUHTLI. The bones are then taken to TAMOAN-CHAN, where the gods grind them like corn into a fine meal. Upon this ground meal, the gods let their BLOOD, thus creating the flesh of the present race of people.

After the creation of people, the gods convene in darkness at TEOTIHUACAN. It is decided that in order to create the fifth sun, Nahui Ollin, one of the gods must throw himself into a great pyre. Two volunteer, the haughty Tecuciztecatl and the diseased and lowly Nanahuatzin. Tecuciztecatl is frightened by the flames, but Nanahuatzin bravely hurls himself into the pyre and is transformed into the SUN. Tecuciztecatl follows to become the MOON. The gods then sacrifice themselves at Teotihuacan and from their remains, sacred BUNDLES or *tlaquimilolli* are fashioned.

Another common Central Mexican creation motif is the emergence of people from the earth. In essence, this differs little from the taking of the bones out of the Underworld, although in this instance, actual living humans emerge out of the earth. One of the most famous versions of the emergence myth concerns CHICOMOZTOC, the seven CAVES of emergence. In the *Historia Tolteca-Chichimeca* account of this episode, the MOUNTAIN containing the seven caves was struck open with a lightning staff. In another version of the emergence, the first people came out after the sun shot an arrow into the House of Mirrors.

Of Mixtec creation mythology little is known in comparison with that of the Maya and peoples of Central Mexico. One brief but important account derives from an early 18th c. work of Fray Gregorio García. During the time of darkness, in the primordial SEA, a creator couple sharing the same calendrical name of 1 Deer create a massive stony mountain upon which they fashion their sumptuous palace. At the peak of the mountain, a great copper axe blade supports the heavens. This creator couple has two male children, one named Wind of Nine Snakes, the other, Wind of Nine Caves. The elder of the sons has the power to transform himself into an EAGLE, whereas the younger son can become a winged SERPENT that can fly through stone as well as air. These two sons create a garden filled with fruit trees, FLOWERS, and herbs. Following the creation of the stony mountain and the brothers and their garden, heaven and earth are fashioned and humans are restored to life. Although only a tangential reference, the mention of humans being restored to life strongly suggests the multiple creations and destructions mentioned in Maya and Central Mexican creation accounts. The Mixtec creator couple are represented in two of the ancient Mixtec screenfolds, the Codex Vindobonensis and the Selden Roll, complete with the calendrical name of 1 Deer.

According to a late 16th c. work of Fray Antonio de los Reyes, the first Mixtecs emerged from the center of the earth, while later gods and rulers were born from trees near the sacred town of Apoala. In the ancient Mixtec codices, the people emerging from the earth are frequently depicted as stone men. This probably refers to an ancient predawn era as, among the Mixtecs and other Mesoamerican peoples, gods and legendary figures were turned to stone at the first dawning. The motif of tree birth, still present in contemporary Mixtec mythology, is also illustrated in both the Vindobonensis and Selden codices. *See also* ANCESTRAL COUPLE.

crossroads In native Mesoamerica, crossroads were widely regarded as dangerous places inhabited by demons and illness. The Aztecs believed that they were the favored place of the fearsome CIHUATETEO, and shrines to these demonic women were frequently placed on major crossroads. It was widely believed that crossroads were an important place to leave dangerous contaminants such as items associated with social misdeeds or DISEASE. Grass brooms, a sign of PURIFICATION, are commonly seen with Central Mexican representations of crossroads.

cuauhxicalli Literally "eagle gourd," the *cuauhxicalli* was the vessel in which the Aztecs made their most sacred offerings, human HEARTS. Real gourds, as well as finely carved stone objects, may have been used for *cuauhxicallis* at the time of the Conquest. The very oldest representations have been found at Chichen Itzá, so the tradition may date to the Toltec era or earlier. In the POPOL VUH, the messenger owls are told to sacrifice Blood Woman, pregnant with the Hero

Mixtec **creation accounts**: a scene of tree birth, Codex Vindobonensis, Late Postclassic period.

A cave sign, a bowl with brooms and *copal*, and the body of a probable executed criminal placed with **crossroads**, Codex Laud, Late Postclassic period. In Mesoamerican thought, crossroads were widely considered to be dangerous places that provided access to the Underworld.

Eagle-plumed **cuauhxicalli** bowl containing hearts and blood, Codex Borbonicus, p. 14, 16th c. Aztec.

Twins, and to bring back her heart in a gourd bowl, perhaps a *cuauhxicalli*.

The largest known *cuauhxicalli* is the heavily maned Jaguar Cuauhxicalli of Tenochtitlan in whose back is carved a deep basin ornamented with the motifs of JADE, feathers, and hearts typical of heart vessels. At the base of the vessel are the depictions of HUITZILO-POCHTLI and TEZCATLIPOCA, both of whom draw BLOOD from their ears. A didactic message is reinforced: as the gods have offered their own blood, so humans must make offerings in the *cuauhxicalli*.

curing Illness was believed to have a number of causes, including the hostile actions of supernaturals or sorcerers, accidents, deficiencies, and excesses such as drunkenness or wanton sexuality. A major cause of sickness was imbalance and disharmony, either with society, the gods and ancestors, or the surrounding world. In order to cure the patient, it was necessary for the curer to divine the particular source of an illness. Hand casting with the 260-day CALENDAR was often used for this purpose, as it still is today in highland Guatemala. Among the common cures was PURIFICATION, such as by CONFESSION or bathing in streams or SWEATBATHS. Along with diviners, important medical specialists included midwives, surgeons and herbalists. Some of the more common forms of surgery included DENTISTRY, the removal of foreign bodies, closing wounds, setting fractures, amputation, and bleeding with obsidian lancets. However, surgery was far less developed than the native knowledge of plants, which appear in an astonishing array of different medical uses.

In the Quiché POPOL VUH, an aged couple pose as curers of broken bones, eyes and teeth in order to trick and destroy the wounded monster bird, VUCUB CAQUIX. In Postclassic Yucatán two aged deities were especially identified with curing. One of these was the old goddess IXCHEL, known as Goddess O or *chac chel* in the codices. Yucatec curers performed a festival in her honor during the 20-day month of Zip. The other aged deity was the creator god, ITZAMNA, who was also invoked during the Zip rites. In Late Post-classic Central Mexico, TLAZOLTEOTL seems to have been an especially important goddess of curing, being closely identified with both confession and the sweatbath.

D

dance Dance played an important role in ancient Mesoamerican religious ritual. Sahagún, for example, describes some sort of dance – sometimes of men, sometimes of women, and sometimes of men and women together – for almost every VEINTENA celebration of the Aztecs, with dancing frequently carried on at the base of the PYRAMID of the god honored on that occasion. The Mixtecs, too, danced to celebrate every major festival, as well as at rites of passage. An elaborate MARRIAGE dance, for example, is depicted in the Codex Selden.

Dancing frequently preceded HUMAN SACRI-FICE. During the *veintena* celebrations of Tititl, a slave woman was fully arrayed as ILAMATECUHTLI. "And before she died, she danced. The old men beat the drums for her; the singers sang for her – they intoned her song. And when she danced, she wept much, and she sighed; she felt anguish. For time was but short; the span was but brief before she would suffer, when she would reach her end on earth." (FC: II)

According to the Aztec 260-day auguries, those born in the *trecena* of 1 Monkey would be dancers, singers, or scribes. Those born on 1 Wind would be necromancers who danced with the forearm of a woman who had died in childbirth; they would be evil people, perhaps even thieves. In general the dancer was a skilled performer, and dance almost always occurred with singing and MUSIC. HUEHUECOYOTL and MACUILXOCHITL were the patrons of music and dance. According to surviving depictions, most Late Postclassic Central Mexican dance follows a counter-clockwise movement.

The reading of a long-undeciphered verb in Maya hieroglyphic writing reveals that the Maya nobility performed a wide range of dances: a snake dance performed with live boa constrictors, dances with bird staffs, God K staffs, basket staffs, and a feather dance performed by rulers and their attendants in great feather backracks. As part of a public performance of ritual BLOODLETTING, Maya lords perforated their phalli with long, colorful pairs of "dancer's wings" – or what may be painted PAPER or cloth strips stretched over wooden supports – and then danced, blood streaming across the "wings."

Other Maya lords donned the costume of the MAIZE GOD, or what has also been called the Holmul Dancer costume, and danced with DWARVES or hunchbacks, frequently with arms and hands waving at mid-body, as if in imitation of waving MAIZE foliage. UNDERWORLD deities frequently dance in procession, usually in a clockwise motion. Dancers may accompany musicians, and sometimes they bear rattles and FANS. Some Maya dance scenes are humorous spoofs. In the POPOL VUH, when commanded to perform in the court of the lords of death, the Hero Twins dance the Weasel, the Poorwill, and the Armadillo.

Many "SMILING FIGURES" of Classic Veracruz may be dancers, with their hands raised in a praying position. Musicians and dancers occur in the art of West Mexico, and the anecdotal groupings include scenes of a cheek perforation dance, in which a stick may pierce two different performers' cheeks, binding dancers together in pain and bloodletting.

The so-called Temple of Danzantes, or dancers, at Monte Albán probably depicts sacrificial victims and not dancers at all.

dawn To the native peoples of Mesoamerica the appearance of the dawn marked more than simply the beginning of day: it constituted the rebirth of the SUN out of the harrowing depths of the deathly UNDERWORLD. It was believed that after the sun set in the west, it traveled at midnight to the nadir of the Underworld and then gradually made its re-ascent to arrive at the east. The Aztecs believed that whereas the female CIHUATETEO pulled the noonday sun from zenith into the Underworld, the youthful souls of warriors slain in battle accompanied the sun in its eastern ascent. The Aztecs also believed that following its passage through the Underworld the sun required sustenance in the form of human BLOOD and HEARTS to begin its arduous ascent into the SKY.

CREATION ACCOUNTS of the first dawning contain profound insights into Mesoamerican conceptions of the sun and the day. At the first dawning at TEOTIHUACAN, the gods sacrificed themselves for the newly created sun. Although this clearly constitutes a Central Mexican charter for HUMAN SACRIFICE in order to nourish the sun, it also describes the end of mythic time. No longer moving, living beings upon the earth, the gods are now represented by their mummy-like *tlaquimilolli* BUNDLES. The now passive and inert

Curing: person with fever, Florentine Codex, Book 10, 16th c. Aztec.

A scene of Aztec **dance**, Manuscrit Tovar, 16th c.

A probable Maya sign of **dawn**: the head of the sun god between signs for earth and sky, detail of a hieroglyphic bench, Copán, Late Classic period.

nature of the gods is reiterated in a curious episode mentioned in the *Leyenda de soles*. TLAHUIZCALPANTECUHTLI, the god of dawn and the morning star, attacked the sun as it hovered over Teotihuacan. The sun, in turn, shot an arrow into the forehead of the morning star, who became the god of cold. Known as ITZTLACOLIUHQUI-IXQUIMILLI, he is also the god of stone. He commonly displays the dart of the sun transfixed through his stony headdress. The transformation of gods into inert stone is graphically described in the POPOL VUH account of the first dawn. Contemporary myths of the Zapotecs and Mixtecs of Oaxaca also mention an early race of people turned to stone at the first appearance of the sun. The first dawning marks the beginning of everyday reality, in which the gods are represented by relatively passive bundles or stone sculptures. But if the dawn and day constitute present ordered reality, the NIGHT by contrast represents the supernatural time of DREAMS and living gods re-enacted in the apparent movements of the starry sky. *See also* CREATION ACCOUNTS.

death In Mesoamerican thought death was closely integrated into the world of the living. Life and death were believed to exist in dynamic and complementary opposition. It was widely recognized that because of the basic need for nourishment, killing and SACRIFICE was a necessary aspect of life. Moreover, deceased ancestors exerted powerful influences upon the living. Not only could they send punishing DISEASES, but they could serve as intermediaries between the living and the gods. During certain of the 20-day VEINTENAS, major festivals honored the dead; the living communicated with their ancestors by means of food, flowers, and other offerings. According to the 16th c. Dominican, Fray Diego Durán, the Aztecs performed festivals for dead children during the 20-day month of Tlaxochimaco, and for adults in the following month of Xocotlhuetzi. With considerable concern, Durán noted that although originally performed in August, many aspects of these native rites were being performed during the Catholic celebrations of All Saints' Day and All Souls' Day. This festival event, now widely referred to as the Day of the Dead, is usually observed during the several days marking the end of October and the beginning of November. Marigolds and other offerings still used today in the Day of the Dead celebrations are clearly of Prehispanic origin.

In ancient Mexico, the AFTERLIFE destination of an individual varied according to his or her status and the mode of death. Most souls, however, had to perform an arduous journey to the UNDERWORLD, for which they were frequently supplied with food and clothing. It was also believed that DOGS knew the way through the Underworld, and thus they too frequently accompanied the dead. For the Aztecs, there are detailed descriptions of the Underworld hazards faced by the soul. Among these dangers are clashing hills and obsidian-edged winds. The Quiché Maya POPOL VUH describes similar hazards faced by the Hero Twins in their journey through the Underworld, including killer BATS, fierce JAGUARS, and numbing cold. The Aztecs believed that the soul was at last extinguished four years after death.

death gods In ancient Mesoamerica, there is commonly a mixture of fear and derision toward the gods of death. Although widely thought to be ruthless and cunning, they are frequently outwitted and defeated in mythological accounts. Thus QUETZALCOATL successfully steals the makings of people from the crafty MICTLANTECUHTLI. In the POPOL VUH, the Hero Twins Xbalanque and Hunahpu trick the gods of death into volunteering themselves to be sacrificed. Thus the lords of Xibalba are defeated and the twins retrieve the remains of their father and uncle. Our very presence is literally a living testimony to the ultimate defeat of the death gods.

In Central Mexico, the preeminent god of death was Mictlantecuhtli, or lord of Mictlan, the UNDERWORLD. He is usually depicted as a skeleton wearing vestments of PAPER, a common offering to the dead. Skeletal death gods are also known for Protoclassic and Classic Veracruz. At times, their animated portrayal suggests a familiarity bordering on affection. The skeletal Maya equivalent of Mictlantecuhtli is today known as God A (*see* SCHELLHAS GODS), and commonly appears in Classic Maya art as well as in the Postclassic codices. In one text from the Madrid Codex, he is referred to as *cizin*, or "flatulent one." *Cizin* is still the name for the death god among both the Yucatec and Lacandon Maya.

deer Two types of deer are native to Mesoamerica, the white-tailed deer (*Odocoileus americana*), and the smaller brocket deer (*Mazama americana*). Of these, the white-tailed deer seems to have had a far more important role in native economy and religion. Deer meat was an esteemed food offering, and the skins could be used as the wrappings of sacred BUNDLES, and as the leaves of screenfold codices (*see* CODEX). As one of the largest game animals, the white-tailed deer plays a fairly passive role in Mesoamerican mythology and is closely identified with gods of the hunt. However, in Classic Maya scenes, the deer appears in an important mythical episode in which the young Moon Goddess flees her attackers on the back of a deer. In certain scenes, this episode seems to have erotic overtones and it is likely that among the Maya, the stag was identified with sexuality.

In many Mesoamerican forms of the 20 day names, including Central Mexican, Zapotec, Mixtec and Maya versions, the term or glyph for deer serves as the seventh day name. In Postclassic Central Mexico, this day was Mazatl, with TLALOC as its presiding god. In Central Mexican sources, a two-headed deer is shot by MIXCOATL, god of the MILKY WAY and the hunt. Transformed into a woman, the deer was impregnated by Mixcoatl, and gave birth to the culture hero QUETZALCOATL.

deformity Since at least the Early Formative period there was a fascination with physical abnormalities. In Olmec art, representations of DWARVES and hunchbacks abound. Rather than being objects of derision, these individuals are often portrayed with great supernatural powers. In one instance, dwarves are represented supporting the SKY, while in another, a chinless dwarf displays heads of the great harpy EAGLE upon his brow. Representations of deformities abound in the Protoclassic ceramic tomb art of West Mexico. Along with dwarves and hunchbacks, double-headed DOGS are among the more common motifs. During the Protoclassic period, another type of deformity appears widely in Mesoamerican art. Commonly referred to by the Spanish term of TUERTO, this form appears as a grotesquely twisted face, with one eye shut, a bent nose, and a frequently extended, sideways-curving tongue.

In Late Postclassic Central Mexico, physical deformities were identified with the AHUIATETEO, gods of pleasure and physical excess. Certain physical deformities and illnesses were probably considered to be punishments

Death: a mortuary bundle placed in the mouth of a cave. Codex Laud, Late Postclassic period.

Mictlantecuhtli, the Central Mexican **death god**. A stone vessel excavated at the Templo Mayor, Tenochtitlan, Late Postclassic Aztec.

Xochipilli wearing a **deer** skin marked with the 20 day names, Codex Borgia, p. 53, Late Postclassic period.

sent by the Ahuiateteo for immoderate behavior. However, the identification of the Ahuiateteo with deformities probably goes further, as it is likely that jesters, musicians and other entertainers were frequently deformed or handicapped. The principal Ahuiateteo was MACUILXOCHITL, or 5 Flower. In the Florentine Codex he is described as a god of the palace folk, which would have included musicians, dwarves, jesters, and other entertainers.

deification Most ancient kings of Mexico and the Maya region were recognized as divine, if not in their lifetimes, then upon their deaths. According to Aztec accounts, Motecuhzoma II surely lived as divine, his feet never touching the earth, avoiding eye contact, and never eating in front of any other person. When Motecuhzoma and Cortés met on the road from Cholula to Tenochtitlan, Cortés sought to greet him as if he were a European mortal and to touch him, an act repellent to the Aztec king. Tizoc, one of Motecuhzoma's predecessors (Aztec ruler 1481-6), commemorated his victories in battle with a monument that depicts him as a conflation of two main deities, the Aztec god of war, HUITZILOPOCHTLI, and TEZCATLIPOCA, with whose serpent foot Tizoc appears.

Maya rulers held divine status after death, and in all likelihood, in life too. Deified ancestors frequently occupy the upper margin of carved stone monuments. At Tikal, Stormy Sky's father and predecessor as king, Curl Snout, looks down on him from above as the sun god. Bird Jaguar of Yaxchilán had his mother and father rendered in the heavens on his monuments, within cartouches of the sun and the moon. King Pacal of Palenque, for example, is rendered in the conflated attire of two gods upon his death: God K and the Tonsured Maize God, with whom he is apparently conjoined. A 7th c. Bonampak king, Chan-muan I, is depicted posthumously as God L; Kan Xul of Palenque appears as CHAC, again posthumously, on the Dumbarton Oaks panel. Even the erection of monumental PYRAMIDS over the tombs of dead kings suggests their apotheosis and a practice of ancestor worship among the ancient Maya. During their own lifetimes, Maya kings often appear in the guise of the MAIZE GOD, with whom they were identified.

deity impersonation Through deity impersonation, a human could become one with the gods. By having a living being perform as the god, individuals played out a collective history and a shared mythic past. Through trance and transformation, the performance of humans as deities distributed magical power and ensured the repeated efficacy of the gods.

Among the Aztecs, the deities celebrated in every VEINTENA of the year were impersonated, sometimes only for the ritual itself, sometimes for days before the culminating festival. In the most elaborate case, for the feast of Toxcatl, a young man lived as TEZCATLIPOCA for a year. In this role, he was much honored, and Motecuhzoma himself adorned him. He was accompanied by eight young men and then, 20 days before his sacrifice, he was married to four women, who themselves personified XOCHIQUETZAL, Xilonen, Atlatonan, and Uixtocihuatl.

According to Sahagún, the impersonator of Tezcatlipoca had to have a specific physical appearance: "He who was chosen was of fair countenance, of good understanding and quick, of clean body – slender like a reed; long and thin like a stout cane; well-built; not of overfed body, not corpulent, and neither very small nor exceedingly tall … [He was] like something smoothed, like a tomato, or like a pebble, as if hewn of wood … no scabs, pustules, or boils on the forehead … not protruding or long ears, nor with torpid neck, nor hunch-backed, nor stiff-necked, nor with neck elongated … not emaciated, nor fat … He who was thus, without flaws, who had no defects" would live as Tezcatlipoca for a year (FC: II).

In the month of Tlacaxipehualiztli, the impersonator of XIPE TOTEC, Our Lord the Flayed One, took on the specific characteristics of that god. For the festival, a Xipe impersonator took on the role 40 days beforehand, and he was glorified and revered as if he were the god himself. On the dawn of the day of celebration he, along with impersonators of eight other gods, among them HUITZILOPOCHTLI, QUETZALCOATL, MACUILXOCHITL, and MAYAHUEL, had their hearts sacrificed and then, immediately, their skins flayed. Other men then donned these flayed skins and the regalia of the various deities in a ceremony Durán calls Neteotoquiliztli, which he translates as "Impersonation of a God." After a ritual combat and more sacrifices, further men borrowed the flayed skins and, adorned as Xipe, begged for 20 days in the streets of Tenochtitlan. At the end of the 20 days, the foul-smelling, putrefied Xipe skins were buried within the Xipe temple. These impersonations and sacrifices of Aztec deities served constantly to renew the vitality of the god himself.

In many cases in ancient Mesoamerica, deity impersonation may have been a shamanic transformation, in which individuals had a "companion self" or TONAL into which they changed under certain conditions. The Maya hieroglyph read UAY links the names of humans with their companion selves, usually animals, and most frequently the JAGUAR. A number of Olmec sculptures show stages of the transformation from human to jaguar form and are in all likelihood shamanic transformations.

In their royal costumes, Maya kings frequently impersonated their gods, most often the MAIZE GOD, but also the JAGUAR GOD of the Underworld, CHAC, and GI of the PALENQUE TRIAD. *See also* SHAMANISM.

dentistry Although little is known of the practice or method of Mesoamerican dentistry, surviving noble skulls frequently reveal filed or inlaid teeth, from 1000 BC on until the Spanish Conquest. Both filing and drilling often left exposed nerves in the teeth and must frequently have resulted in excruciating pain, infection, and even death. Using lapidary skills and techniques, ancient Mesoamericans drilled and inserted into teeth jade beads, bits of turquoise and iron pyrites – among other materials. Dental inlay apparently always functioned cosmetically and not to repair cavities.

Among the Maya, upper incisors were sometimes filed to the T-shape of the sun god, and in this way, a human's visage could be permanently transformed into that of a major deity. The jade mosaic mask constructed directly on King Pacal of Palenque's face after death also featured tesserae that formed a T of upper incisors.

directions The four cardinal directions constitute one of the underlying frameworks of Mesoamerican religion and cosmology. The Olmecs were clearly fascinated by them, and at the Middle Formative Olmec site of La Venta, Tabasco, caches of JADE and serpentine CELTS form crosses oriented to the four directions. The placement of four cleft celts across

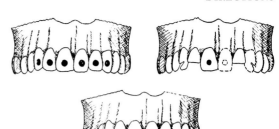

Deliberate mutilation of teeth: examples of **dentistry** from Uaxactún, Late Classic Maya.

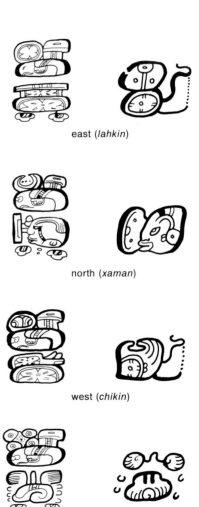

east (*lahkin*)

north (*xaman*)

west (*chikin*)

south (*nohol*)

Comparison of Early Classic and Postclassic Maya **direction** glyphs: left column, Río Azul, Early Classic; right column, Dresden Codex, Postclassic.

the headband or brow of Olmec heads may also be an allusion to the four directions. One late Olmec carving, the Humboldt Celt, may possibly represent particular signs of the four directions, oriented around a central disk containing a cross.

By the Early Classic period among the Maya, there is clear epigraphic evidence of directional glyphs. Early Classic forms of the four directional glyphs are displayed upon the walls of Tomb 12 at Río Azul, Guatemala, where they correspond to the correct cardinal directions, confirming the well-known directional glyphs appearing in the Postclassic Maya codices. Aside from the still undeciphered glyph for south, the Classic and Postclassic directional glyphs provide phonetic values corresponding to Yucatec Mayan directional terms of *lahkin* (east), *xaman* (north), and *chikin* (west).

By the Late Classic period, there is reliable epigraphic evidence for day names and COLORS oriented toward the four directions. Thus in the Classic Maya 819-day cycle, the 20 day names are consistently associated with particular colors and directions. Beginning with the first day name of Imix, the directions and colors shift through the 20 day names in a counter-clockwise motion from east and red to north and white, west and black, south and yellow. The same orientation of day names to colors and directions is well documented for the Postclassic Yucatec Maya.

Although there are no known signs for directions or colors in the writing systems of Central Mexico, directions are frequently indicated by the use of the 20 day names. As in the case of the Classic and Postclassic Maya, the day names pass in counter-clockwise succession, with the first day, Cipactli – corresponding to the Maya Imix – beginning in the east. In other words, both the Maya and Central Mexican versions of the 20 day names are oriented to precisely the same directions. Since the four directions pass five times evenly through the 20 days, each direction has five particular days. For example, the first, fifth, ninth, thirteenth, and seventeenth day names of Cipactli, Coatl, Atl, Acatl, and Ollin all correspond to the east.

In the Central Mexican codices, these four five-day groups are often used to designate the cardinal directions. Thus pages 49 to 52 of the Codex Borgia contain elaborate scenes corresponding to the four directional groupings of day names. Each of the four pages

depicts a different directional god, temple, and tree. Similar directional passages appear in the Fejérváry-Mayer, Vaticanus B, and Cospi codices. Containing references to directional gods, temples, and trees, a very similar sequence appears in the new year pages of the Maya Dresden Codex.

disease In ancient and contemporary Mesoamerica, there is an ambivalence regarding illness. Whereas disease marks an imbalanced and dangerous state, it can also denote a special relationship to supernatural powers. Frequently a person exhibiting a particular illness is believed to have received a supernatural summons. Quite often, people cured of a disease become powerful curers and SHAMANS. Some of the earliest as well as most graphic portrayals of disease appear in the Protoclassic tomb sculpture of West Mexico, especially that of the Ixtlan del Río style of Nayarit.

Diseases are commonly believed to derive from CAVES and the UNDERWORLD. The Quiché Maya POPOL VUH describes particular diseases caused by the Underworld lords of Xibalba. Among these death gods are Ahalpuh and Ahalgan, who cause swelling, pus, and jaundice, Chamiabac and Chamiaholom, makers of extreme wasting and emaciation, and Xic and Patan, bringers of blood vomit. It is probable that many of the Underworld gods and demons in Classic Maya vessel scenes are also personifications of particular diseases. In the Yucatec Maya *Ritual of the Bacabs*, the lord of the Underworld, Hun Ahau, is frequently evoked. In this Colonial text, diseases are treated as personified sentient beings that can be addressed by the curer. Among the maladies mentioned are particular seizures, asthma, and skin eruptions. Among contemporary Yucatec Maya, certain diseases are believed to be caused by insects sent from the Underworld by evil sorcerers.

In many parts of Mesoamerica, diseases are thought to be caused by sorcery. In the early Colonial Yucatec dictionaries, there are terms describing sorcerers who can cause blood or pus in urine, intestinal worms, diarrhea, and other unpleasant complaints. Sorcerers are widely believed to attack the souls or supernatural alter egos of individuals, thereby causing illness and death. A particularly feared form of sorcerer is the individual who can transform into an animal. To the Aztecs, this individual was known as *tlacate-*

colotl, or "owl person." The Aztec Florentine Codex describes the deeds performed by this individual: "He is a hater, a destroyer of people; an implanter of sickness, who bleeds himself over others, who kills them by potions – who makes them drink potions; who burns wooden figures of others."

Impurities caused by excessive sexuality and drunkenness are another cause of disease. Prostitutes, adulterers and drunkards therefore acted as vectors of disease. In Central Mexico, the AHUIATETEO were simultaneously the gods of excess and punishment, frequently in the form of sickness. Thus MACUILXOCHITL, the principal Ahuiateteo, brought diseases of the genitals to those who copulated while under fast. Immoderation represented a dangerous imbalance between the people and the surrounding natural and supernatural worlds and, for this reason, the terrible epidemics of the 16th c. were widely considered to be signs of divine punishment and retribution. To the native sufferers, these plagues were often regarded as signs of profound spiritual as well as physical illness. *See also* CURING; DEFORMITY.

divination Divination is an essential element of Mesoamerican religious life. As a sign of its importance, the primordial ANCESTRAL COUPLE and even the creators themselves are often described as diviners. Thus the Aztec genetrix TOCI was regarded as the goddess of diviners as well as the mother of the gods. It is quite likely that the aged Goddess O of the Maya (*see* SCHELLHAS GODS) was similarly regarded as a diviner as well as an aged creator goddess. In Central Mexico, the primordial couple known as Oxomoco and Cipactonal are described as diviners. According to the Quiché Maya POPOL VUH, the aged couple Xpiyacoc and Xmucane performed divinatory hand casting during the creation of people. Not only do diviners play a role in CREATION ACCOUNTS, but the actual practitioners frequently compare their ritual acts to that of creation. Thus the diviner commonly describes and invokes the images and forces present at the time of creation. This may be seen in a portion of a recent Mazatec divinatory prayer by María Sabina:

From out of the night and darkness, says
Then the trees grew, the mountains and
ridges were formed, says,
He only thought about it and looked into it
to the bottom, says,

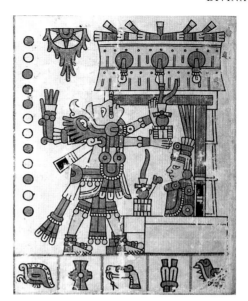

Part of a passage describing temples, gods, and day names of the four **directions**, Codex Fejérváry-Mayer, p. 33, Late Postclassic period. In the lower portion of the scene, the five eastern day names are placed below the sun god, Tonatiuh, who stands before his temple.

Woman performing **divination** by handcasting to determine the outcome of a disease, Codex Magliabechiano, 16th c. Aztec. The starry night symbol behind the diviner indicates that this was a nocturnal rite.

Then the plains and hollows hardened, says
That is what we are going to do, too, says.
(Estrada and Munn 1982: 142)

The Mesoamerican identification of divination with creation is probably because it is, by its nature, a miraculous act. Through ritual and prayer, the diviner summons the godly powers of creation to manifest themselves again in a physical and tangible medium. In contrast to the casting of lots during gambling games, divination was not recreation but *re-creation*.

In ancient Mesoamerica, divination took many forms. The 260-day CALENDAR, so central to Mesoamerican life, served primarily as a divinatory almanac, and probably had its origins in divinatory rites pertaining to midwives and the human gestation period. It was often used in conjunction with sortilage, or the divinatory casting of lots, which was often performed with seeds that were randomly cast and then counted for the augury. It is probable that the vast number of divinatory almanacs in the ancient screenfold books were used with hand casting. Scrying with MIRRORS or pools of water was another form of Mesoamerican divination. Among the Tarascans of Michoacán, the SHAMANS of the king could see all past and future events through bowls of water or mirrors. The events witnessed by these seers could be used as evidence in court cases.

Aside from sortilage and scrying, Mesoamerican diviners commonly used their own bodies for prognostications. Thus diviners could receive messages through muscle twitchings or the pulsing of blood. In Central Mexico, divination was also performed by hand spans. Here the diviner measured the left arm of the patient with the outstretched span of the right hand. Visions derived from HALLUCINOGENS are another important form of divination, and are still widely used among contemporary diviners of Mexico. Among the more common hallucinogenic plants used in divination are morning glory, jinsom weed, and peyote.

Diving God One of the more common sculptural motifs of Late Postclassic Yucatán is a youthful figure that appears to be diving headfirst from the sky. Although the most elaborate and best-known examples occur in the architecture of Tulum, Quintana Roo, the diving god also appears in the sculpture of

Mayapan and other late sites of the northern Maya lowlands. In scholarly literature, this being is often referred to as a bee god but there is little iconographic support for this identification. The vast majority of diving god figures appear to represent the Maya MAIZE GOD, commonly referred to as God E (*see* SCHELLHAS GODS).

dog The tenth day sign in the Central Mexican calendar represented the dog, known as Itzcuintli in Nahuatl; in the Yucatec Maya calendar, the tenth day sign, Oc, probably also refers to the dog, although no such reading is known for the word itself. XIPE TOTEC and QUETZALCOATL presided over the *trecena* 1 Itzcuintli.

The native Mesoamerican dog was a hairless creature, principally raised as a foodstuff. Males were often castrated and force-fed. In Central Mexico, a person born on the day 4 Dog in the *trecena* 1 Deer would be a gifted breeder of dogs and would never lack for food.

XOLOTL, a Central Mexican god with intimate ties to the UNDERWORLD, sometimes has the head of a dog. In both Aztec and Maya belief dogs, perhaps embodying the role of Xolotl, guided their masters into the Underworld after DEATH and were of particular use in crossing bodies of WATER. That this belief is of some antiquity is borne out by carefully buried skeletons of dogs interred with humans at Late Formative Chupicuaro. Dogs also accompanied their masters in Early Classic Maya TOMBS, and frequently appear in Underworld scenes on painted Classic Maya pots. In the POPOL VUH, when they performed in the court of the lords of death, the Hero Twins sacrificed a dog and then brought it back to life; the grateful dog wagged his tail.

Dogs are a frequent subject of West Mexican, particularly Colima, art. While many appear simply to be naturalistic representations of the fat, hairless dog, others wear masks and belong to a supernatural realm.

dreams Mesoamerican peoples recognized dreams as special times of communication between humans and the supernatural world. In dreams, humans can contact companion spirits, or what are called UAYS or TONALS, and enter dialogues with ancestors and gods.

According to Durán, at the time of the landing of the Spanish invaders in Veracruz,

Motecuhzoma II grew preoccupied with omens and dreams; he commanded his people to come forward and relate their dreams, even if they were unfavorable. An old man reported that he had seen the temple of HUITZILOPOCHTLI on fire and fallen; an old woman told of a dream in which a river ripped through the royal palace, destroying it. Motecuhzoma cast the dreamers into jail and left them to die.

Among the modern highland Maya, adolescents – or pre-adolescents – may be called as SHAMANS or calendar keepers through illness and dreams. In Zinacantan, a 10- or 12-year-old boy or girl receives three dreams when called as a shaman.

Effigy vessel in the form of a **dog** wearing a human mask, Colima, Protoclassic period.

duality One of the basic structural principles of Mesoamerican religious thought is the use of paired oppositions. In these pairings, there is a recognition of the essential interdependence of opposites. This complementary opposition is most clearly represented in the sexual pairing of male and female. To the Aztecs, the supreme creative principle was OMETEOTL, the god of duality. In this single self-generating being, the male and female principles were joined. The omnipotent god could also be referred to by its male and female aspects, Ometecuhtli and Omecihuatl. Similarly, the Mixtecs and other Mesoamerican cultures considered creation to be the work of a sexually paired couple.

Two examples of **duality**. (*Right*) Split mask representing living and fleshless face, Tlatilco, Early Formative period. (*Below*) The death god, Mictlantecuhtli (left), with the life-giving god of wind, Ehecatl-Quetzalcoatl; Codex Borgia, p. 56, Late Postclassic period.

Aside from the male and female principles, common oppositional pairings include life and death, sky and earth, zenith and nadir, day and night, sun and moon, fire and water. It can readily be seen that such series of pairings could be easily linked into a larger group of oppositions. Thus, for example, one side could entail male, life, sky, zenith, day, sun, and fire, whereas the other would be female, death, earth, nadir, night, moon, and water. Such larger structural oppositions are evident in both contact period and contemporary Mesoamerican religious systems.

The concept of duality can be traced as far back as the Early Formative art of highland Mexico, where some ceramic masks from the site of Tlatilco are cleft down the middle from brow to chin, a living face on one side and a fleshless skull on the other. In Classic Maya writing, distance numbers used in calendrical references are occasionally introduced with paired couplets. On the Late Classic Tablet of the 96 Glyphs from Palenque, the paired

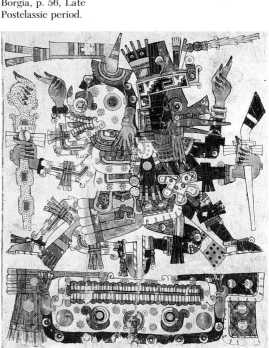

glyphs for sun and darkness, Venus and moon, and wind and water precede distance numbers. The significance of such couplets in Maya calendrical expressions remains to be explained. Perhaps the most advanced literary use of paired expressions appears in Nahuatl ritual speech, where a pair of words is used to refer to a third concept. Known by its Spanish name, *difrasismo*, this literary device is relatively common in Nahuatl. Among the better known examples are fire and water to allude to war (*see* ATL-TLACHIN-OLLI), red and black for writing, and stone and wood for punishment.

dwarves and hunchbacks At the time of the Spanish Conquest, Motecuhzoma II, lord of the Aztecs, kept a troop of dwarves to entertain him and sometimes to advise him on matters of state and religion. But the importance of dwarves – and hunchbacks, with whom they are often paired – in Mesoamerican religion goes back to the earliest times, when the Olmecs paid special attention to dwarves. On Potrero Nuevo Altar 1, dwarves support the symbol for sky, and so may well have been understood to be SKYBEARERS, perhaps akin to the Maya bacabs. Many small, portable Olmec objects feature dwarves and hunchbacks, some occasionally with wings. These images may well be linked to concepts in the Gulf Coast area that have survived into modern times of the *chanekes*, mischievous dwarves and spirits who play unpleasant tricks on humankind.

The Maya believed that dwarves were children of the Chacs (rain gods), and that they could bring rain. Some contemporary highland Mexico Maya peoples believe that dwarves dwell under the surface of the earth. In Yucatec, dwarves are also known as *ciz luum*, or "earth farter," presumably because of their proximity to the ground. On some Classic Maya pots and monuments, dwarves are named as such, and the word for dwarf, *ch'at* is written phonetically. The Zapotecs believed that mountain gods were dwarves.

From abundant Classic Maya depictions of dwarves, it is clear that most suffered short-limb dwarfism, or what is sometimes known as *achondroplasia*. The MAIZE GOD is often shown dancing with a dwarf or a hunchback on painted vases from the Naranjo-Holmul region; perhaps the dwarf is an allusion to the smaller second ear of maize frequently issued by the maize plant, or perhaps to the

edible fungus known today in Central Mexico as *huitlacoche*, which invades and distorts an ear of maize. At Yaxchilán, two dwarves with star markings on their backs attend King Bird Jaguar in a BALLGAME scene and may refer to the constellation Gemini, known as the TURTLE or dwarf star among the Maya.

Among the Aztecs, TLALOC, like the Maya rain god CHAC, was associated with dwarves, hunchbacks, and deformities. The king of Chalco offered a hunchback to the Tlaloque (gods of rain and lightning); he had him carried to a cave in a dormant volcano, where the Tlaloque welcomed him to their palace. When the king later found him alive, he took it as an omen that Chalco would fall, as it did that year, to the Mexica. *See also* AHUIATETEO; DEFORMITY; TUERTOS.

eagle There are two important species of eagle native to Mesoamerica, the harpy eagle (*Harpia harpyja*) and the golden eagle (*Aquila chrysaetos*). Native to the humid lowlands, the harpy eagle is the greatest avian predator of Mesoamerica. With its massive, razor-sharp talons, it is capable of killing adult monkeys. Thus it is not surprising that the harpy eagle plays a major role in Formative Olmec iconography. In Olmec art, the harpy can be readily identified by its sharply downturned raptorial beak and its prominent, forward-sweeping feather crest. The "flame eyebrows" appearing in Olmec iconography are a form of the harpy eagle crest. The Olmec symbolism of the harpy was undoubtedly complex. It often appears on Olmec jadeite "spoons," which were quite possibly receptacles for blood during penis perforation.

Among the Classic Maya, a bird, quite probably the harpy eagle, serves as the personified form of the roughly 20-year *katun*. The same bird also serves for the *baktun* time period, although here it is distinguished by having a human hand serving as the lower jaw. Along with a thick raptorial beak, the bird displays a prominent feather crest upon the brow. The *katun* bird also serves as a symbol for the sky, and in Maya writing can provide the phonetic value of *can* or *chan*, the Mayan term for "sky." The bird head appearing as the Classic form of the day Men

83 EARTH

is probably also an eagle, as the Postclassic
Central Mexican form of this day name is
Cuauhtli, meaning "eagle." In the "flint
shield" war expression of Classic Maya iconography, an eagle head can be substituted
for the sign for FLINT. In Late Postclassic
Central Mexico the eagle was similarly identified with flint.

The eagle plays an especially prominent
role in the religion of Postclassic Central
Mexico. In both Central Mexican and Mixtec
writing, it appears as the 15th day name,
corresponding to the Maya day Men. Rendered with a large feather crest, it is probably
the harpy rather than the golden eagle. In
both writing and art, it is frequently fringed
with flint blades. In Late Postclassic Central
Mexico, the eagle was a symbol of the sun.
Thus in Nahuatl, the terms for ascending
eagle (*cuauhtlehuanitl*) and descending eagle
(*cuauhtemoc*) were used to refer to the rising
and setting of the SUN. For the Aztecs, the
eagle symbolized one of the two military
orders dedicated to the sun, the other being
the JAGUAR (*see* WARRIOR ORDERS). Eagles were
also identified with HUMAN SACRIFICE, one of
the primary means of nourishing the sun.
Thus eagle feather down was a common
symbol of sacrifice in Central Mexico. Human
HEARTS offered to the sun were known as
cuauhnochtli, or "eagle cactus fruit." These
hearts were frequently placed in a stone
vessel known as the CUAUHXICALLI, the "eagle
gourd vessel."

The golden eagle had a special role in the
legendary founding of the Aztec capital of
Tenochtitlan. According to myth, the Aztecs
founded their capital where an eagle fed
upon a nopal cactus. This place corresponds
to Tenochtitlan, or "place of the nopal cactus
rock."

earth The surface of the earth was considered in a variety of ways in ancient
Mesoamerica. Quite frequently, the earth
was regarded as a living entity. Thus in both
Central Mexican and Yucatec Maya thought,
the earth could be viewed as a great CAIMAN
floating upon the SEA. The Aztecs considered
it too as a monstrous devouring being, with
a huge gaping maw, talons, and gnashing
mouths placed on joints of the limbs. Known
as TLALTECUHTLI, or "earth lord," this being is
actually dually sexed, and possesses a strongly
feminine component. The earth was also
regarded as a flat four-sided field, with the

(*Left*) Enthroned **hunchback**, detail of Chenes capstone, Late Classic Maya.

(*Center*) Aztec **eagle** warrior sculpture, Templo Mayor,Tenochtitlan, Late Postclassic period.

(*Below*) Ancestor rising out of the **earth** as a fruit-bearing tree, sarcophagus of Pacal, Temple of the Inscriptions, Palenque, Late Classic Maya.

four DIRECTIONS corresponding to each of the sides. For the Maya, this model is metaphorically compared to the quadrangular maize field. In both Yucatec and Quiché Maya belief, the creation of the world is compared to the making of the maize field. For the Quiché POPOL VUH, this could be viewed as a preparation for the creation of the present human race, the people of corn. Among the modern Sierra Nahuat of Puebla, the earth is seen as a maize field, with people being born or "planted" upon its surface.

Along with the quadrangular model, the earth was considered to be a round disk. Thus the Aztecs referred to it as Anahuatl, a disk surrounded by a ring of water. In Colonial Yucatec Maya writing and maps, a similar conception of the earth as a round disk appears. However, the ancient Maya regarded the circular earth not only as a flat disk, but also as a more rounded ball-like form. There is reliable evidence that the Classic and Postclassic Maya saw the earth as a great tortoise, much like peoples of eastern North America and Asia. *See also* CREATION ACCOUNTS.

eclipse Eclipses were dreaded throughout ancient Mexico and Guatemala. An eclipse occurs when three celestial bodies are aligned in such a way that one body passes between the other two. As far as is known, eclipses in Mesoamerica were universally seen as the biting of the SUN or the biting of the MOON. In Yucatec Mayan, eclipses were called *chibil kin*, or the "biting of the sun." Solar eclipses were thought to be far more dangerous than lunar ones.

The development of an accurate lunar CALENDAR among the Maya guided calculations for solar and lunar eclipses, allowing them to develop eclipse warning dates, although they could not predict whether or not it would be visible. The Dresden Codex eclipse warning tables could have been used to alert PRIESTS and rulers to eclipse possibilities. In this codex, an eclipse of the sun was often pictured as the eating of the *kin* glyph by a sky serpent.

The modern Maya – specifically the Mopan, Tzotzil, Yucatec, and Chol – believe that eclipses occur when the sun and moon fight. In other Maya accounts, the sun is attacked by ants during a solar eclipse. The Maya and other contemporary native peoples believe that pregnant women should not witness an eclipse, lest the fetus be deformed.

The Aztecs held strong beliefs about eclipses. The dreaded TZITZIMIME star demons became visible during an eclipse, descended to EARTH, and consumed humanity. According to Sahagún, the people sought out those of fair face and hair for sacrifice to the sun and drew blood from their own ears, in fear that the sun would not return and that the *tzitzimime* would be unleashed on the earth. To forestall the evil power of an eclipse they raised a great din, shouting and playing musical instruments. Since the time of the Conquest it has been known that the Maya also make great amounts of noise to try to stop an eclipse. In 1991, when a total eclipse was visible in much of Central and Northern Mexico, native peoples in many parts of the country made a commotion to stave off any baleful effects.

Ehecatl Also referred to as Ehecatl-Quetzalcoatl, this god represents QUETZALCOATL in his aspect as god of WIND. In the iconography of Late Postclassic highland Mexico, he is usually black, with a striking red mask resembling a beak. Although this mask probably derives from a duck bill, the corners of the mouth are usually provided with a long pair of curving canines. In addition, Ehecatl wears a great deal of shell JEWELRY, the most important piece being his cut conch pectoral or *ehecailacacozcatl*. The shell jewelry and other elements of his costume suggest that Ehecatl orginally derived from the Huastec area of northern Veracruz. However, two late 9th c. monuments from the Maya site of Seibal portray possible early forms of the beaked Ehecatl. Although both of these stelae exhibit strong Central Mexican influences, there are no known examples of Ehecatl in highland Mexico prior to the Late Postclassic.

In Nahuatl, *ehecatl* signifies "wind," and this deity was credited with "sweeping the way" for the Tlaloque, the gods of RAIN and LIGHTNING. He appears as the patron of Wind, the second of the 20 day names, and of the second TRECENA of 1 Jaguar. However, Ehecatl is best known for his major role in Central Mexican CREATION ACCOUNTS where he figures as a major creator god and culture hero. Along with creating the earth and heavens with TEZCATLIPOCA, Ehecatl also rescued the bones of people from the UNDERWORLD, thereby creating the present race of humankind. According to various accounts he also obtained MAIZE, PULQUE, and MUSIC with which to worship the gods.

The specific temple of Ehecatl was a circular building with a conical roof; quite frequently a great serpent maw serves as the doorway, as if the temple was a symbolic CAVE providing entrance to the winding depths of the Underworld. Due to the common but striking condition of "breathing caves," wind is commonly believed in Mesoamerica to derive from the Underworld.

Among the Late Postclassic Mixtec, Ehecatl was known as 9 Wind. In the Prehispanic Codex Vindobonensis, this Mixtec god was born from a flint on the day 9 Wind in the year of 10 House. According to the Colonial *Telleriano-Remensis*, 9 Wind was also an Aztec birthdate of Ehecatl. The deity 9 Wind plays an important role in the Mixtec codices for, like his Aztec counterpart, he appears as a major culture hero. In several scenes, he is represented receiving his attributes from an aged pair of creator gods. The Codex Vindobonensis also depicts 9 Wind raising the SKY, an episode credited to Ehecatl in Central Mexican creation accounts. In another scene, 9 Wind obtains hallucinogenic mushrooms for the gods. It appears that, much like Quetzalcoatl of legendary TOLLAN, 9 Wind was considered as an ancestor of important Mixtec ruling families.

enemas One of the more curious themes in Classic Maya art is the use of gourd enemas during ritual drinking bouts. Although it has often been suggested that these enemas were used for consuming HALLUCINOGENS, it is far more likely that they contained an alcoholic beverage, such as balché or PULQUE. At times, the enemas are depicted in association with a vessel glyphically labeled *ci* or *chi*, a Mayan term signifying pulque or other alcoholic drinks. According to one 16th c. account, the Huastec Maya of northern Veracruz used enemas during times of extreme intoxication. In fact, many of the Classic Maya scenes represent individuals cavorting, falling, and even vomiting. Given the subject matter, it is not surprising that most of the enema scenes are not on public monuments but rather on ceramic vessels for personal use. One noteworthy exception occurs at the Puuc ruins of Rancho San Diego, close to the site of Uxmal. Here one structure originally displayed at least 14 bas-relief carvings pertaining to enemas and ritual intoxication.

For highland Mexico, there is no concrete evidence for the use of alcoholic enemas.

Maya representation of a solar **eclipse**, Dresden Codex, p. 57, Postclassic period.

(*Below*) Aztec sculpture of **Ehecatl** with his characteristic beak-like mask, Late Postclassic period.

Male self-administering an **enema**, stone panel from Rancho San Diego, Yucatán, Terminal Classic Maya.

However, enemas do appear to have been used for CURING and ritual PURIFICATION. Ruíz de Alarcón records the following cure from the 17th c. Nahuatl inhabitants of Guerrero: if a difficult childbirth was believed to be due to adultery, the woman would be administered an enema containing her own saliva.

excrement In Central Mexico, human excrement symbolized the pollution and filth that occurred from sexual transgressions and other misdeeds. *Cuitlatl*, the Nahuatl term for excrement, also bore connotations of immoral and disgusting behavior. Thus the term *cuitlacoya* signified to be covered with excrement or to have one's reputation stained. In the Central Mexican codices, there are scenes of defecating men eating their own excrement which simultaneously represent both the polluting individual and his self-PURIFICATION. The primary Central Mexican goddess of ritual purification was TLAZOLTEOTL, whose name can be glossed as "eater of filth."

Fecal matter was not only identified with pollution and filth. It is ironic that GOLD, so commonly considered as incorruptible and pure in Western thought, was described as excrement. Thus the Nahuatl term for gold was *teocuitlatl*, or "godly excrement." The Yucatec Mayan term for gold was quite similar: *tahkin*, or "excrement of the sun." This term has continued today as the common Yucatec word for money.

execution Execution constituted a public ritual event distinct from HUMAN SACRIFICE. Instead of serving as an offering, it was a means of punishment and PURIFICATION. Thus there was little interest in extracting BLOOD or HEARTS as offerings and the popular forms of execution were clubbing, stoning, and strangulation. Among the more common causes of execution were adultery, drunkenness, thievery, and treason. Among the Tarascans of Michoacán, the conventional means of execution was by braining with a large wooden club; the parents and relatives of the guilty party were frequently also killed. In Nahuatl, the phrase for punishment was *tetlcuahuitl*, or "wood and stone." In fact, stoning was an especially common form of execution in Mesoamerica, and was frequently used in cases of adultery. At times, the Central Mexican god of stone and castigation, ITZTLACOLIUHQUI-IXQUIMILLI, is shown with a pair of adulterers killed by stoning.

fan Made of feathers or cloth stretched over a frame, or of woven reed, palm, or folded paper, fans were long thought to be specific identifying markers of MERCHANTS, but it is now recognized that travelers, dancers, and occasionally others also bear them. Both Maya and Aztec dancers hold fans, and on Classic Maya pottery, God N sometimes dances with a fan. In the Bonampak murals, a Maya noblewoman holds a fan of either feathers or folded paper while she watches a scene of bloodletting; dancers with blood streaming from their groins in Room 3 of the murals carry fans with bloody handprints.

Fat God The figure known as the Fat God is among the more curious and least understood deities of ancient Mesoamerica. This strange being is found in the Classic period art of Teotihuacan, Veracruz, and the Maya region. He is first known in Late Formative monumental stone sculpture from the piedmont of Guatemala. Appearing at such early sites as Monte Alto and Santa Leticia, the Fat God is represented as either a huge potbellied figure or simply a massive head. In both cases, he appears much like a bloated corpse with heavy, swollen lids covering his eyes. In the case of potbelly sculptures, the navel too is often large and swollen. The Fat God is a common character among Late Classic Maya figurines, occasionally occurring also on ceramic vessels where, like the early piedmont sculptures, he is shown with shut eyes and a swollen belly and navel. In two cases, he is accompanied by a hieroglyphic compound read *sidz*. The term *sidz* signifies gluttony in Chol and excessive desire or gluttony in Yucatec. This possible meaning of the Fat God as an intemperate glutton may explain his frequent role as a dancer or entertainer in Late Classic Maya art. He may have been lampooned as a ritual clown character personifying gluttony and greed, major subjects of derision and social condemnation in Mesoamerica. *See also* CLOWNS.

fire According to Central Mexican sources, QUETZALCOATL, the great creator god, and HUITZILOPOCHTLI, the Aztec cult god, made fire along with a feeble "half-sun" that shone before the DAWN of the era in which humans live. According to other sources it was TEZCAT-LIPOCA who, having changed his name to MIXCOATL, was the first to make fire with FLINTS, or with a fire drill, yielding a flame which then was carried to make great fires.

To initiate a new CALENDAR round, the Aztecs celebrated the ritual of New Fire, perhaps in emulation of these first drillings of fire by the gods. The last New Fire ceremony was celebrated during the month of Panquetzaliztli, a few months after the new year of 2 Acatl had begun in AD 1507. As part of what anthropologists call a TERMINATION RITUAL, all pots were smashed and new ones were prepared for the new era. All fires were extinguished and the land lay in darkness, awaiting the New Fire ceremony that confirmed and renewed the new year. If fire could not be drawn, then the TZITZIMIME would descend from the heavens to consume humankind. Pregnant women, thought to be contaminated, were hidden from view behind stuffed sacks or inside granaries, according to the Codex Borbonicus; any child born in this period would be stigmatized, and all commoners shielded their faces with blue masks. At midnight before the first day of the new year, on a nearby mountain called Citlaltepec ("Hill of the Star"), PRIESTS watched the movement of the STARS we call the Pleiades and which the Aztecs knew as the Tianquiztli, or Market. If they passed overhead at midnight, then the fire priests proceeded: they ripped out the HEART of a sacrificial victim, usually a captive warrior, and started a flame with a fire drill in his open chest cavity. Year BUNDLES of sticks symbolizing the old 52 years were then set afire. The new fire guaranteed the arrival of the morning SUN and the initiation of a new year.

XIUHTECUHTLI was the god of terrestrial fire. His role in the Aztec pantheon may have been diminished by the introduction of Huitzilopochtli, whose cult encompassed sun and fire. HUEHUETEOTL was the old god of fire, usually of the hearth. Basically a domestic god and kept in household shrines, he – along with TLALOC – is a god of great antiquity, and his image was made with little change from Early Classic to Late Postclassic times in Central Mexico. He wears a fire brazier on his head, whose rim is marked with the rhomboid symbol for fire used at TEOTIHUACAN. The XIUHCOATL, or fire serpent, bears the sun

Penitent devouring his own **excrement**: note the excremental stream pouring towards the moon sign; Codex Borgia, p. 10, Late Postclassic period.

Adulterers suffering **execution**, one strangled, one stoned; Codex Telleriano-Remensis, 16th c. Aztec.

Late Classic version of the **Fat God**, termed *sidz uinic*, or "glutton" in accompanying text; detail of polychrome vase.

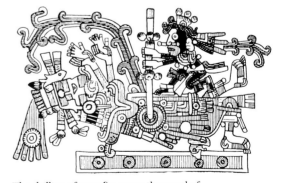

The drilling of new **fire** upon the navel of Xiuhtecuhtli, Codex Borgia, p. 46, Late Postclassic period. During the Aztec New Fire ceremonies, fire was drilled on the chest of a sacrificed captive who had the word *xihuitl* in his actual name.

through the SKY; it is also the weapon carried by Huitzilopochtli. Among the Maya, TOHIL is the god of fire in the POPOL VUH. God K (Palenque Triad GII; *see* PALENQUE TRIAD GODS) may have been a Classic god of fire.

Mesoamerican peoples recognized fire as the fundamental catalyst of change. The Aztecs believed that the current sun and MOON came into existence when two gods, Tecuciztecatl and Nanahuatzin, immolated themselves in a great fire at Teotihuacan. For the Maya, as for other Mesoamerican peoples, fire was a way to communicate with gods and ancestors. Offerings, frequently blood-spattered PAPER, were set on fire in braziers, and in the billowing smoke, the Maya conjured up their gods and ancestors.

The Aztecs also used the metaphor water-fire, ATL-TLACHINOLLI, to mean warfare.

Five Suns The Five Suns constitute the five eras or worlds of Aztec mythology, including the present sun of Nahui Ollin, or 4 Motion. Each of the four previous suns is identified with a particular god and race of people, the generally accepted order of the four earlier suns running as follows: Nahui Ocelotl (4 Jaguar), Nahui Ehecatl (4 Wind), Nahui Qui-ahuitl (4 Rain) and Nahui Atl (4 Water). Following the making of the present people and their corn, the fifth sun was created at TEOTIHUACAN. *See also* CREATION ACCOUNTS.

flint Tougher and more durable than OBSID-IAN, flint was universally used to strike FIRE in the New World. It easily yields sparks, and the rock itself smells of smoke after use. It is a fine-granular quartz which abounds in the Maya lowlands.

As the primary means of striking fire, flint was of inestimable use to humankind and was thus personified and deified; it was also a symbol of HUMAN SACRIFICE and the debt owed by humanity to the GODS. Sacrificial blades everywhere were made of flint and obsidian, and are often depicted at the joints of Aztec deities. Gods and PRIESTS bear flint knives in hand, frequently painted white and red.

In Mesoamerican thought, flint and obsid-ian were both created where lightning strikes. CHAC and TLALOC, respectively the Maya and Central Mexican hurlers of thunderbolts, were thus the creators of these valued materials. According to one Aztec version, Citlalicue (She of the Star Skirt) gave birth to flint, and then hurled it to earth, where it

landed in CHICOMOZTOC, yielding 1600 terres-trial gods. Chac usually carries a personified flint in his hand, but sometimes he is himself a personified flint. Among the Aztecs, flint blades are also personified, frequently with an open, gnawing mouth, indicating their ability to tear flesh. ITZTLACOLIUHQUI-IXQUIMILLI, god of castigation, may be a personified flint.

Flint was widely recognized as a day sign: as Tecpatl among the Aztecs and Edznab among the Maya, for example. Tecpatl was one of the four Aztec YEARBEARER day signs, corresponding to the north, and the TRECENA 1 Tecpatl was presided over by Chalchiutotolin, TEZCATLIPOCA in the form of a blue-green turkey. The usual, iconic form of the Maya day sign bears the same flint markings depicted on Maya weaponry.

flowers Flowers held rich metaphorical meaning in ancient Mesoamerica. Three Aztec deities have particular connections with them: XOCHIPILLI, MACUILXOCHITL, and XOCHIQUETZAL, all of whom serve as patrons of beauty, pleasure, and the arts. Flowers were viewed as sacrificial offerings, and according to some stories, QUETZALCOATL led his people to offer flowers and BUTTERFLIES in lieu of human flesh. Flowers were offered on many occasions: at the beginning of the celebration of the VEINTENA Tlacaxipehualiztli, for exam-ple, a festival of first flowers was held in honor of XIPE TOTEC.

In xochitl in cuicatl was a Nahuatl *difra-sismo*, or metaphorical linking of two phen-omena in Central Mexican hierarchic and priestly address, literally meaning flowers and song but referring to all artistic endeavors and particularly poetry. Another Aztec term incorporating flowers was *xochiyaoyotl*, liter-ally "war of flowers;" it refers to the practice of a particular type of war in Central Mexico carried out by the Aztecs from mid-15th c. on, in which battle was carried out specifically to capture sacrificial victims from nearby, independent polities.

Cempoalxochitl, or marigolds, were ancient offerings to the dead and are still a primary offering on the Day of the Dead, 1 November, All Souls' Day. Some believe that the Central Mexican goddess COYOLXAUHQUI wears a large marigold on her head, and during the *vein-tena* celebrations of Tecuilhuitontli, women danced together, holding marigolds. In the POPOL VUH, marigolds and yarrow are burned together, as a simple offering. *Ololiuhqui,*

morning glories, were valued for the hallucinogenic properties of their seeds, and Durán
describes their consumption during feasts to
TEZCATLIPOCA (*see* HALLUCINOGENS). In the art of
Classic TEOTIHUACAN many varieties of flowers
are depicted.

Dancers in celebration of *veintena* festivals
frequently carried or wore flowers and sometimes distributed them to other participants
or observers. In the celebration of Toxcatl,
the Tezcatlipoca impersonator carried flowers
in his hand. In palace scenes without obvious
sacrificial overtones, Maya kings and nobles
also carry small bouquets of flowers for
sniffing. Maya JADES, particularly those worn
as hair ornaments, were often made in the
four-petal shape characteristic of flowers.

 G

The Aztec Calendar Stone with the **five suns** of
creation, Late Postclassic period.

gods There has been considerable debate
concerning the concept of gods and divinity
in ancient Mesoamerica. The 16th c. Spanish
chronicles make frequent and direct references to *dioses*, or "gods." However, it has
been justly noted that European terminology
may have grossly simplified complex concepts
of sacredness and divinity. Among the 16th
c. Zapotecs, the term *pee*, signifying "breath,
spirit, or WIND," expressed the concept of
divinity. This animistic force caused movement – all phenomena or maternal things that
expresed motion were attributed a certain
degree of sacredness. Among the Aztecs, the
term for sacredness was *teotl* which, like the
Zapotec *pee*, referred to an immaterial energy
or force similar to the Polynesian concept of
mana. In Mayan languages, *ku* or *ch'u* means
sacredness.

Although Mesoamerican peoples did possess concepts of animistic forces, they also
believed in specific gods, that is, animate,
personified beings with their own distinct
mythical cycles. Thus in Mayan languages
and the Nahuatl tongue of the Aztecs the
terms for sacredness could also refer to specific gods. In the case of the Classic period
Zapotecs, anthropomorphic gods are commonly rendered on ceramic urns. Although it
has been recently argued that these images
represent ancestors rather than gods, this is
unlikely. The widespread nature and continuity of certain of the characters, some lasting
over a 1000 years, make it unlikely that these

Eccentric **flint** from Quiriguá, Guatemala, Late
Classic Maya.

are only historical figures. Nonetheless, it does appear that, like the Mixtec gods, Zapotec gods are often identified as the idealized ancestors of particularly important lineages.

gold Gold, or *teocuitlatl*, literally EXCREMENT of the gods, was a precious material to the Aztecs, although not so important as JADE or tropical bird feathers. Motecuhzoma II collected about two tons of gold a year in tribute. So little worked gold survived the Conquest that it is now difficult to reconstruct exactly for which ritual objects it was most used, but when Albrecht Dürer viewed in Brussels the objects that Cortés had shipped back to King Charles V in 1520, he described a SUN made entirely of gold, a fathom wide, and a MOON of silver, of the same size. Because gold was recognized to be a product of the sun, solar gods were associated with the material, particularly HUITZILOPOCHTLI, the Aztec sun god, who wore a gold headband. Gold was also fashioned into JEWELRY for the nobility, particularly for nose ornaments and lip labrets.

Goldworkers, or *teocuitlahuaque*, honored XIPE TOTEC as their patron and made offerings at his temple, Yopico. Goldsmiths held high status and were recognized as craftspeople, or *tolteca*, a term that had lost its ethnic associations with Tula, Hidalgo, by the time of the Conquest.

Goldworking arrived late in Mexico and Central America. Invented millennia before in South America, worked objects of gold turn up in the Maya region no earlier than the 8th c. AD. Metallurgy took hold during the Toltec era in Mesoamerica, and dozens of gold objects were thrown into the Sacred CENOTE at Chichen Itzá. During the Late Postclassic, the Mixtecs carried out the most sophisticated metallurgy in Mesoamerica, perfecting the techniques of lost-wax casting and filigree, while continuing also to use the simpler hammering and repoussé.

In 1932, Mexican archaeologist Alfonso Caso excavated Tomb 7 at Monte Albán and found that the Mixtecs had reused old Zapotec TOMBS to bury their kings in the centuries before the Spanish Conquest. Tomb 7 contained the largest surviving single deposit of Precolumbian gold, along with rock crystal, cave onyx, TURQUOISE, and bone. In 1975, a major cache was discovered by a fisherman near the modern city of Veracruz. Known as the Treasure of the Fisherman,

this Early Colonial cache contained roughly 6 kilos of gold, much of it in the form of Prehispanic Aztec jewelry.

H

hacha *Hacha*, the Spanish word for axe, generally refers in Mesoamerican ritual to a piece of BALLGAME equipment, rather than an axe. Dating from the Classic period, most come from Veracruz and the Pacific slopes of Guatemala. Early *hachas* are frequently heads, perhaps TROPHY HEADS; later ones are narrower and often incorporate bird feathers. Most *hachas* have a tenon; although generally thought of as equipment for play, some may have been designed for architectural placement.

hallucinogens Hallucinogens played and continue to play an important role in Mesoamerican religious life. They have been used for communion with the GODS and ancestors, DIVINATION, personal visions and self-knowledge, and as a source of pleasure and entertainment. Some scholars have suggested that the Formative Olmec used bufotenine, a hallucinogen derived from *Bufo marinus*, a large lowland TOAD. Although this is still uncertain, representations of toads are widespread in the Formative and Late Preclassic art of southern Mesoamerica, and the parotoid glands from which bufotenine is excreted are prominently featured on them.

Psilocybin mushrooms (*Psilocybe mexicana*) may also have been used during the Late Preclassic period. Small stone sculptures in the form of mushrooms have been found at Kaminaljuyú and other Late Preclassic sites of the Maya highlands and Pacific piedmont. Although the resemblance of these carvings to mushrooms may be fortuitous, they are frequently found in association with small grinding stones – among contemporary Mixtecs of Oaxaca, the hallucinogenic mushrooms are first pulverized on grinding stones before being ingested.

The use of psilocybin mushrooms is well documented for Late Postclassic highland Mexico. Page 24 of the Prehispanic Mixtec Codex Vindobonensis contains a scene illustrating the origin and use of the sacred mushroom: 9 Wind, the Mixtec form of

EHECATL, is shown bringing the mushrooms to the gods, and 7 Flower, the most prominent of them, weeps. The mushrooms are personified by two supernatural women, 4 Lizard and 11 Lizard. During the night banquets sponsored by successful Aztec MERCHANTS, participants ate psilocybin with honey. The merchants would frequently cry from the hallucinations, which were regarded as portents of future events.

Another important hallucinogen was morning glory seed (*Turbina corymbosa*), known as *ololiuhqui* in Nahuatl. Detailed accounts of *ololiuhqui* and its use in divination appear in the Colonial treatise of Ruíz de Alarcón. Taken at night by special practitioners, the seeds were used to determine sources of sickness, find thieves, and discover lost objects or people. The *ololiuhqui* was considered to be an actual god that could communicate with the practitioner through visions. As a god, the *ololiuhqui* was treated with tremendous veneration and respect, and was cared for in small baskets passed down through generations of diviners.

A small, spineless cactus, peyote (*Lophophora williamsii*) is native to the deserts of northern Mexico, but was widely traded in ancient times. Ruíz de Alarcón notes its use in 17th c. Guerrero, a region far removed from its natural environment. A Nahuatl term, peyote is well documented for the 16th c. Aztecs. Along with psilocybin and the potent jimson weed (*Datura* spp.), it is described as a fever medicine in the Aztec Florentine Codex. Early representations may appear in the Protoclassic ceramic art of West Mexico. It is still used among the Huichol, Cora, Tarahumara, and other peoples of northwest Mexico.

hearts Mesoamerican peoples valued hearts as sacrificial offerings. They recognized the heart as the vital organ of the body and as such, it was food for the GODS. At the time of the Conquest, the still-beating human heart was the supreme offering, particularly to the SUN and to solar deities. Although long thought to have been a purely Postclassic Central Mexican phenomenon, heart sacrifice can now be identified to have taken place widely in Mesoamerica from Classic times onward and perhaps even earlier, although there is no clear Olmec evidence.

The human heart is often depicted in Mesoamerican art as a trilobed organ, fre-

The preparation of **gold**, Florentine Codex, Book 9, 16th c. Aztec.

Stone **hachas** commonly appear in the form of heads, suggesting a possible symbolic origin as trophy heads associated with the ballgame, Classic Veracruz.

God 7 Flower eating **hallucinogenic** mushrooms while listening to music played by 9 Wind; Codex Vindobonensis, p. 24, Late Postclassic Mixtec.

Pumas tearing the **heart** out of a deer, mural from Techinantitla, Teotihuacan, Late Classic period. Sacrificial hearts are commonly depicted in the art of Teotihuacan.

quently with droplets falling from it. The most explicit evidence that the trilobe *is* the human heart comes from the battle painting at Cacaxtla, where the trilobed symbol itself oozes from the chest cavity of a fallen warrior. At TEOTIHUACAN, where the symbol appears from Early Classic times onward, painted friezes of alternating JAGUARS and coyotes depict hearts in front of their open mouths. In the Techinantitla paintings at Teotihuacan, felines tear out the heart of a DEER. Warriors with goggle masks bear trilobed hearts on the ends of staffs and wear them, usually in rows of three, above the brim of their headdresses.

Although most representations of Classic Maya HUMAN SACRIFICE feature decapitation, heart extrusion is featured from time to time, as in the Bonampak murals. In Veracruz, heart sacrifice follows play of the BALLGAME, among other occasions. Later, at Chichen Itzá, hearts were the featured offerings, and it may have been in Toltec times that hearts became the single most important human sacrifice. As depicted on a hammered GOLD disk from the Sacred CENOTE at Chichen, four assistants hold down the extremities of a victim while a PRIEST or warrior removes the heart with a hafted flint blade under the watchful eye of a cloud serpent, to whom the offering may be made. The WARRIOR ORDERS of the Toltec era, identified with EAGLES, jaguars, and coyotes, all took on associations with heart sacrifice.

In no ancient civilization of the New World were hearts so important as among the Aztecs. Special receptacles for human hearts, known as CUAUHXICALLIS, were made on a large and sometimes colossal scale, and incorporated into other sacrificial sculptures, such as CHACMOOLS. Hearts were worn as necklaces or skirts by earth goddesses, particularly COATLICUE and TLALTECUHTLI, who in some representations wore necklaces of alternating human hands and hearts. Most Aztec agricultural festivals featured human sacrifice by heart extrusion including, for example, rituals in honor of XIPE TOTEC, the flayed god, where heart sacrifice preceded the actual flaying. The Aztecs referred to sacrificed hearts metaphorically as "precious eagle-cactus fruit," and cactus fruits may sometimes be depicted as a visual metaphor when human hearts are the reference.

Hero Twins *see* CREATION ACCOUNTS; POPOL VUH; TWINS

Huehuecoyotl The Aztec god of DANCE, MUSIC, and carnality, Huehuecoyotl ("old coyote") was a patron deity of featherworkers and presided over the TRECENA 1 Flower, a 13-day period dedicated to the artist and artisan. Men born in this period would be singers, storytellers, and craftsmen, but they would also be prone to overindulgence – and thus to a decaying of the genitals and a wasting of the flesh. Women born in the *trecena* would make fine embroidery, but if they failed to be penitent, they would easily fall prey to their own sexual allure and become harlots or courtesans. Although infrequently depicted, when Huehuecoyotl is represented, he usually appears with the body of a human and the head of a coyote.

Huehueteotl was the Old God of the Aztecs, and indeed he was of great antiquity, with a standardized representation continuing with little change from Middle Formative times on. A simple version of a Huehueteotl INCENSE burner has recently been found in a Middle Formative context in Tlaxcala.

Although most revered and honored in Central Mexico, Huehueteotl images have been recovered from West Mexico, Veracruz, Protoclassic Kaminaljuyú and Late Postclassic Yucatán; no representation of him has been found at a Classic Maya site. At Monte Albán, a related old god bore the Zapotec calendrical name 2 Tiger, but no clear identification can be made with any aged Maya gods. Unlike most other gods of Mesoamerica, Huehueteotl seems to have been primarily a household deity, and as the fundamental god of the hearth, his images usually turn up in residential quarters rather than in TEMPLE precincts.

In his standard representation as a stone sculpture, Huehueteotl is a seated figure, legs crossed in front of him, with both hands resting on his knees. His right hand is palm up and his left is clenched as if it once held a banner. He hunches over, with the curved spine of age, and his face is usually heavily wrinkled. Humans are not commonly shown to age in Mesoamerican art and very few gods are depicted as aged either. Although rarely toothless, Huehueteotl is often reduced to only two lower teeth. On his head he usually wears a huge brazier, its rim marked with rhomboid lozenges, symbolic of FIRE at TEOTIHUACAN. The brazier itself may have held smoldering coals or incense. A few ceramic examples are known, most notably the Early Classic Huehueteotl from Cerro de las Mesas. An Aztec example conflates TLALOC, the rain god, with Huehueteotl, perhaps in representation of the Aztec metaphor for war and conflagration, ATL-TLACHINOLLI.

Huitzilopochtli was the supreme deity of the Aztecs, their chief cult god. Associated with SUN and FIRE and the ruling lineage, his introduction to Central Mexico disrupted other established solar gods and patrons of long-standing lineages, particularly XIUHTE-CUHTLI and TONATIUH. In some sources he is also identified as the Blue TEZCATLIPOCA. Literally, Huitzilopochtli means "HUMMING-BIRD on the left" or "hummingbird of the south." The Spaniards called him Huichilobos and saw him as the devil incarnate, the cause of·heart sacrifice (*see* HEARTS), the source of perversion in the New World. Unlike most Aztec gods, Huitzilopochtli's image was generally rendered of wood, rather than stone, and no monumental examples of him survive – indeed, few examples survive in any medium. The main sculpture of Huitzilopochtli was probably removed from his TEMPLE in 1520 and smuggled out of Tenochtitlan. A document of 1539 depicts the bundled Huitzilopochtli sculpture after it was reputedly removed.

What did Huitzilopochtli look like? According to most accounts and to an early post-Conquest illustration, he wore on his head a blue-green hummingbird headdress, a golden tiara, white heron feathers, and the smoking mirror more commonly associated with Tezcatlipoca and probably adopted from him – as is the serpent foot that the Aztec TLATOANI incorporates into his Huitzilopochtli costume on the Stone of Tizoc. His face often bears yellow and blue striped paint, and a black mask dotted with STARS surrounds his eyes. Frequently adorned with PAPER banners and sometimes with shield and darts in hand, he usually carries the XIUHCOATL, or fire serpent.

As the chief Aztec god, Huitzilopochtli occupied the most prominent site within the temple precinct of Tenochtitlan. His temple, together with that of TLALOC, formed what the Aztecs called the Hueteocalli, the Great Temple, a double pyramid. According to one account, Tlaloc had risen from a spring to welcome Huitzilopochtli when the Aztecs fled the mainland and arrived on the island in the middle of Lake Texcoco in 1345. Perhaps

Huehuecoyotl dancing, Codex Borbonicus, p. 4, 16th c. Aztec.

Huehueteotl, the Aztec Old God, stone sculpture from the Templo Mayor, Tenochtitlan.

the very oldest god in the Central Mexican pantheon, Tlaloc offered legitimacy and history to Huitzilopochtli. Together, they also suggested ATL-TLACHINOLLI, or fire-and-water, the Aztec metaphor for war. Huitzilopochtli led the Aztecs in war and in HUMAN SACRIFICE.

Huitzilopochtli's geographical origins remain obscure, but according to Aztec migration legends, he led his people on a journey for generations, commanding them first to leave their island home, AZTLAN, in the early 12th c. and to seek out a new island in a lake. Divided into seven tribes, the Aztecs soon gathered at CHICOMOZTOC, the legendary source of origin for all Central Mexican peoples, and where they, too, sojourned a while, before beginning their wanderings again. Here at Chicomoztoc, Huitzilopochtli's sister, Malinalxochitl (whose powers over SPIDERS, scorpions, and snakes recall the powers held by the principal female goddess of TEOTIHUACAN) had gained followers, and many Aztecs had grown accustomed to civilized life. When a tree split in two Huitzilopochtli interpreted it as a sign to lead the virtuous away, leaving the rest behind. At this point, religion and history intertwine, and the story of a schism among the tribes probably reflects a historical reality in which the group did divide. Those left with Malinalxochitl eventually came to settle at Malinalco, to the west of Tenochtitlan, and Malinalxochitl's son, Copil, would later attempt to avenge his mother's abandonment.

Huitzilopochtli meanwhile led his people on to COATEPEC, Hill of the Serpent, where his miraculous birth – or what we should call a rebirth – then took place. It may also have been at this juncture that a living ruler, Huitzilopochtli, was transformed into the new cult deity. One of the great mountains of Aztec legend, Coatepec was near Tula (see TOLLAN); the Aztecs celebrated a New Fire Ceremony there in 1163, just about the time of the demise and abandonment of Tula – a coincidence suggesting that the nomadic and aggressive Aztecs may have played a role in its downfall.

At Coatepec, the goddess COATLICUE kept and swept the temple. One day, as she swept, she tucked a tuft of feathers in her breast, but when she had completed her task, the feathers were gone and she knew she had become pregnant. Already the mother of 400 sons (known as the Centzon Huitznahua) and a daughter, COYOLXAUHQUI, Coatlicue and her

pregnancy became a source of humiliation to her children, and they plotted to kill her. But from within the womb, Huitzilopochtli comforted her. The Centzon Huitznahua and Coyolxauhqui charged Coatepec, slicing off Coatlicue's head. Out of her truncated body leapt Huitzilopochtli, fully formed and dressed, brandishing his Xiuhcoatl, with which he in turn dismembered his sister Coyolxauhqui, whose body parts tumbled to the foot of Coatepec. Huitzilopochtli then attacked his half-brothers, only a few of whom managed to flee.

Generations later, the Aztecs would reproduce Coatepec in the Temple of Huitzilopochtli at Tenochtitlan. Great serpents flowed down the balustrades while the wooden sculpture of Huitzilopochtli reigned from the shrine at the top – probably in the company of the image of his decapitated mother – and the dismembered Coyolxauhqui lay at the base of the pyramid, her image carved on the surface of a round stone. When bodies were tumbled down the steps, every human sacrifice recreated Coyolxauhqui's fall and public humiliation.

Coyolxauhqui may well have belonged to a group of older fertility goddesses in Central Mexico, and her destruction reveals the rise of Huitzilopochtli's cult. Often identified with the MOON, Coyolxauhqui is in this aspect also destroyed by the solar Huitzilopochtli; in fact, the round Coyolxauhqui stone at the Temple of Huitzilopochtli is periodically sliced by the sun, as if to replicate ongoing solar dominance. The Centzon Huitznahua can be identified with innumerable stars, also chased to the south by the solar Huitzilopochtli. Although often considered to be one of the youthful goddesses, at the Temple of Huitzilopochtli, Coyolxauhqui is rendered as an older woman, with sagging breasts and stretched stomach; the great Coatlicue sculpture (which may or may not have been in the shrine of Huitzilopochtli above), has also lost all trace of feminine beauty. In Huitzilopochtli's company, female goddesses become hideous, subjects for dismemberment.

In the story of Aztec peregrination, Huitzilopochtli led his people on from Coatepec into the Valley of Mexico, where they were settled at Chapultepec by the end of the 13th c. Generally unwelcomed in the Valley, Huitzilopochtli's people soon found themselves at war with their neighbors, led by Copil, the son of Malinalxochitl, the betrayed

sister of Huitzilopochtli left behind at Chicomoztoc. Copil's troops won the battle, but
Copil himself fell and was sacrificed by Huitzilopochtli, who then took Copil's heart and
hurled it onto a rock in Lake Texcoco, giving
rise to the very island on which the Aztecs
would later found their city.

Within a few years, the Aztecs were forced
to leave Chapultepec, and Huitzilopochtli led
them on to Culhuacan, on the other side of
the lake, where they were little more than
slaves to the old Toltec nobility that ruled
there. Compelled to live on the desolate
lava beds at Tizapan, the Aztecs worked as
mercenaries for the lords of Culhuacan and,
against the odds, thrived. Huitzilopochtli saw
that his people had not yet arrived at the
promised destination, and that their success
in Tizapan offered them too much comfort.
He told the tribal leaders therefore to ask the
lords of Culhuacan for a noble bride; fearing
the Aztecs, the lords complied. When the
princess was delivered, the Aztecs immediately flayed her, and a priest put on her skin.
When the Culhua came to celebrate the
arrival of a new goddess among the Aztecs,
they found instead the priest wearing the
princess's skin.   Wildly incensed by this
barbarism, the Culhua set upon the Aztecs,
killing some and driving others into the lake.
The survivors took refuge on the island there,
where they found an eagle sitting on a cactus
growing from a rock, the very image Huitzilopochtli had told them to seek generations
before. The wanderings of Huitzilopochtli
and his people came to an end, according to
most sources, in 1345 with the founding of
Tenochtitlan.

Celebrations in honor of Huitzilopochtli
dominated the religious ceremonies of Tenochtitlan, and he frequently took a role in
festivities dedicated to other gods. Outside
Tenochtitlan, Tezcatlipoca may have been
the most important god, and the two were
often honored together in Tenochtitlan. Thus,
during Toxcatl, the VEINTENA dedicated to
Tezcatlipoca, Huitzilopochtli played a prominent role, and during Panquetzaliztli, the
veintena dedicated to Huitzilopochtli, Tezcatlipoca was also propitiated. Unlike most Aztec
gods, Huitzilopochtli had a stand-in, not just
an impersonator, during many actual festivities. Known as Painal, the substitute wore
Huitzilopochtli's attributes and may be seen
as another aspect of his own numen.

During Toxcatl, a great AMARANTH dough

Huitzilopochtli wielding the Xiuhcoatl fire
serpent, Codex Borbonicus, p. 34, 16th c. Aztec.

Huitzilopochtli in his temple, Codex Azcatitlan,
16th c. Aztec.

figure, or *tzoalli*, was outfitted with Huitzilo-pochtli's attire, carried to his temple, and eventually eaten. Supplicants offered him quail, in particular, and women garlanded with flowers danced the serpent dance for him. Several *veintenas* of preparation led up to Panquetzaliztli, when the anniversary of Huitzilopochtli's miraculous birth at Coate-pec on the day 1 Flint in the year 2 Acatl was celebrated, again with a dough figure of Huitzilopochtli. A PRIEST bearing a figure of Painal led a great procession through Tenochtitlan and neighboring towns before returning to the ceremonial precinct in Ten-ochtitlan. Four victims were sacrificed in the ballcourt, then many more on the Temple of Huitzilopochtli. (Huitzilopochtli was also celebrated during Pachtontli and Tlaxochi-maco.)

human sacrifice Human sacrifice played a vital role in Mesoamerica, probably from early times onward, although it is difficult to document before the Late Preclassic period. According to most native worldviews, the GODS had offered their own BLOOD in order to generate humankind, and the sacrifice most sought by the gods in return was human flesh and blood. After Cortés's arrival in the New World, the Aztecs sent him tamales (ground maize cakes) soaked in blood, a foodstuff appropriate for a god. Humanity lived in the thrall of this blood debt, and human sacrificial victims were offered repeatedly to forestall the demise of the world and to seal the compact made with the gods. The Aztecs, for example, believed that they were living in the fifth sun, the gods having created and destroyed four previous eras, and that human sacrifice helped to keep the gods at bay. Most Mesoamerican peoples probably also recognized that human sacrifice was a way to extinguish enemies, diminish the number of young men in an enemy's army, and to humiliate publicly one's opposition (*see* CAPTIVES). Slaves were purchased for sacrifice, and parents did apparently sell their children for the purpose, but there were probably few willing volunteers, despite the belief that sacrificial victims ascended directly to heaven. Human sacrifice was not used as a punishment within society for crimes; and EXECUTION and human sacrifice were not con-fused.

Truly horrified by the human sacrifice they saw, the Spanish conquerors may have exaggerated its prevalence in order to justify their own violence in the New World. Some students of ancient Mexico, therefore, have wondered whether human sacrifice really did take place at all, and, if so, on what sort of scale. Durán expressed his own incredulity at the 80,400 victims supposedly sacrificed for the rededication of the Temple of HUITZILO-POCHTLI in 1487 – but he also reported that clotted human blood formed great pools within the temple precinct, and that a new skullrack (*see* TZOMPANTLI) had to be built to accommodate the thousands of new offerings. The Telleriano-Remensis, a native post-Con-quest account, specifies the slaughter of 20,000 for that same event.

Archaeologically, a few large deposits of human skeletons have been recovered: 42 children were simultaneously sacrificed to TLALOC and interred on the Tlaloc side of the Great Temple in Tenochtitlan; more recently, a large number of warriors were recovered from the Temple of Quetzalcoatl at TEOTIHU-ACAN, probably a single sacrificial offering for a temple dedication event. Ample evidence of human sacrifice survives from Prehispanic art. That the practice existed is irrefutable. What will probably always remain a mystery is its scale, particularly among the Aztecs.

At Monte Albán, the Temple of the Danz-antes may be a clue to Formative period public human sacrifice among the Zapotecs. Many panels there portray what seem to be sacrificed victims, limp and mutilated, probably displayed as a public memorial of victory.

As depicted in Late Classic art, the Maya generally decapitated their victims, some-times only after agonizing torture. Some were scalped, others burnt or disemboweled and some beaten. Some captives were dressed and then bound as DEER, perhaps as part of a scapedeer ritual; others were trussed up and bounced as if balls in the ritual BALLGAME. Sacrificial victims may have been paraded in litters before sacrifice on scaffolding. Many depictions of human sacrificial victims were carved on the treads or risers of steps, and such architectural features probably served as the sites of repeated sacrifices. Maya lords sought to capture other high-ranking lords in battle, and their subsequent sacrifice offered prestige – and possibly tribute and power – to the victor. No mass interments of Maya sacrificial victims have been recovered archaeologically. One Maya king, Bird Jaguar of Yaxchilán, claimed 21 captives over the course of his lifetime, and if he sacrificed that many over the course of his career, archaeological evidence would be elusive. The Maya often carved human bones, possibly those of sacrificed captives.

Disarticulated skeletons accompanying primary interments may represent slaughtered captives. A few burial configurations have suggested that living offerings accompanied the noble dead: at Palenque, the door to the tomb of Temple 18a was sealed from the inside. A 25-year-old woman left her handprints in the container of plaster that she had used; then, taking a tibia from the fleshless skeleton honored by the TOMB, she sat down in a corner to await her DEATH.

Although depictions of human sacrifices do not survive at Teotihuacan, the presence of human HEARTS on staffs and on costumes argues for the practice there. In Veracruz, sacrifice by flaying took place from Late Formative times onward. At Classic El Tajín, human sacrifice by heart extrusion is depicted as taking place in the ballcourt, but may not have been limited to the ballgame. In the Toltec era, heart sacrifice prevailed at both Tula and Chichen Itzá, and the Chichen examples are the most explicit pre-Conquest depictions of the sacrifice. Given the prominent skullrack (*tzompantli*) at Chichen Itzá, decapitation probably followed, or may have been an independent means of sacrifice.

Human sacrifice occurred with the celebration of most Aztec VEINTENA festivals. The largest number of human sacrifices were made in honor of Huitzilopochtli and TEZCATLIPOCA, as well as at times of dedication. Heart sacrifice dominated the practice, and most flayings took place after the heart had already been extruded. Modern students of heart sacrifice believe it to have been a quick means of death, particularly when carried out by skilled practitioners with FLINT blades. Heads were often severed after death and displayed on the skullrack.

Human imitation of natural events propitiated nature and this mimesis of agricultural phenomena was made sacred through human sacrifice. During Ochpaniztli, in celebration of harvest and CHICOMECOATL (the Aztec MAIZE goddess), a woman was flayed, in this case the flayed human skin representing the ripening husk of corn. For Tlacaxipehualiztli, the XIPE TOTEC impersonator wore the flayed flesh of another human: as the old

Human sacrifice, Codex Laud, Late Postclassic period.

Aztec **human sacrifice**, Florentine Codex, Book 2.

flesh rotted away, the impersonator was like a fresh sprout growing from the rotten hull of a seed. *See also* AUTOSACRIFICE, CREATION ACCOUNTS; DEATH; SACRIFICE.

hummingbird With its diminutive size, brilliant plumage and rapid and erratic flight, the hummingbird is one of the more striking birds of Mesoamerica. But although to the Western mind the hummingbird may be seen primarily as a pretty and diminutive creature, in ancient Mexico it was often identified with BLOOD and war. The peoples of ancient Mesoamerica took special note of its proclivity to suck FLOWERS with its long needle-like beak. Thus both the Classic and Postclassic Maya commonly depict the hummingbird with a perforated flower midway down the beak.

In ancient Mesoamerica, the act of sacrificial BLOODLETTING was commonly compared to the hummingbird sucking nectar from a flower. Among the Middle Formative Olmecs, fine jadeite perforators were frequently carved in the form of a hummingbird, with the long beak serving as the perforator blade. At Early Postclassic Chichen Itzá, the hummingbird is represented in the context of HUMAN SACRIFICE; in the Lower Temple of the Jaguars, a hummingbird pierces the HEART of a man emerging from a flower. In Late Postclassic Central Mexico, both hummingbirds and flowers are widely identified with blood and bloodletting. On page 44 of the Codex Borgia, QUETZALCOATL in the guise of a hummingbird stands in a cascade of blood marked by JADE and flowers. Aztec representations of bone bloodletters commonly portray a flower at the blunt condyle end of the instrument. In many instances, hummingbirds are rendered sucking the nectar of these bloodletter flowers.

The hummingbird is also quite an aggressive and fearless bird that has been known to attack creatures many times its size. Possibly for this reason, it was identified with one of the fiercest and most bellicose gods of Late Postclassic Central Mexico, HUITZILOPOCHTLI, the patron god of the Aztecs. In Nahuatl, Huitzilopochtli signifies "hummingbird on the left," or "hummingbird of the south." In the few known Aztec portrayals of Huitzilopochtli, he is usually shown wearing a long-beaked hummingbird headdress.

Hun Hunahpu One of the most important characters in the POPOL VUH creation account of the Quiché Maya is Hun Hunahpu, father of the Hero Twins Xbalanque and Hunahpu as well as the MONKEY artisans Hun Batz and Hun Chuen. In the *Popol Vuh*, Hun Hunahpu and his brother, Vucub Hunahpu, are defeated and sacrificed in the Underworld. The severed head of Hun Hunahpu is placed in a tree which then magically becomes a gourd. Impregnated by the spittle from this miraculous gourd, the maiden Xquic gives birth to Xbalanque and Hunahpu. After a series of trials, the Hero Twins defeat the gods of death and retrieve the remains of Hun Hunahpu and Vucub Hunahpu.

Representations of Hun Hunahpu are widespread in Late Classic Maya vessel scenes. Quite commonly he is found with the monkey artisans or the Classic versions of Hunahpu and Xbalanque. On one vessel, his head appears on the trunk of a CACAO tree. In the upper branches of the same tree, his head may be seen turning into a cacao pod. Quite clearly this is a Classic form of the episode in which the head of Hun Hunahpu is placed in the gourd tree. It is also now evident that the Classic Hun Hunahpu is a form of the MAIZE GOD. In many vessel scenes he emerges from the earth, much like planted corn sprouting out of the soil.

Hunahpu *see* CREATION ACCOUNTS; POPOL VUH; TWINS

Ilamatecuhtli Also referred to as CIHUACOATL and Quilaztli, Ilamatecuhtli was an Aztec goddess of the EARTH, DEATH, and the MILKY WAY. Portrayed as an aged woman with a fleshless mouth containing large bared teeth, she dressed entirely in white and wore a skirt edged with shells termed the *citlalli icue*, or star skirt, a reference to the Milky Way. Her temple was known as Tlillan, meaning "darkness" and her continually darkened chamber held captive images of GODS from all regions of the Aztec empire. One of her more important festivals occurred during the VEINTENA month of Tititl; during the New Fire ceremonies performed in the year of 2 Reed, Ilamatecuhtli appears to have played a major role in the Tititl burial of the *xiuhmolipilli* BUNDLES marking the completion of a 52-year cycle. *See also* CALENDAR; FIRE.

incense The offering of incense was considered an act of purification that linked a sacrificial object or person to the GODS, thus allowing its acceptance by them. The most common native incense, widely called *copal* – from the Nahuatl *copalli* – and also known as *pom* among the Maya, is the resin from trees of the *Bursera* genus, though gums and resins of other trees are also used as incense. When burnt, *copal* yields abundant smoke, and in this smoke could be seen ancestors as well as the gods to whom an offering was being made. RUBBER, as well as some other saps – regarded as the BLOOD and life forces of trees – made clouds of smoke in which deities might be conjured. Modern Zinacanteco Maya collect two kinds of *pom*, one nodules of resin and the other chips of wood, from two trees of the *Bursera* genus; the nodules are considered the better incense.

In the POPOL VUH, the Quiché Maya lineages offer specialized blends of *copal* to the four DIRECTIONS. In the story of the Hero Twins in the *Popol Vuh*, the UNDERWORLD lords who demand the heart of Xquic are tricked into accepting red nodules of tree sap instead. In the Dresden Codex, gods offer and receive *pom*. In this century, the Lacandon Maya have collected gums and saps for incense and formed it into what they consider male and female nodules on a board for offering to the gods.

The Aztecs frequently censed with a ladle with rattles and proffered the smoke to the four directions. In the VEINTENA Atemoztli, Aztec priests made a special offering of abundant incense to TLALOC, possibly in mimesis of the clouds associated with Tlaloc's RAIN. Archaeologically, incense has been recovered from the Chichen Itzá CENOTE and the Nevado de Toluca.

Itzamna According to Colonial Yucatec accounts, Itzamna was the high god of the Maya. Fitting his role as paramount king, he often bears the title of *ahaulil*, or "lord," in the Postclassic Yucatec codices. Similarly, Classic Maya vessel scenes frequently depict Itzamna as an enthroned king presiding over lesser GODS. However, in Postclassic CODICES he frequently appears wearing priestly accoutrements. In Postclassic Yucatán he was considered as the first PRIEST and the inventor of WRITING. During the month of Uo, priests presented their screenfold books in front of an image of the god. His identification with

The head of **Hun Hunahpu** as an ear of mature maize, detail of a mural from Cacaxtla, Tlaxcala, Late Classic period. Although appearing in a Central Mexican mural, this is a clear representation of a Classic Maya god.

Ilamatecuhtli with shield and baton, Codex Borbonicus, p. 36, 16th c. Aztec.

Copal **incense** placed upon a board, Lacandón Maya, early 20th c.

the scribal arts was also present during the Classic period. In Late Classic vessel scenes, he is often portrayed as a scribe (*see* SCRIBAL GODS). Moreover, at the Terminal Classic site of Xcalumkin, he bears the scribal title of *ah dzib*, or He of the Writing. As with his probable consort IXCHEL, Itzamna was identified with the powers of CURING. Thus during the Yucatec month of Zip, he was invoked as a god of medicine.

In the Postclassic Yucatec codices, Itzamna appears as the aged deity known as God D (*see* SCHELLHAS GODS). During both the Classic and Postclassic periods, he wears a prominent beaded disk upon his brow. A diagnostic element of Itzamna, the same disk also appears in his name glyph. Quite frequently, this disk contains the Akbal sign denoting darkness or blackness, and it is probable that the device represents an OBSIDIAN MIRROR, such as was used in divinatory scrying (*see* DIVINATION). During the Postclassic period, God D can appear in CAIMAN guise and in fact, *itzam* signifies CAIMAN, lizard or large fish in Mayan languages. It is probable that this caiman aspect of Itzamna is identical to the Colonial Yucatec being known as Itzam Cab Ain, the great earth caiman associated with the flood. Itzamna is also closely identified with the PRINCIPAL BIRD DEITY, the Classic Maya form of VUCUB CAQUIX, the monster bird of POPOL VUH fame. The Principal Bird Deity appears to be none other than the celestial aspect of Itzamna.

Itzpapalotl One of the more fearsome goddesses of the Central Mexican pantheon, Itzpapalotl is commonly rendered as a skeletal being with JAGUAR talons and knife-tipped wings. The term *itzpapalotl* can signify either OBSIDIAN butterfly or clawed BUTTERFLY, but it is likely that the second meaning is intended. Rather than obsidian, the wing blades are clearly rendered as FLINT, or *tecpatl*. It is quite possible that the concept of a clawed butterfly refers to the BAT, and in fact, in a number of instances Itzpapalotl appears with bat wings. However, she can also appear with clear butterfly and EAGLE attributes.

Itzpapalotl is patron of the day Cozcacuauhtli and the TRECENA 1 House; the day 1 House is also one of the five western *trecena* dates dedicated to the CIHUATETEO, the demonic women who died in childbirth. Itzpapalotl was not only a *cihuateotl*, but also one of the *tzitzimime*, star demons that

threatened to devour people during solar ECLIPSES. She was a goddess of the paradise realm of TAMOANCHAN, a place identified with the bird of the gods and humankind.

The earliest known representation of Itzpapalotl appears on a fragmentary relief from Early Postclassic Tula, where she appears with a skeletalized head and butterfly wings supplied with stone blades. Although the identity remains to be proven, the Zapotec deity called Goddess 2J by Alfonso Caso and Ignacio Bernal found on ceramic urns may well turn out to be a Classic Zapotec form of Itzpapalotl. In a number of instances, this Zapotec goddess is clearly identified with the bat.

Itztlacoliuhqui-Ixquimilli To the ancient Mexicans, stone and castigation were closely related concepts, since miscreants were frequently punished by stoning. Thus the Nahuatl expression for punishment was *tetl-cuahuitl*, meaning "wood and stone." The Central Mexican deity of castigation, Itztlacoliuhqui-Ixquimilli is also the god of stone and coldness. He frequently appears with a face and curving forehead of banded stone, much like varieties of FLINT or agate. In something like the Western concept of "justice is blind," he is usually blindfolded or sightless. In many cases, he blends with the black TEZCATLIPOCA and in this form appears as a god of the north and patron of the day Acatl. In addition, he serves as the god of the TRECENA 1 Cuetzpalin.

In many instances, Itztlacoliuhqui-Ixquimilli is rendered with a stone-tipped dart in his brow. This probably concerns an episode from the *Leyenda de los soles* account of the creation of the fifth sun at TEOTIHUACAN. As the god of the DAWN and the morning star, TLAHUIZCALPANTECUHTLI shot a dart at the SUN who, in turn, transfixed Tlahuizcalpantecuhtli with a dart through the forehead. The account states that once pierced by this dart, Tlahuizcalpantecuhtli became the god of cold, that is, Itztlacoliuhqui-Ixquimilli. The Central Mexican god of stone, cold, and castigation also appears in the Venus pages of the Maya Dresden Codex. On Dresden page 50, he is rendered not only with the blindfold but also with a flint point projecting from the top of his headdress. It is possible that the codical God Q (*see* SCHELLHAS GODS) is a Postclassic Maya version of Itztlacoliuhqui-Ixquimilli.

Ixchel At the time of the Spanish Conquest,

Ixchel was a prominent Maya goddess, patroness of childbirth, pregnancy, and fertility. Women from all over Yucatán made long pilgrimages to seek her attention at shrines on Cozumel and Isla Mujeres, and the shrines were reputedly filled with sculptures of her image, although none survive. The name Ixchel can be translated as "Lady Rainbow."

In the Dresden Codex, she bears the name Chac Chel, and is depicted as an old lady with snakes in her hair, sometimes with JAGUAR claws and eyes, and occasionally dressed in a skirt patterned with a skull-and-bones motif. She also appears to be a patroness of weaving, DIVINATION, and midwifery, although she is probably not the beautiful young weaving woman given form in a number of Jaina figurines. Nor is there reason to think that she is the beautiful young MOON goddess of Classic Maya art with whom her name has been widely identified: that young woman, sometimes depicted within the crescent of the moon, does not bear the name Ixchel or Chac Chel. Ixchel's closest associations are with certain Central Mexican goddesses, particularly those related to TOCI and ILAMATECUHTLI. *See also* BIRTH; SCHELLHAS GODS.

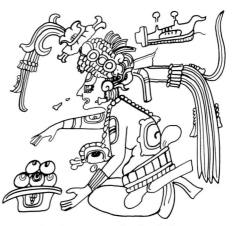

The aged god **Itzamna** with a bowl of maize tamales, detail from a Late Classic Maya vase.

 J

jade The general term jade refers to both jadeite and nephrite. Both are rocks, or mineral aggregates, and both are found in the Old and New Worlds. In Mesoamerica, only jadeite is found, sometimes occurring in lodes of serpentine, a lesser greenstone, and its molecules are rarely pure. Albite and diopside, also greenstones, occur with jadeite and were used for the same precious objects in the ancient New World. Mesoamerican jadeite is a sodium and aluminum silicate, and it is hard, between 6.0 and 7.0 on the Mohs' scale, and so unyielding that tools to work jade were often themselves made of jade. In the Mesoamerican world without metal tools, jade was worked with string saws, tubular drills, and jade tools, but with jade powder or quartz sand as the abrasive. Jade occurs as rocks and boulders, usually along rivers. A field of jade boulders within 30 miles of the Motagua River in Guatemala now supplies a modern jade industry.

Known generically as *chalchihuitl* in Central Mexico, jade was the most precious rock

Itztlacoliuhqui-Ixquimilli, the god of stone, cold, and castigation, Codex Borbonicus, p. 12, 16th c. Aztec.

The aged goddess **Ixchel**, detail from a Late Classic Maya vase.

or mineral in Mesoamerica. Perhaps because of its dominant green and blue-green colors, it was identified with MAIZE, WATER, SKY, vegetation, even life itself. As such, it was sometimes inlaid as the HEART in sculptures and in the mouths of the dead as money – and as a sign of the renewal of life.

The Olmecs were the first Mesoamerican people to locate and carve jade. They preferred the blue-green variety now generally thought to have come from Costa Rica and used the material for their most precious objects: portrait masks, incised depictions of gods, and utensils used in religious rituals. From Olmec times onward, jade had great value as an heirloom, and judging from materials dredged from the Sacred CENOTE at Chichen Itzá, jade was the most important offering. It held great intrinsic value in every Mesoamerican culture, and the Aztecs may have sacked ancient buildings just to retrieve old jade.

The Spanish were interested in *chalchihuitl* only insofar as they were able to promote green and blue glass beads in their trading arrangements. When the Aztecs told them that the stones cured internal ailments, particularly of the spleen, liver and kidney, they called it loin-stone, or *piedra de ijada* in Spanish. Sir Walter Raleigh commented on these miraculous CURING stones of the loins in the 1580s, but the word jade, a corruption of *ijada*, only came into the English language later. When it was catalogued and given a Latin name by Europeans, they called it *lapis nephriticus*, from the Latin word for kidney, *nephrus*, yielding the word nephrite, which they then applied to Asian jade. The confusion was compounded in modern times, when two distinct compounds were identified, nephrite and jadeite.

jaguar Probably the most feared and revered beast in Mesoamerica, the jaguar (*Panthera onca*) played a prominent religious role. Like humankind, the jaguar occupies the top level of the food chain, and people sought to identify themselves with the big cat. Generally nocturnal, the jaguar's eyes are luminous gold disks at night, and a jaguar skull excavated at Kaminaljuyú bears gold pyrite eyes. Distinctive black rosettes characterize jaguar pelage, and they are present even on the rarer all-black jaguar although they can be seen only in raking light. Fishers as well as hunters, jaguars live exclusively in the tropical rain forest but were sought in tribute and trade by all highland civilizations in Mexico. Called *ocelotl* in Nahuatl, the jaguar is not to be confused in English with ocelot (*Panthera pardalis*), the smaller cat of similar pelage. Unlike its more adaptable and silent cousin the puma (*Panthera concolor*), jaguars will roar or grunt. A jaguar's diet includes DEER, agoutis, MONKEYS, waterbirds, fish, TURTLES, and even CAIMANS, and the cat is particularly fond of resting on branches that extend out over water.

JAGUAR GODS were present in every major Mesoamerican civilization, but jaguars were also important shamanic creatures (*see* SHAMAN), and in states of ritual transformation, humans changed themselves into jaguars from at least Olmec times onward. The Maya hieroglyph that is read UAY, meaning animal companion or TONAL, is itself an *ahau* glyph half-covered with jaguar pelt. According to Sahagún, Aztec "conjurers went about carrying its hide – the hide of its forehead and of its chest, and its tail, its nose, and its claws, and its heart, and its fangs, and its snout. It is said that they went about their tasks with them – that with them they did daring deeds, that because of them they were feared" (FC:XI).

To assert lordly power, chiefs and kings wore jaguar pelts, jaguar sandals, headdresses fashioned of jaguar heads, and necklaces made of jaguar teeth – and even necklaces of JADE beads carved as jaguar teeth. Along with the MAT, jaguar pelts and cushions were the symbol of the enthroned lord, and many stone thrones, particularly among the Maya, took the shape of jaguars, sometimes double-headed.

Jaguar offerings were made on important ritual occasions. At Copán, 16 jaguars were sacrificed in conjunction with the installation of the 16th ruler of the dynasty. To be sacrificed, a jaguar might well have had to be drugged! At least three jaguar pelts, along with pelts of three smaller cats, were draped within the so-called Sun God's Tomb at Altun Ha. In the Great Temple of Tenochtitlan, many jaguars were interred, perhaps to symbolize the PYRAMID as a mountain with CAVES, the preferred dwelling of the jaguar.

Sacrificed jaguars were often beheaded, and a headless jaguar glyph in Maya WRITING remains undeciphered. On a series of well-known but poorly understood codex-style Maya pots, CHAC sacrifices a baby jaguar, sometimes pictured naturalistically and other times given human characteristics, in the presence of God A (*see* SCHELLHAS GODS). Such a repeated religious image might refer to a calendrical or astral myth.

jaguar gods Jaguar gods played a prominent role in Mesoamerican religion. Like JAGUARS themselves, these gods were associated with NIGHT, CAVES, the UNDERWORLD, hunting, and stealth. They are also related to transformation figures, and some are known as aspects of other deities.

The Olmecs were long thought to have only one major deity, the WERE-JAGUAR, supposedly derived from the mating of a human and a jaguar. Recent studies have demonstrated that many other animals, including birds and SERPENTS, lie at the root of OLMEC GODS, but Olmec shamanic transformation figures primarily feature the jaguar. Among Olmec deities, the crouching RAIN god frequently has the body of a jaguar, and he may be the most characteristic were-jaguar.

At TEOTIHUACAN, there are numerous jaguar sculptures – some functioning as ritual receptacles – but among the supernatural ones, the Netted Jaguar is probably the most prominent. Characterized by a jaguar body covered in a reticulated interlace, the Netted Jaguar usually features a great panache of trimmed feathers at the back of the head and may have a feather trim along the back, tail, and legs. In depictions of processions where he alternates with coyotes, a human HEART hangs in front of his lolling tongue, suggesting a sacrificial role, and presaging the WARRIOR ORDERS dedicated to totemic animals in Aztec times. The Netted Jaguar often bears MIRRORS and rattles, perhaps because of a relation he may bear to DIVINATION, and he may travel along a path marked by human footprints.

A three-dimensional feathered jaguar with its back carved as a receptacle may have once received human hearts, like the later Aztec CUAUHXICALLIS. The Teotihuacan TLALOC frequently has a jaguar association, particularly in the formation of the Tlaloc A mouth.

At Monte Albán, jaguar urns are featured from an early date. As among the Maya, naturalistic jaguars sometimes bear human scarves, as if to indicate a supernatural association. The jaguar god labeled 1 Tiger by Alfonso Caso and Ignacio Bernal frequently wears a human heart as a pectoral. Their god labeled Old God 5F bears the same twisted

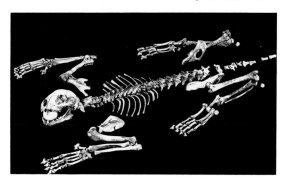

Jaguar with a jade ball in its mouth, found as an offering in the Templo Mayor, Tenochtitlan, Late Postclassic Aztec.

In a state of shamanic transformation, a Maya lord would take on an animal self or *uay*, most commonly the **jaguar**; from a Late Classic Maya vase, Altar de Sacrificios.

Hill of the **Jaguar**, Codex Vindobonensis, p. 9, Late Postclassic Mixtec.

"cruller" (so named because it resembles the twisted pastry) between the nose and under the eyes that characterizes the Maya Jaguar God of the Underworld and is clearly related to that deity.

Perhaps because the Maya and the jaguar shared dominion over the tropical rain forest, the Maya had more jaguar deities and deities with jaguar associations than any other Mesoamerican peoples. The Maya particularly identified the SUN with the jaguar. The daytime sun, often represented as patron of the number 4, can be represented with jaguar features, but the nighttime sun, the Jaguar God of the Underworld, patron of the number 7, is clearly a jaguar in his full-body depictions and generally has jaguar ears in all representations. He may also appear as an anthropomorphic form, with jaguar characteristics limited to the face. The Jaguar God of the Underworld usually has a hank of twisted hair over his forehead, and a "cruller" between his nose that may continue under the eyes. In this form, the Jaguar God of the Underworld is the sun in the Underworld, traveling from west to east, sometimes atop a great CAIMAN. The Jaguar God of the Underworld is particularly associated with Tikal, of which he may be the patron, particularly in the Early Classic; the toponym for Tikal is incorporated into his headdress in some depictions at Tikal and most formal portraiture of Tikal kings incorporates the head of the Jaguar God of the Underworld.

Other Maya jaguar gods include the Water Lily Jaguar, the Jaguar Baby, and the Jaguar Paddler (see PADDLER GODS). Always a zoomorphic form, the Water Lily Jaguar wears a water lily on his head and usually a collar of extruded eyeballs around the neck or a scarf. The Water Lily Jaguar serves as a throne, marches in Underworld processions, appears occasionally with a STAR sign on his back (perhaps to tell us that he is also a constellation), serves as the patron of the month Pop, and functions as an overarching frame for one of the giant Tikal litters. The Jaguar Baby is usually shown as a chubby zoomorphic or anthropomorphic jaguar, almost always set in opposition to CHAC in scenes of SACRIFICE. Chac wields an axe, and the Jaguar Baby usually reclines on a stone ALTAR. One of the pair of PADDLER GODS that guide the MAIZE GOD and others through the waters of the Underworld, the Jaguar Paddler usually handles the fore of the craft. Like his

partner, the Stingray Paddler, the Jaguar Paddler is an old god, with sunken cheeks.

Other Maya supernaturals wear jaguar pelage or are jaguars. The patron of the month Pax is a jaguar god who lacks a lower jaw and who occurs in the company of the Jaguar God of the Underworld on painted ceramics, frequently in the context of HUMAN SACRIFICE. Xbalanque, one of the Hero Twins, often has jaguar pelt on his face, arms, and legs, and is the patron of the number 9.

In Central Mexico, Tepeyollotl was the most important jaguar god, and as a deity related to TEZCATLIPOCA, held a significant place in the Aztec pantheon. Tepeyollotl, "heart of the mountain," dwelt in mountain CAVES, and the very offering of so many jaguars in the Great Temple of their ceremonial precinct suggests that the Aztecs perceived this temple compound, dedicated to TLALOC and HUITZILOPOCHTLI, to be the heart of the mountain where Tepeyollotl dwelt. Tepeyollotl presided over the TRECENA 1 Mazatl and was the eighth Lord of the Night (see CALENDAR). See also KINICH AHAU; TEOTIHUACAN GODS.

jaguar-serpent-bird Terminology that has been used to describe a frontal monster from which a human head protrudes, the "jaguar-serpent-bird" is a frontal version of the WAR SERPENT. Seler linked the imagery to VENUS and the morning star and suggested a relationship to QUETZALCOATL and TLALHUIZCALPANTECUHTLI that can no longer be supported. Rare at TEOTIHUACAN itself, the frontal war serpent is most common among the Maya, at Piedras Negras and Chichen Itzá, and at Tula. The primary association of this composite image is warfare.

Jester God The Jester God takes his name from the head ornament that dangles over his forehead like that of a court jester. Usually trilobed and depicted only as a head (except at Palenque, where a body is included), the distinctive Jester God head ornament makes its first appearance during Olmec times – as a head ornament at La Venta and on braziers from Monte Albán – although the Jester God occurs mainly among the Classic Maya, and makes no Postclassic appearances. During the Early Classic period, some Maya Jester Gods have the characteristics of a SHARK. Generally, the Jester God functions as a head ornament of kings and was made of JADE, but lesser nobles wear Jester Gods of various colors in the Bonampak murals, so it was not the exclusive purview of kingship. The jade Jester God depicted on Pacal's headband on the Palenque Oval Palace Tablet is probably the very one recovered from Pacal's tomb.

jewelry Men and women, GODS and humans all wore jewelry in ancient Mesoamerica. In general, jewelry was made of the most precious materials: JADE, serpentine, and other greenstones, along with amber, pearls, SHELL, quartz, and OBSIDIAN in the Formative and Classic eras, and GOLD, silver, TURQUOISE, obsidian, shell, quartz and greenstones in Postclassic times. Although some mosaic work is known among Classic jewelry, it became more common in the Postclassic era.

In the hair, diadems, tiaras, and headbands of individual carved beads sometimes accompany or supplant headdresses; head-dresses themselves, if they include full heads, might bear ear flares and other ornaments. Hair was also pulled through fancy beads, particularly at the front of the head, and tiny beads were worked into long strands of hair among some 8th c. Maya. Ear flares generally were assemblages in which the large flange at front was anchored to a counterweight behind by a cord that pierced the ear. Nose ornaments, particularly butterfly ornaments, were known at TEOTIHUACAN, Tula, Chichen Itzá, and Tenochtitlan. Noses were pierced to receive nose beads: lords journeyed to Cholula to have their noses pierced and to receive the adornment fitting a king. Central Mexican nobles pierced the lower lip in order to insert a labret, many of which took the form of snakes or birds.

Necklaces were sometimes suspended in multiple strands, forming beaded collars. Beaded wristlets and anklets were additional adornments. Although rarely depicted in art, rings have been found archaeologically, par-ticularly among the Maya. During the Proto-classic and Classic, belt` assemblages, com-posed of a head with three thin dangling plaques, were worn by kings at either the front or back of the waist.

Perhaps because of the green foliage of MAIZE, the Maya maize god HUN HUNAHPU wears abundant jewelry, probably of jade. In preparation for SACRIFICE, Maya captives were often bedecked with jewels and finery. Their sacrifice may have been likened to the harvest of the Maize God.

Crouching **Jaguar-Serpent-Bird**, a version of the War Serpent; Chichen Itzá, Yucatán, Early Postclassic period.

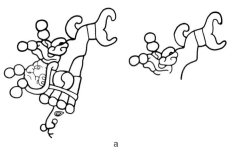

Protoclassic and Classic forms of the shark **Jester God**. *a*, As worn by Protoclassic ruler, Loltun Cave, Yucatán. *b*, Shark Jester God of ruler Stormy Sky, Stela 31, Tikal, Early Classic period. *c*, Shark Jester God of ruler Pacal, Oval Palace Tablet, Palenque, Late Classic period.

Jewelry and regalia worn by a ruler shown on the Leiden Plaque, Early Classic Maya.

K

Kinich Ahau During both the Classic and Postclassic periods the Maya SUN god was termed Kinich Ahau, meaning sun-faced or sun-eyed lord. In profile, the sun god appears much like a younger version of ITZAMNA. The similarities are not coincidental; among the contact period Yucatec, one aspect of the aged creator god was Kinich Ahau Itzamna. For the Postclassic codices, the sun god is commonly referred to as God G (*see* SCHELLHAS GODS). In contrast to Itzamna, the codical sun god is usually bearded and has snake-like elements curving out from the corners of the mouth. However, one of the most distinctive traits of Kinich Ahau, is the four-petaled *kin* often placed upon his brow or body. When viewed face on, it may be seen that the Maya sun god is cross-eyed and has his upper incisors filed into the form of a "T." During both the Classic and Postclassic periods, the sun god is closely identified with JAGUARS, and at times appears with a jaguar ear. In Classic period inscriptions, he serves as the head variant of the number 4, and patron of the month Yaxkin. It is clear that the patron of the month Pax is again the sun god, although without his lower jaw. Along with the Monkey Scribe, the head of the sun god can also denote the Long Count position of Kin, or day (*see* CALENDAR).

The sun god appears in still another epigraphic context, GIII of the PALENQUE TRIAD, where he bears an important title shared with Maya kings. Although this title has been commonly read as *mah kinah*, recent epigraphic research indicates that it is probably to be read *kinich*, a title recorded for the 16th c. highland Maya. The Maya identification of kings with the sun god can be traced to at least as early as the mid-5th c. AD. In the upper portion of Tikal Stela 31, the deceased ruler Curl Snout appears apotheosized as Kinich Ahau. Moreover, at both Late Classic Palenque and Yaxchilán, ancestors are depicted within solar cartouches. *See also* DEIFICATION; JAGUAR GODS; SUN.

Kukulcan *see* QUETZALCOATL

 L

lightning and thunder Among the most potent and dramatic natural phenomena of Mexico are lightning storms which light up the SKY and shake the EARTH with thunder. In particular, lightning is regarded with special interest. Rather than being only a dangerous power, lightning is considered to be life giving and engendering. Because of the basic association of lightning with rain, the gods of lightning are usually also the gods of RAIN. However, lightning itself was clearly considered as a manifestation of powerful fertilizing energy, as, for example, in the widespread myth of the origin of MAIZE, where lightning splits open the rock containing the hidden seed.

In Mesoamerica, the almost instantaneous flash of lightning is represented in a number of ways. Quite commonly, the sinuous aspect of lightning bolts takes the form of undulating SERPENTS. Given the igneous nature of lightning, these lightning snakes are often represented as burning FIRE serpents. The stone axe, usually of FLINT, is another widespread symbol of lightning. Even today, stone axes found in the fields are commonly regarded as spent lightning.

Among the Classic Maya, the so-called MANIKIN SCEPTER refers to lightning simultaneously as a serpent, fire, and axe. The Manikin Scepter takes the form of a deified axe, with one of the legs terminating in a burning serpent foot, and is simply an aspect of the deity commonly known as God K (*see* SCHELLHAS GODS), or *kauil* in the Classic Maya script. CHAC, the Maya god of rain and lightning usually wields the God K serpent axe.

In Central Mexico, the lightning god of the Aztecs and other peoples is the JAGUAR-fanged TLALOC. The earliest known depictions of Tlaloc from Protoclassic Tlapacoya portray the deity flanked by serpentine lightning bolts. Among the Zapotecs of Oaxaca, the god of lightning is COCIJO, a word which means lightning. The Totonac god of lightning, Tajín, is also named by the native word for lightning.

The symbolism of thunder is less evident and developed than that for lightning. According to one Aztec account, thunder is caused by the breaking of great water jars containing rain. Among the contemporary highland Maya, there is a contrast between vigorous and youthful lightning gods and gods of thunder, who tend to be aged gods of the earth and mountains. The aged thunder god is frequently referred to as Mam, and it is probable that the ancient Maya god known as PAUAHTUN or God N is the Prehispanic form of this being. The modern Huastec Maya of northern Veracruz and neighboring San Luis Potosí also possess an aged thunder god known as Mam. He is said to appear bent over his walking stick, and numerous Prehispanic Huastec sculptures similarly portray the old Mam stooped over his staff.

litters Nobles, deity impersonators, sacrificial victims, and images of GODS were often carried in litters, as were wealthy persons who could afford to hire bearers to keep their feet from touching the ground. Presumably it was ennobling to be borne aloft. On long journeys, both Aztec MERCHANTS and ranking Aztec warriors might be carried in litters. The earliest depiction of a litter occurs at Izapa, where a deity watches from a litter while a decapitation takes place. Maya kings were borne in litters, often made of simple rushes and carried by just two bearers. At Tikal, graffiti scratched on palace and temple walls record extremely elaborate litters in the form of giant Water Lily Jaguars and WAR SERPENTS.

The Aztecs frequently carried their sacrificial victims about in litters prior to SACRIFICE. Some Aztec child sacrifices to TLALOC were thus paraded, as were the deity impersonators dressed as MOUNTAINS during the VEINTENA of Tepeilhuitl. During that festival, four of the five mountain impersonators were women, including one dedicated to MAYAHUEL, and all the bearers were women. *See also* DEITY IMPERSONATION; JAGUAR GODS.

long-nosed and long-lipped deities Although these terms have long been in use for Classic Maya and earlier deities, they are confusing and do not allow for discrimination among Maya GODS. SCHELLHAS first used the term "god with long nose" to describe CHAC, but since his day, great numbers of gods have been called long nosed. The more recent term, "long-lipped deity," has been used to describe more accurately the extended upper lip of many Maya and Izapa gods, but this term also tends to group all such deities together without distinction. What can be said about the shape of the lower face – or what can more generally be called the snout –

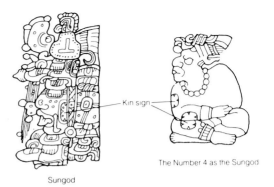

Kin sign

The Number 4 as the Sungod

Sungod

Early Classic (left) and Late Classic representations of **Kinich Ahau**, the Maya sun god.

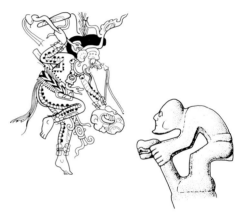

(*Left*) Late Classic form of Chac, the Maya god of rain and **lightning**, wielding a serpent-footed lightning axe; detail from a Maya vase. (*Right*) The aged Mam, the Huastec god of **thunder**, Veracruz, Postclassic period. The staff is in the form of a serpent, probably an allusion to lightning.

Litter topped by a smoking jaguar, Izapa Stela 21, Protoclassic period.

is that it may reveal a zoomorphic origin. Upward-turning snouts, like that of the JESTER GOD, indicate a SERPENT origin. Downward-curving snouts, like that of the PRINCIPAL BIRD DEITY, suggest the beaks of birds. Blunt or square snouts generally reveal a JAGUAR origin.

 M

Macuilxochitl is named for a specific date in the 260-day CALENDAR, 5 Flower. He is the principal god of the AHUIATETEO, who are named after the five southern day names appearing with the coefficient of 5 and who are gods simultaneously of excess pleasure and of consequent punishment. On pages 47 and 48 of the Codex Borgia, they appear with a human hand across the mouth, an important trait of Macuilxochitl. The patron god of palace folk as well as of games and gambling – in particular, the game of PATOLLI – Macuilxochitl is closely related to and frequently overlaps with another youthful god, XOCHI-PILLI, the "flower prince."

maguey Native to highland Mexico, maguey (*Agave* spp.) is a plant of many diverse uses. In ancient Mexico, the thorns tipping the leaves were widely used as BLOODLETTING instruments. The thick fleshy leaves yield tough fiber for rope or coarse CLOTH. However, the most renowned product of maguey is PULQUE, known as *octli* in Nahuatl. The fermented sweet sap, or *aguamiel*, of the maguey plant, pulque is the most important alcoholic drink of native Mexico.

Maguey was frequently personified as a youthful goddess. For the ancient Mixtecs, the maguey goddess is referred to as 11 Serpent, and appears with her severed head falling from her bleeding throat. This may refer to the severing of the central stalk of the maguey plant, a basic process in the production of pulque. To the inhabitants of Central Mexico, MAYAHUEL was the young goddess of maguey. In a 17th c. Nahuatl chant recorded by Ruíz de Alarcón, maguey is referred to by the calendrical name of 8 Flint. The same date of 8 Flint appears on the rim of the Aztec Bilimek Vessel, a Prehispanic stone vase covered with allusions to maguey and pulque.

maize Since the beginning of the Formative period, maize (*Zea mays*) has been the most important food crop of Mexico. The first known domestic maize appears during the Archaic period of the Tehuacan Valley in Puebla at around 3500 BC. However, far larger and more productive forms of maize developed during the Formative period. Many researchers currently believe that ancient people domesticated maize from a closely related grass known as *teosinte* (*Zea mexicana*). The etymology of *teosinte* reveals that the native peoples of highland Mexico also recognized the importance and relevance of this plant to maize. The term derives from the Nahuatl words *teo*, signifying "god" or "sacred," and *cintli*, meaning "maize." Thus a suitable gloss for *teosinte* is "godly corn."

Representations of maize date from as early as the Formative Olmec and abound in the later iconography of Classic and Postclassic Mexico. The Classic Maya seem to have had an especially close relationship with maize, and cranial deformation may have been performed to mimic the elongated form of the maize ear. The Classic and Postclassic Maya also frequently depict maize ears as human heads, as if corn was a sentient being. In the Mixteca-Puebla style of Postclassic highland Mexico, maize ears are also depicted with teeth and open eyes. Entirely dependent upon humans for propagation, maize was considered as a friend and ally of people. In fact, in Maya mythology of highland Guatemala, the present race of humans are the people of maize, and were first fashioned from ground corn and penitential BLOOD. Among Colonial and contemporary highland Maya of Guatemala and neighboring Chiapas, the umbilical cord of the newborn child is cut over a mature maize ear. The bloodied seed is saved and becomes the special crop of the child. Even at the moment of BIRTH, the individual becomes a virtual blood ally of maize. *See also* CINTEOL; CREATION ACCOUNTS; HUN HUNAHPU; MAIZE GODS.

maize gods Although representations of MAIZE are known from the Formative period, the identification of Olmec maize gods is far from clear. God II of the Joralemon Olmec god classification (*see* OLMEC GODS) displays maize sprouting from his or her cleft head. However, it is not certain whether this deity is a personification of maize or perhaps the earth or mountain from which maize originates. Several Olmec representations of chinless DWARVES display maize signs on their bodies. Although it is possible that these dwarves represent maize, they also could refer to LIGHTNING, RAIN, or other forces that create corn. Among the Classic period Zapotecs, one entity commonly formed on Zapotec urns – the God of Glyph L – often appears with ears of maize. For this reason, he has been identified as the Classic form of the Zapotec maize god, known as Pitào Cozobi during the early Colonial period. However, the God of Glyph L shares many characteristics with the Classic form of COCIJO, the Zapotec god of rain and lightning. In fact, Cocijo also generally bears maize ears in his hands or headdress.

The earliest identifiable Mesoamerican maize god appears in Early Classic Maya art as a youthful male with stylized maize placed at the top of the head. During the Late Classic period, two distinct but overlapping forms of this deity develop. One of these, the Tonsured Maize God, appears with a markedly elongated human head often shaved in zones across the flattened brow; he is the Classic Maya prototype of HUN HUNAHPU of the Quiché Maya POPOL VUH. Recently discovered murals at Cacaxtla, Tlaxcala, portray heads of the Tonsured Maize God as ripened ears of yellow corn. He thus represents mature and fertile maize; the other Late Classic maize deity, however, depicts tender growing maize. This figure, the Foliated Maize God, is portrayed with a stylized maize ear sprouting from the top of the head. The Maya maize god continues in this form through the Late Postclassic period. In the codices, he is commonly referred to as God E, following the Schellhas system of deity classification (see SCHELLHAS GODS).

Aside from the notable appearance of the Tonsured Maize God at Cacaxtla, there are no clear representations of maize deities in Central Mexico until the Late Postclassic period. The most important of these is CINTEOTL, who is closely related to two other youthful male gods, XOCHIPILLI and MACUILXOCHITL. Like the Postclassic God E of the Maya codices, Cinteotl typically has a pair of thin, broken, vertical lines passing down across the brow and cheeks. The Aztecs also had female personifications of maize, in particular, CHICOMECOATL, or 7 Serpent. To the Postclassic Mixtecs, maize was commonly conceived of as a woman. In the Codex Vindobonensis, three maize goddesses are

Macuilxochitl, the Central Mexican god of gaming and pleasure, Florentine Codex, Book 1, 16th c. Aztec.

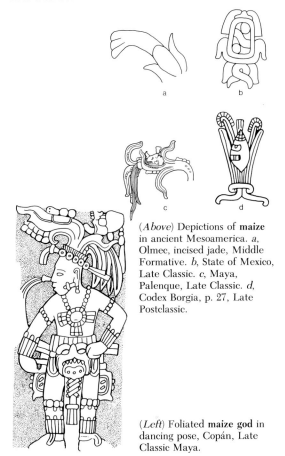

(*Above*) Depictions of **maize** in ancient Mesoamerica. *a*, Olmec, incised jade, Middle Formative. *b*, State of Mexico, Late Classic. *c*, Maya, Palenque, Late Classic. *d*, Codex Borgia, p. 27, Late Postclassic.

(*Left*) Foliated **maize god** in dancing pose, Copán, Late Classic Maya.

mentioned, 5 Flint, 7 Flint, and 7 Grass. *See also* CREATION ACCOUNTS.

Manikin Scepter The Manikin Scepter, a term coined by H. Spinden, is the particular manifestation of a Maya god also known as God K or GII of the PALENQUE TRIAD. His name was Bolon Dzacab in Conquest period Yucatán and he was probably known as Kauil in Classic times. This same deity may have been called Tohil among the Quiché.

In general, the Manikin Scepter is a full-figure but diminutive representation of this god designed to be held in the hand of a ruler as a symbol of rulership itself. When CHAC carries the Manikin Scepter, it symbolizes LIGHTNING. The god is characterized by an axe or smoking tube that pierces his forehead, an upward-turning snout, and, most distinctively, one leg that turns into a SERPENT, like the Central Mexican deity TEZCATLIPOCA, to whom some scholars have linked him. His first clear appearance is on Early Classic monuments, but the Manikin Scepter remains an important attribute of rulership right through the Postclassic at Chichen Itzá and is probably the object held by the patriarch depicted in the 1557 Xiu family tree. The form may well be based on an axe or CELT.

marriage The institution of marriage was not limited in Mesoamerica to the human plane but was present among the GODS as well. In Central Mexico, gods were frequently described as having both female and male aspects, as if they were married couples. Examples include Ometecuhtli and Omecihuatl (*see* OMETEOTL), MICTLANTECUHTLI and Mictecacihuatl, and TONACATECUHTLI and Tonacacihuatl. Marriage also describes particular relationships between deities. Thus for example, CHALCHIUHTLICUE – the goddess of standing WATER and rivers – is the wife of the RAIN and LIGHTNING god TLALOC. Or there is the goddess of MAGUEY, MAYAHUEL, who is the spouse of Patecatl, a PULQUE GOD. In the Maya area, the MOON goddess is frequently described as the wife of the SUN. Pages 57 to 60 of the Central Mexican Codex Borgia contain a remarkable series of 31 god couples, perhaps composed for marriage prognostications. It is possible that the pairing of the youthful Goddess I (*see* SCHELLHAS GODS) with particular gods in the Maya Dresden Codex may similarly have served to determine marriage partners.

In ancient Mesoamerica, marriages were frequently arranged through aged arbitrators or matchmakers. Ritual banquets often formed an essential part of the marriage ceremonies; among both the Aztecs and the Yucatec Maya, the feeding of the groom by the bride was an important rite during the festivities. Thanks to the Florentine Codex and the Codex Mendoza, we know a considerable amount regarding Aztec marriage ceremonies. The Florentine Codex provides part of the speech directed to the future bride:

O my daughter, thou art here. For thy sake thy mothers, thy fathers have become old men, old women. Now thou approachest the old women; already thou commencest the life of an old woman. Forever now leave childishness, girlishness... Be most considerate of one; regard one with respect, speak well, greet one well. By night look to, take care of the sweeping, the laying of the fire. Arise in the deep of night. Do not reject us, do not embarrass us as old men, do not reject thy mothers as old women. (FC: VI)

Among the Aztecs, the bride was carried at dusk to the house of the groom. Seated on a MAT before the household hearth, the couple were presented with gifts. The union of marriage was ritually expressed by the old matchmakers tying together the couple's clothing in a knot.

In highland Mexico, marriage was commonly represented by the couple seated upon a mat or lying together under a single blanket. Among Mesoamerican nobility, marriage cemented alliances and legitimized bloodlines. One of the most detailed scenes of an elite native marriage ceremony appears in the Codex Selden of the Postclassic Mixtecs. Here Lady 6 Monkey of Jaltepec marries a lord named 11 Wind. DANCING and ceremonial bathing by the couple form part of the marriage rites. Among the Classic Maya elite marriage often served to reinforce alliances between cities and revitalize dynasties. The wife of the Copán king Smoke Shell came from the distant site of Palenque. King Flint-Sky-God K of Dos Pilas married a woman from the site of Itzán, and later sent a daughter to be married to a Naranjo lord. One of the greatest kings of Naranjo, Smoking-Squirrel, was born of this union.

mat He of the Mat was an eponym of rulership among most people of ancient Mexico. Not every mat, however, was a key to a ruling lord or high PRIEST himself, for even assistants slept on finely woven mats, according to Burgoa's description of the palaces at Mitla, where mats woven of reed and rush were important furnishings of all noble and priestly dwellings.

Mats, nevertheless, were the settings for many important ritual events. Kings sat on them on the ground or draped them over stone THRONES. In the Codex Mendoza, Mote-cuhzoma himself is shown in his palace on a mat, or *icpalli*. Among the Aztecs, the precious skins that draped thrones were also referred to as special types of mat. Mats were important places for DIVINATION and the casting of lots. Weddings were sometimes conse-crated on mats (*see* MARRIAGE).

The Maya called their ruling lord the *ah pop*, or He of the Mat, and the term was synonymous with *ahau*, or lord, itself. In Yucatán the *popol na*, or mat house, was the young men's community house for DANCE and performance, as well as a place for the community council to meet. Many Puuc Maya buildings have woven mat-like motifs on their exteriors, as do the palaces at Mitla, perhaps because they once served as community coun-cil houses. The POPOL VUH, the surviving Quiché epic, is usually translated as the Book of Council, but the root of *popol* is mat, linking a community council and the mats on which they would sit.

Two Classic Maya stelae bear texts inter-woven in the mat design, perhaps a direct reference to *ah pop*, or ruler.

Mayahuel The Central Mexican goddess of MAGUEY, Mayahuel is usually depicted as a beautiful young woman with a flowering maguey plant. Her earliest known represen-tation occurs in the Toltec-style Early Post-classic rock painting at Ixtapantongo, in the State of Mexico. Dressed in a *quechquemitl* (a draped blouse – *see* COSTUME), the goddess appears within a maguey plant holding two cups probably containing PULQUE. The Late Postclassic Mayahuel frequently displays attributes of the WATER goddess, CHALCHIUH-TLICUE, and, like that goddess, personifies fec-undity and fertility. In one account, she is described as "the woman of four hundred breasts," quite probably a reference to the rich, milky *aguamiel* sap of the maguey plant from which the alcoholic pulque is made.

The *Histoyre du méchique* provides an account of the origin of Mayahuel and

The **Manikin Scepter**, Yaxchilán Lintel 3, Late Classic period.

mirror

celt

god markings

snake foot

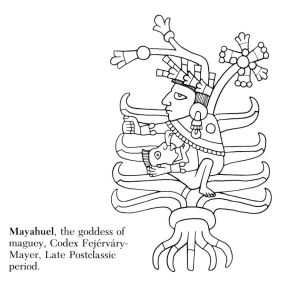

Detail of Aztec **marriage** scene, the garments of bride and groom symbolically tied, Codex Mendoza, 16th c.

Mayahuel, the goddess of maguey, Codex Fejérváry-Mayer, Late Postclassic period.

maguey. In this myth, EHECATL-QUETZALCOATL takes Mayahuel from her grandmother and companions, the fearsome TZITZIMIME star demons. Pursued by the *tzitzimime*, Ehecatl-Quetzalcoatl and Mayahuel disguise themselves as branches of a tree. The *tzitzimime*, however, recognize the branch of Mayahuel, and tear it to bits. Ehecatl-Quetzalcoatl buries her remains, and from her body, the first maguey sprouts forth. In the Central Mexican CALENDAR, Mayahuel is the patron of the day Tochtli, or Rabbit, and the TRECENA of 1 Malinalli.

merchants In Aztec society merchants, or *pochteca* as they were called in Nahuatl, held a very special niche in which they functioned as emissaries, ambassadors, spies, and warriors – not merely as traders. The richest *pochteca* lived in Tlatelolco, just north of Tenochtitlan and on the same island. During the 15th c., Tenochtitlan grew jealous of the wealth of her sister city and in 1473, smote Tlatelolco, essentially uniting the two cities and commanding great quantities of tribute from the wealthy Tlatelolcans.

Central Mexican merchants had their own patron god, Yacatecuhtli, and the auspicious days for embarking on a trading expedition were 1 Coatl or 1 Ozomatli. Like the merchants, Yacatecuhtli bears a walking staff, which itself was an object of reverence. Yacatecuhtli rose to great prominence in the last 30 years of Prehispanic life, but the nature of this god remains obscure.

In making their initial forays into new country, merchants usually traveled in disguise, adopting local dress and manners while they sized up the available luxury goods that they most sought, such as bird feathers, animal pelts, and precious stones. If discovered and attacked, they returned to inform their own ruler, whereupon war was frequently declared upon the hostile region. If the Aztecs won – and they usually did – they imposed unfavorable trade conditions on the losers. Working in this fashion, the merchants professed themselves the allies of HUITZILO-POCHTLI, in whose service they claimed land, goods, and tribute.

Despite their wealth, merchants behaved humbly, if not hypocritically, in order not to draw excessive attention to their success. They practiced self-abasement, and simultaneously offered great feasts with lavish luxuries, usually beginning with the smoking of TOBACCO and the offering of FLOWERS, followed by various courses of food, and ending with hot chocolate and sometimes the consumption of hallucinogenic mushrooms (*see* HALLUCINOGENS). The *pochteca* gave away their merchandise in abundance, particularly capes, mantles, and loincloths. Such exchange fueled the Aztec economy.

Because of the role merchants played in the expansion and mercantile domination of the Aztec realm, they received special honors. Motecuhzoma II brought the *pochteca* into his court and treated them as if they were nobility. In the VEINTENA of Panquetzaliztli, merchants bathed slaves and were able to offer them to Huitzilopochtli along with the CAPTIVES of war offered by great warriors. When a merchant died on a mission, he was gloriously adorned, placed on a LITTER, and borne to a mountain top, where the body was cremated. It was understood, then, that he had died as a warrior for the state, and he proceeded directly to the fourth heaven, that belonging to the SUN.

Among the Classic Maya, God L (*see* SCHELLHAS GODS) was the patron of merchants, and in some of his depictions he carries a merchant pack laden with rich goods. At the time of the Conquest, Ek Chuah was the patron of travelers and, by extension, merchants, in Yucatán. Professional merchants among the Maya were known as *p'olom*, and they burned *copal* to Xaman Ek, the north star, to ensure their safe journey. The Zapotecs named three gods, Pitào peeze, Pitào quille, and Pitàoyàge, as patrons of riches and merchants.

Mexican year sign In Late Postclassic highland Mexico, the YEARBEARER days naming particular years are frequently marked with a specific device, often called the A O sign, or the trapeze-and-ray sign. Due to its prevalence in Mixtec writing, it is also frequently termed the Mixtec year sign. The Postclassic year sign is typically composed of two intertwined elements, a pointed device identical to the solar ray sign, and a squat form resembling a flattened "O." At times, the sign is personified as a frontal face, probably that of the XIUHCOATL fire serpent. In Aztec iconography, the year sign is often placed on the bodies of Xiuhcoatl serpents.

The identification of the Xiuhcoatl with the year sign has a phonetic basis. In Nahuatl, the term *xihuitl* denotes year, TURQUOISE, or grass. In some instances, the Aztec year sign appears with grass BUNDLES, probably a reference to *xihuitl*. Among the Classic Maya, the year sign also appears with tufts of grass. The identification of the year sign with grass may well have begun at the great Classic site of TEOTIHUACAN. In Teotihuacan iconography, grass bundles are bound with a particular triangular knot. This same knot appears as the pointed "ray" portion of early year signs at Teotihuacan, and it is quite likely that the Mexican year sign derives from this bound grass bundle. This identification of grass with the year sign at Teotihuacan supports the possibility that its inhabitants spoke an ancestral form of Nahuatl. *See also* CALENDAR.

Mictlan *see* UNDERWORLD

Mictlantecuhtli The Central Mexican god of DEATH, Mictlantecuhtli ruled over Mictlan, place of the dead (*see* UNDERWORLD), along with his wife, Mictecacihuatl. Sometimes also referred to by the name Tzontemoc, Mictlantecuhtli usually appears as a skeleton of bleached white bones with red, bloody spots. He is often festooned with owl feathers, PAPER head ornaments and banners, and wears a collar of extruded eyeballs. During the VEINTENA of Tititl, the Mictlantecuhtli impersonator was sacrificed at night at the temple named Tlalxicco, meaning navel of the world. Because of the Underworld associations of DOGS, Mictlantecuhtli was the patron of the day Itzcuintli, or dog; he also reigned over the TRECENA 1 Tecpatl. When the impersonator of Mictlantecuhtli died, INCENSE was offered only at night at Tlillan, the temple of CIHUACOATL.

Like other Mesoamerican DEATH GODS, Mictlantecuhtli was fundamentally stupid and vulnerable to the tricks of smarter gods. In the final act of creation, QUETZALCOATL journeyed to Mictlan to retrieve the bones of previous eras of mankind from which to generate a new race of people. Although Mictlantecuhtli first granted the request for bones, he then changed his mind. He gave chase, but Quetzalcoatl escaped with the stolen bones, unfortunately dropping and breaking some of them, and thus yielding a race of humans of mixed sizes. *See also* CALENDAR; CREATION ACCOUNTS.

Milky Way The great band of STARS known as the Milky Way was conceived of in a

(*Top*) **Merchants** traveling with their packs along a road. In Mesoamerica, a tumpline strung across the brow serves as an essential means of carrying loads. (*Above*) Merchants and their goods; along with the carrying pack and frame, one can discern a live bird, a feather bundle, and a string of jade beads; Florentine Codex, Book 9, 16th c.

Aztec sign for **marketplace**, Matrícula de Huexotzinco, 16th c.

Year 1 Rabbit marked with **Mexican year sign**, stone tablet, Late Postclassic Mexico.

variety of ways in ancient Mesoamerica. In Central Mexico, two important deities personified the Milky Way. Dressed in garments of white, the aged goddess ILAMATE-CUHTLI wore a star skirt, or *citlali icue*, an Aztec term for the Milky Way. Another Milky Way deity was MIXCOATL, a god of the hunt whose face is frequently painted with a black field surrounded by stars. The term Mixcoatl signifies "cloud serpent," and could well refer to the cloudy strip of the Milky Way.

Like the Romans (who first gave us the term Via Lactea, or Milky Way), the Central Mexicans considered this band of stars to be a road. According to the *Historia de los mexicanos por sus pinturas*, this became the road of TEZCATLIPOCA and QUETZALCOATL after their creation of the earth. In the Maya region, the Milky Way is conceptualized as the road to Xibalba, the UNDERWORLD, and the entire night sky may replicate the Underworld and the movements of its denizens. In Yucatec, it is termed *zac beh*, or "white road." Another Yucatec Mayan word for it was *tamcaz*, a curious term that also signifies seizures.

milpa The modern Mesoamerican term for MAIZE field, milpa derives from the Nahuatl *milpan*, "in the cultivated field." As the source of maize, beans, squash, and other plants of vital necessity, the milpa field is of central concern. It is thus not surprising that many native peoples are profoundly linked to their fields. The terms for two related Maya peoples, the Chol and Chorti, derive from their native words for milpa, *chol* and *chor*. They are truly the "people of the milpa." In many instances, the milpa represents order and balance, as opposed to the threatening chaos of the surrounding wild bush. In Maya mythology, the cosmic act of creation is compared with making milpa: in the Quiché POPOL VUH, the measuring and the making of the world is cast in terms of preparing the milpa for the present race of humans, the people of corn. Like the milpa farmer, the GODS are supported and nourished by their crop – the people who inhabit the surface of the EARTH. The conceptualization of the earth as a rectangular milpa is also found among other Maya groups, such as the Chorti and Yucatec. In highland Mexico, contemporary Nahuat-speakers in the Sierra de Puebla also describe the world as a milpa. Moreover, the Sierra Nahuat also compare humans to plants that are born or "planted" upon the earth.

mirrors Ancient Mesoamericans used mirrors fashioned of stone in a variety of ways. They could function as ornaments of dress, cosmetic accessories, or as instruments of DIVINATION. One of the most widespread uses of stone mirrors was for divinatory scrying. Among many contact period Mesoamerican peoples, including the Yucatec Maya, Aztecs, and Tarascans, the reflective surfaces of bowls filled with water were also used for divination, and it is possible that this is an especially old tradition, perhaps even dating from before the manufacture of stone mirrors. In Mesoamerica, stone mirrors are known at least as early as the mid-2nd millennium BC, that is, before the appearance of Olmec civilization. Olmec mirrors of the Early and Middle Formative period were usually fashioned of pieces of iron ore, such as magnetite, ilmenite and hematite (*see* CINNABAR AND HEMATITE). Since these mirrors were created from single pieces of stone, they are fairly small, rarely more than 15 cm or 6 inches in total width. Most Olmec mirrors are concave, giving them many unique properties. The reflected image appears inverted as well as reversed, and the larger concave mirrors are capable of starting FIRE. In Olmec art, concave mirrors commonly appear as pectorals worn on the chest.

In Classic Mesoamerica, the favored material for stone mirrors was iron pyrite. In this case, artisans laid cut iron pyrite upon a slate backing, creating a reflective surface of finely fitted mosaic. The slate backing is usually circular and is often beautifully carved. Since the pyrite mirrors were fashioned of mosaic rather than of a single stone, they could be of great size, and certain pictorial Classic scenes suggest that there were mirrors measuring 30 cm (12 inches) or more in diameter. However, unlike the ores used for the concave Olmec mirrors, iron pyrite is not a stable mineral and quickly oxidizes. For this reason, the surfaces of ancient pyrite mirrors tend to be poorly preserved, and now often appear no more than a reddish or yellow coloration upon the slate backing. During the Classic period, nobles wore circular pyrite mirrors on the small of the back, and mirrors have been found so placed in Early Classic burials from TEOTIHUACAN and Kaminaljuyú.

Back mirrors continued to be worn in Postclassic Central Mexico; among the Aztecs they were referred to as *tezcacuitlapilli*. One form of back mirror, a central pyrite disk surrounded by a TURQUOISE mosaic containing representations of XIUHCOATL serpents, was especially common at Early Postclassic Tula. This Toltec form had an unusually broad distribution during the Early Postclassic, and examples have been found at Chichen Itzá, Yucatán, and as far north as distant Casas Grandes in Chihuahua.

The black volcanic glass known as OBSIDIAN was a favored mirror stone in Late Postclassic Central Mexico. Although it is likely that smooth surfaces of fractured obsidian were used in Classic and Formative Mesoamerica, ground and polished obsidian mirrors are not common until the Late Postclassic. The great Central Mexican god TEZCATLIPOCA, He of the Smoking Mirror, appears to have been a personification of the polished obsidian mirror. Quite frequently, a smoking obsidian mirror appears at the back of the head and as one of the feet of Tezcatlipoca.

In ancient Mesoamerica, mirrors often represented objects and concepts occurring in nature and society. By representing a world that could be looked into but not passed through, mirrors could be considered as CAVES or passageways for the supernatural. Because of their bright, reflective surfaces, they were also compared to fiery hearths or shining pools of WATER. Quite frequently, they are identified with the SUN, and this is probably also the case with the turquoise-rimmed pyrite mirrors of the Early Postclassic Toltec. At Teotihuacan, circular mirrors were symbolically linked to eyes, faces, shields, and FLOWERS. Considerable native mirror lore survives among the modern Huichol of Nayarit. Here circular glass mirrors are considered to be supernatural passageways, as well as being conceptually related to the sun, MOON, faces eyes, and flowers.

Mixcoatl Literally "cloud serpent," Mixcoatl may have been physically identified as the MILKY WAY and the very heavens. Primarily a hunting god, he was the patron god of the Otomí and the Chichimecs, and of many communities in Central Mexico that claimed descent from the Chichimecs. He was also worshipped as the principal god of Huejotzingo and Tlaxcala, generally under the name Camaxtli. He may originally have been a legendary hunter and warrior, deified and sanctified, whose traditional role was then displaced by the introduction among the Aztecs of HUITZILOPOCHTLI. Whereas Huitzilo-

Carved slate backing of pyrite mosaic **mirror**, Teotihuacan, Early Classic period. This image appears to represent a fire goddess holding broad torches.

Mixcoatl, god of the hunt, whose name means cloud serpent, signifying the Milky Way; Codex Borgia, p. 25, Late Postclassic period.

pochtli is identified with the SUN, however, Mixcoatl is clearly associated with the STARS.

Mixcoatl's most distinctive physical characteristic is the red and white "candy-cane" striped body paint he wears. He shares this characteristic with TLAHUIZCALPANTECUHTLI, another star god, and they both wear black masks over the eyes, sometimes trimmed with stars. Mixcoatl, unlike Tlahuizcalpantecuhtli, may carry hunting gear, particularly a bow and arrow and a netted basket for carrying slaughtered game.

Mixcoatl plays a number of important roles in scattered references, mainly located in the *Historia de los mexicanos por sus pinturas.* One of the four children of TONACATECUHTLI and Tonacacihuatl, he was also identified as the Red Tezcatlipoca. In another chapter of the account, TEZCATLIPOCA transformed himself into Mixcoatl in order to offer a celebration to the other gods; with his invention of the fire drill, this Tezcatlipoca-Mixcoatl brought FIRE to mankind. The first to use FLINT to strike fire, Mixcoatl took on fire associations along with those of war and the hunt. He was also the father of the 400 sons (the Centzon Huitznahua) and five women created to feed the sun. After the sun had consumed the HEARTS of the 400, one of the surviving women gave BIRTH to Mixcoatl's most famous progeny, QUETZALCOATL.

The 14th VEINTENA, Quecholli, was dedicated to Mixcoatl. The feast was celebrated by one or two days of hunting and feasting in the countryside during which the hunters adorned themselves like Mixcoatl himself and kindled new fire to roast the game. Subsequently, a man and a woman were sacrificed to Mixcoatl in his TEMPLE. The female victim was slain like a wild animal: her head was struck four times against a rock until she was half-conscious; then her throat was slit and the head decapitated. The male victim displayed the head to the assembled crowds before he himself was sacrificed by heart extrusion.

Mixtec gods During the pioneering investigations of the 19th and early 20th c., the gods of the Postclassic Mixtec screenfolds were thought to be essentially identical to those appearing in Aztec and Borgia groups of codices. However, it has become increasingly apparent that the Mixtec pantheon was distinct from that of Late Postclassic Central Mexico. Thus the Mixtec gods tend to have entirely distinct calendrical names, and moreover, certain Mixtec deities appear but rarely or never in Central Mexican iconography. Examples are the fanged stone beings often referred to by the inappropriate Central Mexican term of "XOLOTL." It is now known that these beings were referred to as *ñuhu* by the Mixtecs, and were gods of the EARTH and vegetation. In Central Mexican manuscripts, they appear only in the Borgia and Vaticanus B codices. Still another important Mixtec deity is a flying figure frequently wearing a fire serpent headdress and a TURTLE carapace upon his back. He commonly holds FLINT blades in his hands, and it is possible that he is a LIGHTNING god. To the Mixtecs, this figure was known as YAHUI, and appears among the neighboring Zapotecs as early as the Protoclassic period, or Monte Albán II. For the Mixtecs, this being may be identical to one of the sons of the mythical creator couple 1 Deer recorded by the Dominican Gregorio Garciá. In the Selden Roll, the *yahui* figure is named 1 Jaguar.

The most important pictorial source for Mixtec gods is the obverse side of the screenfold known as the Vindobonensis or Vienna Codex. Typically, the Mixtec gods bear names from the 260-day CALENDAR, presumably referring to dates of birth. The creator couple who are both named 1 Deer in the creation account mentioned by Garciá appear on page 51 of the Codex Vindobonensis with skeletal mouths and wearing the headdress of the culture hero 9 Wind. This same calendrically named couple is also illustrated in the Selden Roll, where they are shown simply as an old man and woman. One of the most important goddesses of the Mixtec pantheon was Lady 9 Grass. Usually depicted with a skeletalized face, she seems to have been a goddess of DEATH and the fertile earth. In the Selden Roll, Lady 6 Monkey of Jaltepec makes pilgrimages to the oracle of 9 Grass at Chalcatongo. In the Codex Vindobonensis, an old man named 2 Dog is portrayed as a PRIEST, and often appears with the TOBACCO gourd of the priestly office. Another aged being, Lady 1 Eagle, is goddess of the SWEATBATH, and by extension, may also have been a goddess of midwives and CURING.

Among the Mixtecs, personifications of particular plants or their products are often portrayed as goddesses. Thus in the Codex Vindobonensis, the goddess of MAGUEY is Lady 11 Serpent, while PULQUE is personified by two goddesses named 2 Flower and 3 Alligator. Young tender MAIZE seems to be embodied by two goddesses named 5 Flint and 7 Flint. Mature maize, however, seems to be identified with a goddess named 7 Grass. In the Codex Vindobonensis, the hallucinogenic psilocybin mushroom is portrayed by two serpent-mouthed goddesses named 4 Lizard and 11 Lizard.

Although the religion of the Postclassic Mixtecs was by no means identical to that of Central Mexico, a number of Mixtec gods have clear analogues with Central Mexican deities. Thus the Mixtec culture hero 9 Wind is very similar to the Central Mexican WIND god, EHECATL-QUETZALCOATL. The solar god 1 Death is the Mixtec form of TONATIUH, the Central Mexican SUN god. Like Tonatiuh, 1 Death is usually red and wears a JADE brow piece and an EAGLE feather headdress. The Mixtec god 7 Flower appears to be related to the youthful solar deity known in Central Mexico as XOCHIPILLI. The Mixtec form of XIPE TOTEC is named 7 Rain, and like his Central Mexican counterpart, commonly wears a flayed human skin and red and white vestments. Finally, the Postclassic Mixtecs had a form of the RAIN and lightning god TLALOC. On page 5 of the Codex Nuttall, he appears with the fanged mouth, goggle eyes, and upwardly turning lip of the Postclassic Tlaloc. In his hands, he wields a burning lightning bolt and jug of outpouring WATER, clearly a portrayal of rain. On page 28 of the Codex Vindobonensis, a similar Tlaloc is named 5 Wind. *See also* CREATION ACCOUNTS; HALLUCINOGENS; MAIZE GODS.

monkey Three species of monkeys once lived in the tropical lowlands of Mexico and Guatemala: spider, howler, and capuchin (although only spider and howler monkeys are found there today). Capuchin monkeys are particularly friendly and adept with their hands, and may have been most commonly adopted as pets in ancient times. Howlers bellow and roar when they vibrate a bone in the larynx, and their calls can be heard for miles. Spider monkeys, social animals that prefer to live in groups of 40 or 50, range farther north than any other New World monkey.

In Central Mexico, the monkey was known as *ozomatli* and was the 11th day sign; among the Maya, the Yucatec day name was Chuen. Generally those born on the day Ozomatli were thought to be lucky and happy persons.

Creator couple 1 Deer | 9 Wind

2 Dog | 1 Death | 5 Flint

7 Rain | 11 Serpent | 9 Grass

Mixtec gods appearing in the Codex Vindobonensis, Late Postclassic period.

Stone sculpture of a spider **monkey**, Late Postclassic Aztec.

Spider monkey serving as the day name **Monkey**, Codex Borgia, p. 13, Late Postclassic period. In the Borgia Group of codices, monkeys frequently appear wearing suits of grass.

MERCHANTS considered a monkey's hand to be a talisman of good luck.

Sahagún describes what is probably a spider monkey: "And as to its actions: it is a shouter, a shrill whistler, making gestures toward one. It stones one, it hurls sticks at one. It has a face which is a little human." (FC: XI)

The monkey is related to QUETZALCOATL in his guise as EHECATL. According to the FIVE SUNS cosmogonic accounts, Quetzalcoatl presided over the second sun, *ehecatonatiuh*, the sun of WIND, until it was destroyed by great winds. The people of that era were turned into monkeys. When the Maya gods destroyed the people formed of wood in the POPOL VUH, they too turned them into monkeys.

Because they had more monkeys close by in the tropical rain forest, the Maya tended to make more distinctions between the spider monkey (*chuen*) and the howler monkey (*batz*). In Classic art, the spider monkey frequently personifies licentiousness and sexual abandon; Maya clowns at highland festivals today often impersonate monkeys when they act out immoral and inappropriate behavior. The presence of great numbers of monkey figures in the art of Classic Veracruz may reflect a similar association of the monkey and sexual license.

In the *Popol Vuh*, Hun Batz (1 Howler Monkey) and Hun Chuen (1 Spider Monkey) were the twin half brothers of the Hero Twins. Gifted in all the arts, particularly song, DANCE, WRITING, and carving, Hun Batz and Hun Chuen were not beyond jealousy of their younger brothers, and tried hard to subdue them, leaving them when young to perish on an anthill and in brambles and later demanding that the younger brothers do their hunting for them. As usual, the Hero Twins had the last laugh: they convinced their twin half brothers to scale a tree to bring down birds stunned by a blowgun. When Hun Batz and Hun Chuen reached the birds, they found that the tree had grown, lifting them so high that they could no longer descend. The Hero Twins advised them to untie their loincloths to trail behind them whereupon these suddenly became tails – Hun Batz and Hun Chuen had turned into monkeys.

These monkey twins occur widely in Classic Maya art as the patron gods of art, writing, and calculating. Sometimes rendered as actual monkeys, at other times as humans with certain monkey attributes, the Monkey

Scribes are often depicted as gifted and industrious. *See also* CREATION ACCOUNTS.

moon The second brightest heavenly body, the moon was uniformly associated with the rabbit in Mesoamerican thought. On the surface of a full moon, the rabbit is visible in profile, and various myths account for its presence. Silver was considered to be an excretion of the moon (*see* EXCREMENT).

According to Central Mexican theology, the SUN and the moon were created together at TEOTIHUACAN, in the dawning of the current era. Nanahuatzin and Tecuciztecatl prepared to immolate themselves before the assembled gods. When Tecuciztecatl hesitated, Nanahuatzin went first, becoming the sun, and then Tecuciztecatl followed, making another sun, but the gods darkened his face, hurling ashes or a rabbit at him to dim his radiance.

The 400 rabbits (*Centzon totochtin*) of Central Mexican lore were drunkards, associated with MAYAHUEL, goddess of PULQUE. Within the TEMPLE precinct of Tenochtitlan, the 44th temple, the *Centzon totochtin in teopan*, was dedicated to these rabbits.

Rabbit, or Tochtli, was the 8th day sign in the Central Mexican CALENDAR and one of the four YEARBEARERS. In the TRECENA 1 Mazatl, the day sign 2 Rabbit was particularly unfortunate: those born on this day and for several thereafter were given to drunkenness.

COYOLXAUHQUI, HUITZILOPOCHTLI's sister, was identified by Eduard Seler as a moon goddess, her own light shattered and diminished by Huitzilopochtli, although there is no textual confirmation of the identification. In two separate images at the sacred precinct of Tenochtitlan, Coyolxauhqui's dismembered two-dimensional image was carved on a round stone at the base of Huitzilopochtli's pyramid, and her large, lifeless, three-dimensional head probably rested on the temple steps, both possibly references to the moon.

Among the Classic Maya, a young, beautiful woman was the moon goddess, and she frequently sits on the crescent of the Maya glyph for moon, bearing a rabbit in her arms. Among the Maya, although the moon was also identified with the rabbit, the full moon in particular – as opposed to any other phase – may have been associated with the moon goddess. The name of this goddess is not known, but she is not IXCHEL, as is often alleged; Ixchel is an old goddess.

Many modern Maya believe that the

female moon was dimmed after a squabble with her husband the sun, and that she may have lost an eye in the quarrel. In a modern Zapotec story, a pair of orphan children who later become the sun and moon escape from a sweathouse before their apotheosis. *See also* CREATION ACCOUNTS.

mortuary bundles In many parts of Mesoamerica, the remains of important individuals were not buried at the time of DEATH, but were rather placed in BUNDLES – a form of the sacred bundle. According to Aztec belief, the sacred god bundles are simply the funerary bundles of those GODS who were sacrificed following the creation of the fifth sun at TEOTIHUACAN. Both deity and funerary bundles took a somewhat human form and wore masks; among these were possibly included the famous stone masks of Teotihuacan. On Stela 4 of Tikal, the Early Classic ruler Curl Snout holds a sacred bundle bearing the mask of TLALOC. At Tikal, masked mortuary bundles appear as early as the Protoclassic period. Burial 85, dating to 50 BC, contained the remains of a mortuary bundle accompanied by a fuchsite mask.

For the Postclassic period mortuary bundles are well documented. Among the Mixtecs, it was usual for kings to be preserved after death in masked funerary bundles; a CAVE at Chalcatongo served as the repository for the bundles of Mixtec kings from the great dynasty of Tilantongo. For the Tarascans of Michoacán, a mortuary bundle was made from the cremated remains of the king. Adorned with a TURQUOISE mask, this bundle was buried in a TOMB placed at the base of the TEMPLE dedicated to the god Curicaveri. The Tarascans also fashioned bundles from the heads of warriors slain in combat. After performing a night vigil with offerings, the Tarascans burned the warrior bundles, with the cremated remains being placed in ceramic vessels. This Tarascan rite relates to the Aztec custom of making bundles from the bodies of slain warriors. Bedecked with PAPER ornaments, these bundles received homage in the form of MUSIC and offerings before being burned. *See also* CREATION ACCOUNTS.

mountains Many mountains in ancient Mexico and Guatemala were held to be sacred. Some of these were active volcanoes, some dormant, while others were not volcanic at all, but rather mountains in prominent and

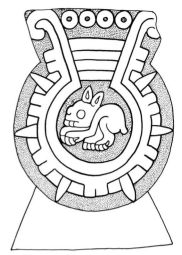

Mixtec **moon** sign containing a rabbit, Stone of Tlaxiaco, Oaxaca, Late Postclassic period.

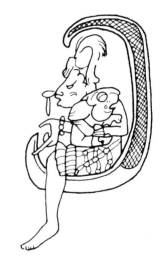

Maya **moon** goddess holding a rabbit, detail of Late Classic incised vase.

Mortuary bundle of dead warrior, Codex Magliabechiano, 16th c. Aztec. The bundle is portrayed as Mixcoatl (left), wearing turquoise regalia.

dramatic locations, frequently with CAVES. Among the Maya, Mixtecs, and Aztecs, communities were named after their mountains; indeed the very Nahuatl word for community, *altepetl*, means water-mountain. Central Mexican place-names often include the mountain glyph, reflecting the great number of places named in this way.

From early times, mountains frequently determined the siting of communities. The Olmec settlement at Chalcatzingo lies in the shadow of a dramatic igneous plug of a mountain, and Monte Albán is a mountain itself, flattened and shaped by generations of people to accommodate human settlement. The unusual fluted shape of the first Olmec PYRAMID, at La Venta, suggests an attempt at making an artificial "volcano" along the non-volcanic Gulf Coast, although some scholars believe that time and weather have simply eroded what was a four-sided pyramid. TEOTIHUACAN's north-south axis leads directly north to Cerro Gordo; traditionally known also as Tenam, Mother of Stone, this dead volcano gurgles from water trapped inside, the very image of the *altepetl*. The Maya city of Aguateca is positioned beside a deep fissure, and this cleft mountain is the actual symbol of that city's toponym in Maya hieroglyphic WRITING.

The twin pyramid dedicated to TLALOC and HUITZILOPOCHTLI in the sacred precinct of Tenochtitlan was positioned against the two smoldering volcanoes to the east – Popocatepetl (Smoking Mountain) and Ixtaccihuatl (White Woman) – whom the Aztecs identified as a married couple, deified and revered. Live rock shrines were carved at Malinalco and Texcotzingo, and, in earlier times, at Dainzú. Shrines were frequently erected at the peaks of mountains.

To the east of Tenochtitlan, the Tlaloque were thought to retreat with their thunderbolts to the Tlaloc Mountains. QUETZALCOATL journeyed to Tonacatepetl (Sustenance Mountain) to find the origin of MAIZE; in order to obtain maize for humankind, he transformed himself into an ant and stole some kernels. Similar accounts of the origin of maize are known among the Maya, and the Quiché called the mountain of origin Paxil.

Mountain shrines are common today among traditional peoples in Mexico and Guatemala. The Maya Zinacantecos, for example, erect crosses at mountain shrines

and visit them in CURING rituals. At each mountain cross, fresh pine boughs and FLOWERS are offered, candles lit, prayers said, and curer and patient drink rounds of homemade sugar cane rum. Ancestors live in the sacred mountains that ring Zinacantan, and each is classified as male or female. Each mountain has specific associations; one can bring RAIN, for example, and another heat. In the 20th c., the Kekchi practiced continence and fasted before making PILGRIMAGES to CAVES on mountain tops.

Mesoamerican peoples frequently built their TEMPLES in the form of symbolic mountains. Maya temples in the Chenes region are entered through great monster mouths that lead symbolically to the heart of the EARTH, or the interior of the mountain. Copán Temple 22 is such a symbolic mountain with a monster mouth forming a cave entrance; the MAIZE GODS flourishing from its cornices suggest that it may have symbolized the mountain where maize originated.

Epigraphic research by David Stuart and Stephen Houston revealed that the Classic and Postclassic Maya referred to pyramids as mountains, or *uitz*. The so-called Cauac Monster, named after the stony *cauac* markings appearing on this beast, is actually a Maya rendering of a zoomorphic mountain. In the sacred precinct of the Aztecs, the twin pyramid dedicated to Tlaloc and Huitzilopochtli symbolically recreated COATEPEC, Hill of the Serpent, where Huitzilopochtli's miraculous BIRTH took place. To drill New Fire, the Aztecs retreated to Citlaltepec, Hill of the Star. CHICOMOZTOC, the Seven Caves, the place of origin for most Central Mexicans, is usually depicted within a mountain, and Culhuacan, Curved Mountain, was a traditional place of ancestors.

In the 13th VEINTENA, Tepeilhuitl, the Aztecs celebrated what was known as the Mountain Feast. Dedicated to Popocatepetl and Iztaccihuatl by the Aztecs, the celebration was widely carried out by Central Mexican peoples in honor of various mountains. Dough images in the shape of mountains were fashioned of ground AMARANTH seeds to honor the dead, particularly those who had died a DEATH associated with the Tlaloque – by flood, drowning, or LIGHTNING – reinforcing the connection between Tlaloc, mountain, and WATER. Five sacrificial victims, four women and one man, then impersonated mountains, were slain by heart extrusion and then decapitated. The dough mountains, finally, were also decapitated and carefully consumed in a ritual communion. The lame and crippled,

whose deformities were thought to have been
sent by Tlaloc (*see* DEFORMITY), sought a cure
in the consumption of the amaranth dough.
See also CALENDAR; CREATION ACCOUNTS; TERM-
INATION RITUALS.

muan owl The screech owl (*Otus asio*) occupies an important role in Classic and Postclassic
Maya iconography. The Maya month of
Muan is named after the Yucatec term for
this bird. The glyph for this month, the head
of the muan owl, is frequently accompanied
by phonetic elements suggesting that the
term *muan* is of considerable antiquity. The
muan owl can be identified by its broad and
sharply tipped beak and spotted feathers.
Quite often, a pair of large spotted feathers
appear on the brow and the back of the head,
probably referring to the horn-like feather
tufts of the screech owl.

In Maya iconography, the muan is identified with RAIN, MAIZE and the UNDERWORLD. In
Yucatec, the term *muan* also bears connotations of clouds, rain and mist. It is probably
for this reason that the rain god CHAC is
frequently associated with the muan owl in
Classic and Postclassic Maya art. On page
78 of the Madrid Codex, Chac paints the
blackened tail feathers of the bird. In Classic
iconography, maize growth commonly
appears with the muan owl, possibly to show
the rain bird as a maize-bringer. The muan
owl is also identified with the major Maya
deity referred to as God L in the Schellhas
system of deity classification. A god of the
Underworld and of MERCHANTS, God L usually
wears a broad hat topped by the muan owl.
See also OWLS; SCHELLHAS GODS.

music Ritual often included the performance
of music. Since there is no Precolumbian
musical notation, the exact nature of
Mesoamerican music remains unknown;
what is known is reconstructed from descriptions, depictions, and surviving instruments
themselves. Singing accompanied instruments, and both singers and players trained
rigorously.

The Mesoamerican ensemble encompassed a standard range of instruments, going
back at least to Classic times: flutes, ocarinas,
gourd rattles, bone rasps, turtle shells struck
with deer antlers, a large, upright drum
(called the *huehuetl* in Nahuatl, the *pax* in
Maya), a slit gong (called the *teponaztli* in
Nahuatl, the *tunkul* in Maya), a hand drum

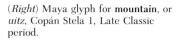

(*Above*) Priest presenting an offering
to a cleft **mountain**, Nochistlan Vase,
Late Postclassic Mixtec, Oaxaca.

(*Right*) Maya glyph for **mountain**, or
uitz, Copán Stela 1, Late Classic
period.

The **Muan Owl**, Dresden
Codex, p. 7, Postclassic
Yucatán. In Maya
iconography, the Muan
Owl frequently appears
with maize foliage upon
its head.

Old man and woman playing **music** with rattles
and drums. While the man beats a *huehuetl*
drum between his legs, the woman strikes a
turtle shell with a deer antler, Codex Laud,
p. 34, Late Postclassic period.

held in the crook of the arm, bells, and trumpets made of conch shells, wood, or gourds. There is no evidence of any stringed instruments before the Conquest, nor for the marimba (xylophone). The Spanish introduced stringed instruments and African slaves brought the marimba.

Bone rasps have been excavated from Early Formative sites, but the first depictions of musicians appear toward the end of the Formative era, in West Mexico. The 8th c. Maya frequently show all or some of the instruments of the Mesoamerican ensemble and confirm that they were played on a wide variety of occasions, including both HUMAN SACRIFICE and ACCESSION, and by UNDERWORLD animals as well as humans. The musicians usually appear in a fixed order, with flutes, rattles and turtle shells appearing before the large drum; trumpets and the hand drum bring up the rear. An abbreviated but similar musical group played at the wedding ceremony of the Mixtec princess 6 Monkey. Mesoamerican music was largely percussive, and nothing like a European scale was known.

The Spanish described Aztec music as doleful and tuneless, but they were nevertheless moved by it, and they recognized the achievements of court performers over the less skilled rural players. Aztec musicians performed a wide repertory of music, all of it by heart, but invention was also considered noble. Just as they credited the Toltecs with the invention of WRITING and counting, the Aztecs attributed the invention of many songs to the Toltecs. Explicit characteristics informed their notions of good and bad music:

The good singer [is] of sound voice. Good, sound [is] his voice; well rounded [are] his words. [He is] of good, sharp memory, keeping the songs in mind; retentive, not forgetful. He sings, cries out, enunciates clearly; [he sings] with well-rounded voice, in full voice, in falsetto. [He sings] softly; he tempers his voice, accompanies judiciously, gives the pitch, lowers [the voice], raises it. He reduces it to medium; he uses it moderately. He practices; he improves his voice. He composes, sets to music, originates [songs]. He sings songs, sings others' songs, provides music for others, instructs others.

The bad singer [is] hoarse, husky, coarse-voiced; crude, dull, heartless, unintelligent. He revolts me; he is fraudulent, vainglorious, arrogant. [He is] haughty, foolish, obstinate,

avaricious, indigent, envious, absconding. He grunts, sounds husky, makes one's ears ring; he is restless, forgetful, violent, indigent; he absconds, he brags; he is presumptuous, vain. (FC: x)

Surviving Aztec musical instruments, particularly the large drums, bear the iconography of war and SACRIFICE, and were probably used most often in sacrificial rituals. Victims themselves frequently made music: the TEZCATLIPOCA impersonator lived for a year in that role and learned to play the flute and whistle. The festivities for the VEINTENA of Toxcatl included constant song and DANCE, but – as if to symbolize his own DEATH – when the impersonator ascended the Tezcatlipoca temple for sacrifice, he broke his flute and whistle and left the shattered pieces on the steps.

Among the Aztecs, the gods MACUILXOCHITL and XOCHIPILLI supervised the domain of music.

nahual A common word in the ethnographic literature of Mexico, *nahual* derives from the Nahuatl term *naualli*, signifying a form-changing sorcerer or witch. To the early Colonial priests, these form-changers were not considered simply to be baseless superstition, but were a source of much concern. Writing in 1600, Fray Juan Bautista warned of native sorcerers that transformed themselves into DOGS, weasels, OWLS, chickens, and JAGUARS. The 17th c. parish priest Ruíz de Alarcón mentioned specific cases of native form-changers and explained their powers by claiming they had pacts with Satan. Although the concept of *nahual* recalls European concepts of witchcraft, it is clearly of native origin and is closely tied to native concepts of shamanic power and transformation. TEZCATLIPOCA, the sorcerer *par excellence* of Late Postclassic Central Mexico, was believed to be able to transform himself into a jaguar. The concept of jaguar form-changers also appears among the Formative Olmecs in the form of "transformation figures," stone sculptures that display a kneeling man being turned into a jaguar. Along with the animal alter-egos, the *nahual* could be transformed into a natural force, such as LIGHTNING. Although *nahual* sorcerers were frequently feared for their ability to commit malignant acts, they could also serve as protectors of the community. During the Colonial era, many nativistic movements were led by *nahual* sorcerers.

The *nahual* is generally identical to the Maya concept of the UAY. Recent epigraphic advances reveal the presence of *uay* alter-egos among the Classic Maya elite. However, it is uncertain whether these Classic texts refer to actual form-changers or to spirit companions. *See also* SHAMANISM; TONAL.

names and titles In many parts of Mesoamerica, individuals were named for the day in the 260-day CALENDAR on which they were born or baptized. Because the 260-day calendar was a divining calendar, these names all had very specific auguries: in the TRECENA 1 Deer, the day 5 Monkey was a good day ("He who was then born was like the workings and qualities of the day: the telling of tales, and jesting ... there was no anger"), but next day, 6 Grass, was evil ("... he who was then born lived only in torment on earth, suffered pain and trouble, and found afflictions"). Calendrical naming prevailed in Central Mexico, Oaxaca, and in parts of the Gulf region. The Mixtec cultural hero 9 Wind, for example, is known generally by his calendrical name, although he is also identified with QUETZALCOATL. In no region of the Maya were calendrical names used (although divinations for birthdays were calculated from the 260-day calendar), and no one knows whether they were used at TEOTIHUACAN.

Individuals carried other names as well as their calendrical ones, and these sometimes ran in families. The Motecuhzoma (He Who is Angry Like a Lord) who ruled at the time of the Conquest bore the same name as his grandfather, who then became known as Huehue Motecuhzoma, that is, Old Motecuhzoma, or Motecuhzoma the Elder. The Mixtec king and hero 8 Deer was also known as Tiger Claw; Princess 6 Monkey was given a new name or title, Serpent Quechquemitl, after her valiant victory over her enemies. Mixtec deities and oracles generally bore calendrical names too: 6 Monkey was given her new name by 9 Grass, a female oracle.

At the time of the Conquest, the Maya of Yucatán bore family lineage names. Among the ruling family names, many of whom dominated individual provinces, were the Cocom, the Xiu, the Cupul, and the Chel. In the case of the Classic Maya, names were often

Aztec **musicians** and dancers, Florentine Codex, Book 4, 16th c.

The Aztec *huehuetl*, or upright wooden drum, used in **music**-making, from Toluca.

characteristic of a particular lineage: Bird Jaguar the Great (reigned AD 752–c. 770), as he has been dubbed by modern investigators (his name glyphs are probably to be read Yaxom Balam) was the fourth king of Yax-chilán to bear that name, and both his father and his son had the name Shield Jaguar (again, a modern nickname: the glyphs may have been read Itz Balam), though his son was also known as Chac Chel. A completely distinctive set of names characterized the Palenque ruling family, and the same can be said of most Maya cities and their ruling families. The evidence from Palenque shows too that women in different generations might have the same name. Maya names frequently incor-porated the significant animals of their natural world: the JAGUAR, SNAKE, QUETZAL, BAT, tapir and PECCARY for example. Often, among the glyphic symbols used for WRITING their own names, Maya kings named their parents as well.

Maya hieroglyphic writing also reveals that the Maya nobility held a great many titles, only some of which can now be deciphered. Specific rankings were spelled out, such as lord (*ahau*), sacred lord (*ch'ul ahau*, applied only to a king), or sun lord (*mah kina* or *chikina* or *kinich*). A secondary stratum of rulers, probably regional governors, were known by the title *sahal*, to which they could be either born or appointed. Both a *sahal* and a *ch'ul ahau* could append CAPTIVES' names to their own (e.g. "captor of Flint Bat") as well as a count of captives. King Bird Jaguar the Great of Yaxchilán counted himself the "captor of 20 captives" most of his life, but on one of his last monuments, his count went up to 21.

Some captives may have been given new names upon their defeat: at Yaxchilán, some captive names refer to the day name on which they were taken: both "Mol" and "Chuen," for example, were captured on those partic-ular days. A famous captive like the Palenque king Kan Xul was publicly named and por-trayed at Tonina after his defeat. Captives' names often appear on their thighs, upper arms, or clothing – perhaps as signs of humiliation or because they were indeed tattooed or emblazoned for public recognition.

Specific titles distinguish other noble mem-bers of society: scribes and artists signed not only their names to works of art but also their titles (*ah dzib*: he of the writing; *idzat*: artist or wise man; *ah naab*: he of the water lily or the daubing). While an artist might sign as maker, the owner too might proclaim possession, e.g. "my cacao pot" or "my ear-spool" or "my temple."

New Fire ceremony *see* CALENDAR; FIRE

night In traditional Mesoamerican thought, the night was widely regarded with a certain amount of dread and fear. At night, form-changers and demons from the perimeters of the social world could wreak havoc upon humans. During the time of darkness, spooks and demons of the UNDERWORLD rose to the surface of the EARTH and the heavens. It was commonly believed that the soul traveled about while one slept, exposing the individual to great danger. Dreams were often consid-ered to be memories of the soul's nocturnal journeys and exploits. Thus in most Mayan lan-guages, the term UAY often bears connotations of sleep, dream, form-changer, or spirit com-panion. The forces of the night often diametri-cally oppose the ordered world of the SUN and daylight. Thus for example, during the New Fire vigil (*see* FIRE), the Aztecs greatly feared that the stellar demons of darkness, the TZITZIMIME, would plunge the entire world into darkness and chaos. *See also* CREATION ACCOUNTS; DAWN.

numbers All Mesoamerican peoples used a vigesimal, or base 20, system for counting, rather than the decimal, or base 10, system developed for Arabic numerals. The Mixtecs and Aztecs, among others, used dots to record numbers: 12 dots would mean 12 things or the coefficient 12, while the Maya used bar-and-dot numeration: the bar equals five, so two bars and two dots would mean 12 things or the coefficient 12. In Central Mexico, the term *centzon* literally meant 400, particularly in counts of tribute, but it could also be used figuratively to mean a large quantity of unspecified amount, as in the *Centzon Huitznahua*, the 400 sons of COATLICUE, per-sonifications of the many STARS of the heavens.

The Classic Maya could configure any number not only in bar-and-dot numeration but by a head or full-figure variant. In this more elaborate format, the numbers 1 to 12 are all distinct, but the numbers 14 to 19 repeat the heads of 4 to 9, with the addition of a skeletal jaw or a skeletal hand over the jaw. This skeletal addition must have had much the same meaning as the "teen" that English speakers add to the numbers 13 to 19.

Number 13 could be represented by a distinct head (*see* WATER LILY SERPENT) or as a "teen." The head variants of 1 to 13 represent various deities: 4, for example, is the sun god, 8 is the MAIZE GOD, and 9 is Xbalanque, one of the Hero Twins – who functioned as the patrons of the numbers.

In Aztec numeration, dots indicate numbers up to 20. A banner equals 20, a feather or leaf represents 400, and a *copal* bag indicates 8000. When the author of the Codex Telleriano-Remensis wanted to indicate that 20,000 captives had been killed in 1487 AD at the rededication of the Templo Mayor, he used 2 *copal* bags and 10 feathers.

Certain numbers also held metaphorical meaning: 1 meant the beginning of things; 9 referred to the levels of the UNDERWORLD; and 13 embodied the strata of the heavens.

The Aztec sign for the starry **night**, Codex Mendoza, 16th c.

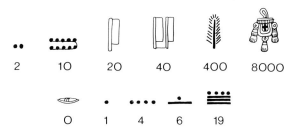

Aztec (top row) and Maya (second row) **numbers**.

obsidian A dark volcanic glass, obsidian was greatly prized for its razor-sharp edge and lustrous sheen. From Early Formative times on, it was traded widely in ancient Mesoamerica. Particular obsidian sources were held in high regard, especially Pachuca, near Tula, which yielded a fine olive green variety. Quite frequently, obsidian was prepared in the form of polyhedral cores, which resemble fluted cones. The prismatic blades obtained from these cores are razor sharp, and served as one of the more common BLOODLETTING instruments in ancient Mesoamerica. Among the Postclassic inhabitants of highland Mexico, the blades were set along the edge of a wooden club, the *macuahuitl*.

Because of its black, lustrous surface, obsidian was also used as a MIRROR stone. During the Protoclassic and Classic periods, a simple fractured plane formed the reflective surface. However, during the Late Postclassic period, ground and polished obsidian mirrors were also present. The Central Mexican deity TEZCATLIPOCA probably personified such a mirror. The 16th c. Cakchiquel Maya communicated with the Chay Abah, the sacred obsidian stone. This stone seems to have had oracular powers and spoke directly to the Cakchiquel. Quite possibly, the Chay Abah was a sacred obsidian mirror. *See also* DIVINATION.

Olmec gods The Olmecs were the first people in Mesoamerica to create a codified religious

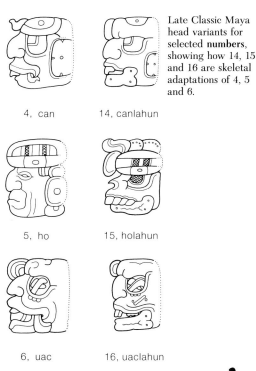

4, can   14, canlahun

5, ho   15, holahun

6, uac   16, uaclahun

Late Classic Maya head variants for selected **numbers**, showing how 14, 15 and 16 are skeletal adaptations of 4, 5 and 6.

The Aztec sign for Itzteyocan, composed of an **obsidian** core and blade atop a stone and the sign for a road; Matrícula de Tributos, 16th c. Central Mexico.

universe that we can recognize today through the surviving art. In fact, it was the existence of a standard symbolic code that forced archaeologists, beginning in the 1930s, to face the fact that some culture had preceded that of the Classic Maya. Before this culture had been documented archaeologically or its date proven, the term "cultura madre," or mother culture, had been introduced. The Olmecs are now recognized to have developed high civilization in Mesoamerica, with a charismatic cast of deities, some of whom were to survive, albeit in a changed form, for 2500 years, until the Spanish Conquest in the 16th c. The term "Olmec" itself is simply the name used by the Aztecs to refer to the "rubber people," meaning the people of the Gulf Coast; there is no clue of the name this civilization may have used to describe itself.

According to the STIRLING HYPOTHESIS, the Olmecs' principal deity was a WERE-JAGUAR, brought to life by the mating of a female human and a male JAGUAR, or a male human and a female jaguar. The "cultura madre" theory proposed that were-jaguars were essentially RAIN gods, and from Olmec rain gods one could see the evolution of all major Maya, Central Mexican, and Zapotec deities. More recently (and with far more examples of Olmec art than were available to an earlier generation) scholars, particularly David Joralemon, have begun to sort out a rich pantheon of Olmec deities as well as to recognize the beginnings of a cosmic structure that endured into later cultural florescences. Given the nascent state of studies of Olmec religion, the following guide to Olmec gods can be neither definitive nor comprehensive.

Olmec deities take the forms of the powerful animals of the tropical rain forest, where the culture itself arose. Principal deities include the SNAKE, harpy eagle (*see* EAGLE), SHARK, CAIMAN, and JAGUAR, and many combinations thereof. None has specific sexual characteristics to indicate gender. The cosmic structure of the Olmecs included a SKY dragon, an EARTH caiman, and the idea that four DWARVES held the sky in place, probably aligned with the cardinal points (*see* DIRECTIONS) and COLORS.

One of the most enduring of Olmec deities is the Rain Baby. Originally identified as a were-jaguar, he certainly has jaguar characteristics, particularly in terms of posture. Joralemon termed this figure God IV. The Rain Baby has a human nose and the squal-

ling, open-mouthed and usually toothless face of an infant; this is the Olmec deity most commonly held in the arms by an adult. Cleft-headed, he wears a headband and wavy PAPER adornments that crinkle along the side of his face, in front of the ears. Crinkled paper ornaments distinguish the rain god of Central Mexico many generations later and may derive from this early characterization.

The most important characteristic of Joralemon God II is the foliage that sprouts from the cleft in his head, possibly indicating a MAIZE god. The nose of this creature seems to be anthropomorphic; the mouth is usually toothless and open, like that of the Rain Baby, but in some cases it has bird characteristics. A full body is rarely depicted. This character may also symbolize the fertile earth or MOUNTAIN from which maize grows.

The Personified Earth Cave (Joralemon God I-B) symbolizes the earth and entry into the earth. It occurs as actual CAVE entrances and also as frames for seated rulers, both on Olmec ALTARS and on Relief 1, Chalcatzingo. Always open-mawed, the image is usually toothless. The eyes have crossed bands; foliage sprouts from the exterior of the maw.

The Olmec Dragon, the principal sky god, probably derives zoomorphically from the crested harpy eagle. One of the most prevalent images of Olmec iconography (Joralemon God I-A), the Olmec Dragon includes many symbols that the Olmecs often chose to represent schematically and independently, such as the paw-wing motif or flame eyebrows. These symbols often appear as the motifs on ceramic seals, and they commonly occur on pottery found far from the Olmec heartland along the Gulf Coast.

The Shark God (Joralemon God VIII) occurs rarely, but has a clearly defined shark tooth when represented. This may be a SEA god.

The Feathered Serpent (Joralemon God VII) often has a crest of feathers, the rattles of a rattlesnake, a forked SERPENT tongue, and may float in cloud symbols, perhaps linking him to the later cloud serpents of the Maya, Toltecs, and Aztecs. The presence of QUETZALS and crossed bands over the head of the human who rests against the serpent's body on La Venta Monument 19 suggests a reading, if written in a Mayan language, of kukulcan (quetzal = kuk; crossed bands = can or chan), or QUETZALCOATL.

Another characteristic Olmec deity with cleft head bears a stripe down the middle of

127 OMETEOTL

the face, usually through the eye (Joralemon God VI). Such face paint characterizes the later god of the Gulf Coast and Central Mexico, XIPE TOTEC, but the Olmec creature has the downturned beak of a bird, and is probably not related to Xipe.

Other Olmec deities await further identification. Some are basic were-jaguars, many have cleft heads; some have interlocking teeth, like those of a caiman, while others have only upper fangs and yet others are toothless. *See also* INTRODUCTION.

omens The peoples of ancient Mesoamerica keenly observed strange behavior and events in the natural world, signs that could portend events of everyday life or even world destruction. Because they regarded the heavenly bodies as especially important, these signs constitute one of the more common subjects in the Prehispanic manuscripts. Possibly because of their proximity to the heavens and their speech-like qualities, birds were widely regarded as omens. Even today, OWLS are considered to be harbingers of DEATH. The Yucatec Mayan term *mut* signifies both bird and augury. In the Postclassic Dresden Codex, this term appears in scenes illustrating the youthful Goddess I (*see* SCHELLHAS GODS) with the MUAN OWL, the QUETZAL, and other birds, here referring to "good" or "bad" auguries.

Many native peoples noted strange, disturbing omens just before the coming of the Spaniards; for the Aztecs, Sahagún records eight evil signs. Among these omens were two probable comets, LIGHTNING striking the TEMPLE of XIUHTECUHTLI, the sound of a crying woman during many nights, and a strange bird with a divinatory MIRROR in its forehead. The Tarascans of Michoacán noted evil omens foretelling the Spanish Conquest. They also described two comets, and added that their temples were continually being destroyed. When rebuilt, these structures would only catch FIRE again, and their walls tumble to the ground. *See also* DIVINATION.

Ometeotl Literally the "two god," Ometeotl embodies the Central Mexican principle of DUALITY. This dual, bisexual god ruled over the highest heaven of the Nahuatl scheme, Omeyocan, "Place of Duality," in the form of Ometecuhtli and his consort Omecihuatl. Together, Ometecuhtli and Omecihuatl were the ever-present progenitors, for they sent

Olmec gods: (*right*) a probable depiction of the Olmec rain baby, San Lorenzo Monument 52, Early Formative period. A deep trough is cut down the back of this sculpture, and it is possible that it served as part of the stone drainage systems used at San Lorenzo.

(*Below*) Joralemon God VI, incised pottery vessel, Tlapacoya, Middle Formative Olmec.

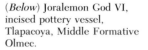

Olmec gods: (*right*) Joralemon God II-B, a possible Olmec maize god; design from an incised celt, La Venta, Middle Formative period.

(*Below*) Goddess I bearing particular birds as **omens**, or *mut*, Dresden Codex, p. 16, Postclassic Yucatán.

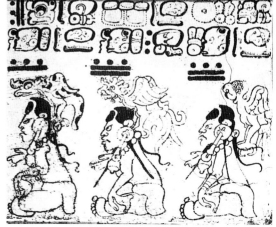

the souls of those about to be born to the surface of the EARTH. Ometecuhtli and Omecihuatl may also be identified with Cipactonal and Oxomoco, aged progenitors and perhaps divine grandparents (*see* ANCESTRAL COUPLE). Generally not a subject of artistic representation, Ometeotl had no specific TEMPLE dedicated to him in the sacred precinct nor an active cult celebrated at one of the annual VEINTENAS, but this being was the subject to whom a multitude of formal prayers were addressed. Some authors have sought to identify an evolution through the worship of Ometeotl toward monotheism in late Central Mexican thought.

Omeyocan *see* OMETEOTL; SKY; TONACATECUHTLI

opossum With its gray fur, shambling gait, and snaggle-toothed mouth, the opossum (*Didelphis marsupialis*) was identified with old age in Mesoamerica. The opossum figures prominently in the new year pages of the Maya Dresden Codex corresponding to the end of the old year. In these scenes, the opossum is labeled *mam*, a term signifying both an aged grandfather and the god of the old year. In Classic Maya iconography, the opossum appears with attributes of the aged deity known as PAUAHTUN, who is probably none other than the god of the dying year.

In the Mixtec codices, the opossum is closely identified with the intoxicating beverage PULQUE. In the Vindobonensis and Nuttall codices, depictions of the decapitated pulque goddess Lady 11 Serpent are accompanied by an opossum holding cups filled with pulque.

owls As a nocturnal bird that frequently resides in CAVES and underground burrows, the owl is widely identified with the NIGHT and the UNDERWORLD. Above the entrance to Oxtotitlan Cave, Guerrero, there is a Middle Formative Olmec painting of a man dressed as a green horned owl. Green owls commonly occur in the art of TEOTIHUACAN, and are quite frequently placed atop MIRRORS, symbols themselves of supernatural caves or passageways. An Early Postclassic cache from the Temple of Chac Mool at Chichen Itzá contained a finch and a burrowing pygmy owl placed atop a pyrite mirror.

Like other birds, owls were considered as OMENS or messengers between humans and the divine. Because of their natural affinities to night and caves, owls held special ties to the dark and deathly Underworld. In the Central Mexican Borgia Group of codices, the owl can appear with a human skull for a head. The owl also often occupies the bone-festooned TEMPLE of MICTLANTECUHTLI, the death god, who frequently wears an owl-feather crest. The Aztecs clearly regarded owls with a certain amount of fear; thus the dreaded nocturnal form-changing sorcerer was termed *tlacatecolotl*, or "owl man."

The ancient Maya seem to have had an ambivalent attitude toward owls, identifying them with both fertility and DEATH. The horned MUAN OWL, for example, brought RAIN and MAIZE and had associations of death and the Underworld. This dual nature can be seen also for the owl messengers of the Quiché Maya POPOL VUH. Although assistants and messengers for the death gods of Xibalba, the owls also assisted Xquic, the pregnant wife of HUN HUNAHPU, in her escape to the surface of the EARTH.

P

Paddler Gods Because one of their primary actions is to paddle a CANOE, two Classic Maya deities have been named the Paddlers. They appear in Classic period art and indicate a specific pair of oppositions, day and NIGHT, apparent through the hieroglyphs that represent them, *akbal*, darkness or night, and *kin*, or day. Unlike most Maya hieroglyphs, those identifying the Paddlers are drawn within identifying cartouches that would seem to represent their canoe, as seen from above.

The Old Jaguar Paddler (night) usually paddles the bow of the canoe while the Old Stingray Paddler (day) handles the stern. Although always anthropomorphic, the Old Jaguar Paddler shares characteristics with a number of aged JAGUAR GODS, including the Jaguar God of the Underworld; he is toothless, wears a jaguar headdress, and usually carries a paddle. The Old Stingray Paddler also has an aged, sagging face, and a perforator, either bone or stingray spine, pierces the septum of his nose. Both Paddlers wear the knotted waist ornament of GI of the PALENQUE TRIAD.

According to Maya hieroglyphic texts, the Paddlers are created or born when a Maya king lets BLOOD. In scenes of BLOODLETTING, they frequently occur in swirls of clouds created when blood is let on PAPER and then set afire. Their presence is most likely to be invoked on period ending dates.

When they paddle their canoe, the Paddlers are often ushering the MAIZE GOD to his next engagement. The canoe itself may have a relationship with bowls used for SACRIFICE and offerings, appropriate for either MAIZE or blood.

Owl, Codex Borgia, p. 71, Late Postclassic period.

Painal *see* HUITZILOPOCHTLI

Palenque Triad Based on hieroglyphic texts at Palenque, Heinrich Berlin identified a trio of gods in 1963. One of the striking characteristics of these gods is that all three appear at other Maya cities individually and over a long period of time, but only at Palenque do they occur as a hieroglyphic triad. Known as GI, GII, and GIII, for Gods 1, 2, and 3, they function as special patron deities for Palenque.

The three births were not actually recorded until Chan Bahlum (reigned AD 684–702) built a group of temples known as the Group of the Cross at the end of the 7th c., but the Triad was referred to by most Palenque kings, from Pacal onward (ruled AD 615–683), and offerings were made to them. On the Group of the Cross, each Initial Series text begins with a date calculated 3000 to 4000 years before it was inscribed. The birth of GI is recorded in the Temple of the Cross, GII in the Temple of the Foliated Cross, and GIII in the Temple of the Sun. It might even be best to consider them triplets for, according to the texts, these gods were all born in 2360 BC over a three-week period. Each birth is accompanied by an 819-day DIVINATION, and an ancestral goddess is named as their collective mother. GI is the first born, followed four days later by GIII, and then 14 days later by GII.

Since Berlin's identification of the Triad in 1963, GI's identity has been scrambled with that of CHAC – whose zoomorphic form, sometimes called the Rain Beast, shares characteristics with GI – and the relationship between the two of them has not been sorted out satisfactorily. GI's Maya name remains unknown; hieroglyphically he is represented by his own distinctive head, whereas Chac's name, sometimes rendered Chac-xib-chac, is well known. GI's BIRTH is the most confused, for he is named as both father (born in 3122

The **Paddler Gods** at fore and aft of a canoe containing the Tonsured Maize God and animal passengers (complete canoe shown together with two details); incised bone, Burial 116, Tikal, Late Classic Maya.

GI   GII   GIII

The **Palenque Triad**, gods GI, GII, and GIII.

BC) and son (born in 2360 BC) on the Temple of the Cross, possibly because the same name was held in two generations.

Whereas GI has a mature, anthropomorphic face, the anthropomorphic Chac is young. GI's squared eye has a curl that turns inward from the exterior corner; his "barbels" or fish fins are at the corner of the mouth, and his only tooth may be a prominent SHARK tooth. Like Chac, he wears large spondylus (spiny oyster) shells as ear flares. Unlike Chac, he frequently wears the same quadripartite headdress worn by the rear head of the BICEPHALIC MONSTER: a stingray spine, spondylus shell, and crossed bands inside a cache vessel, imagery that may be conflated with a heron when worn by GI. His image, usually with the quadripartite headdress, is one of the most common on Early Classic censers from the Petén, and he was a principal recipient of Maya offerings. Maya kings at Copán and Tikal were rendered in the costume of GI. He rarely appears as an actor on Maya polychrome vessels.

GII is one more name for the Maya deity also known as God K in the Schellhas system (see SCHELLHAS GODS) and the MANIKIN SCEPTER. This is a very ancient being, and may be seen on Abaj Takalik Stela 5, a monument dating to the early second century A D. Called Bolon Dzacab at the time of the Conquest, God K was probably known as Kauil during the Classic era, and as Tohil among the Postclassic Quiché. His names suggest bounty and abundance (Bolon Dzacab means nine generations; Kauil, abundance; Tohil, very roughly, storm), and the Temple of the Foliated Cross, where his birth is recorded, depicts abundant MAIZE rising up from a personified kernel. Chan Bahlum, who has attired himself as the MAIZE GOD, stands on a personified mountain in the Temple of the Foliated Cross, in whose eyes are glyphs that read *Uitz nal*, or Hill of Maize, probably analogous to the Sustenance Mountain where QUETZALCOATL sought the source of maize. GII himself does not appear on the Tablet of the Foliated Cross, although he is held in the hands of Chan Bahlum on the Tablet of the Sun.

In his various forms, as the Manikin Scepter or an elongated staff, emerging from a CEREMONIAL BAR, or as a hand-held object, GII is usually shown to be much smaller than humans. His zoomorphic head has a long snout, probably SERPENT in origin, and one of his legs generally turns into a snake. Although

his head has no anthropomorphic form, his body, with the exception of the serpent leg, is human. His forehead is usually punctured by an axe or smoking tube or MIRROR. In one particularly unusual representation on the piers of the Temple of Inscriptions at Palenque, an adult carries a large but infantile GII as if it were a human child; with the adult probably intended to represent Chan Bahlum himself, such a stucco rendering shows the ruling family to be divine in their own lifetime.

On Maya ceramics, GII appears frequently, usually in passive rather than active situations, and rarely in narrative. On some codex-style pots, his serpent leg is a VISION SERPENT. GII's name glyph is a common component of rulers' names. He can symbolize LIGHTNING, and his representation overlaps with that of Chac, linking RAIN and lightning.

GIII is probably the SUN god, KINICH AHAU (lord sun), but GIII is the most obscure member of the Palenque Triad. Probably to be identified with the God of Number 4, GIII appears as the head that frames the earthband on the base of the Tablet of the Sun. The central image of that panel, however, is the Jaguar God of the Underworld (see JAGUAR GODS), the SUN at NIGHT and a principal Classic Maya image of warfare. The relationship of GIII to the Jaguar God of the UNDERWORLD is not clear, but GIII may encompass both diurnal and nocturnal aspects of the sun.

Born only four days apart, GI and GIII have sometimes been identified with the Hero Twins of the POPOL VUH. These pairings occur particularly on codex-style vessels of the 8th c., and suggest the alternating SACRIFICES performed by the Hero Twins. There is every reason, however, to distinguish GI and GIII, as well as Chac and the Jaguar Baby, from the Hero Twins. Paired oppositions (see DUALITY), TWINS, and brothers, however, are all common in Maya and Mexican mythology, and structural parallels with the Hero Twins may well be expected.

palma The tall, palmate stone called the *palma* is one of several standard elements of BALLGAME equipment that survive in stone form, probably as trophies. *Palmas* were worn at the front of the body and inserted into the YOKE. Many take the forms of human arms and hands, standing ballplayers, or fan-tailed birds. If actually worn at the waist, some examples would block the vision of the player. Unlike other items of ballgame equipment, few *palmas* have been recovered away from the Gulf Coast, but they are depicted in the sculpture at Chichen Itzá and Cotzumalhuapa.

paper The peoples of ancient Mesoamerica prepared paper from the pounded inner bark of trees, particularly species of strangler figs, such as *Ficus cotinifolia* and *Ficus padifolia*. Paper was probably present in Mesoamerica by the Early Formative period. Monument 52 from the Olmec site of San Lorenzo portrays a figure wearing ear pennants of folded paper. During the Protoclassic period, people all over Mesoamerica used stone barkbeaters to manufacture paper, and these stone tools may have succeeded wooden barkbeaters, like those of Southeast Asia and Oceania. Although it has been suggested that the Mesoamerican mode of paper manufacture may have originated in Southeast Asia, this paper technology may well have been an independent New World innovation.

In ancient and contemporary Mesoamerica, supplicants splash and daub paper strips with BLOOD, *copal*, RUBBER, or other liquid substances and then burn them as sacrificial offerings. It is perhaps because the RAIN and LIGHTNING gods often receive these offerings that they commonly wear paper ornaments. Paper was also widely used as an offering to the dead. In the iconography of both Central Mexico and the Maya region, paper often appears in DEATH-related scenes. MICTLANTECUHTLI, the skeletal death god of Central Mexico, is usually depicted wearing a pointed cap and other apparel fashioned from paper.

In addition to its uses as offerings and ritual clothing, paper served as an important material for screenfold books. The Maya seem to have especially favored paper screenfold codices (*see* CODEX) and all four of the known Prehispanic Maya codices were fashioned from pounded bark paper. Although the surviving Prehispanic manuscripts of the Mixtecs and peoples of Central Mexico are made of DEER hide rather than paper, codices of paper were probably also common. Nahuatl-speakers called divinatory books *tonalamatl*, a word containing the term for paper, *amatl*.

parrots and macaws Both parrots (*Amazona* sp.) and the related larger macaws (*Arara*

The **Palenque Triad**. (Right) GI, detail from Early Classic carved vessel. (Left) GII, or God K, detail from Abaj Takalik Stela 5, Protoclassic Maya.

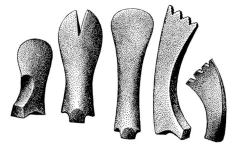

Often elaborately carved, stone **palmas** can also display a subtle elegance of form; from Classic Veracruz.

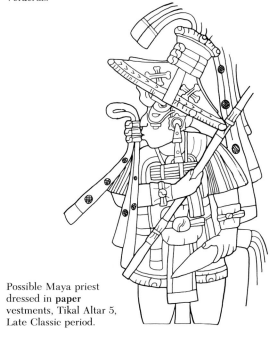

Possible Maya priest dressed in **paper** vestments, Tikal Altar 5, Late Classic period.

sp.) were much esteemed for their brilliant and multihued plumage. Perhaps the most important of these birds of the parrot family were the long-tailed macaws, especially the scarlet macaw (*Ara macao*) and the military macaw (*Ara militaris*). In Mesoamerican art, macaws can often be identified not only by their thick beak and long tail, but also by a beaded ring encircling the eye. Birds of the parrot family are commonly depicted in the Protoclassic TOMB art of West Mexico, and it is probable that many of these birds are tropical macaws that were traded into this region. At the great Early Postclassic site of Casas Grandes, Chihuahua, military macaws (*Ara militaris*) were raised in specially prepared pens.

In ancient Mesoamerica, macaws were often identified with FIRE. The Aztecs called macaw tail feathers *cuezalin*, signifying "flame." In the Maya Dresden and Madrid codices, macaws hold flaming torches. Fray Diego de Landa records that the most massive structure at the site of Izamal, Yucatán, was dedicated to Kinich Kakmo, or "Sun-faded Fire Macaw," a fiery entity that descended at noon to burn and consume sacrificial offerings. The Quiché Maya called the macaw Caquix, meaning "fiery feather." In the POPOL VUH, the Hero Twins trick the gods of DEATH by placing macaw feathers on the tips of their unlit cigars to suggest burning embers. The monster bird slain by the Hero Twins was VUCUB CAQUIX, or 7 Macaw. However, although this important episode is widely depicted in Classic Maya art, the monster bird in this instance bears no direct resemblance to a macaw.

patolli Patolli is a Mesoamerican game of chance in which game piece markers move through a set course depending upon the role of the dice, much like a modern board game. The 19th c. anthropologist Edward B. Tylor noted that patolli is markedly similar to the Indian parchesi, and suggested that patolli originated in Asia. However, although the similarities are indeed striking, there is no evidence that patolli is historically related to parchesi.

Quite commonly, the patolli game course resembles a cross enclosed within a square. They are not discrete units, however, but are interwoven into a single contiguous course. Carved onto flat stones or plaster floors, patolli designs of this form are widespread in Mesoamerica, and often appear at Classic and Postclassic sites of both highland Mexico and the Maya region. A patolli course, along with probable stick, bean, and bone dice, is illustrated on page 20 of the Mixtec Codex Vindobonensis. In the Central Mexican codices, this patolli pattern also occurs in scenes illustrating the TRECENA 1 Cuauhtli, dedicated to the goddess XOCHIQUETZAL. The modern Tarascans of Michoacán still use the cross and square patolli course; the Tarahumara of Chihuahua and Pueblo peoples of the American Southwest also play a modern form of the game.

In ancient Mesoamerica, patolli is best documented for the Aztecs. Here the course was often painted on MATS and commonly took the form of a cross without the encircling square. Players gambled on the patolli game and, at times, people even sold themselves into slavery as a final desperate wager. The patron of this game was MACUILXOCHITL, the most important of the AHUIATETEO gods of excess. According to Diego Durán, Ometochtli, another being of vice and excess and god of the intoxicating PULQUE, also presided over the patolli game. Thus, as in Western society, drinking and gambling were closely related among the ancient Aztecs.

Pauahtun Ancient Mesoamerican peoples widely believed that the cosmic balance of the world rested on the shoulders of four gods situated at the four quarters. For the ancient Maya, this SKYBEARER was glyphically named as Pauahtun. He corresponds to the world DIRECTIONS, and appears in both single and quadripartite form. Ironically, although he bears the weighty office of supporting the SKY, he is frequently portrayed as a drunken and lecherous old man, hardly a paragon of security and responsibility. Along with his distinctive netted cloth headdress, he often appears within a conch or tortoise shell. At times, he wears a spider's web rather than the conch or carapace. As well as being a skybearer, Pauahtun seems to be a god of thunder, MOUNTAINS, and the interior of the EARTH, much like the modern Mam god of highland Guatemala. In the Postclassic codices, he appears as God N in the Schellhas system of deity classification. *See also* LIGHTNING AND THUNDER; SCHELLHAS GODS.

peccary Peccaries, smelly, blunt-snouted wild pigs, generally roam the tropical rain forest of Mesoamerica in small herds; they are omnivores with a keen sense of smell and hearing. Two peccary species are native to Mesoamerica: the collared (*Tayassu angulatus*) and the white-lipped (*Tayassu pecari*).

Peccaries were of interest mainly to the Maya insofar as religious iconography is concerned. A number of Maya nobles included the peccary in their names. In the three bright STARS that modern skywatchers read as the belt of Orion, the Maya saw mating peccaries. In some examples, the Maya god ITZAMNA rides the peccary. Snout-down peccary heads form the legs of Early Classic quadrupod bowls and may bear *caban* curls, or EARTH signs, perhaps in some reference to the pillars of the cosmos. Maya artists may have used sharp peccary tusks to carve stone monuments.

According to one 19th c. account, the peccary was also the earth god of the Huichol.

Parrots and macaws: macaw ballcourt marker, Xochicalco, Morelos, Late Classic period. Macaw head ballcourt markers are also known for Late Classic Copán, and it appears that the macaw had a special association with the ballgame.

pilgrimage Certain MOUNTAINS, shrines, and cities became objects of Mesoamerican religious pilgrimages. Motecuhzoma II himself reputedly walked to TEOTIHUACAN regularly to worship there. As the setting for the creation of the fifth sun (*see* FIVE SUNS), Teotihuacan held great power for the Aztecs, and they left testimony of their visits there in the form of broken Aztec pottery. They treated Tula, Hidalgo, as a site of pilgrimage too, but they also removed many of its visible sculptures and hauled them back to Tenochtitlan. As the traditional refuge of QUETZALCOATL, Cholula was also an important pilgrimage destination.

After the Zapotecs abandoned Monte Albán, the Mixtecs treated the mountain with reverence and as a place of pilgrimage. They honored it by placing their own dead in ancient Zapotec TOMBS (which they first emptied and presumably desecrated).

Pilgrimages were carried out to sanctify rulership, to seek advice, and to change one's fortune. A Mixtec princess, 6 Monkey, journeyed with the well-known lord 10 Wind to seek the advice of 9 Grass, a priestess or goddess who guarded an important oracle, probably at Chalcatongo.

Little is known of Classic Maya pilgrimages, although there is evidence for royal visits. At the time of the Spanish Conquest, Landa noted that "they held Cozumel and the well of Chichen Itzá in the same veneration as we have for pilgrimages to Jerusalem and

Macuilxochitl presiding over a **patolli** game, Codex Magliabechiano, 16th c. Aztec.

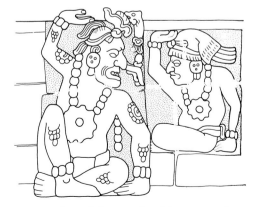

Two **Pauahtun** skybearers, detail from a carved bench, Copán, Late Classic Maya.

Rome, and so they used to go to visit these places and to offer presents there, especially to Cozumel, as we do to holy places; and if they did not go themselves, they always sent their offerings, and those who went there were in the habit of entering the abandoned temples also, as they passed by them, to offer prayers there and to burn copal."

In the Postclassic period, beginning with the fall of Classic cities, the Sacred CENOTE at Chichen Itzá was the most important pilgrimage destination for the Maya, and so it remained until 1539. Although Landa considered Cozumel the greater pilgrimage destination, it was probably in fact the lesser. IXCHEL's cult was celebrated there, as it was on the neighboring island, Isla Mujeres, and many pilgrims to these islands were women who sought fertility and guidance from the goddess. According to Landa, pilgrims came from great distances – sometimes from as far away as the Putún Maya region, or what is the modern Mexican state of Tabasco.

Religious pilgrimages remain important in Mexico and Guatemala today, based on practices coincident both from the past in the New World and from Europe. The shrine of the Virgin of Guadalupe at the hill of Tepeyac, the most important pilgrimage destination for Mexican Catholics today, was once the site of worship to Tonantzin, a Central Mexican goddess related to TOCI. Chalma, a town once known for its ancient CAVE shrine, now houses within its Catholic church a black Christ claimed to work miracles, and an adjacent sacred *ahuehuetl* tree receives modern offerings from the pilgrims who flock to the town.

Popol Vuh The most important surviving sacred book of the Quiché Maya is called the *Popol Vuh*, or "council book." As the Dennis Tedlock translation of the text tells us, "there is the original book and ancient writing, but he who reads and ponders it hides his face," so early in the era of Christianity, some time in the mid-16th c., a Quiché nobleman sat down with what must have been a hieroglyphic book and wrote a transcription in the Roman alphabet. At the beginning of the 18th c., a Quiché-speaking Spanish friar, Francisco Ximénez, learned of the manuscript in Chichicastenango. He copied the Quiché text and wrote a parallel Spanish text: his is the earliest surviving version of the *Popol Vuh*, and it is preserved today in the Newberry Library in Chicago. The book has been translated many times and into many languages.

The *Popol Vuh* has essentially three parts: first, the creation of the EARTH and its first inhabitants; second, the story of the Hero Twins and their forebears; and third, the legendary history of the founding of the Quiché dynasties, continuing up to the years following the Spanish Conquest. The middle section of the *Popol Vuh*, treating not only of the Hero Twins but also of their father, HUN HUNAHPU, is the most ancient, appearing in art from Late Formative times onward. From that point on, Maya kings seem to have emulated the Hero Twins and their exploits. The tales are not related in a linear fashion and presume a familiarity with the characters on the part of the audience.

Unlike the creation at the beginning of the Bible, the Maya creation in the *Popol Vuh* takes place in great quiet. Gugumatz, the Quiché translation of QUETZALCOATL, and Hurucan, probably to be identified with TOHIL/God K (*see* SCHELLHAS GODS), first shape the earth and its features, and then raise the SKY overhead. The SUN does not rise until much later. The gods then populated the earth with all its animals, but when they found that the animals were unable to speak and praise their makers, they condemned them forever to being the food of higher beings.

In a second attempt to create a being that would praise its makers, the gods shaped a human of mud, but it dissolved in front of them. For a third attempt, Hurucan and Gugumatz called on ancestral diviners, Xpiacoc and Xmucane, to generate mankind. This time humans were carved of wood, and although they quickly populated the earth, they forgot their makers and were destroyed by the gods, who sent various destructions from the sky and who turned the pots, the griddles, the grinding stones, and even the DOGS, against the people of wood.

After this destruction, the *Popol Vuh* begins to relate stories of the Hero Twins, Hunahpu and Xbalanque. Demigods, the Hero Twins defeat the false sun and vanquish the gods of the Xibalba, or UNDERWORLD, setting the stage for the generation of true humans later in the *Popol Vuh*.

Hunahpu and Xbalanque took on VUCUB CAQUIX (7 Macaw), who had set himself up as a false sun with the support of his sons Zipacna and Cabracan. Great blowgunners, the Twins took their weapons and struck the bejeweled teeth of Vucub Caquix, and then tricked him into accepting ground corn as the replacement. Unable to eat and deprived of the jewels that gave him his false radiance, Vucub Caquix was defeated, and his sons were defeated thereafter.

The story then flashes back to the generation of Hun Hunahpu and his brother Vucub Hunahpu, such skillful ballplayers (*see* BALLGAME) that their constant play disturbed the lords of Xibalba, who commanded that they come to Xibalba for a contest. Messenger OWLS from Xibalba guided the brothers into the Underworld, where they failed one test after another. The day after they arrived, they were sacrificed by the lords of Xibalba and buried in the ballcourt, with the exception of the head of Hun Hunahpu, which was stuck in a calabash tree, as if it were a skullrack, or TZOMPANTLI.

When Xquic, a young Xibalba goddess, learned of the strange fruit of this tree, she visited it, and Hun Hunahpu's head spat into her hand, impregnating her with what would be Hunahpu and Xbalanque. When her condition became apparent, she was driven out of Xibalba and went to live with Hun Hunahpu's mother, who tested her before allowing her to stay and deliver the Twins. Hun Hunahpu had already fathered another pair of twins, Hun Batz and Hun Chuen, great artists and musicians, who resented, abused, and took advantage of their baby brothers. But when they grew old enough, the Hero Twins outsmarted their brothers and lured them into a tree, where, unable to get down, they became MONKEYS.

Their grandmother hid their father's ballgame equipment from the Hero Twins, but they tricked her and became even more proficient ballplayers than their father and uncle. Once again, the lords of Xibalba summoned the ballplayers to the Underworld, but the Hero Twins were not defeated by the tests and traps set for them. Instead, the gods fell into the Twins' traps. They used a mosquito to bite each god in sequence, and so the gods revealed their names, part of their defeat. Each day, the Hero Twins played the Xibalba lords on the ballcourt; each night, they were sent to a different house to be tested. When told to keep their cigars lit for a night, they complied by using fireflies on the ends; when told to provide cut FLOWERS, the Twins summoned cutter ants to cut the flowers of the Xibalba. When sent to the Cold

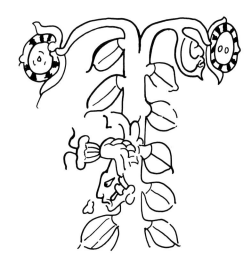

Head of Hun Hunahpu, father of the **Popol Vuh** Hero Twins, placed in a fruit-laden tree, detail from a Late Classic Maya vase. Although the Popol Vuh states that the head of Hun Hunahpu was placed in a gourd tree, this image clearly represents a cacao tree. A cacao pod with human features can be seen in an upper branch, which probably refers to the transformation of Hun Hunahpu's head into the fruit.

A monkey scribe dancing with a mirror, detail from a Late Classic Maya vase. The monkey scribes appearing in Classic Maya iconography are now known to be early forms of Hun Batz and Hun Chuen of the **Popol Vuh**. Although widely recognized to be gods of the scribal arts, Hun Batz and Hun Chuen were also identified with music and dance.

House, the Twins drove the cold away; when sent to the Jaguar House, the Twins offered the JAGUARS the flesh of all other animals. In the Fire House, FIRE did not consume the Twins. In the Bat House, however, although the Twins slept inside their blowguns, when Hunahpu stuck his head out early in the morning, a killer BAT sliced off his head.

Xbalanque called the animals to help him, and they fashioned a new head for Hunahpu from a pumpkin, but when they got to the ballcourt, the lords of Xibalba introduced the head of Hunahpu as the ball. Xbalanque struck the head out of the court, and a RABBIT curled up and bounced away as if it were the ball, leading the Xibalbans on a wild chase and giving Xbalanque time to restore Hunahpu's head. But the Twins then let themselves be defeated, cooked in an oven, and their bones ground and tossed into the river.

Five days later the Twins reappeared from the river, first as catfish, then disguised as wandering magicians and performers. The lords of Xibalba summoned them to their court, where the Twins performed great feats: they danced, they sacrificed a dog and brought him back to life, they sacrificed a human and brought him back to life, and Xbalanque sacrificed Hunahpu and brought him back to life. The lords of Xibalba grew ecstatic at the sight and begged to be sacrificed themselves. The Twins obliged, of course, but did not revive the DEATH gods. They dug up the bodies of Hun Hunahpu and Vucub Hunahpu and revived them before walking into the sky to reign as the sun and MOON.

The final and longest section of the *Popol Vuh* begins with the ANCESTRAL COUPLE attempting once again to make a creature that would praise the gods. This time, the four founders of the Quiché lineages were formed of MAIZE. They praised their makers and flourished. In their near perfection, these men of maize alarmed the gods, who curtailed their vision to only what was nearby. All this took place before the true sun rose.

The four founders journeyed to Tulan Zuyua, the MOUNTAIN of the seven CAVES, and there they received the gods, whom they then carried home in BUNDLES on their backs. Balam Quitze received TOHIL, who gave humans fire, but only after HUMAN SACRIFICE to him had begun. At last the true sun rose in the east. The *Popol Vuh* closes by listing the lineage heads in each generation, 14 from Balam Quitze to his descendants in the middle of the 16th c. *See also* CREATION ACCOUNTS.

priests The priest held one of the most important public offices in ancient Mesoamerican society. Intermediaries between humans and the supernatural, priests were fulltime specialists who possessed a vast amount of esoteric knowledge concerning such subjects as calendrics, WRITING, rituals and mythology. Typically, priests were males culled from the elite ranks of society. They endured a life of penitence and fasting, and rarely cohabited with women. According to Burgoa, the Zapotecs castrated the elite children to become neophyte priests known as *pixana*. Unlike SHAMANS, who frequently engaged in trances and spirit possession, priests usually served in the more detached position of a mediator or spokesperson between humans and the GODS. Thus one of their more important roles was that of presenting sacrificial offerings to the gods. However, the distinction between priest and shaman was far from fast: the Zapotec high priest of Mitla for example, the Uija Tao, would communicate with the supernatural through ecstatic trance.

Although priests were undoubtedly present in Formative and Classic Mesoamerica, it is difficult to identify their offices in the ancient writing and art, even in the naturalistic art and detailed writing of the Maya. As it currently stands, there is no known glyph or reading for the office of priest in ancient Maya script. Nonetheless, it is quite possible that priests, religious experts fully versed in courtly esoteric knowledge, created a great deal of the fine elite art.

Priests are well documented for the Late Postclassic period in detailed early Colonial accounts. Among the Aztecs and other peoples of Central Mexico, as well as among the Mixtecs of Oaxaca and the Tarascans of Michoacán, priests commonly wore gourds filled with TOBACCO upon their backs. Today, the tobacco gourd is still an important accessory of the Huichol *mara'akame* shaman priest. Along with the tobacco gourd, Aztec priests usually wore a white *xicolli* jacket and a knotted cotton INCENSE bag. In addition, the Aztec priest is often represented with BLOOD in the area of his temples, indicating his role as penitential bloodletter. The ethnohistorical accounts reveal that among the Aztecs, Zapotecs, Tarascans, and Yucatec Maya, complex hierarchies of priestly offices specified particular roles and responsibilities.

In Postclassic Mesoamerica, particular gods were identified with the office of priest. For the Aztecs, QUETZALCOATL was the paramount god of priests, and the *calmecac* school of noble youths and neophyte priests was dedicated to him. In addition, the two highest priests of the Aztecs bore the title of Quetzalcoatl. Among the Mixtecs, the deity known as 2 Dog appears as an aged priest wearing a prominent tobacco gourd upon his back. For the Postclassic Yucatec Maya, ITZAMNA frequently serves as a priest, complete with priestly accoutrements as mentioned by the early Colonial chroniclers. However, the Yucatec priests were also identified with the SUN, and bore the title of Ah Kin, or He of the Sun. Possibly, this is a reference to the aspect of Itzamna known as KINICH AHAU Itzamna, meaning "sun-faced lord Itzamna."

primordial couple *see* ANCESTRAL COUPLE

Principal Bird Deity At the beginning of Maya civilization, one of the first deities to take consistent, public form is the Principal Bird Deity, a great avian creature that may be based on the king vulture. In all likelihood, this god is to be identified with VUCUB CAQUIX of the POPOL VUH, a bird god who sets himself up as a false SUN before the DAWN of time. In the *Popol Vuh*, the Hero Twins shoot down Vucub Caquix with blowguns, and his demise sets the stage for the rising of the true sun at the dawn of the era of the current race of humanity. The Maya did not view the Principal Bird as an unmitigated evil power, however, and particularly in early representations, the Principal Bird is presented in a positive light. In fact, there may well have been a shift in the perception of this god over time.

Very early versions of the Principal Bird Deity formed huge stucco sculptures on the exteriors of pyramids at Cerros and Nakbe, perhaps by as early as 300 BC. Early portrayals emphasize a long, downward-curving beak and wings bordered by serpent faces. Although the Principal Bird is considered a Maya deity, the powerful lord on La Mojarra Stela 1, from outside the Maya area, wears a large head of the Principal Bird as his headdress and a smaller version as his pectoral. Early Maya kings at Kaminaljuyú also adopted the Principal Bird as an important symbol of power. Later lords rarely include the Principal Bird Deity in their regalia.

An Aztec **priest** with his tobacco gourd, *copal* incense pouch, and long-handled censer, Codex Mendoza, 16th c.

The **Principal Bird Deity** was one of the major gods of the Protoclassic Maya; in many scenes, such as the one here, the bird is represented holding a snake in its mouth, possibly a reference to storms and lightning; El Mirador Stela 2, Guatemala, Protoclassic Maya.

El Ave de Pico Ancho, the Zapotec form of the Maya **Principal Bird Deity**, is common in Protoclassic and Classic period Zapotec iconography; detail from a Classic Zapotec urn, Oaxaca.

During the Classic period, the Principal Bird often bears aspects of ITZAMNA. Although the relationship between the two gods is not clear, the Principal Bird may be the UAY, or spirit companion, of Itzamna.

On painted pottery, the Principal Bird Deity appears with the Hero Twins in scenes closely paralleling the much-later text of the *Popol Vuh*. The monster bird of the *Popol Vuh* also appears on two stelae from Izapa.

The Principal Bird Deity likewise appears in ancient Zapotec art, where it has been labeled *El Ave de Pico Ancho*, or "the bird with the broad beak." The Zapotec motif known as the *Fauces de Cielo*, or "jaws of heaven," is formed by two profile faces of this bird joined at the eye. Although the Zapotec entity is virtually identical in form to the Maya one it is not known whether the Principal Bird Deity played the same mythological role among the Zapotecs. *See also* VUCUB CAQUIX.

pulque An alcoholic beverage derived from the fermented sap of the MAGUEY (*Agave* sp.), pulque played an important role in public ceremonies and festivities. The peoples of Central Mexico frequently fortified the relatively mild pulque with certain roots to increase its potency.

Pulque was a vitamin-rich milky liquid, and was identified with mother's milk in Central Mexico. On the stone Aztec Bilimek Pulque Vessel, pulque is represented cascading into a pulque pot from the breasts of a fearsome EARTH goddess. The Aztecs clearly had an ambivalent attitude concerning pulque, for although a fertile and intoxicating fluid, it also caused drunkenness and social discord. According to Aztec legend, QUETZALCOATL slept with his sister while in a drunken stupor. Thus shamed, he left his capital of TOLLAN.

Pulque played a major ceremonial role among the ancient Mixtecs and Zapotecs of Oaxaca. On page 25 of the Mixtec Codex Vindobonensis, a series of 12 deities drink pulque from small cups. Among the neighboring Zapotecs, pulque appears in elite MARRIAGE scenes depicted on monuments dating from roughly AD 800 to 1000. The Aztecs considered the Huastec Maya of northern Veracruz to be great drinkers of pulque. Thus according to the Florentine Codex, the king of the Huastecs became so drunk with pulque that he cast off his loincloth. Because of this, the Huastecs moved in disgrace to the present region of Panuco. The ancient Maya of southeastern Mesoamerica probably also had pulque. In a number of Colonial Mayan dictionaries, forms of the term *ci* or *chi* are glossed as maguey and pulque. In Classic Maya vessel scenes of drinking, pots are frequently labeled with a glyph denoting the phonetic value *ci* or *chi*. Moreover, recent excavations have revealed that maguey was cultivated in Classic times at the site of Cerén, El Salvador. *See also* MAYAHUEL; PULQUE GODS.

pulque gods The first known personification of PULQUE in Mesoamerica appears at the Classic site of TEOTIHUACAN. Here a number of scenes depict a masked individual with white gouts of milky pulque. In one instance, the head of this figure is surrounded by the long pointed leaves, or *pencas*, of the MAGUEY plant. Among the Postclassic Mixtecs, the pulque deities appear to have been distinguished from the goddess of maguey: thus while maguey is represented by the goddess 11 Serpent, pulque is personified by goddesses 2 Flower and 3 Alligator. In Central Mexican iconography, the pulque gods are similarly distinguished from maguey: MAYAHUEL is the female divinity of maguey while the pulque gods are generally male. A noteworthy exception is the aged EARTH goddess upon the Bilimek Pulque Vessel, who has pulque squirting from her pendent breasts.

The concept of pulque gods was very highly developed among the Aztecs. Collectively known as the Centzon Totochtin, or "400 Rabbits," these beings took a great many forms and permutations. A number of pulque gods were buried at the base of an early phase of the Templo Mayor, on the HUITZILOPOCHTLI side of the TEMPLE, laid out like victims, possibly identifying the Centzon Totochtin as the Centzon Huitznahua, the 400 youths slain by Huitzilopochtli.

Many of these pulque gods are illustrated in the Colonial Aztec Codex Magliabechiano. Certain pulque gods reigned over particular regions: Tepoztecatl, for example, was the god of Tepoztlan, and the remains of his temple still survive above the contemporary town. The pulque gods were represented collectively by the deity Ome Tochtli, or 2 Rabbit. Another important pulque god, Patecatl, presided over the day Malinalli and the TRECENA 1 Ozomatli.

purification Much like the English adage of

"cleanliness is next to godliness," purification was a major concern in Mesoamerican ritual. The success of many ceremonies depended on physical and moral cleanliness. In many cases, there were restrictions on sexual behavior during important ceremonies, particularly for PRIESTS, who usually abstained from contact with women. But the concern for purity was by no means limited to ritual events; purification was also necessary to achieve a healthy and successful life. Misdeeds, frequently of a sexual nature, possessed an almost palpable form that could accrue like filth around the individual, the household, and even the entire community. For this reason, calendrically timed events ensured the purification and harmony of communities. Among the Late Postclassic Yucatec Maya, the new year was marked by the casting out of sweepings and old household utensils. The Aztecs of Tenochtitlan repeated this purification event on a massive scale: all household debris was removed during the New Fire ceremonies performed at the completion of a 52-year cycle (see CALENDAR; FIRE).

In Mesoamerica, moral impurity was considered much like contaminating dirt or dust. For this reason, brooms and sweeping were symbols of ceremonial purification. In the Central Mexican codices, grass brooms are often placed by CROSSROADS, popular places for depositing dangerous and contaminating impurities. WATER also symbolized purification, and washing or aspersing (sprinkling with water) were common ritual forms of cleansing. SWEATBATHS were widely used for spiritual as well as physical purification. Fire, an important component of the sweatbath, could also purify: the burning of sweet-smelling INCENSE was often used to cleanse and purify. Individuals frequently performed personal acts of purification, such as sexual abstention, fasting, penitential BLOODLETTING, and CONFESSION. See also TLAZOLTEOTL.

pyramid Mesoamerican pyramids are stable forms that resist destruction in a land prone to earthquakes. Generally rising as a four-sided form with stairs only on one side, a pyramid usually supports a TEMPLE on its broad, flat summit. Although often now considered mysterious, pyramids had quite specific religious functions.

Many pyramids were dedicated to particular cult deities. Sahagún lists over 70 deities

Pulque pouring from the breasts of an earth goddess, detail of Bilimek Pulque Vessel, Late Postclassic Aztec.

Pulque god, Codex Magliabechiano, 16th c. Aztec.

that had their own raised temples in the sacred precinct at Tenochtitlan, and among these were QUETZALCOATL, TEZCATLIPOCA, XIPE TOTEC, HUITZILOPOCHTLI, and TLALOC. Surviving illustrations of Aztec pyramids show that the iconography of the roofcombs revealed particular associations: Tlaloc's pyramid, for example, had a blue roofcomb with aquatic motifs. Dual pyramids, such as the Templo Mayor of Tenochtitlan, had a single great platform, two staircases, and individual shrines at the top, and were generally dedicated to two distinct cults.

For earlier Mesoamerican civilizations such specific associations are not known with assurance. At TEOTIHUACAN, the principal pyramids were said by the Aztecs to be dedicated to the SUN and MOON, and this may well be true. Because of its association with the long dormant, gurgling volcano which frames it, the Pyramid of the Moon at Teotihuacan was quite possibly dedicated to a WATER or fertility cult. At Monte Albán, little elucidating iconography survives to identify any pyramid other than the Danzantes, which, with its iconography of sacrificial victims and humiliation, may well have been dedicated to a cult of war.

Some Maya pyramids were dedicated to specific deity cults, for example, the Group of the Cross at Palenque, with its dedicatory links between the BIRTH of the PALENQUE TRIAD gods and the rulership of Chan Bahlum. More characteristically, though, Maya pyramids were dedicated to ancestor worship. When kings and other high-ranking nobles died, pyramids were raised over their TOMBS. Temple I at Tikal housed Ruler A and the Temple of Inscriptions at Palenque held the remains of Pacal: from the time these pyramids were completed, they embodied great kings and acted as the center of their worship.

Although most Maya pyramids held the tombs of ancestors, some were dedicated to other purposes. Radial pyramids, such as E-VII-sub at Uaxactún or the Castillo (Temple of Kukulcan) at Chichen Itzá, were places of celebration for the completion of periods of time. Pyramids with surrounding colonnades at Chichen Itzá, such as the Temple of the Warriors, may have been dedicated to rulership and warfare.

Pyramids often replicate MOUNTAINS, particularly sacred mountains. The dual pyramid dedicated to Huitzilopochtli and Tlaloc at Tenochtitlan symbolically recreates COATEPEC,

the hill of Huitzilopochtli's birth, while at the same time the offerings deposited in the two temples suggest that the temples were conceived of as one of the mountains dedicated to Tlaloc. The deposit of cremated ashes of noble predecessors demonstrates that such pyramids were also centers of ancestor worship for powerful lineages.

The earliest pyramid in Mexico, the earthen mound at La Venta from c. 800 BC, is roughly in the form a fluted cupcake and may well be an effigy of a volcano, although its unusual contours may simply be the result of natural erosion of a four-sided structure. Natural rises are used to elevate pyramids, such as the Temple of Inscriptions at Palenque, and in the rolling plain of the Petén, the great pyramids of Tikal appear like man-made mountains, cresting above the canopy of the tropical rain forest.

Quadripartite monster *see* BICEPHALIC MONSTER; PALENQUE TRIAD

quetzal Known as the *quetzalli* in Nahuatl and *kuk* in Maya, the resplendent trogon, *Pharomachrus mocinno*, was prized for its extraordinary feathers. The quetzal lives in cloud forest, that rare and vulnerable ecological niche of tropical rain forest between 3000 and 4000 feet (about 900 m and 1200 m) in altitude. Solitary creatures that are rarely glimpsed other than at DAWN or dusk, quetzals feed on the wing and often hover while eating fruits, bugs, tree frogs, or snails. Although both male and female of the species are brilliantly colored, with blue-green feathers on wings, tail, and crest, and scarlet ones on the breast, it is the iridescence and unusual length of the male tail feathers – often about a yard in length – that made the bird the most desired in all Mesoamerica.

Because of their role in elite and ritual costumes, quetzal feathers were an important element in Mesoamerican tribute. The famous headdress housed in Vienna that is often called Motecuhzoma's headdress (but which he probably never wore) includes 500 quetzal feathers. Hunters were forbidden to kill the birds; rather, they stunned them with a blowgun, removed the feathers, and set them free. The males are best spotted during the

nesting season: the birds nest in holes in tree
trunks and when the male sits on the eggs,
his long tail feathers trail out of the nest.

Although few Mexican or Maya ancient
cities were in quetzal habitat (the Maya city
of Chinkultik is an exception), the bird and
its distinctive crest and feathers were well
known throughout Mesoamerica. Bernal Diaz
reported seeing quetzals in Motecuhzoma II's
zoo. *Kuk* was included in the name of a
number of Maya kings, and *quetzal*, of course,
formed part of QUETZALCOATL. In Nahuatl
poetry, the quetzal feather was often mentioned metaphorically, and the idea of its
tearing or decay referred to the transience of
life on EARTH.

Quetzalcoatl One of the great gods of ancient
Mesoamerica, Quetzalcoatl is a miraculous
synthesis of SERPENT and bird. The Postclassic
Nahuatl name Quetzalcoatl derives from the
Nahuatl terms for the emerald plumed QUET-
ZAL (*Pharomachrus mocinno*) and the SERPENT,
or *coatl*. Thus the term could be glossed as
"quetzal serpent," although the serpent is
specifically a rattlesnake. The earliest known
representations of this avian serpent appear
among the Formative Olmecs. Monument 19
from La Venta portrays a rattlesnake with an
avian beak and feather crest. Next to this
snake, two quetzal birds flank a SKY BAND.
Although the language of the Olmecs is still
unknown, in Mayan languages the words for
snake and SKY are identical. Thus it is possible
that this sign is a reference to quetzal sky or
quetzal snake.

The earliest known appearance of the quetzal serpent in Central Mexico occurs at the
Temple of Quetzalcoatl at TEOTIHUACAN, dating
to the 3rd c. AD. Representations of plumed
serpents alternating with the mosaic headdress of the WAR SERPENT – a probable ancestor
of the XIUHCOATL fire serpent – cover this
remarkable structure. In the murals of Teotihuacan and the later site of Cacaxtla, Quetzalcoatl is rendered as a snake covered with
quetzal plumes. At both sites, this being
appears with both drops of RAIN and standing
WATER, suggesting that it was considered a
spirit or deity of water.

Modern Pueblo peoples of the American
Southwest identify a plumed serpent with
water. Like Quetzalcoatl, the Zuni Kolowisi
and the Hopi Palulukong plumed water serpents can bring abundance and fertility.

Although the feathered serpent appears at

(*Above*) Disguised Aztec
merchants obtaining
quetzal plumes from
Zinacantan, Chiapas,
Florentine Codex, Book 9.

(*Above*) **Quetzalcoatl** atop a
pyramid, Codex Telleriano-
Remensis, 16th c. Aztec.

(*Right*) **Quetzalcoatl** with
bicephalic serpents, cut conch
pectoral and hands in the form
of quetzal heads, detail of a
Late Classic *palma*, Veracruz.

such Classic sites as Teotihuacan, Xochicalco, and Cacaxtla, few human forms of this being occur during the Classic period. One noteworthy example appears on a stone PALMA from Late Classic Veracruz, where Quetzalcoatl is shown with human hands cleverly rendered as quetzal heads. Combined with the bicephalic serpents covering the body, these quetzal heads provide an explicit reference to Quetzalcoatl. An especially important detail is the sectioned conch whorl worn on the chest of the figure. This is identical to the cut conch "wind jewel," or *ehecailacacozcatl* of the Postclassic Quetzalcoatl. During the Late Postclassic period, Quetzalcoatl usually appears in human form, often with a conical cap, the WIND jewel, and other shell JEWELRY. A rare Maya form of Quetzalcoatl may be found on page 4a of the Dresden Codex.

In Late Postclassic Central Mexico, Quetzalcoatl often takes the form of the god of wind, Ehecatl-Quetzalcoatl. In this context, Quetzalcoatl appears as the life-giving aspect of wind. According to the Aztec Florentine Codex, Quetzalcoatl was the roadsweeper of the Tlaloque rain gods, that is, the wind that brings the rain clouds. Along with the conical hat and shell jewelry, Ehecatl-Quetzalcoatl typically wears a red buccal mask resembling a duck beak. Patron of the day Ehecatl and the TRECENA 1 Ocelotl, Ehecatl-Quetzalcoatl was the great culture hero, and plays an important role in Central Mexican CREATION ACCOUNTS. Among the Mixtecs of Oaxaca, this figure was known by the calendrical name 9 Wind.

In the ethnohistorical documents of 16th c. Mexico, the ancient deity known as Quetzalcoatl is confused with the historical figure Ce Acatl Topiltzin Quetzalcoatl, the king of legendary TOLLAN, now known to be the site of Tula. According to Aztec belief, Ce Acatl Topiltzin Quetzalcoatl departed TOLLAN for the red lands of the east, an event corroborated by Colonial documents from Yucatán which mention the coming of an individual named Kukulcan, the Yucatec term for quetzal serpent. In these accounts, Kukulcan is said to have come to Chichen Itzá, a site with striking similarities to Tula. At Chichen Itzá, depictions of a masked individual backed by a green-plumed feathered serpent may refer to the actual historical individual. However, the historical figure may have been apotheosized at DEATH as his namesake, thus further blurring the distinction between the man and the god.

Quetzalcoatl was closely identified with the site of Cholula which became the great PILGRIMAGE center for devotees of Quetzalcoatl during the Late Postclassic period. Frequently the patron of rulership, Quetzalcoatl was also considered to be a god of PRIESTS and MERCHANTS in Late Postclassic Central Mexico. *See also* CREATION ACCOUNTS; EHECATL; MIXTEC GODS; PULQUE; TEOTIHUACAN GODS.

R

rabbit Along with the DEER, the rabbit (*Sylbilagus* spp.) was one of the favored creatures of the hunt. For this reason, the Aztecs often identified rabbits with the hunter-gatherer Chichimecs and their patron hunting god, MIXCOATL. During the Aztec VEINTENA of Quecholli, dedicated to Mixcoatl, there was a ceremonial hunt during which deer, rabbits, and other animals were routed and killed on Zacatepetl MOUNTAIN. However, in ancient Mesoamerican religion, the rabbit is best known as a symbol of the MOON. Many peoples of the New World and Asia observe the pattern of a rabbit upon the face of the moon. Depictions of the lunar rabbit may be seen in Prehispanic Central Mexico, the Classic Maya area, and the ceramic Mimbres art of the American Southwest.

In Postclassic Central Mexico, the rabbit was also closely identified with the intoxicating drink PULQUE. This association is well documented in the day name Tochtli, meaning rabbit in Nahuatl. The patron of Tochtli was MAYAHUEL, the goddess of MAGUEY and by extension its principal product, pulque. Moreover, the many PULQUE GODS were known collectively as the *centzon totochtin*, meaning 400 rabbits, or by the calendrical name Ome Tochtli, or 2 Rabbit.

In Classic Maya art, the rabbit steals the broad hat and other regalia of God L. The significance of this mythological episode is now unknown.

rain To the farming peoples of ancient Mesoamerica, rain was of great importance. At Chalcatzingo, Morelos, explicit portrayals of rain occur as early as the Middle Formative period, where an Olmec-style rock carving shows rain falling from clouds above young growing MAIZE and a mist-filled zoomorphic CAVE. Furthermore, the gods of rain and

LIGHTNING are among the most continuously worshipped deities in ancient Mesoamerica, and TLALOC of Central Mexico, the Zapotec COCIJO, and the Maya CHAC can all be easily traced to the beginnings of the Postclassic period. In the Maya region, offerings continue to be made to Chac to this day.

Auguries for rain were of great importance. On page 28 of the Codex Borgia, five Tlaloque rain gods water maize fields with various types of rain. Beneficial rain is marked with flowery JADE signs, but the four other forms are depicted as destroyers of corn, specifically fiery rain (possibly drought), fungus rain, wind rain, and flint blade rain, the last probably a reference to cutting hail. The later pages of the Maya Dresden codex are filled with almanacs concerning the Chacs and rain. In the Colonial Yucatec Books of Chilam Balam, auguries describe specific types of rain; in the *Chilam Balam of Chumayel*, RABBIT sky rains, parched sky rains, woodpecker sky rains, vulture sky rains and DEER rains, are all set in relation to Katun 3 Ahau.

A **rabbit** holding the headdress and staff of God L, detail of a Late Classic Maya vase.

reptile eye The reptile eye sign is both an iconographic element and a day name. In both cases, its meaning is still unknown. At TEOTIHUACAN, the probable place of origin for this sign, the reptile eye appears primarily as an iconographic device. Commonly occurring within circular medallions at Teotihuacan, it tends to have a large curl placed against an eye-like element at the lower portion of the device. Because of this semicircular lower element, the sign has been widely interpreted as a reptile's eye. However, rather than referring primarily to an eye, the device may represent brilliance or FIRE. In Teotihuacan iconography, eyes are frequently used to depict shining or reflective surfaces, such as MIRRORS or WATER. In addition, the Teotihuacan sign is often accompanied by secondary devices denoting fire.

During the Late Classic period in highland Mexico, the reptile eye sign is widely used as one of the 20 day names of the 260-day CALENDAR. As a day name, it appears at such sites as Teotenango, Xochicalco, and Cacaxtla. At Xochicalco and Piedra Labrada, Veracruz, the day glyph is depicted with flaming fire elements. Although present at the Early Postclassic site of Tula, the reptile eye day glyph was no longer used during the Late Postclassic period. For this reason, the day sign cannot be readily correlated with

A **rabbit** in the moon, Florentine Codex, 16th c. Aztec.

The **reptile eye** glyph, detail from a Teotihuacan vessel, Early Classic period.

the known day glyphs of the contact period.

rubber Obtained from the latex sap of the rubber tree (*Castilla elastica*), rubber had a variety of uses in ancient Mesoamerica. To the Aztecs, rubber was known as *olli*, from which the Spanish word for rubber, *hule*, derives. The word *olli* clearly relates to the Nahuatl term *ollin*, or motion, probably because of the remarkable bouncing and elastic qualities of rubber. The best-known use of rubber was as the ball played in the Mesoamerican BALLGAME, known as *ollama* or *ullama* in Nahuatl. Recent excavations at the Olmec site of El Manatí have yielded the first known rubber balls in Mesoamerica. Dating roughly to the 9th c. BC, the balls are part of a rich assemblage of offerings placed in a SPRING. It is entirely appropriate that the first known rubber derives from the Olmecs, whose name (given to them by the Aztecs) can be translated as "the rubber people." The humid Olmec heartland of the southern Gulf Coast was a well-known rubber producing region.

In addition to its use in the Mesoamerican ballgame, rubber also served medicinal purposes. According to the Florentine Codex, the latex was drunk with chocolate to relieve stomach and intestinal upset. As a sap, rubber was also treated as an INCENSE much like *copal*. In the offerings recovered from the Sacred Cenote of Chichen Itzá, rubber was frequently mixed with *copal*. The rubber latex was often burned as a ball, in effigy form, or as drops sprinkled upon PAPER. Because of the thick cloud-like smoke, rubber was a favored offering to the RAIN gods.

sacrifice Mesoamerican GODS required sacrifice. According to the POPOL VUH of the Quiché Maya, the gods required praise from their subjects, whom they had made; when praise was not forthcoming, they destroyed them. Once the gods had created humans who did praise them, these people were given their own god BUNDLES, and the chief Quiché lineage received TOHIL, who demanded the sacrifice of HEARTS in exchange for his gift of FIRE. The tribal leaders offered precious metal, but Tohil insisted on costlier sacrifice: human flesh. Tohil then made further demands of the lineage heads: "It remains for you to give thanks, since you have yet to take care of bleeding your ears and passing a cord through your elbows. You must worship. This is your way of giving thanks before your god."

At the time of the Conquest, HUMAN SACRIFICE was seen as the fair exchange for the sacrifices that the gods had made to create the EARTH and humanity. The violence of human sacrifice was also part of the appeasement of the violence of creation itself. According to the version of the creation of the earth in the *Histoyre du méchique*, QUETZALCOATL and TEZCATLIPOCA took TLALTECUHTLI from the heavens, turned themselves into two SERPENTS, and then, each taking a hand and opposite foot of the goddess, squeezed her until she split in half. Of one half, they formed the SKY and of the other half, the earth. All the gods then descended to console her, "and they ordained that from her would spring all the fruit necessary for the life of man. And in order to do this, they made of her hair trees and flowers and grasses, of her skin many common and small flowers, of her eyes wells and fountains and little caverns, of her nose valleys and mountains, and of her shoulders mountains. And this goddess cried many times in the night desiring the hearts of men to eat. And she would not be quiet just with those that were given her, nor would she take fruit unless it was sprinkled with the blood of men." Humans lived in the debt of, and at the grace of, the gods: the ravaged body of Tlaltecuhtli provided the sustenance for humanity, and she howled at NIGHT unless offered human BLOOD.

Mesoamerican gods could see through insincerity. In the Aztec account of the creation of the fifth sun (*see* FIVE SUNS), the gods sought volunteers to become the SUN. Tecuciztecatl put himself forward, and then, more hesitantly, Nanahuatzin came forward when called to do so. As a preparatory sacrifice, the two fasted for four days and performed penance. According to Sahagun, "that with which [Tecuciztecatl] did penance was all costly. His fir branches [were] quetzal feathers, and his grass balls of gold; his maguey spines of green stone; the reddened, bloodied spines of coral. And his incense was very good incense. And [as for] Nanahuatzin, his fir branches were made only of green water rushes – green reeds bound in threes ... And his grass balls [were] only dried pine needles.

And his maguey spines were these same maguey spines. And the blood with which they were covered [was] his own blood. And [for] his incense, he used only the scabs from his sores ..." (FC: VII)

Nanahuatzin's spines to pierce the flesh, then, were red with his own blood, while Tecuciztecatl's were of a precious red coral. Even Nanahuatzin's incense was of his own flesh. The four days of penance completed, these two were to become gods by immolating themselves in the bonfire made by the gods. Four times Tecuciztecatl ran up to the fire but leapt back. Only when Nanahuatzin took his turn and hurled himself into the fire did Tecuciztecatl follow. Nanahuatzin rose as the sun. When Tecuciztecatl rose with equal brilliance, one of the gods darkened the face of Tecuciztecatl with a RABBIT, and he was made the lesser heavenly body, the MOON. In this story, the sincerity, generosity, and immediacy of sacrifice are the keys to Nanahuatzin's transformation.

Generally the most important forms of sacrifice were the most precious: human flesh and blood, whether drawn from one's own body or from a sacrificial victim. Such offerings could be made through anointment of sculptures of gods or through offerings in special vessels, or through their transformation into fire and smoke. AUTOSACRIFICE in particular was frequently collected on strips of bark PAPER and then set afire. In the resulting smoke, a supplicant would see the ancestor or god to whom the sacrifice was made. An offering of INCENSE or TOBACCO also generated copious smoke and often accompanied other sacrifices.

Other offerings were also important as sacrifices, and at times, may have preempted human blood. When Quetzalcoatl came to Tula, he supposedly commanded only a perfect devotion and the offering of serpents and BUTTERFLIES. In both Central Mexico and among the Maya, DOGS, quail, and turkeys were all regular offerings, as were foodstuffs. The offerings recovered from the Sacred Cenote at Chichen Itzá reveal the importance of precious metals and JADE as sacrificial offerings, and the abundant vessels offered there and in other places of sacrificial deposit, such as CAVES, dedication caches, and mountaintop shrines, surely held varied offerings, including balls of incense and foodstuffs.

The offering of dough images formed another means of sacrifice to the gods. Known as *tzoalli*, these dough images were made of

Sacrifice: Lady Xoc kneels before the ruler of Yaxchilán, Shield Jaguar, and performs a bloodletting ritual by passing a spiny chord through her tongue. Whereas ancient Maya men commonly performed bloodletting from the penis, the tongue appears to have been the favored organ for Maya women. Yaxchilán Lintel 24, Late Classic Maya.

Penitent priest in the act of self-**sacrifice**, Codex Borgia, p. 10, Late Postclassic period. In the Borgia Group of codices, the act of piercing the eye serves as a symbol of penance.

ground AMARANTH mixed with human blood and a sticky sweetener, often honey, to bind the mixture together. During celebrations for the VEINTENA of Panquetzaliztli, a large dough image of HUITZILOPOCHTLI was made over a wooden frame; during Tepeilhuitl, dough mountain effigies were made. Usually in conjunction with human sacrifice, celebrants ritually broke apart the *tzoalli* and ate them to commune with the gods. *See also* CREATION ACCOUNTS; CUAUHXICALLI.

Schellhas gods During the pioneering efforts of the late 19th c., researchers faced a complex and poorly understood array of supernatural beings in the three ancient Maya screenfolds known as the Dresden, Paris, and Madrid codices. Paul Schellhas, the first to identify systematically the various gods and accompanying name glyphs occurring in these Postclassic screenfolds, organized and labeled the various gods according to the Latin alphabet. Beginning with A, each isolated god was thus provided with a letter designation.

The Schellhas system of letter designation has proven to be of great use for several reasons. For one, the poorly understood identities of particular gods can be referred to by non-committal letters, rather than by a tenuous or uncertain meaning, such as WIND God, or EARTH God. Furthermore, letter designations avoid the use of wholly inappropriate Mayan terms. Although the MAIZE GOD, God E, is frequently referred to as Yum Kaax in modern literature, this term simply means "lord of the forest bush" and bears no direct relation to maize or even the corn field. In addition, the Yucatec Maya often called a particular god by a number of epithets, and it is frequently difficult to select which term is the most appropriate. Again, recent research indicates that the majority of Postclassic codical gods isolated by Schellhas also appear in the Classic period, and it is unwarranted to assume that the Yucatec deity terms recorded for the early Colonial period were also present during the Classic era. Aside from a few emendations and additions, the Schellhas god list continues to be widely used in Maya studies.

God A: The skeletal god of DEATH, God A is equivalent to MICTLANTECUHTLI of Central Mexico. On page 77 of the Madrid Codex, he is phonetically named Cizin, or "flatulent one," a common term for the devil in contemporary Yucatec.

God A': Although not isolated by Schellhas, God A' is a distinct death god who usually has a horizontal black band across the eyes and the Akbal sign of darkness upon his brow. This god is of considerable antiquity, appearing in Early Classic Maya art as well as in the Postclassic codices. God A' is a deity of violent SACRIFICE, such as decapitation.

God B: This deity is the Postclassic form of CHAC, one of the most continuously worshipped gods of ancient Mesoamerica. The Maya god of RAIN and LIGHTNING, Chac is represented on Stela 1 from Protoclassic Izapa. Maya epigraphy reveals that during both the Classic and Postclassic periods, this deity was actually named Chac.

God C: Although frequently and erroneously identified as the god of the north star, God C is actually a personification of the concept of sacredness. Thus during both the Classic and Postclassic periods, the portrait of this god provided the phonetic value of *ku* or *ch'u*, a pan-Mayan term signifying deity or sacredness.

God D: One of the great gods of the Maya pantheon, God D appears to be the Maya form of the aged creator god, much like TONACATECUHTLI of Central Mexico. During both the Classic and Postclassic periods, God D was referred to as ITZAMNA. He seems to be a god closely identified with esoteric priestly knowledge, such as DIVINATION and WRITING.

God E: The Maya god of MAIZE, the Postclassic God E usually has a human head that merges into a growing maize ear. During the Classic period, there were two related forms of the maize god. One of these, the Foliated Maize God, is essentially identical in form to the Postclassic God E. The other Classic form, the Tonsured Maize God, has a human head flattened by cranial deformation to resemble a mature maize ear. The Tonsured Maize God is the Classic prototype of HUN HUNAHPU, the father of the Quiché Hero Twins.

God F: Unfortunately, with this letter designation Schellhas conflated and confused three distinct gods. One of these was the aforementioned God A', whereas the other two were coined God Q and God R by J. Eric S. Thompson. Thus in contemporary usage, there is no specific deity correlating to God F.

God G: The SUN god of the Maya, God G commonly appears with the solar *kin* glyph upon his head or body. In the codices, he seems be named KINICH AHAU, or "sun-faced lord." During the Classic period, this being appears as the head coefficient of the numeral 4.

Gods H and CH: Under the letter H, Schellhas conflated two distinct gods. One of these is a poorly understood youthful male deity that may be a Maya version of the wind god. Although this being is still known as God H, the other figure has been termed God CH by G. Zimmermann. Erroneously called the "Chicchan God," God CH is the Postclassic codical form of the Classic Headband Twin with JAGUAR pelt markings. This being is the Prehispanic form of Xbalanque, one of the Hero Twins of the Quiché POPOL VUH.

Goddess I: Although Schellhas identified this goddess as an old woman, subsequent scholars have considered Goddess I to be a different being, a youthful and beautiful woman. Although this youthful goddess has often been identified as IXCHEL and the MOON goddess, there is no concrete evidence that she was either. In fact, Ixchel appears to have been the aged Goddess O, not Goddess I. In the codices, the lovely Goddess I is often coupled with various male gods, and it is likely that she is identified with human fertility and sensual love.

God K: During the Postclassic period, God K appears with a large upwardly turned snout. The Classic form of God K displays a similar upturned nose, although in this case the deity typically has a burning torch or CELT in his forehead and a smoking SERPENT foot. The Classic God K also occurs as the MANIKIN SCEPTER held by Chac and Maya rulers. It appears that God K was identified with lightning, FIRE, and dynastic descent. Epigraphic evidence indicates that God K was anciently known as Kauil, a deity name also appearing in early Colonial Yucatec texts.

God L: An aged and frequently black JAGUAR GOD, God L commonly wears an ornamented back cape and a large, broad-brimmed headdress topped by the MUAN OWL. An important god of the UNDERWORLD, God L was also a merchant god. Thus during the Classic period, God L commonly appears with a merchant bundle (*see* MERCHANTS). Recent excavations at the Late Classic site of Cacaxtla, Tlaxcala, have uncovered a mural depicting God L with a merchant bundle complete with feathers and other trading goods.

God M: One of the most striking gods of the Maya codices, God M is a black deity with a

The **Schellhas god** list published in 1904.

pendulous lower lip and long Pinocchio-like nose. This deity is a Maya form of Yacate-cuhtli, the long-nosed merchant god of Central Mexico. God M is primarily a Postclassic Maya god that appears to have gradually eclipsed the earlier Maya merchant deity, God L. The contact period name of this god was Ek Chuah, *ek* being the Mayan word for black.

God N: In the codices and Classic Maya art, the aged God N commonly appears wearing a TURTLE carapace or conch upon his back. During both the Classic and Postclassic periods, the name of this god was phonetically written as PAUAHTUN. Quadripartite in nature, God N seems to have had the weighty responsibility of supporting the SKY.

Goddess O: An aged and fearsome goddess, Goddess O usually has jaguar claws as hands and wears a serpent in her headdress. In the codices she is phonetically named Chac Chel. Goddess O appears to be an aged genetrix, much like the Aztec ILAMATECUHTLI-CIHUA-COATL.

God P: Although termed a frog god by Schellhas, God P may not be a distinct deity. Appearing only in the Madrid Codex, this being may simply be a version of God N.

scribal gods A number of Mesoamerican gods served as the patrons of WRITING and the arts. The Aztecs attributed all such lore generically to the Toltecs: "they were thinkers, for they originated the year count, the day count; they established the way in which the night, the day, would work; which sign was good, favorable; and which was evil, the day sign of wild beasts. All their discoveries formed the book for interpreting dreams." (FC: x) Those born during the TRECENA 1 Monkey were most likely to be artists and scribes. As patron of the *trecena* 1 Monkey, XOCHIPILLI may be the Central Mexican patron of scribes and WRITING.

For the Maya, scribal gods are both more explicit and more numerous. According to various sources, ITZAMNA invented writing, and he appears as a scribe on Classic Maya pots; occasionally he teaches other scribes and instructs them in their counting. A supernatural RABBIT scribe sits as if he were a stenographer and records a scene on a Maya pot. In the Madrid Codex, CHAC writes, paints, and spews a stream of "print-out," as Mayanists have termed numbered strips of paper that scribal gods occasionally bear. The most

commonly depicted patrons of writing and timekeeping, however, are the monkey scribes and artists of the POPOL VUH, Hun Batz and Hun Chuen (*see* MONKEY). They usually have a DEER ear over the human one, and hold an ink pot, pen, or CODEX; the face may be a monkey grotesque or that of a beautiful young human, and a strip of "print-out" may be attached to the body.

sea The sea was widely believed to be the primordial WATER upon which the EARTH floated. Since this water lay underneath the earth, subterranean and surface bodies of fresh water were also identified with the sea. In an early Classic mural from the Temple of Agriculture at TEOTIHUACAN, freshwater WATER LILIES float atop waves containing sea SHELLS. Marine shells from both the Gulf Coast and the Pacific abound in Teotihuacan representations. At the Teotihuacan apartment compound of Tetitla, a pair of murals illustrates divers collecting shells in netted bags.

The Classic Maya clearly identified the sea with fresh water and the watery UNDERWORLD. As at Teotihuacan, the water lily is identified with the primordial sea. The Mayan word for water lily, *nab*, can also denote the sea and other standing bodies of water. One head variant of the numeral 13, the WATER LILY SERPENT, typically appears with a bound water lily pad headdress. An elaborate stucco frieze at the Temple of the Seven Dolls at Dzibilchaltun depicts this water lily serpent with water signs and marine life; accompanying caches contained abundant remains of marine shell. It is quite possible that this being is a sea god.

The Aztec Templo Mayor contains one of the clearest identifications of the sea with fresh water and agricultural fertility. On the TLALOC side of the temple, corresponding to the watery mountain of fertility and sustenance, elaborate caches contained sea shells, coral, and even marine fish.

serpent In religious terms, serpents may have been the most important fauna of Mesoamerica. No single other type of creature receives such elaborate treatment in Sahagún's Florentine Codex, for example, in terms of either text or illustration. And although many powerful animals – JAGUARS and EAGLES, most notably – play an important role in iconography, snakes, perhaps because of their number and variety in the natural world, have the broadest and most varied roles in religion and religious symbolism: in states of ecstasy, lords dance a serpent DANCE; great descending rattlesnakes adorn and support buildings from Chichen Itzá to Tenochtitlan, and the Nahuatl word *coatl*, meaning serpent or twin, forms part of the names of primary deities such as MIXCOATL, QUETZAL-COATL, and COATLICUE.

Among the most important snakes in Mesoamerica are the boa constrictor, the fer-de-lance, the rattlesnake, and the bushmaster. The harmless boa constrictor (*Constrictor constrictor*), called *chicchan* by the Maya and *mazacoatl* by the Aztecs, made a prized costume element, as evidenced by the stuffed boa skins worn by Maya lords in the Bonampak murals. The fer-de-lance (*Bothrops atrox*), silently coils before striking, unlike its fellow pit viper, the rattlesnake (*Crotalus durissus*), which gives a warning with its twitching rattles. The deadly bushmaster of Central America (*Lechesis muta*) is second in size only to the Indian king cobra among the world's poisonous snakes and often reaches 10′ (3 m) in length.

The Aztecs made a large number of sculptures of rattlesnakes, many of them extremely naturalistic, and they are characteristically carved on all sides, including the underside. In both Central Mexican and Maya day counts, the fifth day is snake. Snakeskin, with its dramatic geometric patterning, is frequently emulated in textiles and architectural ornament. Explicit rattlesnakes are rare in Classic Maya art but occur with great frequency in the art of Chichen Itzá. Although serpents combine with other creatures to make many fantastic animals found in no zoological guide, the open snake mouth is the feature on which many deities, generally those with upturned snouts, are based. The forked tongue is a characteristic unique to serpents; it is not to be confused with the long, curling proboscis of the BUTTERFLY.

Two features of serpentine behavior were probably of paramount interest to Mesoamerican peoples: first, snakes swallow their prey whole, letting it decompose inside their bodies; and second, snakes shed their skins. The skins split along their backs, allowing the snake to slither out, leaving behind the old skin, and in the case of rattlesnakes, even the rattles. Both these features of snake behavior may have supported the pan-Mesoamerican notion that snakes were vehicles of rebirth

The monkey **scribal gods** painting a codex, detail from a Late Classic Maya vase.

Coral, shell, and other **sea** offerings deposited in a cache on the Tlaloc side of the Templo Mayor, Tenochtitlan, Late Postclassic Aztec.

and transformation, for great supernatural serpents frequently belch another creature from their mouths – a warrior, a human, a god, or a skeleton.

Three fundamental notions accompany the Mesoamerican serpent: one, that the serpent is WATER, the conduit of water, or the bearer of water; two, that its mouth opens to a CAVE; and three, that the serpent is the SKY. Among the Maya, linguistic support survives for the latter concept: the words snake and sky are homophones, generally *caan* or *chan*, depending on the language, and the same word is usually the number 4 as well. Many Mesoamerican deities, including serpent deities, are considered to exist as fours, or as four-in-one, often with separate color and directional associations.

Mesoamerican people believed in serpent deities from earliest times. The feathered serpent occurs from Olmec times on, and although it is rare among the Classic Maya, it is common at contemporary TEOTIHUACAN. At Postclassic Tula, Chichen Itzá, and Tenochtitlan, the feathered serpent was generally known as Quetzalcoatl, and until the Spanish Conquest, was generally configured as a rattlesnake with bright green parrot or QUETZAL feathers, rather than as a human. The feathered serpents rarely hold another creature in their mouths; when they do, it is often the human impersonator of Quetzalcoatl. In various Aztec accounts, Quetzalcoatl turns himself into a serpent and then back into an anthropomorphic god.

The feathered serpents at Teotihuacan and Cacaxtla have specific aquatic associations. On the Temple of Quetzalcoatl at Teotihuacan, feathered serpents with ruffed collars flow down the balustrades and form undulating friezes across the temple; marine SHELLS – conch, pecten, and spondylus – fill the interstices and great WAR SERPENT headdresses jut out from the frieze at regular intervals. In the murals at Cacaxtla, a lord in a bird suit stands on top of a brilliant green feathered serpent who flows down the side to the base of the painting, all the while atop freshwater aquatic life. The feathered serpents that function as columns (i.e. serpent columns) at Chichen Itzá, Tula, and other Postclassic cities may well indicate the channeling of water and life-giving forces from the sky to the EARTH.

Both TLALOC and CHAC carry snakes in their hands from time to time; these snakes are the LIGHTNING bolts they hurl from the MOUNTAINS where RAIN gods make their retreat. Although Europeans generally see lightning as jagged rather than undulating like a serpent, when lightning strikes sand it can form an undulating solid strand of glass, and Mesoamerican peoples may have been familiar with this phenomenon.

The serpent was the body for many specifically Maya gods and deified objects. The earliest versions of the CEREMONIAL BAR are floppy double-headed serpents from which emerge the heads of gods and ancestors; later examples are generally stiff stylized bars. Occasionally bearing iconography of the sky band, the ceremonial bar probably symbolized the sky itself. The ruler who held it thus held the sky.

With his upturned snout and serpent leg, GII of the PALENQUE TRIAD gods is based on the serpent. The serpent leg forms the staff to be held by rulers when GII is in the form of the MANIKIN SCEPTER. The only analogous feature of any Central Mexican god is the serpent foot that sometimes replaces one of TEZCATLIPOCA's feet.

In states of ecstasy and usually following BLOODLETTING, particularly as graphically depicted at Yaxchilán, Maya nobility conjure up the VISION SERPENT. This great undulating serpent rises from burning bloody PAPER, and from its mouth emerges an ancestor or, occasionally, a deity. The serpent itself, then, is probably what one sees in the clouds of smoke rising from the burning SACRIFICE, and cloud symbols may flank the vision serpent's body. The vision serpent can be the vehicle by which ancestors or deities make themselves manifest for humanity, and is probably the sky serpent commonly depicted at Chichen Itzá, particularly on the gold plates dredged from the Sacred Cenote.

A similar deified serpent, the XIUHCOATL, known as the fire serpent, but more literally turquoise snake, plays an important role in Aztec religious iconography. HUITZILOPOCHTLI brandished the Xiuhcoatl as his weapon when he was born, and the Xiuhcoatl frequently appears independently. On the Aztec Calendar Stone, however, two Xiuhcoatls carry the SUN on their backs, and from their mouths emerge what may be deified ancestors; the tied knots of paper on their bodies are the same bloodletting knots used a millennium before by the Maya. The snakes, then, are the vehicle for the movement of the sun, the bearers of ancestors, and carry references to bloodletting.

A COATEPANTLI, or snake wall, was constructed at many Postclassic cities to shield sacred buildings or precincts. The earliest known example is at Tula, where a frieze of rattlesnakes spews or devours human skeletons.

The main Central Mexican serpent gods at the time of the Spanish Conquest were Quetzalcoatl and Mixcoatl. They were both celestial serpents, Quetzalcoatl as the WIND, a sky serpent, and the bearer of bounty; Mixcoatl as the personification of the MILKY WAY. Coatlicue is characterized by her skirt of snakes, but she does not take the form of a serpent. CHICOMECOATL, 7 Snake, is a MAIZE GODDESS with a calendrical name; in one instance she is vividly represented by cobs of maize carved on a rattlesnake tail.

Dances with snakes or in imitation of serpentine movements played an important role in ancient rituals (*see* DANCE). Both Maya pots and carved monuments depict dances with snakes, and in at least one case, the text specifically reads that a Maya king "performed the snake dance." During the Aztec VEINTENA of Pachtontli, men, women, and children adorned in feathers linked hands and sang while performing the serpent dance. During Toxcatl, young seasoned warriors linked hands and moved in an undulating pattern, performing the serpent dance while young women simultaneously danced the popcorn dance, with careful supervision all the while that none of the women be seduced by the serpent dancers.

Aztec **serpent** sculptures. (*Top*) Turquoise mosaic pectoral of a double-headed rattlesnake. (*Above*) Stone carving of a coiled rattlesnake.

7 and 9 zoomorphic heads Two distinct heads often appear as a pair in Classic Maya iconography, and each bears a coefficient in bar and dot numeration, one of 7 and the other of 9. Both heads have long, upturned snouts based on the shape of a SERPENT head, but the lower jaw (and sometimes the entire head) is skeletal. The 7 head bears the glyphs *ek* (black), *nal* (ear of MAIZE), and *kan* (sometimes a reference to maize); the 9 head includes a rare glyph for 20 (*may*) and might refer to an obscure deity – Bolon Mayel – known in Conquest-era Yucatán.

The 7 and 9 zoomorphic heads may be carried in the hand, rest on CEREMONIAL BARS, or set floating in space. Incised obsidians may depict the heads, as may the exterior surfaces of cache vessels. The meaning of these heads

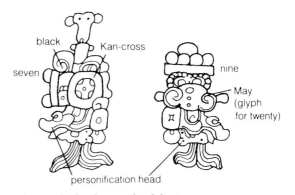

The **7 and 9 heads**, Temple of the Sun, Palenque, Late Classic Maya.

is not clear, but they might function as toponyms referring to supernatural places.

shaman In anthropological literature, there is frequently a distinction between the ceremonial roles of PRIEST and shaman. Whereas a priest tends to communicate with the divine through offerings and prayer, the shaman becomes an actual vehicle for the supernatural through ecstatic trance and spirit-possession. During ecstatic trances – often brought on by DANCE, HALLUCINOGENS, or deprivation – the shaman interacts directly with the spirit world. Whereas priests are part of an established religious bureaucracy, shamans tend to be more independent, with their power based upon personal charisma and expertise. Although the contrast between priest and shaman is a useful dichotomy, the distinction is not hard and fast. In actual practice, the roles of shaman and priest overlap considerably. Although priestly offices were common in the complex urban societies of Postclassic Mesoamerica, many priestly roles suggest an older substratum of shamanic belief and practice.

The term shaman is not native to Mesoamerica or even to the New World but rather derives from the Tungus language of Siberia. Nonetheless, many of the traits observed in Siberian shamanism, such as ecstatic trance, supernatural flight, and animal spirit companions, are also present in much of the New World, including Mesoamerica. Many features of Mesoamerican shamanism are of considerable antiquity, and were probably brought from Asia by the first Paleoindian inhabitants of the New World. The shamanic importance of animal transformation and animal spirits in Mesoamerica suggests remote hunter and gatherer origins from before the development of agriculture and food production.

Although shamanism was probably present in Mesoamerica well before the appearance of agriculture and settled village life, it can be first documented among the Formative Olmecs. Peter Furst has called attention to a fascinating theme in Olmec stone sculpture, a kneeling man that becomes a JAGUAR – what he terms transformation figures. Furst has suggested that these sculptures depict the shaman being transformed into his alter ego, the jaguar. Whereas the bear is frequently the creature of powerful shamans and curers in North America, below the Tropic of Can-

cer, the jaguar is the shamanic spirit companion *par excellence*. Among the Classic Maya, the glyph denoting a UAY, or spiritual alter ego, is a stylized human face half covered by a jaguar skin. The deity of shamans and sorcerers of Late Postclassic Central Mexico, TEZCATLIPOCA also appears to have had the jaguar as his spiritual co-essence. *See also* NAHUAL; TONAL; UAY.

shark Recently, Tom Jones has determined that the English word shark is borrowed from the Maya *xoc*, as introduced by English sailors who had encountered the creature in the Caribbean Sea. Because the bull or cub shark leaves the SEA and travels into fresh WATER, the creature was familiar not only to Mesoamericans who lived along the sea coast but probably also to those who lived well upriver, such as the Maya of Piedras Negras and Yaxchilán or the Olmecs of San Lorenzo.

A terrifying creature to humans, the shark was deified early on in Mesoamerican society. The Olmecs had a shark god, clearly marked by a shark tooth, and fossilized Great White Shark teeth have been found at Olmec sites. A shark may very well be the basis for the Maya JESTER GOD, very early versions of which have a defined shark tooth, and the shark tooth of GI of the PALENQUE TRIAD also indicates a relationship with the shark. The Aztecs cached shark teeth into the Templo Mayor along with other marine material.

shell Nobles in ancient Mexico and Guatemala imported sea shells to inland centers from both coasts through trade and tribute. At the time of the Conquest, the Aztecs demanded 1600 spondylus shells a year in tribute from coastal regions. The Aztecs deposited thousands of shells along with other marine and aquatic materials, including corals, snail shells, and skeletons of SEA creatures, in caches in the Templo Mayor. The conch shells included in Offering 48, a deposit of sacrificed children, referred to the aquatic nature of TLALOC, to whom the offering was dedicated. Giant stone effigies of conchs rested along the Tlaloc side of the Twin Pyramid. Abalone shells, which occur naturally no farther south than the coast of Baja California, made their way into Aztec caches, giving us some sense of the long-distance trade that the Aztecs managed.

At Tikal, archaeologists found spondylus shells of both Atlantic and Pacific species, and the pearls from such thorny oysters were worn as jewelry by the Maya elite. Many spondylus shells were scraped to reveal a bright red or orange concavity; when thus carved, the shells were sewn onto cloaks, worn as necklaces or worn at the waist. The MAIZE GOD, for example, often wears such a shell at the waist, as do many women who wear the costume, perhaps signifying female fertility. At Copán, an excavated cached spondylus shell still held traces of human BLOOD. Along with strings of dots, alternating cutaways and profiles of spondylus shells were used by the Maya to indicate water in their representations. Maya lords wore oliva shells as noisemaking tinklers at the waist. In Postclassic Maya hieroglyphic writing, a shell functions as the completion sign, probably indicating that shells were used in counting out sums.

Conch, spondylus, and pecten shells flank the undulating body of QUETZALCOATL on the Temple of Quetzalcoatl at TEOTIHUACAN. Since the variety and number of shells increased dramatically at Tikal after it came in contact with Teotihuacan, the Teotihuacanos may have dominated the shell trade during the Classic period. At Cacaxtla, paintings of shells, sometimes inhabited by creatures that never dwelt in such shells, form aquatic borders around regal lords. The Olmecs carved JADE into the shapes of clamshells and then strung these large disks into necklaces. During the Late Formative period West Mexican artists made clay figures of musicians playing conch shell trumpets, a practice well documented at the time of the Conquest. Some West Mexican nobles wore conch shells on their heads to signify high status.

Worn around the neck as a pendant or chest ornament, a cross-sectioned slice of conch shell is one of Quetzalcoatl's identifying characteristics. Dozens of such pieces of conch have been found, particularly in Veracruz. The Maya God N (see SCHELLHAS GODS) usually emerges from a shell, either a conch or a snail shell. The Central Mexican god Tepeyollotl, Heart of the Mountain, is often depicted with conch shells, which may be why the Templo Mayor, conceived to be a symbolic MOUNTAIN, held so many shells.

skullrack *see* TZOMPANTLI

sky Unlike the realms of the EARTH and UNDERWORLD, which could be penetrated by humans,

Olmec portrayal of a **shark**, San Lorenzo Monument 58, Early Formative period.

Youth fishing for marine **shells**, Tetitla, Teotihuacan, Classic period. Shells are widespread in the iconography of Teotihuacan.

Tonacatecuhtli in the highest realm of the **sky**, Omeyocan, the place of duality; Codex Vaticanus A, 16th c. Aztec.

the sky was a source of mystery, a supernatural realm entirely distinct from that of human beings. The concept of sacredness was often tied to the degree of proximity to the heavens. Thus sacred shrines and TEMPLES were frequently placed atop especially high promontories, such as MOUNTAINS and PYRAMIDS.

Since at least the Formative Olmec period, specific signs delineated the sky. In the art of Classic Mesoamerica, deities frequently emerge from the sky or heavens. Among the Zapotecs, the motif known as the "jaws of the sky" is based on the joined profiles of the entity known as *El Ave de Pico Ancho*, the Zapotec version of the PRINCIPAL BIRD DEITY. In Late Classic Zapotec art, figures descend from these celestial jaws. Ancestors and deities are frequently depicted in the upper portion of Classic Maya stelae, in the region corresponding to the sky.

In ancient Mesoamerica, the sky was believed to have distinct levels, often cited as 13, particularly among the Classic and Postclassic Maya. A sky sign with the coefficient of 13 frequently accompanies the MUAN OWL in Maya representations. The Colonial Aztec Vaticanus A manuscript provides us with a detailed account of the 13 levels of the sky, with the creator couple TONACATE-CUHTLI and Tonacacihuatl residing in the highest level also known as Omeyocan, "place of duality." *See also* SKY BANDS; SKYBEARERS.

sky bands In southern Mesoamerica, the sky was frequently rendered as a band marked with diagonal and vertical elements. The sky band first appears with the Formative Olmecs, and continues in the Maya region until the Spanish Conquest, a clear example of continuity from the Olmecs to the later Maya. One of the earliest known sky bands appears on Potrero Nuevo Monument 2, an Early Formative ALTAR-throne. Quite probably, this Olmec monument was considered as a celestial THRONE, much like the sky band thrones of the later Classic Maya. Stela 1 from the Middle Formative Olmec site of La Venta displays a sky band in its upper portion. The band contains the same inverted "U" elements which appear on the earlier Potrero Nuevo Monument, although here they are topped by a pair of outwardly leaning diagonal bands. The Alvarado Stela, a Protoclassic monument written in the script of the Tuxtla Statuette and La Mojarra Stela 1, contains a

sky band with the same outwardly sloping diagonal bars and inverted "U" elements as those that appear on Stela 1 at La Venta.

Carved some 500 years after La Venta Stela 1, the Alvarado Stela is roughly contemporaneous with Izapa, Kaminaljuyú and other Protoclassic sites of the Maya region. At Izapa, sky bands also appear with the pair of outwardly leaning diagonal bands, although here the lower inverted "U" elements are missing. Instead, the lower portion typically contains a central vertical tab flanked by a pair of outwardly curling elements. Classic Maya sky bands are usually represented by a segmented band. Within the regularly spaced segments are signs delineating the SUN, MOON, STARS, darkness, and other celestial phenomena. At times, the lower portion of the sky band may be marked with the belly scutes of the SERPENT. This probably derives from the fact that the Mayan words snake and sky are homonyms. The same punning of snake and sky may be seen in many instances of the Classic Maya CEREMONIAL BAR, which can appear as a bicephalic serpent with a sky band body. The segmented sky band continues in Maya art until the Late Postclassic, and may be seen in the murals of Tulum as well as in the Maya codices. *See also* SKY; SKYBEARERS.

skybearers According to Postclassic Central Mexican belief, particular gods had the role of sustaining the SKY. According to the *Historia de los mexicanos por sus pinturas*, the heavens were raised by the four sons of the creator couple along with four other gods. To assist in this effort, QUETZALCOATL and TEZCATLIPOCA transformed themselves into two great trees. In the Vaticanus B and Borgia codices, parallel passages illustrate four skybearers, each oriented to a specific world DIRECTION and YEARBEARER. In both codices the four gods, directions and yearbearer days run as follows: TLAHUIZCALPANTECUHTLI with the east and Acatl, XIUHTECUHTLI with the north and Tecpatl, EHECATL-QUETZALCOATL with the west and Calli, and finally, MICTLANTECUHTLI with the south and Tochtli. The Central Mexican skybearers were far from being entirely benevolent. According to Tezozomoc, the skybearers were TZITZIMIME, the fierce STAR demons of darkness that threatened to descend and destroy the world during ECLIPSES and the NIGHT vigil marking the end of the 52-year cycle.

The Mixtec form of Ehecatl-Quetzalcoatl, 9 Wind, was also regarded as a skybearer. Thus on page 47 of the Codex Vindobonensis, 9 Wind supports the sky. However, in this instance, the SEA filled with marine SHELLS is depicted lying above the sky. What particular cosmic event this scene refers to is still unknown.

The ancient Maya had highly developed concepts regarding the skybearers. According to Diego de Landa, the Postclassic Yucatec Maya had four skybearers known as the bacabs. As in Central Mexico, each of the four bacabs was associated with a particular yearbearer day as well as direction. Increasing evidence suggests that the bacabs are identical to the aged quadripartite deity known as PAUAHTUN. Although some have suggested that Pauahtun supported the EARTH rather than the heavens, there are explicit examples of Pauahtun supporting celestial THRONES rendered with a seat in the form of a SKY BAND or SERPENT.

In ancient Mesoamerica, the skybearers were widely identified with the office of rulership. Tezozomoc mentions an Aztec term for the skybearers, "sustainers of the cane mat," which refer to the woven cane MAT that symbolized the seat of kings. The concept of skybearers supporting celestial thrones extends even as far back as the Early Formative Olmec period. Two DWARVES support a sky band on Potrero Nuevo Monument 2. The role of skybearers probably related to the Mesoamerican concept of public office as an elevated burden or CARGO to be passed from one office-holder to another.

smiling figures Smiling faces characterize many small, solid figurines as well as larger, hollow-bodied ceramic sculptures from Classic period Veracruz, and they have come to be known by this distinctive facial expression. Traditionally, such figures have been associated with the site of Remojadas, from which large numbers are reputed to come, but they have also been found at many other sites, including Nopiloa and Dicha Tuerta. Little is known about them archaeologically, but most come from Late Classic burials.

Smiling figures usually engage in pleasurable activities: many DANCE, others make MUSIC; still others hold out their arms in the orant or praying position. Most wear costumes of richly patterned cotton CLOTH.

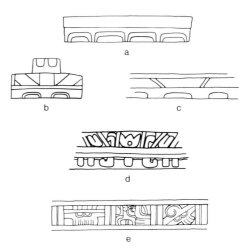

Examples of **sky bands**. *a*, Potrero Nuevo Monument 2, Early Formative Olmec. *b*, La Venta Stela 1, Middle Formative Olmec. *c*, Alvarado Stela, Late Formative. *d*, Izapa Stela 12, Protoclassic Maya. *e*, Sarcophagus lid of Pacal, Palenque, Late Classic Maya.

Two **skybearer** dwarves supporting the sky, Potrero Nuevo Monument 2, Early Formative Olmec.

Smiling figure with monkey tail on headdress, Late Classic Veracruz.

Lively MONKEYS join humans, and a few other animals, such as DEER and RABBITS, are associated with the smiling figurines, though few of the animals smile. Some of the animals turn on wheeled feet, and such toys are the only known examples of the wheel in ancient Mesoamerica.

The sheer delight of these figurines long made them a focus for collectors who sought an alternative to the iconographically dense art of the Maya or Aztecs. Some investigators have suggested that the smiling figures may be in states of ecstatic transformation or perhaps drug-induced trances; however, it is more likely that many of the smiling figures represent performers.

snake *see* SERPENT

spider In ancient Mesoamerica, spiders were commonly identified with female goddesses and the EARTH. At TEOTIHUACAN, an important goddess identified by a fanged nose bar appears with spiders. It seems that this entity was considered to be a spider earth goddess, much like Spider Grandmother of the contemporary American Southwest. IXCHEL, the aged Postclassic Yucatec goddess of DIVINATION, midwifery and CURING, was also identified with the spider. Divination stones referred to as spiders played an important part in the ceremonies dedicated to Ixchel during the month of Zip. In the Colonial *Ritual of the Bacabs*, Ixchel is mentioned prominently in a prayer concerning venomous spiders.

In Classic and Postclassic Maya iconography, the old Pauahtun SKYBEARER can appear wearing a spider's web. This correlated with Central Mexican conceptions of the skybearers, who threatened to descend to the earth in the form of demonic TZITZIMIME. Because of their headlong descent, the *tzitzimime* were compared to the spider descending by its thread. On an Aztec stone copy of the *xiuhmolpilli* year BUNDLE, a *tzitzimitl* star demon is depicted descending from the starry sky as a spider, complete with a web placed at the tip of the abdomen. Although by no means a natural trait, the curious pair of antennae is found with other Aztec spider representations.

springs From the Formative period to contemporary times, springs have been places of religious worship. In many religions, springs are regarded as the source of WATER, including even the RAIN clouds. The recently discovered Olmec site of El Manatí, Veracruz, has yielded offerings of carved wood, JADE, RUBBER, and other goods that were placed in the crystal clear waters of a natural spring. The many CENOTES and water-filled CAVES of Yucatán can be considered as forms of springs, and have been places of worship for millennia. For rain ceremonies, the contemporary Yucatec Maya still collect the sacred "virgin water," or *zuhuy ha*, from isolated subterranean pools. During the Tarascan festival of Sicuindiro, the BLOOD from two sacrificed slaves was poured into two hot springs dedicated to Cueravaperi, the mother of the gods, and vapors rising from these hot springs brought the rain clouds. Among the Aztecs of Central Mexico, springs were frequently identified with the *ahuehuetl*, or "water drum" tree (*Taxodium mucronatum*). According to Fray Diego Durán, these great trees always grew at springs. Still today, pilgrims collect spring water from the roots of a great *ahuehuetl* tree on the outskirts of Chalma.

stars and planets Ancient skywatchers keenly observed the movements of all heavenly bodies in Mesoamerica that could be observed with the naked eye, including the SUN, MOON, Mercury, VENUS, Mars, Jupiter, and Saturn. They observed the MILKY WAY, perceived groups of stars to form constellations, and Maya astronomers – like their counterparts in the ancient Old World – may have recognized a zodiac along the ecliptic. Glass, and, by extension, lenses, were never invented in the New World; astronomers used pairs of crossed sticks and observed features on the horizon through the notches. The anomalous round building called the Caracol ("snail") at Chichen Itzá probably functioned as an observatory, its narrow windows at the uppermost story guiding observations of the movements of Venus. One Mixtec city was known as Ndisi nuu (now Tlaxiaco), or "clearly seen"; it was the site of a prominent observatory. Mound J, one of the oldest buildings at Monte Albán, probably acted as an observatory for the rising of the star Capella, which may have been understood to guide the sun on the day of the first zenith passage at the latitude of Monte Albán. (Zenith passage occurs when the sun passes directly overhead, a phenomenon which occurs twice annually at the Equator, on the equinoxes, once annually at the Tropic of Cancer and the Tropic of Capricorn, at their respective summer solstices, and twice annually in between, ranging according to latitude.)

Although neither the first nor last astronomers in Mesoamerica, the Classic Maya became the most skillful skywatchers we know of. Recent investigations into Classic texts have revealed a high level of sophistication in Maya observations, particularly of planets. The Maya viewed the Milky Way as the road to Xibalba and saw in the seasonal movements of constellations along the ecliptic their fundamental CREATION story. They timed events of war and SACRIFICE to coincide with the movements of Venus and Jupiter. According to his inscriptions, Chan Bahlum, a late 7th c. Palenque king, not only lived by the movements of Jupiter, but the major events of his life dovetailed with the movements of that planet deep in the past.

stela Mesoamerican peoples erected prismatic stone slabs called stelas or stelae to celebrate the reigns and ritual passages of the ruling elite, and usually of the supreme ruler himself. The impetus to erect stelae first came in the Middle Formative among the Olmec, when other efforts to record history also developed. Stelae at La Venta depict historical rulers attired in regalia that symbolized and reinforced the office and power of an early king.

The custom of erecting stelae subsequently took root in the Isthmian region during the Late Formative and Protoclassic, part of the constellation of traditions characterizing eastern Mesoamerica. At Chiapa de Corzo and Tres Zapotes, Mesoamericans began to inscribe long count dates (CALENDAR) on stelae, fixing them in time. At Abaj Takalik and Izapa, altars were paired with stelae, a pattern that continued at most Classic Maya sites. Izapa stelae feature mythical scenes and generally lack dates; the Abaj Takalik monuments depict rulers in Early Classic Maya poses, and the human figures are accompanied by dates and long texts.

Classic Maya stelae bear texts that reveal some ancient perceptions of the monuments. Following the katun ending date, the glyphs on Stela 9 at Lamanai can be read *dzapah te tun* or "the setting of the stone tree," as recently deciphered by David Stuart and Nikolai Grube. These stelae, then, were individual

(*Right*) **Spider** descending from the starry sky as a *tzitzimitl*; note the web at the tip of its abdomen. Detail from a stone copy of a year bundle, Late Postclassic Aztec.

(*Below*) **Stela** D, Quiriguá, Late Classic Maya.

trees; as time passed and dozens of monuments clustered on a central plaza they formed what Linda Schele and David Freidel have called a "forest of kings."

The Classic builders of Cholula in Central Mexico adopted the custom of erecting stelae and ALTARS, although no figurative carved imagery survives; at Xochicalco and Tula, before AD 900, ruling lords adopted the practice of erecting stelae with their portraits. In Yucatán, stelae were erected throughout the Postclassic, but the imagery shifted, the dynastic ruler giving way to representations of the setting of the supernatural lords of the katun, reflecting a changed society more concerned with the collective community than the single all-powerful ruler.

Stirling Hypothesis In 1955, the noted Olmec archaeologist Matthew Stirling suggested that many "WERE-JAGUAR" figures appearing in Olmec art derived from an ancient Olmec origin myth in which a JAGUAR copulated with woman. Thus the Olmecs may have considered themselves as "people of the jaguar," a union of jaguar and human. However attractive or intriguing this concept may be, there is little material evidence for such a creation myth among the Olmecs.

Stirling based his theory on two badly damaged Early Formative Olmec monuments from the region of San Lorenzo, Tenochtitlan Monument 1 and Potrero Nuevo Monument 3. According to Stirling, Tenochtitlan Monument 1 represents an anthropomorphized jaguar copulating with a supine woman. However, on close inspection, it can be seen that the upper figure displays no jaguar attributes but is fully human. Moreover, the figure appears to be in ballplayer garb, much like the contemporaneous ballplayer figurines from Las Bocas. Although it is possible that the lower figure is a woman, the ankles are crossed and bound. Instead of representing a mythical copulation, this monument may depict the SACRIFICE of a CAPTIVE in association with the BALLGAME. The other sculpture, Potrero Nuevo Monument 3, clearly displays a rampant jaguar over a human. Unfortunately, the monument is too damaged to provide any indication of the gender of either figure or to determine whether copulation is intended. It is quite possible that the monument depicts a jaguar attacking a hapless human. In theme, the sculpture is notably similar to an Olmec-style relief from the Middle Formative site of Chalcatzingo, Morelos, depicting two jaguars climbing atop and attacking human victims, with no indication of any sexual act. See also JAGUAR GODS; OLMEC GODS.

sun Although the sun was undoubtedly worshipped from remote antiquity, the first clear representation of it appears among the Protoclassic Maya in the form of the four-petaled element commonly referred to as the *kin* sign, *kin* being the Mayan term for "sun" or "day." At the Protoclassic site of Cerros, Belize, the *kin* sign appears on the cheek of a blunt-snouted mask, probably to identify this entity as the solar JAGUAR. The *kin* glyph continued to serve as the Maya solar sign until the Spanish Conquest.

In highland Mexico, solar signs cannot be readily identified until the Terminal Classic period. In this case, the sun is indicated by a disk with radiating triangular elements representing solar rays. One of the earliest occurrences of the rayed solar disk appears on the abdomen of a standing jaguar on the Terminal Classic Nevado de Toluca Stela. The rayed solar disk is especially common in the art and writing of Late Postclassic Central Mexico. In many instances, the disk bears the date 4 Ollin, the name of the present sun created at TEOTIHUACAN.

In ancient Mesoamerica, solar gods tend to be youthful males, consistent with the vigor and power of the rising sun. In the Maya region, the sun was also identified with the most powerful creature of the forest, the JAGUAR. The Nevado de Toluca Stela suggests that the jaguar was also considered a solar creature in Central Mexico during the Terminal Classic period. In the Aztec myth of the creation of the fifth and present sun, both the jaguar and the EAGLE were born out of the solar pyre at Teotihuacan. In Late Postclassic Central Mexico, the sun was personified by the youthful TONATIUH, who tends to be portrayed with red skin, golden hair and a prominent rayed solar disk. See also CREATION ACCOUNTS; DAWN; FIVE SUNS; SCHELLHAS GODS.

sun god see KINICH AHAU

sweatbath The sweatbath served the ancient Mesoamerican community as a place of CURING, rest, and maintenance of health. Traditional native communities today often construct sweathouses and continue to use them as places of healing. In Mesoamerica, rituals of healing were religious rites, in which appropriate gods were invoked. The process of retreating to the sweatbath offered seclusion from society, in itself a purifying act, but the treatment by moist heat was seen as a pinnacle of PURIFICATION. When a person emerged from a sweatbath, that person was as if "reborn" from the womb of the EARTH.

Ancient Mesoamerican sweatbaths have been found near the ritual precincts of cities, as well as in domestic sectors. At the Maya city of Piedras Negras, at least eight elaborate, masonry sweatbaths served the core of the city, some directly adjacent to the king's palace and TEMPLES. Unlike simpler contemporary examples, each of these Piedras Negras sweatbaths was encompassed within a larger structure, perhaps a place of additional ritual, but also, surely, for the mundane needs of privacy and dressing. To increase the temperature within the bath itself, the steam chamber was a small, low, vaulted room within the larger structure, with room for two benches and a firebox. As in most ancient sweatbaths, the Piedras Negras examples included fireboxes lined with broken pottery for repeated heatings. WATER would have been thrown on this firebox to release clouds of steam into the chamber, and a channel led outside to carry away the water.

The recognition of sweatbaths at Piedras Negras led to further such identifications in other Mesoamerican cities, but at no other place have they been found in such abundance or on such a scale. As the ethnohistoric record makes clear, however, the sweatbath was a standard feature of Mesoamerican cities, and many of the modern, ethnographically documented examples are small and would be more difficult to recognize in an archaeological context.

Known in Central Mexico as the *temascal*, the sweatbath was dedicated to the god TEZCATLIPOCA, according to the gloss of the Codex Magliabechiano, but the picture of the same manuscript shows the frontal face of the goddess TLAZOLTEOTL over the doorway, and most sweatbaths were probably dedicated to her or to TOCI, a related female goddess. Tlazolteotl was the Aztec goddess known by the epithet "eater of filth," and she was the one to whom CONFESSIONS were made, so she is the most appropriate deity for the dedication of the purifying sweatbath.

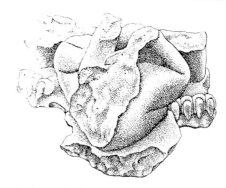

Stirling Hypothesis: Potrero Nuevo Monument 3, a sculpture purportedly showing the copulation between a jaguar and a woman, Early Formative Olmec.

Tonatiuh, the Central Mexican **sun** god, Codex Borgia, p. 23, Late Postclassic period.

The *temascal*, or **sweatbath**, Codex Magliabechiano, 16th c. Aztec.

The Codex Magliabechiano also informs us that "when any sick person went to the bath house, [that sick person] offered incense, which they call *copal*, to the idol and covered the body in black in veneration of the idol they call Tezcatepocatl [Tezcatlipoca], who is one of their major gods."

The sweatbath was especially important to midwives and their patients, pregnant or recently delivered women, for whom Tlazolteotl was also patroness. Sahagún cites the formal speech of a midwife, who addresses herself to the parents of a pregnant woman: he specifies Yoalticitl as the mother of the gods, with dominion over sweatbaths, known in some cases as *xochicalli*, or flower houses. Once inside the sweatbath, attending PRIESTS and priestesses (or the supplicants themselves) struck the bodies of the supplicants with various grasses, herbs, and sticks, but pregnant women were sometimes excused from such rigors. After a BIRTH, a woman repaired to the sweatbath for massage by the midwife, probably to help shrink the uterus. Recently delivered highland Maya women and their midwives in Guatemala still frequent the sweatbath.

T

Tamoanchan In Late Postclassic Central Mexico, Tamoanchan was considered a mythical and paradisiacal place of origin. At Tamoanchan, the gods fashioned the present race of humans from penitential BLOOD and ground human bones stolen from the UNDERWORLD (*see* CREATION ACCOUNTS). The Florentine Codex relates that PULQUE was also discovered at Tamoanchan. In the Florentine Codex account, Tamoanchan appears to be placed in the general Gulf Coast region of the Huastec Maya. In fact, the term Tamoanchan is a Mayan word, and could be paraphrased as "place of the misty sky," an appropriate description of the humid Gulf Coast.

In the Central Mexican codices, Tamoanchan is represented by a flowering cleft tree emitting blood. The significance of this toponym is uncertain, although it may relate to the Aztec origin legend of MAYAHUEL, in which TZITZIMIME demons tore apart the tree containing Mayahuel and QUETZALCOATL. In the codices, Tamoanchan commonly appears in illustrations for the TRECENA of 1 Calli. The goddess presiding over this *trecena* is ITZPAPALOTL, one of the principal *tzitzimime* demons.

Tecpatl *see* CALENDAR; FLINT; YEARBEARERS

temalacatl According to various accounts, in order to humiliate the defeated Tepanecs and to reenact their demise in a public forum, Motecuhzoma I invented a sort of gladiatorial SACRIFICE subsequently used to celebrate generations of Aztec victories. In these contests, an Aztec warrior tied a hapless prisoner to a sacrificial stone called the *temalacatl* and forced him to engage in combat until DEATH or defeat. These round stones were perforated by a hole at the center, and a rope ran from the CAPTIVE's leg and through the stone, handicapping the victim. In such gladiatorial combat, the victorious warrior usually donned the attire of a JAGUAR knight while the defeated one wore a feather costume; the victorious warrior armed himself with a *macuahuitl*, or club with embedded OBSIDIAN blades disguised by feathers while the defeated one wielded a club with only feathers. Despite such odds, the captive tied to the *temalacatl* occasionally succeeded at beating off his enemy, and perhaps several of them in succession. In some cases, the captive immediately achieved his liberty; in others he was nonetheless sacrificed. In still others, the valiant captive then faced a left-handed warrior, who was almost certain to slash and defeat his enemy.

Large crowds observed such gladiatorial combat within the sacred precinct of Tenochtitlan, adjacent to the TZOMPANTLI or skullrack, and near XIPE TOTEC's temple Yopico, whence the defeated captives were removed for sacrifice by HEART extrusion.

temple The Spanish word "templo" and English "temple" have come to refer to what the Aztecs called a *teocalli*, or literally god house, and generally indicate a place of worship. Throughout Mesoamerica, PRIESTS and supplicants repaired to temples to communicate with their GODS, to make offerings to the gods in exchange for divine intervention, and to make themselves one with the gods. In their sacred precinct, the Aztecs constructed 78 different structures, most of them temples dedicated to particular gods or cults. (Other buildings included priestly residences and schools.) The *Hueteocalli* (Great Temple or Templo Mayor) referred specifically to the great dual PYRAMID dedicated to HUITZILOPOCHTLI and TLALOC. The Templo Mayor precinct, like those throughout Mesoamerica, was the heart of the city, and it was roughly at the center of Tenochtitlan. To show conquest, the Aztecs depicted the falling, burning temple of their foes; they often hauled the sculptures of enemy gods back to Tenochtitlan, where they kept them in a separate temple of captive deities. Individual temples within the precinct may have been thought to encapsulate the mountain homes of various deities. Research at the Tlaloc side of the dual pyramid has shown that the Aztecs created the manmade embodiment of Tlaloc's mountain through offerings and deposits.

Among Mesoamerican cities known only archaeologically, the word temple has often been applied without specific knowledge of any religious practices that may have taken place there. What have been termed Maya "temples" and "palaces," for example, seem to grade into one another, and in recent years, archaeologists have preferred to give structures neutral numbers rather than nicknames like "Temple of the Giant Jaguar." Nevertheless, Maya temples can generally be identified: a temple has a high platform topped by small chambers; access is limited and is usually by a single staircase, although a few examples have other arrangements. Most such temples were constructed at the death of a king to enshrine his TOMB, as for example, at Tikal, although occasionally, as at Palenque, such a temple was constructed beforehand, leaving access to a sarcophagal chamber. Although clearly associated with specific deities, these Maya temples primarily commemorated royal ancestors and the gods with whom the kings were united in death. *See also* MOUNTAINS.

Templo Mayor *see* TEMPLE

Teotihuacan The Aztecs believed in serial creations, that the SUN and the population of the EARTH had been generated five times, with the current sun and humankind having been made in the fifth and last creation. This final creation of the fifth sun took place at Teotihuacan. Although a real place, where high civilization in Central Mexico thrived in the first millennium AD, it was also a place

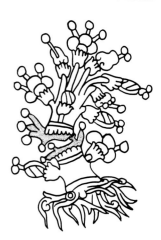

The Aztec sign for **Tamoanchan**, Codex Vaticanus A, 16th c.

(*Below*) Gladiatorial sacrifice: an Aztec warrior attacks a prisoner tethered to the **temalacatl**, or sacrificial stone, Codex Magliabechiano, 16th c. Aztec.

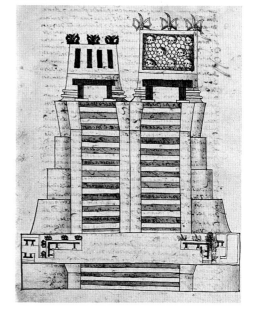

(*Below*) The double **temple**: the Templo Mayor at Tenochtitlan, with its two shrines dedicated to Tlaloc and Huitzilopochtli; Codex Ixtlilxochitl, 16th c. Aztec.

of the imagination, the locus of religious generation, where the Aztecs believed the gods had conjoined to create the fifth sun. According to some accounts, Teotihuacan was also the birthplace of the gods themselves. According to the Florentine Codex, during the long peregrination from AZTLAN that eventually led to Tenochtitlan, the Aztecs went from TAMOANCHAN to Teotihuacan, where they made offerings and built PYRAMIDS over the burials of rulers, thus giving them life everlasting.

In 1971, archaeologists found the opening to a CAVE under the Pyramid of the Sun at Teotihuacan. Archaeologists found that this cave extended far beneath the Pyramid of the Sun, with small ancillary chambers radiating from the central passageway. Ceramic evidence indicates that the cave was in use from Protoclassic until Aztec times, and it may well have been an ancient site of worship hallowed by the construction of the great pyramid above it. The Aztecs claimed to have come from a place called CHICOMOZTOC, or Seven Caves: perhaps this sacred place lay under the ground at Teotihuacan. In any case, the Aztecs certainly considered the abandoned city sacred: they carried out rituals there, brought pieces of its sculpture and painting back to Tenochtitlan, and made it the site of royal PILGRIMAGE. See also CREATION ACCOUNTS; FIVE SUNS.

Teotihuacan gods In the complex and poorly known iconography of Teotihuacan, a series of characters that appear to portray distinct deities occur time and time again. Although certain of these gods can be readily identified as ancestral forms of deities known among the Late Postclassic Aztecs, other figures appear to be unique to Teotihuacan. In contrast to the Classic Maya, female divinities have a prominent position. In this respect, Teotihuacan is similar to Late Postclassic Central Mexican religion, which also has a great many goddesses.

Tlaloc: Until recently, many distinct Teotihuacan gods were confused with Tlaloc, the Central Mexican god of RAIN and LIGHTNING. Although Alfonso Caso and Laurette Séjourné both made progress in determining Tlaloc's characteristics, Esther Pasztory first successfully isolated and defined the Teotihuacan Tlaloc from other gods. At Teotihuacan, Tlaloc typically appears with goggle eyes and a prominent upper lip containing a set of

large teeth. Pasztory identified two forms of Tlaloc. One form, Tlaloc A, displays a prominent set of JAGUAR canines; quite frequently, a WATER LILY is placed in the mouth. The other aspect, Tlaloc B, has a set of identically sized conical teeth and a prominent bifurcated tongue, much like the pendulous tongue of COCIJO, the Zapotec god of rain and lightning.

Great Goddess: Although this term is widely used in recent literature, it probably subsumes a number of distinct goddesses. One female entity currently placed in this category wears a fanged nose bar. Due to the appearance of SPIDERS with this figure, she has been termed the Teotihuacan Spider Woman. Yet another Teotihuacan goddess appears with a stepped facial patterning around the mouth and lower cheeks. The significance of this goddess is still unknown.

Netted Jaguar: This poorly understood entity is a JAGUAR covered with interlaced cords, resembling a net. This net patterning is also found on Teotihuacan representations of MIRRORS, and it is possible that like the Postclassic TEZCATLIPOCA, the Netted Jaguar represents a personification of the stone mirror.

Huehueteotl: The aged FIRE god of the hearth, Huehueteotl commonly appears at Teotihuacan in the form of a stone effigy censer. Ceramic Huehueteotl censers can be traced back to Protoclassic Cuicuilco, and there are still earlier Middle Formative examples from Tlaxcala.

Quetzalcoatl: One of the earliest appearances of the plumed SERPENT at Teotihuacan occurs upon the original facade of the Temple of Quetzalcoatl. Here feathered serpents pass through feathered mirror rims and swim in a SHELL-filled SEA. At Teotihuacan, the feathered serpent is usually depicted with symbols of rain and standing WATER. The Teotihuacan plumed serpent is typically represented with a canine-like muzzle and a rattlesnake body covered with the green plumes of the QUETZAL. Although anthropomorphic forms of Quetzalcoatl are virtually unknown at Teotihuacan, the plumed serpent can appear upon a woven MAT, a widespread symbol of rulership in Mesoamerica. It is thus possible that as in Postclassic Meosamerica, the Teotihuacan Quetzalcoatl was identified with an important office of rulership.

War Serpent: On the Temple of Quetzalcoatl, the projecting feathered serpent heads alternate with another being frequently misidenti-

ified as Tlaloc. Rather than Tlaloc, this form
depicts a mosaic headdress in the form of a
serpent head. Although probably originating
at Teotihuacan, this serpent being is also
commonly found in Classic Maya art. Either
as a headdress or as a complete serpent, it
occurs in the context of war. Frequently
appearing with smoke or flames, the WAR
SERPENT is probably an ancestral form of the
XIUHCOATL fire serpent of Postclassic Central
Mexico.

Pulque God: Since the time of the Spanish
Conquest, Teotihuacan has been a famed
center for the production of PULQUE. Although
rare, there are examples of a Teotihuacan
pulque deity. This being appears with a
simple mask, possibly of the paper-like MAGUEY
skin. Underneath the mask, in the region of
the eyes and mouth, it may be seen that the
face is blackened. In one instance, the head
is surrounded by pointed maguey leaves
spouting white pulque. In another example,
the pulque spills from the mouth of the god.

Fat God: A common deity of Classic
Mesoamerica, the FAT GOD often appears on
mold-made Teotihuacan figurines. Invari-
ably, the heavily lidded eyes are shut, as if
the figure is dead. In a number of instances,
the Fat God appears with the sign of the
REPTILE EYE or a FLOWER upon his forehead.
See also FAT GOD; HUEHUETEOTL; PULQUE GODS;
QUETZALCOATL; TLALOC.

termination rituals When Mesoamerican
peoples came to the end of their use of a
building or even of a period of time, they
engaged in what anthropologists have called
termination rituals, in which they ritually
"killed" certain material manifestations. The
defacing of Olmec sculpture may be among
the earliest indications of this practice. An
army of workers ground down the colossal
heads and table-top ALTARS, leaving systematic
round pits; in some cases the effort of destruction equaled that of the original creation.
They then buried the defaced monuments
with layers of specially prepared sand and
stone. The Olmecs may have thought that
through such efforts they neutralized the
power inherent in such representational
sculpture. Wherever the oversized masks of
the Protoclassic period are uncovered,
whether at El Mirador or Cerros, there is
evidence that the faces suffered active damage before being covered. During the reign
of Ruler A, Tikal Maya lords smashed the

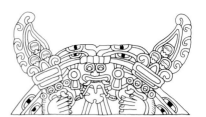

Tlaloc A

Netted Jaguar

Great Goddess

Pulque God

Classic period **Teotihuacan gods**.

base of Stela 31, cached the upper part of the monument in Structure 33 together with burnt offerings, and then built a new super-structure. The subject of Stela 31, King Stormy Sky, may well be the interred subject of the tomb below Structure 33, and this destruction of his stela was quite possibly part of a termination ritual in which the last vestige of his presence was removed from view. At Lagartero, Susanna Ekholm un-covered middens of smashed ceremonial pottery free of any household debris, and despite the presence of vast quantities of figurine bodies, no matching heads were found. In all likelihood, such a deposit was made as a termination ritual, perhaps to mark the completion of a period of time.

Before the drilling of the last New Fire (*see* FIRE) before the Spanish Conquest, the Aztecs carried out a termination ritual: all the old pots were smashed, all fires extinguished, and pregnant women hidden from view in order to start the mundane world anew once the New Fire was kindled in the open chest of a slain CAPTIVE.

textiles *see* CLOTH; COTTON

Tezcatlipoca One of the more fascinating gods of Postclassic Central Mexico, Tezcatli-poca was the ominipotent god of rulers, sorcerers and warriors. The name of this being signifies "smoking mirror," and is a term rich in symbolic meaning. For one, MIRRORS of OBSIDIAN and other stone were widely used in necromancy and sorcery in ancient Mesoamerica. However, in the early 17th c. chants recorded by Ruíz de Alarcón, the surface of the EARTH itself is referred to as a smoking mirror. In the myth of the FIVE SUNS, Tezcatlipoca presided over the SUN of earth. According to the *Historia de los mex-icanos por sus pinturas*, a battle raged between the god of this first sun, the sun of earth, and QUETZALCOATL, the god of the following sun of WATER. Thus the first sun ended when Quetzalcoatl struck Tezcatlipoca down, turning him into a JAGUAR. In turn, Tezcatlipoca terminated the sun of WIND by knocking over Quetzalcoatl. This cosmic bat-tle between Tezcatlipoca and Quetzalcoatl is also reflected in the legends of TOLLAN, in which Tezcatlipoca eventually bests Quetzal-coatl through a series of ruses. The conflict between Tezcatlipoca and Quetzalcoatl could be viewed in terms of a dualistic opposition

of earth and wind, or by extension, matter and spirit. However, Tezcatlipoca encompasses more than the earth. According to the Floren-tine Codex, Tezcatlipoca is omnipresent, and causes discord and conflict everywhere he passes. Nonetheless, the same passage also describes him as a creator as well as destroyer, a bringer of fortune as well as disaster. In Central Mexican beliefs, Tezcatlipoca not only battles against but also assists Quetzal-coatl in the creation of the world and its inhabitants. More than anything, Tezcatli-poca appears to be the embodiment of change through conflict.

In view of his omnipresent and volatile nature, it is not surprising that Tezcatlipoca was referred to by many epithets. Doris Heyden has counted an astonishing 360 dis-tinct phrases for him in Book 6 of the Floren-tine Codex. Among them are *titlacuahuan*, "he whose slaves we are," *yaotl*, "the enemy," *youalli ehecatl*, "night wind," and *ilhuicahua tlalticpaque*, "possessor of the sky and earth."

The first clear representations of Tezcatli-poca appear on Toltec-style stone sculptures from Early Postclassic Chichen Itzá. Like later images of this being, he displays a smoking mirror upon his head and a SERPENT foot. During the Late Postclassic period, Tez-catlipoca may appear with a serpent foot, although in this case the serpent usually appears emerging from the smoking mirror that typically replaces his foot. The mirror or serpent foot probably alludes to the creation myth in which Tezcatlipoca loses his foot while battling with the earth monster. Aside from the smoking obsidian mirrors marking his head and foot, the Late Postclassic Tezcat-lipoca tends to have broad alternating bands of yellow and black across the face. The nocturnal JAGUAR, the most powerful animal of Mesoamerica, was the animal counterpart of Tezcatlipoca. Tepeyollotl, or Heart of the Mountain, was a jaguar aspect of Tezcatli-poca. It is thus entirely fitting that Tezcatli-poca was patron of the TRECENA 1 Ocelotl. An omnipotent god of fate and punitive justice, he often merges into ITZTLACOLIUHQUI-IXQUI-MILLI, the blindfolded god of stone and casti-gation. In this composite form, Tezcatlipoca appears as the black god of the north, and patron of the day Acatl.

Michael Coe first noted a series of striking correspondences between Tezcatlipoca and the ancient Maya deity commonly known as

God K (*see* SCHELLHAS GODS). Like Tezcatlipoca, God K has a serpent foot and usually displays a smoking mirror on his head. In addition, both Tezcatlipoca and God K are closely tied into the supreme office of rulership. Nonetheless, despite these direct and important parallels, these gods are not entirely equivalent. Whereas the jaguar constitutes the faunal counterpart of Tezcatlipoca, God K clearly has serpentine characteristics. In addition, the lightning and agricultural component of God K is not readily evident in the attributes of Tezcatlipoca. *See also* CREATION ACCOUNTS.

throne Mesoamerican lords ruled from elevated seats of power, or what we call thrones, from around 1200 BC until the transfer of power to the Spanish conquerors. The so-called "table-top altars" of the Olmecs are probably the oldest permanent thrones that survive in Mesoamerica, and they are among the largest ever made. A huge stone from Kaminaljuyú depicts some of the early Maya of the Guatemala highlands presiding from small thrones during the Protoclassic. CAPTIVES kneel before the enthroned rulers, each of whom bears what may be a name glyph in his headdress, and the sequence may record a series of rulers or a genealogical chart.

During the Late Classic, wedge-legged thrones predominated in the western Maya region, particularly at Palenque, Yaxchilán, and Piedras Negras, where artists carved thrones with elaborate reliefs. The richly ornamented throne, installed by Pacal in House E of the Palenque Palace in the 7th c., was replaced by a larger version in an extension of the Palace at the beginning of the 8th c. Both sculpture and painting indicate that Maya thrones were often painted, particularly in bright red and green; ruling lords draped them with jaguar pelts and reclined against jaguar-covered cushions. According to the Florentine Codex, rulers sat on several different types of pelts, including puma, JAGUAR, wolf, coyote, and various cured leathers with painted designs.

The Aztec Temple Stone, long called the Monument of Sacred War, has been recognized as the official throne commissioned by Motecuhzoma II to commemorate the New Fire ceremony of 1507. A flight of stairs leads up to the seat of the throne, inscribed with the image of TLALTECUHTLI, the Aztec EARTH

The smoking mirror of **Tezcatlipoca**, Aztec stone sculpture, Late Postclassic period.

(*Below*) **Tezcatlipoca** with the twenty *trecena* periods, Codex Fejérváry-Mayer, Late Postclassic period.

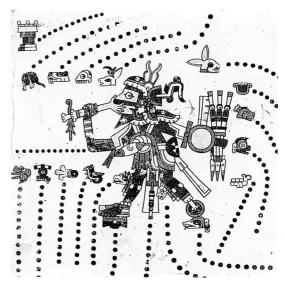

(*Below*) The Aztec Temple Stone, in fact the **throne** of Motecuhzoma II, 16th c.

monster; what would be a temple chamber forms the backrest, and it features the rayed diadem of the SUN. When the throne was occupied by the TLATOANI, or ruler, his role in sustaining the earth and SUN in their proper places was explicit.

Gods, too, reigned from thrones, and among the Maya, the hierarchy among certain deities is particularly notable. ITZAMNA, for example, often receives the appeals of other gods. In one striking example, God L (*see* SCHELLHAS GODS), who often presides from a throne himself, appears humbly before God G, the sun god, after losing his ritual attire to a RABBIT. Although Mixtec lords often sit or squat on MATS to symbolize their authority, Mixtec gods and oracles may offer counsel from elevated seats. Aztec figurines often take the form of small TEMPLES that are probably thrones for the gods seated on them. In the 260-day *tonalamatls* (*see* CALENDAR) of Late Postclassic Central Mexican manuscripts, enthroned gods reign over individual TRECENAS, and iconographic details of the thrones themselves often reveal aspects of the divination.

Tlahuizcalpantecuhtli In Central Mexico, the god of the morning STAR was known as Tlahuizcalpantecuhtli, meaning Lord of the Dawn. Tlahuizcalpantecuhtli represented an especially fierce and dangerous aspect of VENUS. According to Mesoamerican belief, the rays of the morning star at heliacal rising could inflict great damage upon particular classes of people as well as on MAIZE and WATER. In the Borgia, Cospi, and Vaticanus B codices, Venus tables predict the days and victims of the heliacal appearance of the morning star. In these pages and other scenes, Tlahuizcalpantecuhtli hurls his baleful rays in the form of *atl-atl* darts (*see* WEAPONRY). In the *Leyenda de los soles,* Tlahuizcalpantecuhtli hurls a dart at the newly created SUN at TEOTIHUACAN. In response, the sun god transfixes Tlahuizcalpantecuhtli, transforming him into ITZTLACOLIUHQUI-IXQUIMILLI, the god of coldness, stone, and castigation.

The first clear representations of Tlahuizcalpantecuhtli appear during the Early Postclassic period. The Toltec-style rock painting at Ixtapantongo bears an eroded but identifiable representation of the skull-faced Tlahuizcalpantecuhtli with a plumed SERPENT marked with star signs. At Ixtapantongo and Chichen Itzá, the Early Postclassic Tlahuizcalpante-

cuhtli is clearly identified with the plumed serpent, or QUETZALCOATL. The Colonial *Anales de Cuauhtitlan* states that after being burned upon the funeral pyre, Quetzalcoatl was reborn as Tlahuizcalpantecuhtli. The god of the morning star was also closely identified with the star god MIXCOATL, and in a number of instances appears with the facial markings of Mixcoatl, a field of black surrounded by white spots denoting stars. However, the typical star markings of Tlahuizcalpantecuhtli are five white spots upon the nose, brow, cheeks, and chin. Tlahuizcalpantecuhtli appears as one of the four SKYBEARERS, in this case the skybearer corresponding to the eastern YEARBEARER Acatl.

Tlaloc The Central Mexican god of RAIN and LIGHTNING, Tlaloc first appears on ceramic vases from Tlapacoya that date to the 1st c. BC and portray Tlaloc with serpentine lightning bolts. Tlaloc is one of the most common deities at TEOTIHUACAN and often appears with lightning, MAIZE, and WATER. Like Postclassic examples, the Teotihuacan Tlaloc typically has goggled eyes and large, jaguar teeth. In contrast to the Maya CHAC, Tlaloc is clearly part JAGUAR, and it is possible that the rumblings of thunder were compared to the bellows of the jaguar.

In Postclassic Mexico, Tlaloc was believed to reside in mountain CAVES. These caves were considered to be miraculous treasure houses filled with wealth and prosperity. To the Aztecs, Tlaloc was known as "the provider," and depending on the rains, could be either generous or miserly. One of the dual TEMPLES upon the Templo Mayor of Tenochtitlan was dedicated to Tlaloc, and this side of the PYRAMID was apparently considered as his MOUNTAIN abode. Excavations in the foundations of this temple have revealed rich offerings, many of which are related to water and the SEA. Near Tenochtitlan, there was a special mountain temple dedicated to Tlaloc. Located on the peak of Mount Tlaloc, some 13,500′ (*c.* 4100 m) above sea level, it housed a shrine containing stone images of Mount Tlaloc and other neighboring hills and mountains.

Patron of the day Mazatl and the TRECENA of 1 Quiahuitl, Tlaloc also presided over the third sun or world, 4 Quiahuitl, the sun of rain destroyed by a fiery deluge.

Tlaloc and his consort CHALCHIUHTLICUE governed the Tlaloque, literally the "Tlalocs," who were recognized to be the multiple spirits of mountains and powerful weather phenomena. *See also* COCIJO; FIVE SUNS; LIGHTNING AND THUNDER; MOUNTAINS; RAIN; TEOTIHUACAN GODS.

Tlalocan Nahuatl-speaking Central Mexicans at the time of the Conquest called the fourth level of the heavens or upper world Tlalocan, meaning the place of TLALOC. Because it was in the heavens, Tlalocan is often thought of as Tlaloc's paradise. According to the Vaticanus A codex, those who drown or die from other aspects of WATER, such as floods and the striking of LIGHTNING, go directly to Tlalocan, as do the deformed – DWARVES, cripples, and so forth – that are the special charges of Tlaloc. The Florentine Codex notes that Tlalocan is verdant, a place of endless spring, abounding in green and yellow plants: MAIZE, chilis, squash, AMARANTH, tomatoes, beans, and marigolds. Tlaloc's TEMPLE was also known as the Tlalocan.

Although the Classic period painting at Tepantitla has been called the Tlalocan, the watery land of abundance that it depicts is probably not an illustration of this later concept.

Tlaltecuhtli Tlaltecuhtli literally means "earth lord," but most Aztec representations clearly depict this creature as female, and despite the male gender of the name, some sources call Tlaltecuhtli a goddess. Usually in a *hocker*, or birth-giving squat, with head flung backwards and her mouth of FLINT blades open, Tlaltecuhtli menaces humanity and demands constant appeasement. Tlaltecuhtli's image is usually carved on the bottom of Aztec sculptures, where it makes contact with the EARTH. This image on the base of monuments may merge with aspects of TLALOC and MICTLANTECUHTLI. On the Stone of Tizoc, Tlaltecuhtli is configured by the open-mouthed frontal face and markings of CAIMAN skin, the surface of the earth.

According to the *Histoyre du méchique*, QUETZALCOATL and TEZCATLIPOCA carried Tlaltecuhtli down from the heavens and turned themselves into great SERPENTS. One grasped the right hand and left foot and the other took the left hand and right foot; they squeezed Tlaltecuhtli until they had rent her body asunder. After they had taken one half away to the SKY, other gods descended to the earth to console her, and from the remaining,

The Central Mexican god of the morning star, **Tlahuizcalpantecuhtli**, Codex Telleriano-Remensis, 16th c. Aztec. In this scene, Tlahuizcalpantecuhtli is named 1 Reed, the calendrical name of Quetzalcoatl.

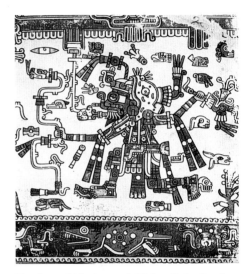

The Central Mexican god, **Tlaloc**, Codex Laud, p. 2, Late Postclassic period.

The earth monster **Tlaltecuhtli**, Aztec sculpture, Late Postclassic period.

violated half of her body they formed the surface of the earth, making of her hair "trees and flowers and grasses, of her skin ... flowers, of her eyes wells and fountains and little caverns, of her nose valleys and mountains, and of her shoulders mountains. And this goddess cried many times in the night desiring the hearts of men to eat. And she would not be quiet just with ... fruit unless it was sprinkled with the blood of men."

Midwives exhorted Tlaltecuhtli to come to their aid when an infant warrior threatened to kill the mother during a difficult labor. Along with preparations for war, prayers to Tezcatlipoca often invoked Tlaltecuhtli as the SUN.

Although represented in the sculpture of Mayapan, Tlaltecuhtli cannot be located in Classic Maya art, and her origins remain obscure.

tlatoani With their rise to power in the Valley of Mexico in the 15th c., the Aztecs replaced their traditional tribal administrative arrangement of four lineage heads with the position of *tlatoani*, a ruler who was in turn advised by a four-man council, including the CIHUACOATL. Literally meaning "he who speaks" in Nahuatl, the *tlatoani* was the supreme Aztec ruler in political affairs, and sometimes in religious ones as well. Although in theory a new *tlatoani* could be selected or elected by the council from one of hundreds of male nobles, in practice the new ruler was always brother, son, or grandson of a previous *tlatoani*. For example, at the time of the Conquest, the *tlatoani* Motecuhzoma II, known also as Motecuhzoma Xocoyotzin, was the grandson of Motecuhzoma I, the longest reigning Aztec ruler. The Aztecs treated the *tlatoani* as a divine being, and the public rarely saw their sovereign. Perhaps because a divine being did not reveal mundane bodily functions, the *tlatoani* ate in solitude, a carpet protected his feet from touching the soil of the EARTH wherever he walked, and other humans did not touch him in public, a taboo violated when the Spaniard Cortés reached out to embrace Motecuhzoma at their first meeting. *See also* ACCESSION.

Tlazolteotl As a Central Mexican goddess of purification, Tlazolteotl was also identified with filth, or *tlazolli*. In Nahuatl, the term *tlazolli* can refer to both vices and DISEASES. As the goddess of *tlazolli*, Tlazolteotl was a

goddess of PURIFICATION and CURING, particularly of diseases caused by sexual misdeeds or excess. According to Fray Diego Durán, penitent individuals would perform CONFESSION and BLOODLETTING in front of an image of Tlazolteotl. As an indication of her cleansing role, she is commonly depicted with a grass broom. In the codices, she can be readily identified by a black zone around her mouth and spools of COTTON in her headdress. She appears to derive from the Gulf Coast and may have originally been a Huastec goddess. Tlazolteotl is patron of the day Ocelotl and the TRECENA 1 Ollin.

toad Amphibians of the genus *Bufo*, toads played an important and early role in the religious symbolism of ancient Mesoamerica. Depictions of toads first appear in Formative Olmec art, and it is likely that many of the "WERE-JAGUAR" figures are actually toads. One species, *Bufo marinus*, a giant toad that produces a powerful HALLUCINOGEN known as bufotenine through glands at the back of the head, was of special importance. Stela 6 from the Protoclassic site of Izapa portrays a seated toad with the pitted paratoid gland prominently displayed. The scrolls swirling from this area probably refer to bufotenine exuded from the gland. At Izapa, Kaminaljuyú, and other Protoclassic Maya sites, toads commonly appear in the form of massive ALTARS. These toad-altars are usually placed in front of STELAE, and constitute an early component of the Maya stela-altar complex.

Among the Classic Maya, the toad serves as the zoomorphic form of the 20-day *uinal* period of the Long Count. Quite probably, this derives from the fact that toads, like people, possess 20 digits. Thus in Yucatec Mayan, whereas the name for the 20-day period is *uinal*, the term for person is *uinic*. In recently discovered Early Classic stucco reliefs from Balamkú, Campeche, there are full-figure toads with upwardly facing heads. Seated lords are positioned in their mouths, as if the toads were metaphorically giving BIRTH to the kings. In Classic Maya art, there is a clear iconographic overlap between toads and JAGUARS, as if toads were considered the great predators of their diminutive world. Thus for example, a three-spotted circular element probably referring to the parotoid gland of the toad can substitute for a jaguar ear in representations of the patron god of Pax. In the Maya-style murals from the Red

Temple at Cacaxtla, a toad displays the black-spotted yellow coloration of the jaguar.

tobacco Tobacco (*Nicotiana* sp.), one of the most important ritual plants of ancient Mesoamerica, was consumed in two principal ways, either chewed with powdered lime or smoked. In many regions of Mesoamerica, dried tobacco was ground and mixed with lime to increase the stimulating effects of nicotine. The discovery of lime-filled pits in the center of Tierras Largas phase public buildings at San Jose Mogoté, Oaxaca, suggests that the practice of chewing tobacco with lime may have been present during the Early Formative period. During the Postclassic period, bottle gourds filled with tobacco and lime served as insignia for PRIESTS. The tobacco was chewed to relieve fatigue during long vigils and other ceremonies and possibly to induce visions as well. The Huichol, Tzeltal Maya, and other contemporary peoples of Mesoamerica continue to carry ground tobacco in bottle gourd containers.

Among the ancient Maya, cigars seem to have been the preferred means of consuming tobacco. In fact, Pierre Ventur has noted that our word cigar derives from the highland Mayan *sikar*, signifying cigar or tobacco. Classic and Postclassic Maya art contains abundant scenes of actual people and gods smoking cigars. One deity in particular, the aged God L (*see* SCHELLHAS GODS), is commonly shown smoking a large cigar. Among the Postclassic Tarascans of Michoacán, tobacco was usually smoked in long-stemmed ceramic pipes. Elbow-shaped pipes seem to have been the preferred means of smoking tobacco over much of Postclassic West Mexico.

According to Mendieta, the Aztecs considered tobacco to be the embodiment of CIHUACOATL, an aspect of ILAMATECUHTLI, the great goddess of the MILKY WAY. In the early 17th c. treatise of Ruíz de Alarcón, tobacco was said to have been born of the Star-Skirted One, that is, the Milky Way.

Tochtli *see* CALENDAR; MAYAHUEL; RABBIT; YEAR-BEARERS

Toci A form of the aged genetrix, Toci, Our Grandmother, was a major Aztec goddess. Among her other epithets were Teteo Innan, or Mother of the Gods, and Tlalli Iyollo, meaning Heart of the Earth. An EARTH goddess, Toci was a patroness of midwives and

MOTECUHZOMA I 1440–1469   MOTECUHZOMA II 1502–1520

The Aztec king or **tlatoani**, Motecuhzoma I (Motecuhzoma Ihuilcamina), with his grandson Motecuhzoma II (Motecuhzoma Xocoyotzin), Codex Mendoza, 16th c.

The goddess **Tlazolteotl**, detail from a Huastec conch shell pectoral, Postclassic Veracruz.

Seated **toad**, Izapa Stela 6, Protoclassic Maya. The curls emanating from its shoulder probably refer to poisons exuded from the parotoid glands of particular toad species.

Tobacco: God L smoking a cigar, detail from a Late Classic Maya vase.

curers, and was closely identified with the *temascal*, or SWEATBATH. According to Sahagún, Toci was also termed Temazcalteci, or Grandmother of the Sweatbaths. She was clearly related to TLAZOLTEOTL, and frequently displayed the same black facial markings and COTTON spool headdress. The major festival of Toci was the harvest rite performed during the VEINTENA of Ochpaniztli.

Along with being a goddess of the earth and CURING, Toci was identified with war, and was also called the Woman of Discord. According to Aztec legend, while serving as mercenaries for the Culhua, the Aztecs received a daughter of the ruler of Culhuacan. Although the ruler intended his daughter to marry an important Aztec, HUITZILOPOCHTLI instructed that the maiden be sacrificed and flayed to become Toci. Enraged by this brutal act, the ruler of Culhuacan banished the Aztecs. Forced onto Lake Texcoco, they discovered and founded their capital of Tenochtitlan.

Tohil Patron deity of the Quiché at the time of the Spanish Conquest, Tohil is a principal god named in the POPOL VUH and guides the lineages at the beginning of their peregrinations. He is the deity who demands BLOOD offerings from his people, and so they sacrifice to him both their own blood and the blood of CAPTIVES of war. In the *Popol Vuh*, Tohil insists on the right to suckle from his people, meaning to drink not milk from the breast, but blood: to be suckled by Tohil is to have one's HEART ripped out. The Quiché established his principal TEMPLE at Utatlan, their capital, and brought offerings to him on the day *Toh*, one of the 20 days and corresponding to the Yucatec day Muluc. Tohil means OBSIDIAN, is cognate with Tahil in other Mayan languages, and probably can be identified with the Classic God K (*see* SCHELLHAS GODS).

Tollan The Aztecs and most other Central Mexican peoples believed that there had once been a more glorious era, when the Toltecs had reigned at Tollan, or Tula, as it is also called. But the name Tollan can also simply mean "place of rushes" and, as such, was the term applied to any great city. At the time of the Conquest, Tenochtitlan itself was a Tollan, and the archaeological sites of both TEOTIHUACAN and Tula, Hidalgo, were Tollans. All across Mesoamerica, from the Chichimecs to the Maya, noble lineages claimed descent

and legitimacy from Tollan and the Toltecs. Who were the Toltecs, and where exactly was Tollan?

According to the Aztecs, these Toltecs were held to be the inventors of all artistry, from WRITING to goldworking to medicine, and the very word "toltec" meant artist or craftsman. They lived in unparalleled majesty, reigned over by QUETZALCOATL, who dwelt in a palace of four buildings oriented to the four DIRECTIONS, one ornamented with sheets of GOLD, another with JADE and TURQUOISE, another of SHELLS and silver, and a last one embedded with red shells and precious stones. In this Tollan there was abundance; the QUETZAL flew and the blue cotinga dazzled. The Florentine Codex places Tollan along the banks of the Xicocotitlan, and acknowledges that this is the place where Toltec treasures and pots can be dug from the earth. In fact, the Aztecs did indeed sack the cities of their predecessors, especially Tula, Hidalgo, and they hauled the booty back to Tenochtitlan, but the description of tropical birds and a paradisiacal abundance sounds less like a place in the Central Mexican highlands and more like TAMOANCHAN, a mythical place usually thought to be down in the tropical lowlands, perhaps even in the Maya area. In the POPOL VUH, the Quiché Maya tell of a journey to the east, to Tulan, and their Tollan may well have meant Chichen Itzá or perhaps one of the great trading ports along the Gulf Coast.

The idea of Tollan may well date to the rise of the historical Toltecs in Mesoamerica, who, around the year AD 900, controlled trading networks extending from the American Southwest down into Central America. The two largest cities of the Toltec network were Tula, Hidalgo, and Chichen Itzá; Cholula also thrived in that era. By Aztec times, the great cities of the past and their achievements may well have been conflated into a single concept of a glorious past, tropical abundance, and invention, with Tollan more an idea than a single place.

tombs Some Mesoamerican nobles were interred in tombs upon their DEATH, while others were wrapped into BUNDLES with layers of CLOTH and then burnt or interred, or both, depending on the customs of the culture. In Central Mexico, for example, the noble dead were wrapped into mummy bundles. Many of the great TEOTIHUACAN masks were probably

once sewn onto such bundles and then interred. The Aztecs cremated their dead, and
then interred the ashes, although victims of
death by drowning were buried. The Codex
Magliabechiano illustrates the mummy bundle of a MERCHANT accompanied by the tokens
of his wealth – JAGUAR pelt, GOLD, and valuable
beads – with which his ashes would be
interred in case he chose to take up his
profession in the UNDERWORLD.

But throughout most of the rest of
Mesoamerica, in West Mexico, in Oaxaca,
along the Gulf Coast, and in the Maya lands,
nobles and royalty began their journey into
the AFTERLIFE once their bodies had been
placed in tombs. The stone sarcophagus first
appeared at La Venta, in Olmec times, within
a tomb framed by basalt columns. The most
extraordinary sarcophagus known belongs
to Pacal at Palenque and is carved on sides
and top with the images of Pacal's descent
into the Underworld and his reception
by his forebears. Pacal's sarcophagus lies
inside a tomb deep within the Temple of
Inscriptions, reached only by an interior,
secret staircase.

The imagery of the Maya tomb sometimes
suggested the entry into the Underworld but
at other times the foundation of a MOUNTAIN.
Artists painted the fine masonry tombs at Río
Azul and elsewhere during the Early Classic
period with symbols of transition from this
world to another, frequently with symbols
of WATER and BLOOD. Like the later Aztec
merchants, Maya nobles took with them the
things they would need in another world. A
Kaminaljuyú lord was interred with the tools
for working jade; a Copán lineage head was
accompanied by the materials a PRIEST or
scribe would need. At Uaxactún, small
TEMPLES were erected over the burials of Early
Classic rulers in Group A; during the Late
Classic, the same building complex received
simpler burials of women and children. When
Ruler A of Tikal died in AD 725, a tomb was
dug into the bedrock of the Great Plaza, and
over his mortal remains, his successors raised
up Temple I, permanently enshrining the
king. Many Maya PYRAMIDS, then, were great
tomb structures.

At Monte Albán, the Zapotecs buried their
noble dead in tombs at the centers of their
patios, in underground chambers reached by
a single flight of stairs. Niches for offerings
interrupt rich paintings of parading deities;
perhaps if the offerings sufficed, the interred

Two nobles seated before the sign for **Tollan**, or
"place of rushes." The central mountain marked
by a snake refers to Coatepec, the birthplace of
Huitzilopochtli; Manuscrit Tovar, 16th c. Aztec.

Tomb of the Late Classic Maya king, Pacal, in
the Temple of the Inscriptions at Palenque.

noble made an easy transition. The Zapotecs at Mitla built cruciform tombs under their palaces. During the Late Postclassic, when the Mixtecs held greater political authority in Oaxaca, they went to ancient Monte Albán, emptied some of the Zapotec tombs, and buried their own noble dead in the old tombs together with abundant new offerings, including the largest single deposit of Mesoamerican gold discovered in its Prehispanic context this century.

In West Mexico, in the 1st millennium BC, the peoples of Colima, Jalisco, and Nayarit dug shaft tombs into the bedrock, like their contemporaries in Ecuador, a fact which raises questions about contact between North and South America. Frequently multichambered, these shaft tombs received the interments of a family or lineage, and have yielded the most dramatic West Mexican figures. The living marked the surrounding surface area above the shaft tombs with stones, possibly to demarcate a place of interface between the living and the dead. *See also* DEATH.

Tonacatecuhtli Lord of Our Sustenance, Tonacatecuhtli was a Central Mexican form of the aged creator god. According to the Vaticanus A codex, this deity and his consort, Tonacacihuatl, resided in the 13th and uppermost heaven, Omeyocan. From Omeyocan, the creator gods sent down the souls of infants to be born. Tonacatecuhtli is identified with the miracle of procreation, and in a number of scenes appears with copulating human couples. As a god of creations and beginnings, it is appropriate that he is patron of Cipactli, the first of the 20 days, and the TRECENA 1 Cipactli, the first of the 20 *trecenas*.

tonal In contemporary ethnographic literature, the term *tonal* is frequently used in contrast to NAHUAL. Whereas *nahual* generally signifies a form-changer, frequently in the form of an animal, *tonal* is used to refer to a spirit-familiar or soul. Among contemporary Mesoamerican peoples, the *tonal* is generally synonymous with the concept of the "shadow" spirit of an individual. Among a number of Mesoamerican peoples, the *tonal* of an individual is discovered soon after BIRTH, frequently by contact with a particular animal. The term *tonal* derives from the Nahuatl *tonalli*, a word bearing such connotations as solar heat, day, day name, destiny, and soul or spirit. According to Sahagún, the

tonalli soul of an infant was sent from the highest heaven of Omeyocan, the Place of Duality. This soul was inextricably tied into the *tonalpohualli* CALENDAR of 260 days. Quite frequently, the *tonalli* corresponded to the day of birth, with this particular day becoming the personal name of an individual. *See also* NAMES AND TITLES; TONACATECUHTLI; UAY.

Tonatiuh The sun god of Postclassic Central Mexico, Tonatiuh typically appears with red body paint, an EAGLE feather headdress, and a large rayed solar disk. He is first found in Early Postclassic Toltec art from Ixtapantongo and Chichen Itzá. The Toltec Tonatiuh is frequently paired with QUETZALCOATL in his aspect as the morning star. At Chichen Itzá and Ixtapantongo, the costume of Tonatiuh seems to be based on that of a Maya king. In terms of Central Mexican cosmography, the identification of Tonatiuh with the Maya is apt, since he is the god of the east, that is, the region of the Maya. In the Late Postclassic CALENDAR, he serves as the patron of the day Quiahuitl. In the TRECENA of 1 Miquiztli, or 1 Death, he appears with the lunar god Tecuciztecatl, and in this regard it is interesting to note that the Postclassic Mixtec sun god was known as 1 Death.

To the peoples of Central Mexico, Tonatiuh was a fierce and warlike god. During the wars of Spanish Conquest, the 16th c. Aztecs called Pedro de Alvarado – a vicious conquistador – Tonatiuh. *See also* MIXTEC GODS; SUN.

traders *see* MERCHANTS

trecena In the *tonalamatl* (*see* CALENDAR), the period of 260 days was divided into *trecenas* (the Nahuatl word is no longer known, and Mesoamericanists use the Spanish term), or periods of 13 days, counted 1–13, with each new *trecena* beginning with 1. The first day of the *trecena* and its auguries, as well as one or two gods, reigned over the entire 13-day period. According to the Codex Borbonicus, for example, those born in the *trecena* 1 Atl would be impoverished, and the entire 13-day period begun on that particular day was in general a bad one. However, the Borbonicus and the Florentine codices, the two most complete sources for the auguries of the *trecenas*, do not always agree on the DIVINATION for the *trecena*.

The Aztec *trecenas* and their patron deities ran as follows:

	trecena	patron deities of each trecena
1	1 Cipactli	Tonacatecuhtli
2	1 Ocelotl	Quetzalcoatl
3	1 Mazatl	Tepeyollotl, Quetzalcoatl, or Tlazolteotl
4	1 Xochitl	Huehuecoyotl or Macuilxochitl
5	1 Acatl	Chalchiuhtlicue and Tlazolteotl
6	1 Miquiztli	Tonatiuh and Tecuciztecatl
7	1 Quiahuitl	Tlaloc and Chicomecoatl or 4 Ehecatl
8	1 Malinalli	Mayahuel and Xochipilli or Cinteotl
9	1 Coatl	Tlahuizcalpantecuhtli or Xiuhtecuhtli
10	1 Tecpatl	Tonatiuh and Mictlantecuhtli
11	1 Ozomatli	Patecatl and Cuauhtliocelotl
12	1 Cuetzpallin	Itztlacoliuhqui
13	1 Ollin	Ixcuina or Tlazolteotl and Tezcatlipoca or Uactli
14	1 Itzcuintli	Xipe Totec and Quetzalcoatl
15	1 Calli	Itzpapalotl
16	1 Cozcacuauhtli	Xolotl and Tlalchitonatiuh or 4 Ollin
17	1 Atl	Chalchiuhtototl
18	1 Ehecatl	Chantico and 1 Acatl or 1 Cipactli
19	1 Cuauhtli	Xochiquetzal and Tezcatlipoca
20	1 Tochtli	Iztapaltotec and Xiuhtecuhtli

trophy heads Like peoples of Central and South America, the ancient Maya preserved the severed heads of CAPTIVES as trophies. In addition, these heads may have been considered as a source of supernatural power, the repository of the spirit of the defeated warrior. Depictions of trophy heads abound in Protoclassic art from the Maya region. Frequently they are held in the hand, in the crook of the arm, or worn on belt assemblages. The mask and triple CELT belt assemblage commonly worn by Classic Maya rulers probably derives from trophy heads worn upon the belt. The peoples of Classic Veracruz also seem to have had trophy heads. The stone HACHAS associated with ballgame belts appear to be based on the concept of trophy heads. Thus the earlier examples are not blade-like but rounded, and commonly portray lifeless human heads. The identification of trophy heads with ballgame belts concerns the wider association of decapitation with the BALLGAME. In Mesoamerica, the ball was often metaphorically considered as a severed human head. It is even possible that among the Maya, human skulls were placed in larger RUBBER balls, giving them lightness and bounce. Perhaps the most developed use of trophy heads with the ballgame is the TZOMPANTLI skullrack. A wooden rack with impaled human skulls, the *tzompantli* appears to have been specifically identified with ballcourts.

The aged creator god, **Tonacatecuhtli**, as patron of the day Cipactli, Codex Borgia, p. 9, Late Postclassic period.

The sun god, **Tonatiuh**, detail from a wooden lintel at the Upper Temple of the Jaguar, Chichen Itzá, Early Postclassic period.

tuerto Signifying an individual blind in one eye, the Spanish term *tuerto* is used to refer to a peculiar ancient motif, a grotesquely deformed and twisted face. Typically, the face appears with one eye shut and the nose and mouth twisted to one side. At times, the tongue curves sideways out of the mouth. The *tuerto* motif seems to date to as early as the Formative Olmec, for an example appears on an Olmec-style stone *yuguito* (a small U-shaped stone object, possibly used in the BALLGAME). During the Classic period, *tuertos* are known for TEOTIHUACAN, central Veracruz, and the Maya area. Although rare, the *tuerto* motif continues into the Late Postclassic period. At the Aztec capital of Tenochtitlan, a stone *tuerto* head was discovered within the Stage II platform of the Templo Mayor, a constructional phase dating to approximately AD 1390. The sculpture was found on the Tlaloc side of the Templo Mayor, that is the side dedicated to RAIN and agricultural fertility.

To the Aztecs and possibly the earlier peoples of Mesoamerica, the *tuerto* face may have been identified with gods of rain. Among the Aztecs, the *tepictoton* mountain gods were considered to be aspects of TLALOC. According to the Aztec Florentine Codex, the *tepictoton* punished those who tasted PULQUE before it was fully prepared: "And of him who secretly tasted it, who in secret drank some, even tasting only a little, it was said that his mouth would become twisted, it would stretch to one side; to one side his mouth would shift; it would be drawn over." This ailment sounds very like the *tuerto* face. Matos Moctecuma suggests that the *tuerto* portrays the facial paralysis known as Bell's palsy, which can derive from trauma or exposure to extreme cold. Such a condition could easily occur among individuals who visited the windy and icy fastness of high mountains, the realm of the Tlaloque and the *tepictoton*. *See also* DEFORMITY.

turquoise An entirely opaque stone of aquamarine color, turquoise was one of the treasured gemstones of ancient Mesoamerica. However, turquoise does not occur naturally within the confines of Mesoamerica. Most turquoise appearing there derives from the Cerillos region of New Mexico. This turquoise does not appear in Mesoamerica until the advent of the Toltecs during the Early Postclassic period. They probably secured the Cerillos turquoise through the trading center of Casas Grandes in northern Chihuahua. Toltec figures, especially warriors, are frequently represented wearing costume elements covered with turquoise mosaic. Some of the common turquoise mosaic elements are large back MIRRORS, pointed crowns, and pectorals in the form of stylized BUTTERFLIES or DOGS. During the Late Postclassic period, Central Mexican warriors were similarly identified with turquoise. The Codex Magliabechiano illustrates a MORTUARY BUNDLE prior to burning. The dead warrior is dressed in paper copies of turquoise ornaments, these being a pointed crown, a nose piece, and a dog-shaped pectoral. In Central Mexico, the turquoise nose piece, or *yacaxihuitl*, was emblematic of the soul of the dead warrior.

Perhaps because of the blue color at the heart of intense flames, turquoise was identified with FIRE in Late Postclassic Central Mexico. The god of fire, XIUHTECUHTLI, or Turquoise Lord, was richly costumed in turquoise, including a pointed crown, breast pendant, and shield of turquoise mosaic. During the Late Postclassic period, the pointed turquoise *xiuhuitzolli* crown was an important distinguishing mark of rulers.

In Nahuatl, the term *xihuitl* signifies "grass" and "solar year" as well as turquoise. In Central Mexican WRITING and art, these three distinct meanings are deliberately associated with one another. Thus the Postclassic XIUHCOATL fire serpent is frequently portrayed with grass and the trapeze-and-ray year sign. During the Late Postclassic period, turquoise is represented either as a quincunx, or as a circle containing a central element of roughly hourglass form. *See also* JADE.

turtle Both marine and terrestrial turtles were often identified with WATER in ancient Mesoamerica. In large part, this clearly derives from the common occurrence of turtles in aquatic habitats. However, the identification with water may also be due to the use of turtle shells as musical instruments, possibly as an allusion to thunder. Turtle carapaces were widely used as drums, and were struck with an antler, stick, or other hard implement.

Because their bodies form an instrument, turtles may have been identified with MUSIC in Central Mexico. On page 24 of the Codex Borgia, a turtle plays a drum while blowing a conch trumpet. The YAHUI figure of the

Mixtecs and Zapotecs frequently wears a turtle carapace, possibly as an allusion to the rumble of thunder. The turtle shell often worn by the Maya deity PAUAHTUN may also be a reference to thunder. On one Late Classic vessel, four Pauahtuns are accompanied by four CHACS, the gods of RAIN and LIGHTNING. Three of the Chacs are playing music, one with a turtle carapace and antler.

For the ancient Maya, the turtle shell described the circular and rounded EARTH. A number of Late Classic ALTARS are carved in the form of turtles. One such monument, Itzimte Altar 1, depicts Caban curls – a well-known earth sign – upon the shell. The Tonsured Maize God is often represented rising out of the turtle shell earth. In Late Postclassic Yucatán, small stone turtles served as the locus for penis perforation. Page 19 of the Codex Madrid illustrate five gods engaged in BLOODLETTING around a turtle altar. Quite possibly, this rite was to fertilize the earth with blood during calendrical period-ending celebrations. At Mayapan, some stone turtles bear probable *katun* ending dates. In one instance, an entire round of 13 *katuns* is represented on the rim of the shell, making this sculpture a Prehispanic Katun Wheel.

twins Mesoamerican peoples generally believed twins to be dangerous. The Aztecs considered the birth of twins a malevolent omen and to be such a source of misfortune that one of them should be killed at birth. XOLOTL is the patron of twins and other deformities, and the very word *xolotl* means twin in Nahuatl, and may also mean a doubled MAIZE plant or, as *mexolotl*, a doubled MAGUEY plant. Xolotl and QUETZALCOATL are often paired, although probably not twins; because of this relationship, *coatl* has been corrupted in Mexican Spanish to *cuate*, pal or buddy, and *cuates*, twins.

In the Codex Borgia, TEZCATLIPOCA and Quetzalcoatl are twins as they journey through the UNDERWORLD. The POPOL VUH relates the adventures of two sets of twins fathered by HUN HUNAHPU: Hunahpu and Xbalanque, the Hero Twins, and Hun Batz and Hun Chuen, the Monkey Scribe twins (*see* MONKEY). Painted Maya ceramics reveal other paired individuals, but no other pairs of twins can be surely identified. Some Maya pairs, such as the PADDLER GODS, express opposition rather than identity and can be likened to Aztec *difrasismos*, paired oppositions. *See also* BIRTH; DEFORMITY; DUALITY.

Tuerto, detail from a Late Classic stone yoke, Veracruz.

Place sign for Xiuhtepec, meaning **turquoise** or grass mountain, Matrícula de Tributos, 16th c. Aztec.

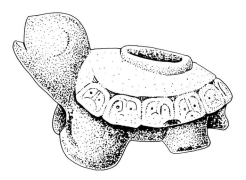
Stone **turtle** bearing a Katun Wheel on its back, Mayapan, Late Postclassic Maya. This sculpture constitutes the only Prehispanic Katun Wheel known.

The Hero **Twins**, Hunahpu and Xbalanque, painted within Naj Tunich Cave, Guatemala, Late Classic Maya.

tzitzimime Among the most feared supernatural beings of Late Postclassic Central Mexico were the *tzitzimime* (singular *tzitzimitl*), the star demons of darkness. According to Central Mexican belief, planets and constellations could be transformed into fierce devouring demons during particular calendrical and celestial events. Solar ECLIPSES were an especially feared phenomenon, since it was believed that the star demons were attacking the SUN. This concept is probably based on the fact that during total solar eclipses, STARS can be discerned close to the sun, as if they were attacking and overpowering it. For the Aztecs, the end of the 52-year cycle was another fearful time. If New Fire was not created on the Hill of the Star (*see* FIRE), the *tzitzimime* would descend and destroy the world.

The *tzitzimime* were believed to dive head-first from the heavens, and for this reason, they were compared to the SPIDER hanging head downward from its thread. The four SKY-BEARERS, TLAHUIZCALPANTECUHTLI, XIUHTECUHTLI, EHECATL-QUETZALCOATL and MICTLANTECUHTLI, could also take on the role of *tzitzimime* star demons, but the *tzitzimime* themselves were usually considered to be female. The Codex Magliabechiano contains skeletal *tzitzimime* wearing shell-fringed skirts. Among the most important *tzitzimime* was the skeletal *Itzpapalotl*, the goddess of TAMOANCHAN.

tzompantli One of the more striking structures of Mesoamerican public architecture was the *tzompantli*, or skullrack. This was a wooden scaffold containing human skulls pierced horizontally by crossbeams. The term *tzompantli* is Nahuatl, and it has been widely assumed that this structure derives from Postclassic Central Mexico. However, a probable Protoclassic *tzompantli* was excavated at La Coyotera, Oaxaca. Moreover, there are indications that they were present at Uxmal and other Terminal Classic Maya sites in the Puuc region of Yucatán.

In the Quiché Maya POPOL VUH, the severed head of HUN HUNAHPU was placed in a gourd tree next to the ballcourt. This gourd tree is clearly a reference to the *tzompantli* filled with human skulls. In Nahuatl, the term for head is *tzontecomatl*, with *tecomatl* signifying gourd tree. It appears that like the Sumbanese skull trees of Indonesia, the *tzompantli* was considered as a tree laden with fruit. In a Toltec-style rock painting at Ixtapantango, there is a *tzompantli* portrayed as a tree

containing skulls and banners, or *pantli*. On page 19 of the Codex Borgia, the *tzompantli* is also depicted as a tree with *pantli* banners. *See also* TROPHY HEADS.

U

uay In Mayan languages, the term *uay* commonly refers to sorcerers and form-changers. Among contemporary Yucatec, there is a great deal of concern and fear regarding *uay* sorcerers. In fact, the word even appears in local Spanish as an expression of alarm and fear. But although the *uay* sorcerer corresponds closely with the highland Mexican NAHUAL, in certain Mayan languages the term signifies a soul-like spirit companion similar to the Mexican TONAL. In Mayan languages, *uay* can also mean dreaming or sleep. This may well refer to the widespread Maya belief that the soul or spirit companion travels in dreams while one is asleep.

Stephen Houston and David Stuart have isolated a glyph denoting *uay*. This sign is composed of a stylized human face serving as the sign for *ahau* or king, but with one important difference – half the face is covered by a JAGUAR pelt. In Classic texts, animals and supernatural figures commonly serve as the *uay* of particular Maya lords. Even gods are described as having *uay* counterparts. Thus a skeletal SERPENT is described as being the *uay* of God K, or Kauil (*see* SCHELLHAS GODS). In the Classic inscriptions, it is uncertain whether form-changers or spirit companions are being described. For this reason, Houston and Stuart prefer to describe the *uay* as a "co-essence." *See also* TONAL.

Uayeb Among the most important ceremonies described for the contact-period Maya of Yucatán were the rites concerning the Uayeb, the five unlucky days at the end of the year. Detailed descriptions of the Uayeb rites appear in the 16th c. account by Diego de Landa, and in the Colonial Yucatec *Cantares de Dzitbalché*. In addition, passages pertaining to the Uayeb rites appear in the Prehispanic Dresden, Paris, and Madrid codices.

The Yucatec term Uayeb probably signifies the sleeping or resting place of the year. However, the Uayeb period clearly had more sinister connotations. The *Cantares de Dzitbalché* describes this period as a time of evil when the UNDERWORLD is open. The Prehispanic glyph for the Uayeb period is the 360-day *tun* sign topped by a U-shaped skeletal maw, quite probably the cave-like entrance to the Underworld. The Uayeb ceremony continues to be celebrated by the Tzotzil of Chamula as a native form of Catholic Carnival. In this five-day festival, performers impersonating MONKEYS and other demons from the perimeters of the social world take control of the community. According to the Chamula people, this festival is performed during the five days of Uayeb. *See also* CALENDAR.

Underworld The Mesoamerican Underworld was a fearsome and dreaded place. For example, the Quiché Maya word Xibalba means "place of fright," and that it was indeed. But unlike hell in the Christian world, the Mesoamerican Underworld was not the preserve of sinners, but rather the destination of all those who escaped violent death, for it was only these latter who went directly to one of the heavens. In their preaching, the Spanish friars generally translated the word for the Christian hell as Mictlan, but threats of an eternity in Mictlan had little effect, since the audience already knew that all souls, whether rich or poor, good or evil, must go there.

At the time of the Conquest, most Central Mexican people believed in the cosmographical scheme of nine levels of the Underworld, with 13 levels of upper world. According to the Codex Vaticanus A, where the 9–13 scheme receives its most explicit and ample presentation, Tlalticpac, literally "on the surface of the earth," belongs to both sequences, and so was considered the first level of both worlds. The Maya certainly perceived layers of both Underworld and upper world but the notion of nine levels of the Underworld is not specific or universal for the Maya, nor is it for either the Mixtecs or the Zapotecs. Nevertheless, the construction of numerous nine-level PYRAMIDS during the Classic and Terminal Classic era (e.g. Temple I at Tikal, Temple of Inscriptions at Palenque, and the Castillo at Chichen Itzá) might reflect such a conceit, particularly in the case of funerary pyramids. The notion of "houses" in which the Hero Twins undergo ordeals in Xibalba also suggests compartments, if not exactly levels, in the Underworld.

Xibalba, and the Maya Underworld in general, could be entered through a CAVE, or

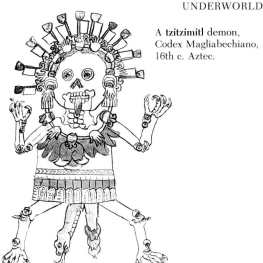

A **tzitzimitl** demon, Codex Magliabechiano, 16th c. Aztec.

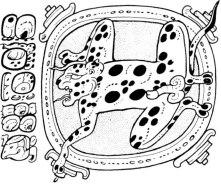

(*Right*) A **tzompantli** skullrack, Codex Durán, 16th c. Aztec

(*Below*) A water jaguar described as the **uay** of a Seibal lord, detail from a Late Classic Maya vase.

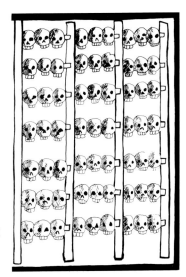

(*Right*) The sign for the five-day **Uayeb** period, Palenque, Late Classic Maya.

still, standing WATER. From wherever one stood, the Underworld lay to the west, which may be why the islands off Campeche, including Jaina, received so many burials: they were the last land masses to the west of the Yucatán peninsula. In the POPOL VUH, the Underworld geography includes at least two rivers and varies much like the geography of the surface world, and its realm is vast. When preparing for death and a journey into the Underworld, a Maya steeled himself to be like a Hero Twin, that is, to be able to overcome the Underworld gods and their trials through wit and perseverance.

In Central Mexico, the eight layers under the surface of the EARTH offered discrete hazards that had to be endured by the souls of the dead: dangerous waters, clashing MOUNTAINS, OBSIDIAN blades, arrow SACRIFICE, and HEART sacrifice among them, before the souls finally reached Mictlan, where MICTLANTECUHTLI and his wife Mictecacihuatl reigned over the deepest nether region. To aid the dead soul in the perilous journey, the dead were cremated with their worldly possessions, particularly their tools – such as a woman's weaving kit – as well as precious items from the surface that might speed the ordeal – such as JADE beads and frothy hot chocolate (*see* CACAO). When the souls of the dead finally arrived in Mictlan, they offered up the materials with which the bodies had been burned.

Some gods traveled in and out of the Underworld: to create a new generation of mankind, for example, QUETZALCOATL descended into Mictlan to steal the bones of a previous race of humans.

Throughout Mesoamerica, DOGS were considered valuable companions and guides for the dead spirit, and dog skeletons are occasionally found in TOMBS from the beginning of Classic times onward. In West Mexico, particularly in Colima, mourners placed pottery dogs in shaft tombs, probably as an expression of a similar concept. In the Florentine Codex, only a yellow dog could ferry his master across the treacherous waters of the Underworld. *See also* AFTERLIFE; DEATH.

veintena The *veintena*, or 20-day period, or "month," in the Aztec calendar, received great attention from the Spanish at the time of the Conquest, perhaps because the series of 18 agricultural festivals offered closer analogies to European months and Christian feast days than any other aspect of the Mesoamerican CALENDAR. Unfortunately, the Nahuatl term for the time period has been lost; no record of the *veintena* survives in a Central Mexican manuscript made before the Conquest, probably because it did not play the same role in DIVINATION that the TRECENA, as part of the *tonalpohualli*, did. Nevertheless, because religious festivals were organized for each *veintena*, the Spanish studied them assiduously, and from their accounts emerge some of the most detailed descriptions of Aztec religious practices. The *veintena* festivals were largely agricultural, with many dedicated to the RAIN gods and the MAIZE GODS. *Veintena* ceremonies were widely celebrated throughout Mesoamerica, but usually the term is reserved for the peoples of Central Mexico. We can also consider the Maya count of months to have been *veintenas*.

The 18 Aztec *veintenas* ran as follows, to be succeeded by the *nemontemi*, or nameless days, after Tititl, before the beginning of a new 365-day year. There is some disagreement about the timing of the principal feasts.

	veintena name	principal deities	principal celebrations
1	Izcalli	Tlaloc, Xiuhtecuhtli	*Huauhquiltamalcualiztli* (meal of amaranth tamales); feast for Xiuhtecuhtli every four years
2	Atlcahualo, Xilomanaliztli	Tlaloque	Cuauhuitlehua (lifting of posts, planting of trees, stretching of limbs); young maize
3	Tlacaxipehualiztli	Xipe Totec	Feast of Xipe, god of spring; flaying of captives
4	Tozoztontli	Tlaloque, Tlaltecuhtli, Xipe Totec	Bloodletting; first flowers
5	Hueytozoztli	Tlaloque, Cinteotl, Chicomecoatl	Bloodletting; feasts to Tlaloc, maize gods; first fruits
6	Toxcatl, Tepopochtli	Tezcatlipoca, Huitzilopochtli	Feasts to Tezcatlipoca and Huitzilopochtli
7	Etzalcualiztli	Tlaloc	Feasts to young crops
8	Tecuilhuitontli	Huixtocihuatl, Xochipilli	Feast to goddess of salt, Huixtocihuatl; exchange of noble clothing and flowers
9	Hueytecuihuitl	Xilonen, maize gods	Feast of Xilonen
10	Tlaxochimaco, Miccailhuitontli	Huitzilopochtli	Feast of merchants; small feast for the dead
11	Xocotlhuetzi, Hueymiccailhuitl	Huehueteotl, Xiuhtecuhtli	Feast of the *xocotl* pole
12	Ochpaniztli	Tlazolteotl, Toci	*Veintena* of sweeping and bathing; feast of Tlazolteotl, Toci; scaffold sacrifice; harvest feasts
13	Teotleco or Pachtontli	Xiuhtecuhtli, Huitzilopochtli	Bloodletting; feast of Huitzilopochtli
14	Hueypachtli or Tepeilhuitl	Tlaloque, Xochiquetzal	Mountain feasts to Tlaloc; sacrifice of Xochiquetzal impersonator
15	Quecholli	Mixcoatl or Camaxtli	Feasts of Mixcoatl; ritual hunts
16	Panquetzaliztli	Huitzilopochtli	Main festival to Huitzilopochtli; banners
17	Atemoztli	Tlaloque	Feasts to water deities
18	Tititl	Ilamatecuhtli	Feasts to Ilamatecuhtli, old people

(*Opposite*) Celebrants dance around a Xocotl pole erected during the **veintena** of Xocotlhuetzi. This rite featured a climbing competition in which noble youths tried to obtain an image placed at the top of the pole, Codex Borbonicus, p. 28, 16th c. Aztec.

As recorded in the *Relación de Michoacán*, the Tarascans also celebrated *veintenas*, although the surviving list is incomplete. Only Cuingo, "flaying," can be surely linked to a specific Mexican festival, Tlacaxipehualiztli, although Johanna Broda has investigated other parallels. Alfonso Caso offered a reconstruction:

	Tarascan veintena	Aztec veintena
1	Tzitacuarenscuaro	Izcalli
2	Purecoracua	Atlcahualo
3	Cuingo	Tlacaxipehualiztli
4	Unisperacuaro	Tozoztontli
5	n/a	Hueytozoztli
6	n/a	Toxcatl
7	Mazcuto	Etzalcualiztli
8	Uazcata cónscuaro	Tecuilhuitontli
9	Caheri cónscuaro	Hueytecuihuitl
10	Hanciñáscuaro	Tlaxochimaco
11	Hicuandiro	Xocotlhuetzi
12	Sicuindiro	Ochpaniztli
13	Charapu zapi	Pachtontli
14	Uapánscuaro	Hueypachtli
15	Caheri uapánscuaro	Quecholli
16	n/a	Panquetzaliztli
17	Peuánscuaro	Atemoztli
18	Curindaro	Tititl

Caso, Jacques Soustelle, Pedro Carrasco, and Johanna Broda have also investigated the Otomi *veintenas*, and these align clearly with Aztec counterparts:

	Otomi veintena	Aztec veintena
1	Anthudoeni	Izcalli
2	Abuoentaxi	Xilomanaliztli
3	Anttzayoh	Tlacaxipehualiztli
4	Atzhotho	Tozoztontli
5	Antatzhoni	Hueytozoztli
6	Atzibiphi	Toxcatl
7	Aneguoeni	Etzalcualiztli
8	Anttzengohmuh	Tecuilhuitontli
9	Antangohmuh	Hueytecuihuitl
10	Anttzengotu	Miccailhuitontli, Tlaxochimaco
11	Antangotu	Hueymiccailhuitl, Xocotlhuetzi
12	Ambaxi	Ochpaniztli
13	Anttzenboxegui	Pachtontli
14	Atamaxegui	Hueypachtli
15	Antzhoni	Quecholli
16	Anthaxme	Panquetzaliztli
17	Ancandehe	Atemoztli
18	Ambue	Tititl

Venus No female symbol of erotic love, in Mesoamerica the planet Venus embodied danger, and always took anthropomorphic form as a male god. The periodic movements of Venus offered warnings of drought, danger, and warfare. TLAHUIZCALPANTECUHTLI, Central Mexican god of the morning star, is the principal Venus god, but other gods may hurl darts and preside over these baleful periods. QUETZALCOATL is also a god of the morning star; XOLOTL has sometimes been considered to be his twin and to represent the evening star, but there is no evidence for these associations, and it may have been that Tlahuizcalpantecuhtli presided over the evening star as well. Among the Postclassic Maya, Lahun Chan was a malevolent Venus god. For the Classic period Maya, a skeletal deity whose name is unknown was the god of the evening star.

According to the Florentine Codex, the influence of Venus could be good or evil, but the instructions for dealing with it reveal that most people perceived it to be the source of dangerous rays: those afraid of its pernicious light sealed any openings in their houses lest it bring on sickness and misfortune.

Venus lies closer to the SUN than the EARTH and orbits the sun more quickly, but seen from the vantage point of the earth, it takes 584 days for the earth, sun, and Venus to return to a specific alignment. From at least Early Classic times onward, the Maya kept track of the cycle (as the Teotihuacanos may well have done too, although they have left us no specific records), recognizing that this brightest "star" of two distinct phases, morning and evening star, was a single heavenly body. When Venus rises as the morning star, it appears before sunrise and leads the sun out of the UNDERWORLD; when Venus rises as the evening star, it comes into view just after sunset and then follows the sun into the Underworld.

When Venus passes directly in front of the sun, modern astronomers call its position *inferior conjunction*, and it generally cannot be observed for a few days (usually 8) before its *heliacal rising* as the morning star; it then rises as the morning star for roughly 263 days. Its orbit then takes Venus behind the sun for *superior conjunction*, a period of 55 to 60 days when again the planet cannot be seen, before it makes it first appearance as the evening star, in which position it remains for 263 days before vanishing in front of the sun again. The cycle takes 584 days to complete;

irregularities generally occur in days of viewing at a particular station rather than in the cycle over all. Curiously, according to both Maya and Central Mexican manuscripts, Mesoamerican astronomers regularized the Venus periods, extending superior conjunction and abbreviating both the morning and evening star, but particularly the former, to create unequal periods, whereas, in fact, the times of visibility are roughly equal. Accordingly, inferior conjunction lasted 8 days, the morning star 236 days, superior conjunction 90 days, and the evening star 250 days. Five complete Venus cycles = 2920 days = 8×365 days, so the Venus cycle easily interlocked with the solar year (*see* CALENDAR).

Several Precolumbian books carefully chart Venus, most notably the Dresden and Grolier codices (Maya) and the Borgia, Vaticanus B, and Cospi (Central Mexican). Both sets show stabbings and destruction under the auspices of the Venus gods, usually at heliacal rising. In both Central Mexico and among the Maya, Venus calendars are read from 1 Xochitl or 1 Ahau, the base day for heliacal rising. Long thought to have been a Postclassic religious construct, the baleful influence of Venus is now known to be of greater antiquity in Mesoamerica.

Classic Maya inscriptions recording "star wars," or wars timed to coincide with the movements of Venus and sometimes Jupiter, indicate that many battles were scheduled to occur on the days when Venus rose for the first time after its inferior or superior conjunction. The inscriptions also indicate that Maya astronomers charted both maximum brightness and greatest elongation of both morning and evening star and timed battles accordingly. These "star wars" were the greatest conflagrations in Classic Maya times and took place with increasing frequency during the 8th c., probably contributing to the Classic Maya collapse. Victorious Maya lords of Venus warfare donned costumes laden with Central Mexican imagery, including BUTTERFLIES, TLALOC faces, OWLS, the WAR SERPENT, and the MEXICAN YEAR SIGN.

Vision Serpent Through rituals of BLOODLETTING, Classic Maya nobles conjured up images of rearing SERPENTS whose mouths belch gods, ancestors, and other nobles. At Yaxchilán, such images are specifically linked to penis and tongue bloodletting and are generated in clouds of smoke rising from the burning

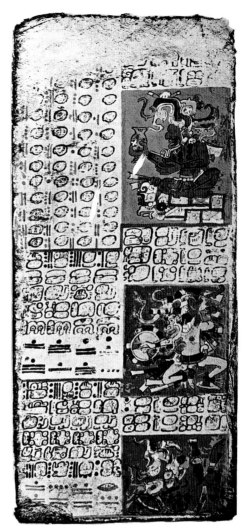

(*Above*) A section from the **Venus** pages of the Dresden Codex, Postclassic Yucatán.

(*Right*) A **Vision Serpent** rising from a burning blood offering, Yaxchilán Lintel 15, Late Classic Maya.

BLOOD offering. In all likelihood, these Vision Serpents function as visual metaphors for BIRTH and rebirth, whether of divinities or humans. Vision Serpents usually have a single head and prominent snake markings; they may undulate, although they rarely appear on the ground, and they sometimes have feather crests.

As SKY deities, Vision Serpents also appear on the Chichen Itzá gold disks, some with cloud markings along their bodies. Some codex-style Classic vases depict the serpent foot of God K (*see* SCHELLHAS GODS) as a Vision Serpent or in the process of becoming one, linking the Vision Serpent to the Maya god of LIGHTNING. Morphologically, the Maya vision serpent closely resembles the Postclassic Central Mexican XIUHCOATL, or fire serpent. Like the Xiuhcoatl, the Vision Serpent may appear in clouds, embodying lightning and FIRE, and perhaps, by extension, powerful storms.

Vucub Caquix In the POPOL VUH (the creation epic describing the deeds of the Hero Twins) a great monster bird known as Vucub Caquix, or 7 Macaw, presides over the murky twilight world following the flood. Although he proclaims himself to be the SUN and MOON, the dawning and separation of day and NIGHT have not yet occurred. Angered by his arrogance, Hunahpu and Xbalanque wait for the monster bird under his favorite fruit tree, and then shoot him down with their blowguns. During the fierce battle that ensues, Hunahpu loses his arm. However, through magic and trickery, the Hero Twins eventually defeat and kill Vucub Caquix and restore the arm of Hunahpu.

Although the *Popol Vuh* is a Colonial Maya document, the episode of Vucub Caquix can be traced to the Protoclassic beginnings of Maya civilization. Stela 2 from the site of Izapa portrays the two Hero Twins running toward Vucub Caquix, who is descending to his fruit tree. At the base of the tree, one can discern the crumpled remains of the defeated bird with a bone jaw. The monster bird also appears on Izapa Stela 25, above a male with a bleeding stump for an arm. Clearly, this scene portrays the fight in which Vucub Caquix tears off Hunahpu's arm.

Representations of the PRINCIPAL BIRD DEITY abound in the art of Protoclassic and Classic Maya and can be identified with Vucub Caquix. Although Vucub Caquix signified 7 Macaw in Quiché, the Protoclassic and

Classic entity does not display the beaded round eye and thick beak of the macaw, and may rather be based upon the king VULTURE (*Sarcoramphus papa*). Supplied with a WATER LILY pad headdress and a SERPENT body, this bird head can serve as the head variant of the 360-day *tun* period and the numeral 13. In addition, this same character is represented as the personified bloodletter rendered with a headdress of tied knots. *See also* WATER LILY SERPENT.

vulture The king vulture (*Sarcoramphus papa*), one of the largest birds of Mesoamerica, reaching a size roughly equivalent to the harpy EAGLE, rarely ventures above 4000' (*c.* 1200 m), and so was best known to Mesoamerican civilizations outside the Valley of Mexico, although the smaller turkey vulture (*Cathartes aura*) and the black vulture (*Coragypes atratus*) are common everywhere in Mesoamerica. The Central Mexican day sign Cozcacuauhtli is the vulture.

Alfonso Caso and Ignacio Bernal identified a Zapotec deity, El Ave de Pico Ancho, as a vulture. This Zapotec deity is identical to the PRINCIPAL BIRD DEITY of the Maya, who is also a vulture. Protoclassic kings at Kaminaljuyú and La Mojarra arrayed themselves as this god. Often adorned with a headband, the king vulture head substitutes for *ahau* in Mayan WRITING, both for the day sign and to mean "lord."

War Serpent Created during the 3rd c. AD, the Temple of Quetzalcoatl originally contained one of the most elaborate architectural facades known in ancient Mesoamerica. Two forms of tenoned sculpture project out of the facade. One of these heads is clearly the plumed serpent, or QUETZALCOATL. However, the other entity has been more difficult to identify. Although it has been widely interpreted as the head of Tlaloc, it is actually a mosaic headdress portraying a serpent being with jaguar attributes. Because of its frequent appearance with weapons and warrior figures, this entity can be called the War Serpent.

The War Serpent is probably an ancestral form of the XIUHCOATL, the fire serpent of Postclassic Central Mexico. Although the war serpent probably originates at TEOTIHUACAN, it is also commonly found in Classic Maya and Zapotec art. *See also* TEOTIHUACAN GODS.

warrior orders At the time of the Spanish Conquest, certain Aztec warriors were identified with powerful predators of the natural world, particularly EAGLES and JAGUARS, and these have come to be called the eagle knights and the jaguar or tiger knights. (In modern Mesoamerica, there are no tigers, but all wild cats, particularly pumas and jaguars, are often called *tigre* in Spanish.) The Nahuatl metaphor for warriors, *in cuauhtli in ocelotl*, "the eagles, the jaguars," expressed the oppositions of SKY and EARTH and of day and NIGHT. The eagle and jaguar knights served HUITZILO-POCHTLI, the SUN, and the Aztec cult god *par excellence*. At the creation of the fifth sun at Teotihuacan (*see* CREATION ACCOUNTS), the eagle and jaguar hurled themselves into the burning pyre after Nanahuatzin and Tecuciztecatl to generate the first eagle and jaguar knights. The Aztec myth thus suggests an antiquity to the warrior orders.

Although there was no standing Aztec army, members of the eagle and jaguar knights came from elite society and dedicated their lives to their roles. They frequently participated in public celebrations, particularly of the VEINTENAS. During the month of Tlacaxipehualiztli, for example, the eagle and jaguar knights fought CAPTIVES tied to the TEMALACATL in gladiatorial bouts, and engaged in street skirmishes with the Xipe impersonators. Recent excavations in Tenochtitlan have revealed a temple to the eagle knights adjacent to the dual PYRAMID dedicated to TLALOC and Huitzilopochtli.

Painted friezes of alternating coyotes and pumas or jaguars at TEOTIHUACAN may symbolize early warrior orders there, and the cults may have been quickly adopted by the Maya, for some Early Classic warriors at Tikal and elsewhere include coyote fur in their costumes. At the end of the 8th c., the chief victorious warriors in the Bonampak murals all wear jaguar costumes; in contemporaneous paintings at Cacaxtla, a noble eagle warrior and jaguar warrior frame a doorway. Eagle and jaguar warriors parade at both Tula (*see* TOLLAN) and Chichen Itzá, and the presence of coyotes at Tula and bears at Chichen Itzá suggest additional orders there as well.

water Because of their dependence upon agriculture, water has been of central concern

The defeat of **Vucub Caquix**, Izapa Stela 2, Protoclassic Maya. In this scene, the descending bird is being attacked by the two Hero Twins. Vucub Caquix appears a second time, now defeated, at the base of the fruit tree.

(*Right*) Maya figure wearing **War Serpent** headdress, vessel sherd, Belize, Late Classic Maya.

(*Below*) The eagle and jaguar **warrior orders**, Codex Borbonicus, p. 11, 16th c. Aztec.

to both ancient and contemporary peoples of Mesoamerica. Particular regions, such as the ocean, SPRINGS, and MOUNTAINS are frequently worshipped as magical sources of water. In Mesoamerica, the gods of water – especially RAIN – are among the most ancient and pervasive deities, particularly the Maya CHAC, the Zapotec COCIJO, and TLALOC of Central Mexico.

Often, male gods of rain are distinguished from female deities of standing water. The name of the Central Mexican goddess CHALCHIUHTLICUE, She of the Jade Skirt, is a metaphoric allusion to a shining expanse of verdant water.

As well as a source of agricultural fertility, water was also an important means of ceremonial PURIFICATION. Among the Maya of Yucatán, native PRIESTS consecrated an area by scattering water from a serpent-tailed aspergillum. The water used in this act of purification derived from dew gathered from leaves or from virgin water, *zuhuy ha*, collected in distant locations removed from the presence of women; *zuhuy ha* continues to be an important component of modern Maya agricultural ceremonies. Among both the Postclassic Yucatec Maya and Central Mexican Aztecs, water was used in BAPTISM ceremonies as a means of purifying the child.

water lily One of the more lovely flowering plants of Mesoamerica, the water lily (*Nymphaea* spp.) grows in relatively still waters such as ponds, lakes, and slow-moving rivers. These conditions correspond well to the humid Maya lowlands, and it is thus not surprising that this plant abounds in Classic Maya art.

In Maya iconography, the water lily frequently denotes standing WATER, including the surrounding and sustaining SEA. Perhaps because of its almost miraculous emergence out of the still water, the water lily may have served as a model for the creation of the EARTH. The lid of one Early Classic Maya ceramic vessel depicts a pair of fish and birds nibbling a water lily, as if the plant is the terrestrial interface between the SKY and the watery UNDERWORLD. Moreover, the veined surface of the water lily leaf is frequently marked with a net-like pattern also used to depict the surface of turtle shells. Among the Maya, the TURTLE was another model for the circular earth floating upon the sea. The role of the water lily in Maya creation mythology continued into this century. According to one

Lacandon account, the great god Kakoch created a water lily from which all the other gods were born.

In Maya iconography, two gods are particularly associated with the water lily. One of these is the Underworld denizen known as the Water Lily Jaguar, whose modern name derives from the water lily flower placed prominently on his brow. The other being is the WATER LILY SERPENT, identified by its SERPENT body, beak-like face, and the bound water lily pad and flower serving as its headdress. The Water Lily Serpent serves as head variants of the numeral 13 and the 360-day *tun* period. *See also* JAGUAR GODS.

Water Lily Serpent Known only among the Maya, the Water Lily Serpent symbolizes the surface of still WATER. Although the body is an undulating SERPENT, the head has the downward curving beak of a bird, often with crossed bands infixed in the lower jaw. A WATER LILY pad and FLOWER form the headdress, and a fish often nibbles at the flower. He is a supernatural patron of the NUMBER 13 and substitutes for that number, and may also figure as the personified *tun*, or year, sign. At Dzibilchaltún, Water Lily Serpents undulate along the upper frieze of the Temple of the Seven Dolls, and abundant adjacent sea SHELL offerings suggest that the ancient city may have represented the image of an oasis in hot, dry northern Yucatán. Today, water lilies float on the Dzibilchaltún CENOTE.

Classic Maya kings and other lords often wear the head of the Water Lily Serpent as a headdress, sometimes in contexts of aspersion and daubing of paint. The Water Lily Serpent is closely related to the Shell/ Wing dragon, who sometimes rests on the Water Lily Serpent's headdress. The Kancross Water Lily Monster, or Tubular Headdress Monster, is probably a variant of the Water Lily Serpent.

weaponry Mesoamerican deities, like their mortal counterparts, carried weapons, and some Mesoamerican weapons were themselves deities. The following list is not comprehensive, but it includes the weapons most commonly carried by the gods.

Even among the Olmecs, some deities were armed: the early flying figures bear clubs, and seated figures – supernatural or divine – often hold "knuckledusters:" hand stones that may have been some sort of weapon.

By Classic times, weaponry is far more elaborate: both gods and humans wear armor, bear shields and carry a wide variety of weapons. In Central Mexico, at Teotihuacan, warriors bear OBSIDIAN-tipped lances, arrows, and *atlatls*, or dart throwers, and this latter weapon retains an identification with Central Mexico throughout time. The Maya adorn their shields with the face of the Jaguar God of the Underworld (*see* JAGUAR GODS), a patron of war, and sometimes the Jaguar God of the Underworld himself is armed. Maya kings sometimes bear the MANIKIN SCEPTER in hand as if it were a weapon; held in the hands of CHAC, the Manikin Scepter embodies LIGHTNING. Deities and warriors both hold hafted axes, often with bloody tips. The Hero Twins shoot pellets from their blowguns.

In the Postclassic era, perhaps most important among deified weapons is the XIUHCOATL, or fire serpent, the weapon that HUITZILOPOCHTLI bears in his hand at birth and uses to kill his half-sister, COYOLXAUHQUI, and to banish his half-brothers, the Centzon Huitznahua. Other Aztec deities also carry weapons, usually the *atlatl*, but occasionally long spears. In close combat, the Aztecs fought with the *macuahuitl*, a club imbedded with obsidian blades.

Across Mesoamerica and throughout time, weapons were in most cases used in combat to disable but not to kill the opponent. Victorious lords dispatched their captured enemies publicly, using knives with hafted obsidian blades either to decapitate or to remove the HEART.

were-jaguar As the Olmec civilization began to be recognized early in this century, many of its zoomorphic figures were thought to be of feline derivation and the anthropomorphic ones of a human-feline blend – or what have come to be called were-jaguars. Were there half human, half JAGUAR creatures? In his famous hypothesis, Matthew Stirling argued that the Olmecs believed in a supernatural mating between humans and jaguars, leading to a special race of were-jaguars, but this overarching theory cannot explain the diversity and complexity of Olmec supernaturals. Only one, the Rain Baby, clearly seems to be a human-jaguar blend. Another class of figures that demonstrates the change of humans into jaguars and other animals probably illustrates shamanic transformation. *See also* JAGUAR; NAHUAL; OLMEC GODS; SHAMAN; STIRLING HYPOTHESIS; TONAL; UAY.

Water lily pad and flowers with fish and birds, lid of a ceramic bowl, Early Classic Maya.

Ruler wearing the mask and headdress of **Water Lily Serpent**, Machaquilá Stela 4, Late Classic Maya.

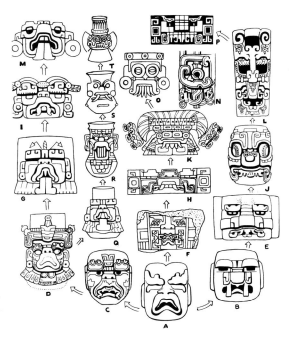

Were-jaguar: a chart by Miguel Covarrubias suggesting the evolution of Mesoamerican rain gods from the Olmec jaguar god.

wind Something that moves but cannot be seen, the wind commonly symbolizes the engendering, creative spirit from which life derives. Among the Zapotecs, this force was known as *pee*, signifying wind, breath, or spirit. It was believed to reside in all things that moved and thus showed life. Among the Maya, wind was represented by a sign resembling the letter "T" of the Latin alphabet. In Maya WRITING, this T-shaped device is the identifying element of the second day name, Ik, signifying "wind" in Yucatec. During the Classic period, the head variant of the number 3 frequently displays the wind sign upon his cheek, possibly denoting him as the god of wind.

Perhaps the best-known wind god of ancient Mesoamerica is EHECATL-QUETZAL-COATL, that is, Quetzalcoatl in his aspect as god of wind. In Late Postclassic Central Mexico, he typically appears with a red buccal mask resembling a duck beak, and shell JEWELRY, including particularly his "wind jewel," a pectoral formed from the cut cross-section of a conch whorl. According to the myth of the FIVE SUNS, Ehecatl-Quetzalcoatl presided over the sun of Nahui Ehecatl, or 4 Wind, the world destroyed by winds. In Aztec mythology, Ehecatl-Quetzalcoatl is also a great culture hero who creates the world, humans, and MAIZE. Scenes in the Prehispanic Codex Vindobonensis reveal that 9 Wind, the Mixtec equivalent of Ehecatl-Quetzalcoatl, had a similar role in Mixtec mythology. *See also* CREATION ACCOUNTS; MIXTEC GODS.

world trees In Mesoamerican thought, the cardinal DIRECTIONS were associated with a broad spectrum of things from the natural and cultural worlds. One of the most important and pervasive of these embodiments of the directions were world trees, each oriented to a specific direction. These trees seem to express the four-fold nature of a single great tree, or *axis mundi*, located at the center of the world.

Among the Yucatec Maya, this central tree was a *yaxché* (*Ceiba* spp.), the national tree of modern Guatemala. With its roots in the UNDERWORLD and its branches in the heavens, this great tree connected the planes of SKY, EARTH, and Underworld. In Yucatec, the term *yaxché* signifies first or green tree. Although the concept of first tree is entirely apt for the cosmic tree at the center of the world, the reference to green is also appropriate; in

ancient Maya religion, green is the color associated with the central place. The Colonial Yucatec *Chilam Balam of Chumayel* describes four *imix yaxche* set up at the four corners of the world, each associated with the cardinal directional COLORS of red, white, black and yellow. Thus the *yaxche* world tree is simultaneously a single green tree and four trees associated with a directional color. On pages 25 to 28 of the Postclassic Maya Codex Dresden the four directional trees are illustrated with a particular god and cardinal region.

In the Dresden passage, the world trees are associated with the four YEARBEARERS, the days by which the 365-day year was named. A markedly similar passage occurs on pages 49 to 52 of the Central Mexican Codex Borgia, where four trees are oriented to the four yearbearers and directional gods. A fifth, central tree of growing MAIZE appears on page 53, here flanked by QUETZALCOATL and the green Ahuiateotl named 5 Malinalli. In Central Mexican iconography the four directional trees are distinguished by species and by a particular animal, usually a bird, appearing at the top of the tree. On page 1 of the Codex Féjerváry-Mayer, the four directional trees appear with their accompanying birds, gods, days, and YEARBEARERS.

The placing of birds in world trees is of considerable antiquity in the Maya region. At Late Classic Palenque, this motif occurs on the Tablet of the Cross, the Tablet of the Foliated Cross, and the sarcophagus lid from Pacal's tomb in the Temple of the Inscriptions. Stela 25 from the Protoclassic site of Izapa, Chiapas, portrays a bird atop a tree-like CAIMAN for a trunk, probably a reference to the spiny green trunk of the *yaxché*. Izapa Stela 5 bears one of the most complex representations of a world tree ever carved, but extensive erosion of the monument prohibits a clear understanding of this early and important scene. *See also* CREATION ACCOUNTS.

writing Certainly no later than 600 BC some Mesoamerican peoples knew how to write, for by that date, carved inscriptions appear at San José Mogote, Oaxaca. During the Protoclassic, writing thrived and developed in Veracruz and Oaxaca, and a few carved monuments, such as the La Mojarra stela, reveal that the system was fully developed, although it remains impenetrable to modern scholars. By the 1st c. BC complex calendrics were inscribed in the Maya area, where Mesoamerican writing eventually achieved its greatest sophistication.

During the Classic period, the Maya wrote in what linguists called a "mixed" script, composed of both phonetic syllables and logographs (that is, word pictures) that allowed them to replicate most of the nuances of speech. The word jaguar, *balam*, could be written by a jaguar head, or by the phonetic syllables *ba-la-ma*, with the final vowel silent, or even by a mix of the two, a jaguar head with a phonetic complement, such as *ma* underneath, probably to make it plain that the *balam* word was meant for jaguar and not some other synonym. During the Postclassic, perhaps because of the dearth of public monuments, writing grew ever more phonetic and thus less accessible to those not trained to read and write.

At the time of the Conquest, the Spanish described writing in both Central Mexico and among the Maya as the preserve of PRIESTS, and most writing was considered sacred. For the Classic Maya, literacy was probably the province of the nobility, but noble women may also have learned to read and write: at least one noble woman, Lady Ahau Katun of Piedras Negras, bore the title Ahau Kin, or lord sun, one of the highest noble titles, probably indicating her literacy.

At TEOTIHUACAN, despite what must have been a familiarity with Maya script, there was little interest in writing, and even when it grew more common in Postclassic Central Mexico, few phonetic elements were added until after the Conquest, when Precolumbian writing flourished for several decades before dying out altogether.

According to sources from separate Mesoamerican regions, the gods invented writing. The Maya attributed the invention to ITZAMNA, who may be called *ah dzib*, He of the Writing. In the POPOL VUH, the older brothers of the Hero Twins, the Monkey Scribes, are the patrons of writing and the arts. The Aztecs called writing by a metaphor, *tlilli tlapalli*, "the black, the red," which, as Michael Coe has suggested, may refer to a Maya origin for Central Mexican books and writing, since the surviving Maya books are written in red and black while the Central Mexican ones are not. *See also* SCRIBAL GODS.

The **wind** god Ehecatl-Quetzalcoatl or 9 Wind in front of his wind temple, Nochistlan Vase, Late Postclassic Mixtec. The cut conch wind jewel of Quetzalcoatl can be seen on the thatched roof of the temple.

World trees oriented to the four directions, Codex Fejérváry-Mayer, p. 1, Late Postclassic period.

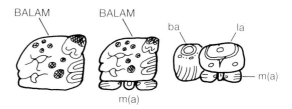

Writing: the Mayan word *balam*, meaning jaguar, could be written logographically (left), phonetically (right), or logographically with a phonetic complement (center).

Xbalanque *see* CREATION ACCOUNTS; POPOL VUH; TWINS

Xibalba *see* UNDERWORLD

Xipe Totec Xipe Totec, Our Lord the Flayed One, had achieved a large cult following in Central Mexico at the time of the Conquest, and the celebration of his festival, Tlacaxipe-hualiztli, reverberated beyond the normal VEINTENA, or 20-day period. Alfonso Caso and Ignacio Bernal identified Xipe with the Zapotec god Yopi and found him commonly represented in Classic period urns, and Sahagún attributed his origins to the Zapotecs. Among the Mixtecs, Xipe was known as the god 7 Rain. The celebration of Xipe Totec flourished along the Gulf Coast in the early Postclassic before gaining a prominent place in the Aztec pantheon, probably as a result of the Aztec domination of the Gulf Coast after the famines of the mid-15th c. According to Aztec sources, Xipe was born in the first genesis of the gods, and is identified also as the Red TEZCATLIPOCA.

Most Xipe figures vividly depict a human inside the flayed skin of another man, the extra flayed hands hanging like mittens. Characteristic vertical stripes run from forehead to chin, running over or broken by the eyes. Puckered and bubbled, the flayed skin usually displays an incision where the HEART was removed; the penis is absent; the skin is elaborately tied on at the back. Conceptually, the flayed skin may suggest a glorified foreskin. Some Aztec stone sculptures may have been attired in a flayed human skin.

Goldsmiths regarded Xipe Totec as their patron, and they made rich offerings at his TEMPLE, Yopico, within the Templo Mayor. During the Tlacaxipehualiztli festival, a man donned the skin of a slain CAPTIVE, which the goldsmiths likened to a golden sheathing, and they adorned the impersonator with red spoonbill feathers and golden jewelry. Xipe also had the power to cure eye ailments, and offerings were made to him at Yopico by those who sought miraculous cures.

Tlacaxipehualiztli, usually calculated as the third *veintena* of the solar year, began with the flaying of captives of war, usually following gladiatorial combat, of which Xipe was also a patron. Victorious warriors donned the skins of their captives and wore them for days, engaging in mock skirmishes throughout Tenochtitlan, begging alms and then blessing those who gave them food and offerings. The stinking skins were worn for 20 days, by which time they had nearly rotten off, and then, or 20 days hence, thrown by some accounts into a CAVE, or by others into a hole.

At the time of the Conquest the Xipe festival fell during the spring, in our month of March, and much of its imagery suggests agricultural renewal: as a seed germinates, it feeds off the rotting hull around it, finally letting the new shoot emerge. The Xipe impersonators wore the old skins until they were rotten, when the young man once again emerged. *See also* DEITY IMPERSONATION.

Xiuhcoatl According to Aztec accounts, the newly born HUITZILOPOCHTLI destroyed COYOLXAUHQUI and the Centzon Huitznahua with a fiery SERPENT known as the Xiuhcoatl, as illustrated on a fragmentary Coyolxauhqui sculpture excavated at the Templo Mayor. Like the better known Coyolxauhqui monument discovered in 1978, this was originally a great stone disk depicting the slain Coyolxauhqui. However, in this case, the Xiuhcoatl serpent actually penetrates the chest of the goddess, with the body and tasseled tail projecting out of the wound.

In Aztec iconography, the Xiuhcoatl typically has a sharply back-turning snout, a segmented body, and a tail resembling the trapeze-and-ray year sign. This tail device probably does refer to the year sign; *xihuitl* signifies "year," "turquoise," and "grass" in Nahuatl, and in many cases the tail is marked with the sign for grass, parallel rods tipped with circular elements. Double and triple knotted strips of PAPER (sometimes called "bow-ties") wrap the fire serpent's body and link it to SACRIFICE and BLOODLETTING.

During the Postclassic period, the Xiuhcoatl appears with all three concepts: TURQUOISE, grass, and the vague solar year (*see* CALENDAR). On page 46 of the Codex Borgia, four smoking Xiuhcoatl serpents surround a burning turquoise mirror. Similar turquoise-rimmed MIRRORS are known from Early Postclassic Tula (*see* TOLLAN) and Chichen Itzá, where four Xiuhcoatls in turquoise mosaic circle the mirror rim. The atlantean warrior columns from Mound B at Tula wear precisely this type of mirror upon their backs. In this case, the bodies of the four smoking serpents display the grass motif of parallel lines tipped with dots.

The association of the Xiuhcoatl with turquoise, grass and the solar year relates to its essential meaning of FIRE and solar heat. Turquoise, dry grass, and the vague year were all identified with fire in Postclassic Central Mexico. The Xiuhcoatl is emblematic of the Central Mexican god of fire, XIUHTE-CUHTLI, the Turquoise Lord. The Xiuhcoatl wielded by the newly born Huitzilopochtli represents the fiery rays of the SUN dispelling the forces of darkness.

Although the Xiuhcoatl can be readily traced back to Early Postclassic Tula, its ultimate origins are still obscure. Nonetheless, the TEOTIHUACAN War Serpent probably constitutes an ancestral form of the Xiuhcoatl; in Classic period iconography, the WAR SERPENT appears with flames, the grass motif, and the trapeze-and-ray year sign. *See also* TEOTI-HUACAN GODS.

The flayed god, **Xipe Totec**. (*Left*) Xipe impersonator dressed in a human skin, Florentine Codex, Book 2, 16th c. Aztec. (*Right*) Aztec sculpture of Xipe, Late Postclassic period.

Xiuhtecuhtli A Central Mexican god of FIRE, Xiuhtecuhtli overlaps with the aged fire god, HUEHUETEOTL. According to the Florentine Codex, Huehueteotl was but another epithet of Xiuhtecuhtli. But whereas Huehueteotl is depicted as a markedly aged being, Xiuhtecuhtli displays no indications of infirm old age: he is strongly identified with youthful warriors and rulership.

The name Xiuhtecuhtli signifies Turquoise Lord, and he usually appears richly bedecked in TURQUOISE mosaic, the *xiuhuitzolli* crown of rulership, and a turquoise pectoral often in the form of a stylized BUTTERFLY. Xiuhtecuhtli commonly wears a descending turquoise-colored bird, the *xiuhtototl* (*Cotinga amabilus*), against his brow and the XIUHCOATL fire serpent on his back. Many of these turquoise costume elements of Xiuhtecuhtli appear together on Early Postclassic Toltec warriors, and are also associated with the MORTUARY BUNDLES of Aztec warriors, as illustrated in the Codex Magliabechiano. However, clear depictions of Xiuhtecuhtli are not common until the Late Postclassic period. The depiction of Xiuhtecuhtli on page 49 of the Codex Dresden constitutes a rare Maya example of this Central Mexican being. The accompanying Maya hieroglyphic text phonetically names him *chac xiutei*, a close gloss to the Nahuatl Xiuhtecuhtli.

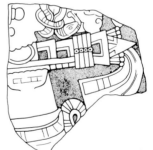

Fragment of a monument depicting a **Xiuhcoatl** serpent tearing open the chest of Coyolxauhqui, Templo Mayor, Tenochtitlan.

Xiuhtecuhtli, the Central Mexican god of fire and time, Florentine Codex, Book 1, 16th c. Aztec.

In Nahuatl, *xihuitl* signifies year as well as turquoise, and according to a number of sources, Xiuhtecuhtli was the god of the year, and by extension, of time itself. In the 260-day CALENDAR, Xiuhtecuhtli serves as the patron of the day Atl and the TRECENA 1 Coatl.

Xochipilli Xochipilli, whose name means "Flower Prince," is closely identified with Macuilxochitl, 5 Flower, one of the AHUIATE-TEO, or gods of excess. Sahagún attributes to Xochipilli the meting out of hemorrhoids, venereal disease and boils to those who violate times of fasting with sexual intercourse, but he is also a god of positive creative energies, and as such is a patron of FLOWERS, dancing, feasting, painting, and game-playing. Because of his generative powers, he is also closely linked to CINTEOTL, the young maize god. Xochipilli was feted early in the growing season, during Tecuilhuitontli, when his impersonator (*see* DEITY IMPERSONATION) was sacrificed. *See also* VEINTENA.

Xochiquetzal Literally "Flower Quetzal," Xochiquetzal epitomized young female sexual power, FLOWERS, and pleasure, and in this regard, was related to the AHUIATETEO and excess. But she was also a patroness of weavers and the arts practiced by noblewomen; she presided over childbirth and pregnancy and served as the guardian of the young mother. In these ways she bears relationship to TOCI, TLAZOLTEOTL, and the other mother goddesses, but unlike those female deities, Xochiquetzal remained ever young and beautiful, ever alluring. Depictions generally show her in luxurious attire and wearing GOLD ornaments.

The patron of the TRECENA 1 Xochitl, Xochiquetzal was feted during the VEINTENA Hueypachtli, especially by the practitioners of luxury arts – metalsmiths, sculptors, painters, weavers, featherworkers and embroiderers, in particular – who presented a woman to impersonate the goddess (*see* DEITY IMPERSON-ATION). After PRIESTS sacrificed and flayed her, a man donned the skin and fancy attire, sat at a loom, and pretended to weave, while the master craftspeople danced around in costumes of MONKEYS, JAGUARS, DOGS, coyotes, and pumas. Subsequently the worshippers confessed their sins to her idol through penitential tongue BLOODLETTING and completed their atonement with a ritual bath. A Xochiquetzal impersonator was one of the four brides taken by the HUITZILOPOCHTLI impersonator before his sacrifice during the feast of Toxcatl.

Xolotl Although living in intimate proximity to humans, the DOG breaks on a daily basis many basic social conventions observed by people; perhaps for this reason, dogs were considered filthy and immoral in Mesoamerica. The canine god Xolotl embodies many of the characteristics ascribed to them. This Central Mexican god appears to have served as the *nahualli*, or double, of QUETZALCOATL, and he accompanied Quetzalcoatl in his descent to the UNDERWORLD to retrieve the bones of mankind. As the canine companion of Quetzalcoatl, Xolotl wears the cut conch pectoral and other costume elements of Ehecatl-Quetzalcoatl.

Although the faithful assistant and companion to the great culture hero Quetzalcoatl, Xolotl was also identified with sickness and physical DEFORMITY. In the codices, he commonly displays a ragged-edged ear, generally believed to be due to the running sores which often occur on dogs' ears. The name Xolotl relates to concepts of TWINS and deformity. In Nahuatl, *xolochaui* signifies "to wrinkle or double over," and in fact Xolotl is frequently depicted with a deeply furrowed face. However, the word *xolotl* also frequently refers to twinned objects in Nahuatl; thus the term for a doubled MAIZE plant is *xolotl*, and doubled MAGUEY, *mexolotl*. In Postclassic Central Mexico, twins were feared much like monstrous births or deformities. According to Tezozomoc, DWARVES AND HUNCHBACKS were termed *xolome* and the name may explain why *xolotl* also signified a courtly page, since dwarves, hunchbacks and other physically deformed individuals often served in the palace court. The identification of the dog with twinning and deformities is of great antiquity in Mesoamerica: two-headed dogs are commonly found in the Protoclassic ceramic sculpture of West Mexico.

Xolotl plays an important role in certain Aztec accounts of the creation of the fifth sun at TEOTIHUACAN (*see* CREATION ACCOUNTS). According to Sahagún, during the SACRIFICE of the gods at the first dawning, Xolotl unsuccessfully tries to escape by first turning into the doubled maize plant, then the doubled *mexolotl*, or maguey, and finally the salamander known as the *axolotl*, or "water xolotl." However, in the Mendieta account of this mass sacrifice, Xolotl is described as the sacrificer rather than the victim. In codical depictions of the TRECENA 1 Cozcacuauhtli, Xolotl holds the FLINT blade of sacrifice. He also serves as the patron of the day Ollin.

Xochipilli, the god of flowers and music, seated upon a drum, Aztec, Late Postclassic period.

Yacatecuhtli *see* MERCHANTS

yahui Among the more important supernaturals appearing in the Postclassic Mixtec codices is a character wearing a XIUHCOATL serpent headdress and tail and the shell of a TURTLE upon his body. As an indication of its fiery nature, the Xiuhcoatl occasionally sprouts flaming volutes from the head and tail. At times, the figure carries a conch trumpet and FLINT blades in his hands; in many instances he appears flying or in the role of a sacrificer tearing the HEART out of a victim. Mary Elizabeth Smith has noted that in the Codex Muro and Codex Sánchez-Solís, this turtle-fire-serpent character is named *yahui*. In the Colonial Mixtec Alvarado Dictionary, *yahui* is defined as a certain wizard that can fly through the air. According to Smith, this flying *yahui* may be identical to one of the two sons born to the creator couple 1 Deer.

Xochiquetzal, the Central Mexican goddess of love, Codex Borbonicus, p. 19, 16th c. Aztec.

Among the Mixtecs, the *yahui* may have been the companion spirit of powerful transformational sorcerers, much like the *nahualli* sorcerers of Central Mexico (*see* NAHUAL). One of the most common companion spirits of Mesoamerican sorcerers is lightning, which provides the SHAMAN with rapid flight and omnipotent power. The *yahui* may allude to both LIGHTNING AND THUNDER. Whereas his ability to fly, the fire serpent attributes, and the flint blades may refer to lightning, the turtle shell and conch could be allusions to thunder-making instruments. Although the *yahui* character is found widely in Mixtec codices, he was probably borrowed from the Zapotecs. The serpent and turtle shell *yahui* often occurs in Zapotec iconography and appears in ceramic art as early as Monte Albán II.

Xolotl, patron of the day Ollin, in the form of a diseased *ahuiateotl*, Codex Borgia, p. 10, Late Postclassic period.

yearbearers To distinguish one 365-day year from another in the 52-year CALENDAR, Mesoamerican peoples named each year after a particular day in the coincident 260-day calendar. These days are called year-

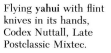

Flying **yahui** with flint knives in its hands, Codex Nuttall, Late Postclassic Mixtec.

bearers. Among the Postclassic Maya of Yucatán, the yearbearer occurred on the first day
of the solar year, while the Aztecs named
their years after the day in the 260-day
calendar falling on the 360th day of the 365-
day calendar.

To calculate the yearbearer in either system requires two basic calculations relating
the 260-day (13×20) and 365-day
$(18 \times 20 + 5)$ calendars. First, dividing the
number of day names, 20, into 365 yields a
remainder of 5; thus for each successive solar
year, the day names move five places forward.
After four years, the day naming the year
has moved 20 places, returning it to the
original day name that started the series, so
only four days can be yearbearers. Second,
dividing the day numbers, 13, into 365 leaves
a remainder of 1. So while the day names
progress by five each year, the numerals
increase by one until reaching 13 when they
begin again. For the 16th c. Aztecs, the order
of the 52 years ran as follows: 2 Acatl, 3
Tecpatl, 4 Calli, 5 Tochtli, 6 Acatl, and so on,
until the final year of 1 Tochtli, which would
then be followed by 2 Acatl, the first year of
the next 52-year cycle.

Yearbearers often bore special signs to cue
the reader to the meaning. Among the Classic
period Zapotecs, a headband containing a
cross in the form of a diadem signaled
yearbearer dates. This convention occurred
as early as Monte Albán I and appears on
Stela 12, a monument that dates to c.500 BC.

In Central Mexico, the Late Classic writing
of Xochicalco indicates a yearbearer with
a looped cord. In full-figure forms of this
convention, it can be seen that the cord is a
tumpline or sling for carrying the year glyph,
as if the year were a burden to be supported.
The looped cord convention also occurs at the
contemporaneous sites of Central Mexican
Teotenango del Valle and Maltrata, Veracruz.
At Early Postclassic Tula, the looped cord
occurs as the tumpline borne by an old man
carrying the year. Among the Postclassic
Mixtecs, yearbearer dates were designated
by the MEXICAN YEAR SIGN. In their books, the
Aztecs marked the year by placing it in a
turquoise-blue square, a convention with a
linguistic base: in Nahuatl *xihuitl* signifies
"turquoise" as well as "year." Among the
Maya, despite their use of the yearbearer
system, there is no known yearbearer sign,
possibly because for recording history the
Maya favored units of the Long Count rather
than the succession of yearbearers.

The particular four days selected as yearbearers varied widely in Mesoamerica. The
most common sequence was the 3rd, 8th,
13th, and 18th day names, corresponding to
Calli (House), Tochtli (Rabbit), Acatl (Reed),
and Tecpatl (Flint) in the Aztec series of day
names. This series is found at Xochicalco,
Teotenango del Valle, Maltrata, among the
Postclassic Toltecs, Mixtecs, Aztecs, and other
peoples of highland Mexico, and in the Paris
and Dresden codices of the Postclassic Yuca-

tec Maya. However, among the Zapotecs and in neighboring Guerrero, the yearbearers were the 2nd, 7th, 12th, and 17th day names. During the Late Postclassic, some Yucatec Maya used yet another yearbearer system, in this case, the 4th, 9th, 14th, and 19th day names, corresponding to Kan, Muluc, Ix, and Cauac. *See also* CARGO.

yoke A yoke (sometimes known by the Spanish word *yugo*), the U-shaped element of the BALLGAME costume, was worn around the waist to deflect blows from the center of the body. Slipped on sideways, the front, back, and one side of the body were always protected. Hundreds, if not thousands, of stone ballgame yokes have been found in tombs along the Veracruz coast and the Pacific slope of Guatemala, almost exclusively from the Classic period, and they have also been recovered from surface remains at Copán and Palenque. Most stone yokes weigh 25–35 lb (*c.* 11.5–15.5 kg), and although a trained player could move wearing one, these stone yokes were probably reserved for ceremonial use, perhaps as a sort of trophy – stone versions of what was probably a wooden piece of protective armor. A few have no opening and could not have been worn. Many, particularly those from Veracruz, bear complicated iconography that is difficult to decipher without a modern drawing. Common imagery includes TOADS, sacrificial victims, and TUERTOS. *See also* HACHA.

Toltec representation of a **yearbearer** flint; the figure carries the year 11 Flint. Tula, Early Postclassic period.

The stone **yokes** associated with the ballgame can be either enclosed or open-ended, Classic Veracruz.

Guide to Sources and Bibliography

The reader may well wonder how the authors have come to the conclusions presented in this book. The sources for the Precolumbian past in Mesoamerica are many and diverse, and the piecing together of gods, iconography, and meaning rarely depends on just a single source but rather on the more convincing evidence that comes from finding patterns that are reflected in archaeology or ethnohistory. In general, we have made direct citations in this book only from 16th c. sources, and we have tried to attribute important post-1950 discoveries to those responsible. The following discussion and bibliography are by no means exhaustive or complete (and the reader is advised to look elsewhere for a history of Mesoamerican archaeology*) but what follows is a description of sources, how they have come down to us, and how scholars have come to understand them.

Prehispanic Books

Despite the concerted effort by religious and civil authorities to destroy any native manifestation of "idolatry" after the Conquest, a number of Prehispanic books – screenfolds of deerskin or fig paper painted with fine brushes – have survived. Some were shipped to Europe before the zeal to destroy overcame the conquerors, while others were hidden for generations and came to light in the 19th c. Of primary importance for studying gods and symbols is the Borgia group of manuscripts, named after the largest and finest among them. Although it may have been painted in Puebla or Cholula or perhaps even in Veracruz, the Codex Borgia is the best surviving example of a Central Mexican book, containing a divinatory 260-day calendar, sections on yearbearers and Venus, and a long, poorly understood section ("middle pages") that depicts the journey of Quetzalcoatl and Tezcatlipoca to the nadir of the Underworld. Other manuscripts in the Borgia group lack these middle pages, but all share a similar style and a similar constellation of gods. Most are named for their original collector and all reside in European libraries: Borgia, Laud, Fejérváry-Mayer, Cospi, and the Vaticanus B. Donald Robertson demonstrated that the Codex Borbonicus, long thought to be a Prehispanic book, was made after the Conquest, but probably before 1530; its first part, a tonalamatl, or 260-day calendar, replicates a luxurious Aztec model. Because of the size and detail of the Borbonicus, it offers one of the best guides to *trecena* patrons and *veintena* festivals.

Several Mixtec Prehispanic codices have survived, perhaps because of their predominantly historical and genealogical content, or it may simply be that

---

* For histories of Mesoamerican archaeology, the reader should consult Bernal 1962, Adams 1969, Bernal 1980, and Willey and Sabloff 1980. The history of the recognition of art in the New World is treated in Kubler 1990. See Keen 1971 and Boone 1987 for a consideration of Aztec historiography; for the Maya, see Schele and Miller 1986, Miller 1989, Coe 1992 and Stuart 1992.

manuscripts treating other subjects were usually destroyed. New genealogies in Prehispanic style continued to be made during the 16th c. and Prehispanic manuscripts received continued annotation after the Conquest. Some were later presented in Colonial courts as evidence in cases involving land tenure; owners scraped manuscripts of all "idolatrous" imagery in order that they be accepted by the court as evidence, and as a result, a manuscript like the Bodley was badly mutilated. The best preserved of the Mixtec books are the Selden, Nuttall, Colombino, Bodley, and the Vindobonensis (or Vienna), and several are kept at the Bodleian Library in Oxford. Of these the Vindobonensis is the richest source for Mixtec gods. No Prehispanic Zapotec manuscripts survive.

Four Maya screenfolds – the Dresden, Madrid, Paris, and Grolier – escaped the bonfires of Diego de Landa, the Franciscan later tried for excessive zeal in enforcing the notorious *auto da fé* in Maní, Yucatán. The Grolier may have been written several centuries before the Conquest, but the others were probably painted within 100 years of the Spanish arrival. The Dresden Codex is a particularly important source for studying the gods and religious practices of Late Postclassic Yucatán. Yucatec scribes wrote these books with texts in red and black pigments and illustrated them with pictures of gods and rituals in the same colors.

Sixteenth-century European Sources

Sixteenth-century sources provide the most broad and accurate descriptions of Mesoamerican life, and some of these, such as the *Second Letter* of Cortés to King Charles V or the much later *Discovery and Conquest of Mexico* by Bernal Diaz offer vivid eye-witness descriptions of the Aztecs and their neighbors, their cities, temples, and gods. Without such accounts, we would know nothing about such things as the elaborate cuisine prepared for Motecuhzoma II or the sort of zoo for exotic animals that he kept or the nature and abundance of the Aztec marketplace.

From across all Europe Charles V called Apostolic Twelves from various Catholic religious orders – Franciscans, Dominicans, and Augustinians – to carry out the conversion of New Spain, or Mexico, as the Spaniards soon began to call the land. ("Mexico" is a corruption of Mexica-Tenochtitlan, the Aztec name for their capital city.) Educated men truly interested in the land and people, these first friars soon began to make systematic records of the New World, largely in order to speed conversion and to understand the language and religion of the people they sought to bring under control. Among the authors of the 16th c. sources, one name stands above all others: Father Bernardino de Sahagún, a Franciscan friar who arrived just a few years after the original Twelve, but who knew most of them and drew on their experiences as well as his own.

Sahagún devoted his life to understanding the Aztecs and their neighbors in the Valley of Mexico. He became fluent in Nahuatl and wrote dozens of sermons in it that his minions then preached throughout the countryside. But, most importantly, he began to gather systematically the knowledge of the Precolumbian world and to present it in volumes along the lines of a late medieval encyclopedia. A preliminary effort, the Primeros Memoriales (sometimes known as the Codices Matritenses), was finished in 1560 or so, but his lifework, the *General History of the Things of New Spain*, was completed and produced in subsequent decades. Usually known as the *Florentine Codex*, the name given to the sole surviving holograph (considered subversive, other copies sent to Spain were confiscated and presumably destroyed by Spanish authorities), the 12-volume work is a major encyclopedia assembled by

Sahagún and a troop of Nahuatl-speaking nobles, and the text is written in parallel columns of Nahuatl and Spanish. The work treats the gods, religion, history, temples and cities, ceremonies, omens, auguries, natural history, cosmography, moral rhetoric, calendar; describes different ethnic groups; and relates the Conquest itself, as told from the native point of view. A separate Spanish-only text also survives. Despite the lens of the Spanish Conquest, the Florentine Codex is the single greatest source for understanding the native New World.

Anonymous authors, including friars and natives, also made other early records – probably in the first generation after the Conquest – of Aztec gods and religion that survive only as fragments: *Historia de los mexicanos por sus pinturas, Leyenda de los soles,* and *Histoyre du mechique.* These extremely important texts recount the deities, religion, and cosmography and describe now-lost manuscripts, probably as presented to the friars by Aztec interlocutors. Many other friars wrote important documents for understanding the Conquest and the social environment of the 16th c., but they offered only a few insights into the religious iconography of the past. The well-known Dominican, Bartolomé de Las Casas, for example, wrote lengthy tracts describing indigenous conditions and advocating social reform, but offers little information on Mesoamerican gods not expounded more explicitly elsewhere.

Toward the end of the century, two major efforts at documentation were completed. First, in 1577 Philip II conducted a census of New Spain, demanding that each province answer 50 questions about its people, wealth, geography, local administration, religious practices, and provide a map. Six years later, most of these *relaciones geográficas* were completed, many with the assistance of native informants. In this same period, Diego Durán, a fierce Dominican priest who both loved Mexico and lamented the tenacity of native religion, completed a series of important studies known today as *The Book of the Gods and Rites, The Ancient Calendar,* and *The History of the Indies*; the last is the most comprehensive history of the Aztec state.

The friars concentrated on the Valley of Mexico, so it is little wonder that few records survive for other regions. Diego de Landa wrote his *Relación de las cosas de Yucatán* in the 1560s while awaiting trial in Spain for his overenthusiastic enforcement of the Inquisition. Although this document is extremely useful – Landa, for example, wrote down the 30 characters in Maya phonetic, syllabic script that led eventually to the phonetic decipherment of Maya hieroglyphic writing – it lacks the richness of detail that characterizes the Central Mexican documents. In the 17th c., Father Francisco de Burgoa made an important record of the Zapotecs, although nothing comparable survives for the Mixtecs.

Native Documents after the Conquest

After the Spanish Conquest, native scribes worked for their new masters and made dozens of manuscripts that survive, even though far more were lost. Some books took on new content to suit the audience: religious iconography was spelled out in order that a priest recognize his enemy; histories recounted peregrinations of different ethnic groups, partly in order to express grievances regarding land distribution or privileges; and native books turned up in Colonial legal proceedings. The Spanish commissioned tribute records to assess the wealth of their colony and maps to guide them to its sources. Many books required a hybrid effort: native scribes painted the illustrations and Europeans added interpretive glosses. Where Mesoamericans learned to represent their languages in the European alphabet, they began to write books of their own in this new system, occasionally transcribing an ancient picture book, as in the case of the *Popol Vuh*. As the 16th c. progressed, the Spanish Crown passed from Charles V to Philip II, who had less desire to understand Mesoamerica and less patience with the eclectic sort of books made there: his subordinates must have destroyed the missing copies of Sahagún's encyclopedia, although he did commission the *Relaciones geográficas*, completed in 1583. After the English defeat of the Spanish Armada in 1588, Spain wanted little from her colonies but precious minerals. By the end of the 16th c., 90 percent of the indigenous population had died; the generation that had known Preconquest life was gone, and sympathetic friars had generally given way to less educated priests dependent on local Colonial patronage. The Crown forbade foreigners (i.e. non-Spanish born) to visit the colonies. The Precolumbian past was passively abandoned or actively destroyed.

The major groups of 16th c. native or hybrid works can be roughly classified as follows (some are written on native paper, others on European paper; a *lienzo* is painted on cloth; the catalogue in the *Handbook of Middle American Indians*, particularly Glass 1975, should be consulted):

MAPS: including Plano en Papel de Maguey, Mapa de Coatlinchan, Mapas de Cuauhtinchan, Mapa Quinatzin, Mapa de Santa Cruz, among others

HISTORICAL/RELIGIOUS CHRONICLES: including Relación de Michoacán, Codex Boturini, Codex Mendoza, part 1, Lienzo de Tlaxcala (orig. lost), Historia Tolteca-Chichimeca, the Popol Vuh

TRIBUTE LISTS: Codex Mendoza, part 2, and Matrícula de Tributos

DESCRIPTIONS OF FESTIVALS AND CUSTOMS: including the Codex Magliabechiano and its group; the paired manuscripts Codex Telleriano-Remensis and Codex Rios, or Vaticanus A; the Tovar Calendar; and Codex Mendoza, part 3

Other manuscripts, including an herbal, Codex Badianus, written in Latin by a learned Nahuatl speaker, survive from the 16th c., but few have played a seminal role in the decipherment of Mesoamerican gods and symbols. Some later Colonial sources, including Tezozómoc's *Crónica mexicana* (c. 1600), Torquemada's *Monar-chía indiana* (c. 1613), Chimalpahín's *Relaciones* (c. 1625), Ixtlilxochitl's *Relaciones* and *Historia chichimeca*, and the various Mayan Books of Chilam Balam (all 18th c.) include information not available from other sources.

The End of the Spanish Colonial Era

Perhaps in response to the general intellectual climate of the Enlightenment, Charles III of Spain took a renewed scientific interest in the Americas and the Prehispanic past, and so inaugurated the modern era in Mesoamerican studies. In 1786, he sent out explorers to document Palenque, Chiapas, and at the beginning of the 19th c., his son, Charles IV, commissioned further study of abandoned archaeological sites, their merit and contents, including Monte Albán and Mitla. The Mexican scholar José Antonio Alzate published drawings and commentary on El Tajín and Xochicalco. The German nobleman and scholar Alexander von Humboldt was granted leave to carry out scientific study in the Spanish colonies, resulting in his 1810 *Vues des cordillères et monuments des peuple indigènes de l'Amérique*. By the time of Mexican independence, the regional styles of Mesoamerican art and the presence of different gods and religious practices began to be recognized.

In 1790 and 1791, when workmen uncovered three Aztec monoliths, the Stone of Tizoc, the Calendar Stone, and the large Coatlicue, they were preserved rather than destroyed, and the scholar Antonio Léon y Gama began deciphering their meaning. He was the first student to publish accurate, measured drawings of Aztec religious art. Although he thought the Calender Stone to be a true calendar, recording hours, days, weeks, months, years, and other cycles, a reading no longer tenable, he nevertheless correctly identified many symbols and gods (while misidentifying others), and we may consider Léon y Gama's efforts as the first scientific study of Mesoamerican iconography.

Following the Mexican declaration of independence in 1810 and the withdrawal of Spanish authority in 1821 (and the independence of Central America in 1825, opening up yet more lands), European, North American, and Mexican investigators surged across the countryside, exploring, studying, and collecting evidence of the past. And when the Spanish left, they took with them quantities of documents, including, for example, the works of Diego Durán.

The Precolumbian past and the sophisticated cultures whose wreckage lay on and under the ground puzzled its 19th c. students and many offered fantastic explanations, some of which the Spanish had already put forth, such as the notion that Mesoamerican civilization was founded by the Lost Tribes of Israel or by strayed Egyptians (see Wauchope 1962). Soon Atlantis, India, China, and Africa were added to the stew; the Mormons saw Mesoamerican civilization as the locus for a separate resurrection of Christ. Authors argued about the possibility for high civilization to have flourished at all in Mesoamerica, but by the end of the century there was near-universal consensus among scholars that it had, that there was more time depth and antiquity than previously thought, and more diversity of cultures; among competing explanations, the idea that these cultures had grown up in the New World without Old World stimuli began to take root.

John Lloyd Stephens and Frederick Catherwood explored what are now Guatemala, Belize, Honduras, and the Mexican states of Chiapas, Yucatán, Campeche, and Quintana Roo in 1839–42, documenting dozens of Maya cities with lively descriptions and generally accurate illustrations. Unlike most of their contemporaries, they believed that the living Maya descended from the city-builders, and they recognized the uniformity of Maya writing across the vast geographic realm they traveled. They had no reason to believe that the cities had been abandoned any earlier than the time of the Conquest and so knew nothing of the antiquity of Maya cities. Stephens' four volumes were bestsellers; they went through dozens of editions and printings, perhaps creating the first large audience of armchair archaeologists in history, and they undoubtedly sparked interest in those who would later be scholars of ancient Mesoamerica.

Between 1831 and 1846, Edward King, Lord Kingsborough, drove himself into bankruptcy by bankrolling and publishing nine elephantine folios of facsimile reproductions of Precolumbian and Postconquest Mesoamerican codices and manuscripts known in European collections. Despite some serious handicaps – the copyist Agostino Aglio misinterpreted unfamiliar imagery and inevitably changed details in his interpretations of the manuscripts, and the enormous volumes could be bought only by major libraries or by the very wealthy – for the first time, the rich iconography in these books could be consulted widely, and dozens of Precolumbian sculptures were also illustrated. With this documentation, scholars could assemble and study the temples, books and gods of Mesoamerica, from Teotihuacan and Tenochtitlan in the north, on through Xochicalco, El Tajín, Monte Albán, and Mitla, to the Maya sites in the south.

Aztec history had been described many times by the 19th c., but the American historian William H. Prescott wrote what we might call the first "modern" history of the Aztecs, a 3-volume study published in 1843, using voluminous sources, particularly Precolumbian and early Postconquest manuscripts, to build a picture of the Aztecs that included their religious life. Sahagún's works began to be rediscovered, and a 3-volume Spanish edition of the *General History* text was published in 1829–30. And as museums around the world were founded, Mesoamerican antiquities began to receive a permanent, stable home. Founded in 1825, the Mexican National Museum has always housed the world's largest collection of Aztec antiquities. By the end of the century, the Trocadero, British Museum, American Museum of Natural History, and Smithsonian Institution, among others, would all amass significant collections of Mesoamerican materials.

At mid-century, several scholars competed to collect Precolumbian and Colonial manuscripts, prying them loose from archives, churches, and small towns. In the 18th c., Lorenzo Boturini had bought some 500 manuscripts before xenophobic Spanish officals deported him, confiscated the collection and then let it be dismantled. J. M. A. Aubin spent a decade collecting manuscripts around Mexico City and succeeded in reassembling many pieces of the Boturini corpus, which he then took to Paris in 1840 and spent the rest of his life studying. In Mexico, despite his antipathy for the Aztecs, Joaquín García Icazbalceta assembled previously unpublished documents relating to Mexico's history and began publishing them in 1858. Considering himself Aubin's heir, Abbé Charles-Etienne Brasseur de Bourbourg traveled among the Maya and sought out manuscripts and documents that he hoped would unravel their past. His perserverance and luck led him to make several important discoveries: first, in Guatemala, he came upon the 18th c. copy of the 16th c. *Popol Vuh*, translated it into French and published it; then, back in Spain, he found the Madrid Codex and a copy of Landa's *Relación* and published them as well.

Brasseur's discoveries ushered in a new phase of study, in which 16th c. commentaries were used to decipher Precolumbian books and art. Using the variety of sources now available to them, scholars in Mexico, the United States, and Europe began to identify gods, symbols, and iconography. Books and journals proliferated, fueling greater interest; national governments, academic institutions and private backers sponsored campaigns of exploration, and eventually, of excavation.

During the long, stable reign of Porfirio Díaz in Mexico (1876–1911), Mexican scholars began to study the Aztecs and their predecessors with care. Because of their identification with the despised Porfirio Díaz regime, however, some of their works have been unjustly neglected, or even condemned. Manuel Orozco y Berra, Jesús Sánchez, Alfredo Chavero, Justo Sierra, José Fernando Ramírez, Cecilio Robelo, and Jesús Galindo y Villa, among others, read manuscripts, published previously unknown documents, and began interpreting Aztec art, life and religion. Robelo published his 2-volume *Diccionario de Mitología Nahuatl* in 1905, a compendium of Central Mexican religion that was rarely cited by his contemporaries (and even less frequently today) but which must have been heavily consulted by his contemporaries and successors. Based on the sources unearthed or published by his learned colleagues, Robelo's dictionary is useful for any student of Aztec gods and symbols today and has remained surprisingly current. Of his Mexican contemporaries, Francisco Paso y Troncoso made the greatest contribution. A skilled *nahuatlato*, or Nahuatl-speaker and translator, Paso y Troncoso dedicated much of his life to rediscovering the works of Bernardino de Sahagún and making them available to scholars, although his vast project of translation and publication was left unfinished upon his death in Europe in 1916.

Leopold Batres carried out excavations at Mitla, Teotihuacan, and Tenochtitlan, and although the following generation of archaeologists harshly criticized Batres' techniques and results, his efforts laid the groundwork for modern archaeology in Mexico. After the Mexican Revolution, Manuel Gamio carried out the first stratigraphic excavations in Mexico, at Atzcapotzalco, opening up the possibility of documenting civilized life in the first millennium BC.

In France, E.-T. Hamy studied and separated Aztec from non-Aztec works in Paris museums, publishing dozens of articles in his journal *Décades americaines*, identifying gods and relating Teotihuacan representations to Aztec deities in useful investigations, although he shared with Brasseur a passion for theories of non-native origins of Mesoamerican civilization. He published the first edition of the Codex Borbonicus in 1899. Désiré Charnay had visited Mexico in 1857, but his 1880 trip produced his most important observations, the identification of Tula, Hidalgo, with the home of the Toltecs, and the linking of it culturally and temporally to Chichen Itzá, but unfortunately he then went on to attribute all civilization in Mesoamerica to Toltec genius.

Several German scholars made important contributions to the deciphering of Mesoamerican religious imagery at the end of the 19th c., but the wide-ranging efforts of Eduard Seler remain the most important today, perhaps because his commentaries are almost always rooted in an object or corpus: only rarely did Seler begin with an idea that he sought to prove, rather than starting with a text, an object, or a building. Sponsored by the Duc de Loubat, a wealthy New Yorker, from 1887 onward, Seler wrote commentaries to new facsimile editions of many codices in which he identified the gods, explicated the calendrics and related patterns to ethnohistoric documents. Although more skilled in his manipulation of Central Mexican materials, Seler was the first to compare Maya and Mexican materials systematically; more profoundly than any of his contemporaries, Seler drew his interpretations from the widest possible range of sources, including history, ethnohistory, and archaeological remains. Seler's writings began to be collected in the 5-volume *Gesammelte Abhandlungen* in 1902, and the final volume was issued posthumously in 1923. Seler's vast corpus remains the point of departure for most modern iconographic inquiries.

Once Ernst Förstemann, Royal Librarian in Dresden, began to prepare a facsimile edition of the Dresden Codex (pub. 1880), he worked with the manuscript until he had broken the code of the Maya calendar and mathematics, making possible the decipherment of the Long Count of the monuments and its correlation to the Christian calendar, as later propounded by the American journalist J. T. Goodman in 1905. From that point on, the antiquity of the Maya monuments later attributed to the "Classic" period was known, and the dichotomy of "Maya: Greeks of the New World" vs. "Aztecs: Romans of the New World" took root. The sudden cessation of Maya monuments with Long Count dates in the 9th c. came to be called the "collapse," a problem for scholars from that time onward. In 1897, Paul Schellhas inaugurated modern Maya iconographic studies with his investigation of the deities of the Maya codices in which he carefully isolated separate iconographic entities, recognized their name glyphs, and assigned neutral letters of the alphabet to individual gods.

In the United States, Daniel Brinton translated Nahuatl poetry into English (1887) and reacted against the excesses of enthusiasts like Charnay with skeptical attacks on the very existence of the Toltecs, invoking, in turn, the wrath of Seler. Zelia Nuttall, the first woman scholar to study Mesoamerica, published commentaries on Precolumbian manuscripts, correctly identified the large piece of featherwork in the Vienna Museum as a headdress, perhaps Motecuhzoma's, rather than a standard, and offered hypotheses for the meanings of some Mesoamerican calendrical cycles that her male colleagues found laughable, although some have been shown to be probable today. She correctly proposed that a Mixtec codex (like her contemporaries, she thought the Mixtec books were Aztec) depicted largely historical, not religious, iconography; in her honor, the book, the Codex Nuttall, was given her name.

Probably inspired by the writings of Stephens, scholars in the United States and England focused their attention on the Maya, particularly the discovery and exploration of archaeological sites. Alfred P. Maudslay made extensive Maya art available to study through publication of drawings of monuments at Copán, Quiriguá, Palenque, Yaxchilán, and Chichen Itzá. Despite efforts by Cyrus Thomas and others to use the Landa "alphabet" to decipher Maya texts, the nature of the script remained unknown until Yuri Knorosov tackled it after World War II. J. T. Goodman recognized the head and full-figure variants for numbers and period glyphs, some of which turned out to be gods. Herbert Spinden built on Schellhas's 1897 list of Postclassic Maya gods by identifying some of them and isolating yet others in the earlier Classic art for his 1909 Harvard dissertation, later published as *A Study of Maya Art* in 1913. George Vaillant established the basic chronological sequence for Maya ceramics still in use today. Harvard sponsored campaigns of archaeological exploration and documentation, and the Carnegie Institution of Washington dominated Maya archaeology between the World Wars, publishing vast quantities of material for later iconographic exegesis.

The Problems of Early 20th c. Mesoamerican Studies

With the correlation of the Maya and European calendars settled, the Maya were seen by many as the inventors of the calendar and gods. But problems remained with such a construct, particularly as evidenced by the corpus of art that came to be called "Olmec." Non-Mayanist Mesoamericanists, among them Marshall Saville, George Vaillant, Matthew Stirling, Alfonso Caso, and Miguel Covarrubias believed that the Olmec aesthetic and iconographic enigma, present both in Central Mexico and in Veracruz, predated the Maya. Covarrubias earned the wrath of Mayanists when he drew a now-famous flow chart (see illustration under WERE-JAGUAR, p. 185) to show how what he called Olmec were-jaguars preceded all other rain gods in Mesoamerica, and he called the Olmec the *cultura madre*. After World War II, radiocarbon dating would prove the chronological primacy of the Olmec as Mesoamerica's first complex culture and the Gulf Coast as its hearth.

Alfonso Caso excavated Monte Albán for several seasons in the 1930s, establishing a stratigraphically based chronology for Oaxaca and vastly amplifying the corpus of religious art. Caso and Ignacio Bernal studied Zapotec ceramic urns, isolating deity complexes and relating them to both Colonial god lists made by Francisco de Burgoa and to known Aztec gods. Unlike his predecessors, including Seler and Nuttall, Caso recognized that the Mixtec codices were distinct from Aztec ones, and he unraveled the major genealogies, identifying them with known places, although scholars now believe that he pushed the antiquity of these lineages back too far into the past.

Knowledgeable in all aspects of Mesoamerica except the Maya, Caso explored Aztec religion and iconography and offered what until recently were the most explicit studies of Mesoamerican calendars, and many of his interpretations have remained in favor.

Unlike many other Mesoamerican sites, Teotihuacan was never lost from view. But although Charnay had identified Tula, Hidalgo, as the historical home of the Toltecs, Teotihuacan had come to be considered Tula for most of the century. The discovery in the late 1930s of Teotihuacan-style pottery in contexts with datable Early Classic Maya pottery at Kaminaljuyú pushed Teotihuacan back into the first millennium AD and opened a place for Tula, confirmed as the Toltec capital by Wigberto Jiménez-Moreno at the first round table of the Sociedad mexicana de antropología in 1941.

As professor of anthropology at the National Autonomous University of Mexico in the 1920s, Seler's student Hermann Beyer carried on Mesoamerican iconographic studies, particularly of Aztec art, as did Walter Lehmann in Germany. Angel María Garibay offered the first comprehensive translations of Nahuatl texts. Ignacio Marquina explored the iconography of Mesoamerican architecture. Ignacio Bernal carried on Caso and Covarrubias's Olmec studies.

After World War II, scholars sought unified terminologies to refer to both time and place. Spinden and Morley's notion of Old and New Empires for the Maya, for example, had never applied to other parts of Mesoamerica, and evidence for early occupation of Yucatán made it impossible to believe the Maya collapse to have been a wholesale movement of peoples. A. V. Kidder and Tatiana Proskouriakoff of the Carnegie Institution of Washington began to refer in published works to what had also been called the "Initial Series Period" as the Classic era, roughly AD 300–900, and they used the term to refer to other contemporaneous cultures at Monte Albán and Teotihuacan. The Postclassic era, then, began with the rise of the Toltecs at Tula; the Olmec and other early developments were Preclassic, and fell in the first millennium BC. Such terms implied a value judgment that the "Classic" era achieved some ideal, a notion now out of favor, and so other terms have been proposed, but only the substitution of "Formative" for Preclassic has taken hold.

In 1943, Paul Kirchhoff suggested the name Mesoamerica to refer to an area of shared cultural traditions from 14 to 21 degrees north latitude, encompassing much of Mexico, all of Guatemala and Belize, and the northern strip of Honduras and El Salvador. This term has successfully replaced "Middle America," "Nuclear America," or the names of modern nation-states in scholarly discussion of the region.

Later 20th c. Studies: Maya

Sir Eric Thompson dominated studies of Maya religion and iconography for most of the 20th c. as surely as Eduard Seler had reigned over the Mesoamerican scene at the turn of the century. (Thompson's prominent colleague Sylvanus G. Morley operated more in the archaeological realm and ultimately followed many of Thompson's views in his synthetic writings.) Thompson sprinkled his writings with quotations from English literature which he used to idealize Maya gods and religion, heightening differences between what he characterized as the peaceful Classic period and the warlike Postclassic era. Based on his knowledge of Central Mexican iconography – a knowledge vastly expanded by his supervision of a translation of Seler's collected works during World War II – Thompson wrote *Maya Hieroglyphic Writing* (1950), a compendium of iconography as well as of Maya writing. In *Maya*

History and Religion (1970) he offered a new model of Maya religion, with many
gods subsumed under Itzamna.

The Carnegie Institution of Washington began to phase out its program of Maya
research after World War II, and Maya archaeologists turned away from the
excavation of major ceremonial architecture and the documentation of stone
monuments. In the field, archaeologists sought to determine the nature of Maya
settlement, without any special consideration of the elite and their art, yielding few
studies of religion, gods, and iconography, intellectual territory they had ceded to
Thompson. The contributions of Günter Zimmermann (1956) and Ferdinand Anders
(1963), updating the works of Schellhas and other German scholars, were among
only a very few such studies of the period.

Since 1970, however, studies of Maya religion have flourished, dependent in part
on the decipherment of Maya hieroglyphic writing that began with Yuri Knorosov
(first comprehensively published in English in 1967), Heinrich Berlin (1958), Tatiana
Proskouriakoff (1960, 1963, 1964), David Kelley (1962, 1976) and continued on with
Victoria Bricker, Federico Fahsen, Nikolai Grube, Stephen Houston, John Justeson,
Floyd Lounsbury, Berthold Riese, Linda Schele, and David Stuart, among others.
It took hieroglyphic decipherment, for example, for Proskouriakoff to prove that
Maya depictions represented named nobility, including women (1960), or to see
that the Classic Maya were a warlike people (e.g. Miller 1986). The 8 volumes
issued to date of the Palenque Round Table have been a forum for discussions of
Maya art and writing (1974–). Linda Schele has tackled dozens of iconographic
problems, with many of the results published in *The Blood of Kings* (1986) and *A
Forest of Kings* (1990), and she initiated *Copan Notes* and *Texas Notes*, privately
published iconographic and epigraphic commentaries. *Research Reports on Ancient
Maya Writing*, published by George Stuart, also treat religion and iconography. Karl
Taube has made a systematic reassessment of Postclassic Maya deities (1992).
Decipherment of Maya writing has meant not only the identification of deity names
but also the recognition of verbs marking religious events, among them bloodletting,
war, sacrifice, dreaming, dancing, death, and burial. Stephen Houston and David
Stuart recently cracked the pattern of naming places in Maya script and found the
names of supernatural places along with those of the mundane world.

Iconographic studies have also grown because of a near-explosion of new materials
for study from both archaeology and looting. Michael Coe has studied the new
corpus of Classic Maya ceramics and used the *Popol Vuh* to decipher iconography
and identify gods (1973, 1975, 1977, 1978, 1982); Clemency Coggins analyzed the
Tikal corpus (1975), while Francis Robicsek and Donald Hales considered others
without provenience (1981, 1982). Karl Herbert Mayer has assembled photographs
of looted monuments (1980, 1991). Since 1970, Nicholas Hellmuth has been
photographing Maya vessels, building a photographic archive kept at the University
of Texas at San Antonio (e.g. Quirarte 1979) and several museums; using the archive,
Hellmuth has analyzed Early Classic iconography (1987). Justin Kerr is publishing
the corpus of Maya vessels he has photographed with his rollout camera (1989,
1990, 1992). New editions and translations of the *Popol Vuh* have been useful
(Edmonson 1971; Tedlock 1985), as are new facsimile editions of the Maya codices
and the identification of a fourth Preconquest book, the Grolier Codex (Coe 1973).
Archaeological exploration has promoted study of gods and iconography, particularly
with the careful line drawings of monuments now considered obligatory for any
archaeological project (Jones and Satterthwaite 1982; Beetz and Satterthwaite 1981),

and the Corpus project directed by Ian Graham has set a high standard for all other line drawings (Corpus of Maya Hieroglyphic Inscriptions 1975–). The tomb paintings at Río Azul have amplified an understanding of the Maya iconography of death and the cave paintings at Naj Tunich have revealed the world of cave rituals. Ongoing projects at Copán and Dos Pilas continue to yield iconographic materials without precedent.

Some archaeological discoveries also reshaped fundamental thinking about Maya gods and religion, and discoveries at Cerros, El Mirador, and Kohunlich have shown that those gods were known by at least 100 BC; some of the Postconquest *Popol Vuh* narrative appears to be explicit on highland monuments and at Izapa by no later than AD 100. The murals of Bonampak and the discovery of the secret tomb within the Temple of Inscriptions at Palenque both suggested personal aggrandizement rather than paeans to Maya gods; the subsequent discovery of a major tomb at the base of Tikal Temple I confirmed the pattern of tombs within temples, ultimately leading Mayanists to recognize the role of ancestor worship in religion. Settlement studies have revealed the complexity of urban and rural life for the Maya; ecological archaeology has frequently resonated with iconographic patterns (Puleston 1976).

Recognition of war iconography among the Classic Maya (Riese 1984, Schele and Miller 1986; Schele and Freidel 1990) has narrowed the perceived intellectual and moral rift between the Classic Maya and the Maya at Chichen Itzá, raising questions of dating, provoking new iconographic studies of Postclassic Yucatán, and forcing a reevaluation of the role played by Tula at Chichen Itzá (Coggins and Shane 1984; Lincoln 1990).

Later 20th c. Studies: Central Mexico

In 1978, excavations began again at the Templo Mayor compound, the Aztec sacred precinct within Tenochtitlan, initiating a new era of Aztec archaeological and iconographic studies under Eduardo Matos Moctezuma. New major monuments such as the Coyolxauhqui stone came to light, as did abundant caches and offerings, allowing new understandings of Aztec religious practice and meaning (Boone 1987; Broda, Carrasco, and Matos Moctezuma 1987; Matos Moctezuma 1988), and the provincial Aztec record has also received incisive documentation (Solís 1981). Although buoyed by the new archaeological discoveries, Aztec textual and iconographic studies had long flourished, particularly in Mexico under the stewardship of Miguel Léon-Portilla, Alfredo López Austin, and Eduardo Matos Moctezuma; in the United States led by H.B. Nicholson; and in Germany, most recently headed by Karl Nowotny and Ferdinand Anders. Nicholson's 1971 synthesis remains a model of understatement, the single best guide to Aztec gods and religious complexes. Other contributors to the study of Aztec iconography and religion include Carmen Aguilera, Patricia Anawalt, Johanna Broda, Jacqueline de Durand-Forest, Doris Heyden, Cecilia Klein, Esther Pasztory, Hanns Prem, Bodo Spranz, Richard Townsend, and Emily Umberger. Arthur J. O. Anderson and Charles Dibble have systematically translated the Nahuatl Florentine Codex into English (Sahagún 1950–1982); Thelma Sullivan also translated selections of the corpus of Sahagún and his contemporaries. In *Aztecs*, Inga Clendinnen (1991) paints a rich picture of the Aztec religious world.

New facsimile editions, particularly those published by the Akademische Druck-und Verlaganstalt in Graz, Austria, of Central Mexican Prehispanic and Postconquest books have increased their availability for study, as have accompanying iconographic studies (e.g. Codex Mendoza 1992). Major international exhibitions featuring or including Aztec art have improved its documentation (e.g. Nicholson with Quiñones Keber 1983; Paz et al 1990; Levenson 1991).

Jorge Acosta long directed excavations at Tula (and at Teotihuacan) and offered interpretations of Toltec art and gods, although the material is still poorly understood. The role of major Terminal Classic sites in the power vacuum after the fall of Teotihuacan has come to be recognized, particularly after the 1976 discovery of complex paintings in Maya style at Cacaxtla, Tlaxcala (McVicker 1985; Lombardo de Ruíz 1986), reviving interest in Xochicalco and its iconography, as well as the general problem of an "international" iconography (Berlo and Diehl, eds., 1989).

Poorly documented before World War II, Teotihuacan received massive archaeological study starting in 1960, followed more recently by iconographic inquiries. Esther Pasztory (1974) sorted out the goggle-eyed gods, bringing to an end the practice of calling all such figures "Tlaloc," and together with George Kubler (1967), initiated the introduction of neutral names for Teotihuacan gods. Female deities have been recognized as well as male (Taube 1983), and shared iconographic traits with the rest of Mesoamerica have been considered (Berlo, ed. in press). Hasso von Winning has assembled a corpus of Teotihuacan iconographic signs (1987). Many Teotihuacan mural paintings have come to light, including the recently documented Techinantitla corpus (Berrin 1988) that features hieroglyphs, but no texts have been surely deciphered and a linguistic decipherment will languish as long as the language spoken at Teotihuacan remains an enigma.

Later 20th c. Studies: Oaxaca
The antiquity and importance of writing to the early Zapotecs has gained recognition (Marcus 1980; Urcid 1992), Zapotec civilization has been studied at sites other than Monte Albán (e.g. Bernal 1979), and the Danzantes at Monte Albán have been shown to be mutilated victims rather than "dancers" (Scott 1980). First built upon by Mary Elizabeth Smith, Caso's studies of Mixtec codices have now been amplified and in some cases superseded by those of Jill Furst, Maarten Jansen, John Monaghan, John Pohl, and Nancy Troike, with new decipherments of history and places of the Mixtec.

Later 20th c. Studies: Formative Olmec and the Protoclassic Era
Radiocarbon dating has confirmed the early date of the Olmecs, and although their lowland origin has been settled in the minds of most investigators, discoveries at Teopantecuanitlan, Guerrero (Martinez Donjuan 1985), have reinforced the importance of highland Mexico in this early orbit. The excavation and documentation of La Venta, San Lorenzo, and Chalcatzingo (Drucker, Heizer and Squier 1959; Coe and Diehl 1980; Grove 1987), as well as the publication of looted materials from Las Choapas (Joralemon 1971) vastly amplified the Olmec materials available for study, leading to serious iconographic inquiry. Coe (1968) proposed a series of gods based on incised markings of the Las Limas figure, a suggestion later systematized by Joralemon as Gods I-X, although the meanings of these figures are still not clear (1971, 1976; see also Pohorilenko 1990 and Reilly 1990).

Although it is not well understood, Mesoamerican culture thrived along the Isthmus of Tehuantepec, from Atlantic to Pacific, at the end of the Formative era, or what is often called the Protoclassic. Even though the art of the period is often called Izapa-style, Izapa probably did not function as a center of diffusion, nor did

Abaj Takalik, despite its importance in this era and to the later Classic Maya. The art and religion of this period and place may be better represented in recent discoveries at La Mojarra, discovered in 1986 (Winfield Capitaine 1988). Bearing dates in AD 143 and 156, the La Mojarra stela shows the sophisticated development of writing, advanced calendrical notation, iconography and ideology that encompasses and includes the Olmec while pointing the way to the Classic Maya.

Later 20th c. Studies: Classic Veracruz
Much of the art and iconography of Classic Veracruz remains a mystery, plagued by centuries of looting, insufficient documentation of both archaeological works and those without provenience, and uncertainty about fundamental cultural associations between place and ethnicity. Excavations at El Zapotal have yielded life-sized tomb figures of deities; paintings at Las Higueras depict lords festooned with paper strips carrying out sacrificial rituals. Catalogues of Huastec and El Tajín sculptures have improved access to materials (de la Fuente and Gutiérrez Solana 1980; Kampen 1972).

Later 20th c. Studies: West Mexico
Although long thought to be anecdotal and free of the religious meaning of the Aztecs or Maya, the art of West Mexico has been studied for its iconographic complexity in recent years (Furst 1965; Von Winning 1974; Gallagher 1983; Graham n.d.), following publication of quantities of looted material, some of which has suggested patterns of meaning and a highly stratified society. Recent excavation and reconnaissance has revealed intersections with the rest of Mesoamerica (Foster and Weigand 1985; Schöndube and Galván 1978).

Later 20th c. Studies: Other Problems
Anthony Aveni, Horst Hartung, and John Carlson have all demonstrated the importance of geomancy and astronomy for ancient America (Aveni 1980; Aveni 1988; Aveni and Brotherston, eds. 1983). Johanna Broda has published a useful synthesis and commentary of comparative Mesoamerican calendars (1969). New journals, including *Mexikon, RES, Latin American Antiquity* and *Ancient Mesoamerica*, have increased the ability of specialists to communicate their findings to one another. Major dictionary and linguistic projects have drawn upon both modern and Colonial sources, yielding in some cases new dictionaries (Barrera Vásquez 1980, Laughlin 1975, Kartunnen 1983, Summer Institute of Linguistics 1974, 1985) and new guides to older dictionaries (e.g. Campbell 1985). Ethnographers and linguists have worked all across Mesoamerica (Bricker and Gossen 1989, Fought 1972, Furst 1965, Girard 1966, Gossen 1974 and 1986, Ichon 1973, Jansen, van der Loo, and Manning, eds., 1988, Mendelson 1959, Sandstrom 1991, Taggart 1983, Tedlock 1982, and Vogt 1968, among many others), and ethnohistorians have worked through documents to offer a new view of native Mesoamerica in the years following the Conquest (Burkhart 1989, Klor de Alva 1981, Carmack 1981).

Sources of Quotations
Direct citations from the Florentine Codex in *Gods and Symbols of Ancient Mexico and the Maya* are labelled FC in the main entries and come from the A. J. O. Anderson and C. E. Dibble translations, 1950–1982 (listed under Sahagún in the Bibliography).

Direct citations of the *Popol Vuh* are from the Dennis Tedlock translation, 1985.

Abbreviations
BAE   Bureau of American Ethnology
CIW   Carnegie Institution of Washington
DOS   Dumbarton Oaks Studies in Pre-Columbian
        Art and Archaeology
ECM   Estudios de Cultura Maya
ECN   Estudios de Cultura Nahuatl
HMAI Handbook of Middle American Indians
ICA   Proceedings of the International Congress
        of Americanists
IMS   Institute for Mesoamerican Studies, SUNY
        Albany

MAI   Museum of the American Indian, Heye
        Foundation, New York
MARI Middle American Research Institute
PMM   Peabody Museum Memoirs
PMP   Peabody Museum Papers
PRT   Palenque Mesa Redonda or Palenque
        Round Table, ed. M. G. Robertson
RRAMW Research Reports on Ancient Maya
        Writing
RMEA Revista Mexicana de Estudios Antropo-
        lógicos
TR   Tikal Report, University Museum

Acosta, Jorge R., 1940, "Exploraciones en Tula, Hidalgo 1940," *RMEA*, 14, 172–94
——, 1957, "Interpretación de algunos de los datos obtenidos en Tula relativos a la época Tolteca," *RMEA*, 14, 75–100
Adams, Richard E. W., 1969, "Maya Archaeology 1958–1968, A Review," *Latin American Research Review*, 4:2, 3–45
Alcorn, Janis B., 1984, *Huastec Mayan Ethnobotany*, Austin
Alva Ixtlilxóchitl, Fernando de, 1965, *Obras históricas de Don Fernando de Alva Ixtlilxóchitl*, 2 vols. Mexico City
Alzate y Ramírez, José Antonio, 1791, "Descripción de las antigüedades de Xochicalco," Supplement to *Gaceta de literatura*, No. 31, Mexico
Anawalt, Patricia, 1981, *Indian Clothing Before Cortés*, Norman, Okla
Anders, Ferdinand, 1963, *Das Pantheon der Maya*, Graz
——, and **Maarten Jansen**, eds., 1988, *Schrift und Buch im alten Mexiko*, Graz
Aubin, J. M. A., 1849, *Mémoire sur la peinture didactique et l'écriture figurative des anciens mexicains*, Paris
Aveni, Anthony F., 1980, *Skywatchers of Ancient Mexico*, Austin
——, ed., 1988, *New Directions in American Archaeoastronomy*, Oxford
——, and **Brotherston, Gordon**, 1983, *Calendars in Mexico and Peru and Native American Computations of Time*, Oxford
Badianus Manuscript: An Aztec Herbal of 1552, 1940, ed. E. W. Emmart, Baltimore
Bardawil, Lawrence, 1976, "The Principal Bird Deity in Maya Art," *PRT* 2, Part III, 195–209
Barlow, Robert, 1949, The Extent of the Empire of the Culhua Mexica, *Ibero-Americana* 28
Barrera Vásquez, Alfredo, ed., 1980, *Diccionario Maya Cordemex: Maya-Español, Español-Maya*, Merida
Batres, Leopoldo, 1889, *Teotihuacan, o la ciudad sagrada de los Toltecas*, Mexico City
——, 1902, *Exploraciones en Monte Albán*, Mexico City
Baudez, Claude F., 1985, "The Knife and the Lancet: the Iconography of Sacrifice at Copan," Fourth *PRT* 1980, 201–210
Beetz, Carl P., and Linton Satterthwaite, 1981, *The Monuments and Inscriptions of Caracol, Belize*, Univ. Mus. Monograph 45, Philadelphia

Bell, Betty, ed., 1974, *The Archaeology of West Mexico*, Ajijic, Jalisco
Benson, Elizabeth P., ed., 1968, *The Dumbarton Oaks Conference on the Olmec*, Washington, D.C.
——, ed., 1972, *The Cult of the Feline*, Washington, D.C.
——, ed., 1973, *Mesoamerican Writing Systems*, Washington, D.C.
——, ed., 1981, *Mesoamerican Sites and World-Views*, Washington, D.C.
——, ed., 1987, *City-States of the Maya: Art and Architecture*, Denver
——, and **Coe, Michael**, eds., 1981, *The Olmec and Their Neighbors: Essays in Memory of M. W. Stirling*, Washington D.C.
Benson, Elizabeth P., and Griffin, Gillett, eds., 1989, *Maya Iconography*, Princeton
Berlin, Heinrich, 1958, "El glifo emblema en las inscripciones mayas," *Journal de la Société des Americanistes*, N.S. 47, 111–19
——, 1963, "The Palenque Triad," *Journal de la Société des Americanistes*, N.S. 52, 91–99
——, and **Kelley, David H.**, 1970, The 819-Day Count and Color-Direction Symbolism Among the Classic Maya, MARI Pub. 26, 9–20
Berlo, Janet Catherine, ed., 1983, *Text and Image in Pre-Columbian Art: Essays on the Interrelationship of the Verbal and the Visual Arts*, Oxford
——, 1984, *Teotihuacan Art Abroad: A Study of Metropolitan Style and Provincial Transformation in Incensario Workshops*, Oxford
——, ed., in press, *Art, Polity, and the City of Teotihuacan*
——, and **Diehl, Richard**, eds., 1989, *Mesoamerica After the Decline of Teotihuacan*, Washington, D.C.
Bernal, Ignacio, 1962, *Bibliografía de arqueología e etnografía: Mesoamerica y Norte de México*, Mexico City
——, 1979, *The Ballplayers of Dainzú*, Graz
——, 1980, *A History of Mexican Archaeology*, London and New York
Berrin, Kathleen, 1988, *Feathered Serpents and Flowering Trees*, San Francisco
Beyer, Hermann, 1921, *El llamado 'Calendario Azteca,'* Mexico City
——, 1965, *Mito y simbolismo del méxico antiguo*, Mexico City

Bierhorst, John, trans., 1985, *Cantares Mexicanos: Songs of the Aztecs*, Stanford

Blom, Frans, 1950, "A Polychrome Plate from Quintana Roo," *Notes on Middle American Archaeology and Ethnology No. 98*, CIW

——, and La Farge, Oliver, 1925, *Tribes and Temples*, MARI Pub. 1, 2 vols.

Boone, Elizabeth Hill, ed., 1982, *The Art and Iconography of Late Post-Classic Central Mexico*, Washington, D.C.

——, 1983, *The Codex Magliabechiano and the Lost Prototype of the Magliabechiano Group*, Berkeley

——, ed., 1984, *Ritual Human Sacrifice in Mesoamerica*, Washington, D.C.

——, ed., 1987, *The Aztec Templo Mayor*, Washington, D.C.

——, 1987, "Temple Mayor Research, 1521–1978," in *The Aztec Templo Mayor*, ed. E. H. Boone, Washington, D.C.

——, 1989, *Incarnations of the Supernatural: The Image of Huitzilopochtli in Mexico and Europe*, Philadelphia

Bowditch, Charles P., ed., 1904, *Mexican and Central American Antiquities, Calendar Systems, and History: 24 Papers by Eduard Seler et al*, BAEB 28

Brasseur de Bourbourg, Charles E., 1861, *Popol Vuh: Le livre sacré et les mythes de l'antiquité américaine*, Paris

——, 1869, *Manuscrit Troano: Etudes sur le système graphique et la langue des Mayas*, Paris

Breton, Adela C., 1917, "Preliminary Study of the North Building (Chamber C), Great Ball Court, Chichen Itzá, Yucatán," *19th ICA*, 187–94

Bricker, Victoria R., 1986, *A Grammar of Maya Hieroglyphs*, MARI Pub. 56

——, and Gossen, Gary H., 1989, *Ethnographic Encounters in Southern Mesoamerica: Essays in Honor of Evon Z. Vogt*, Albany

Brinton, Daniel, 1887, *Ancient Nahuatl Poetry*, Philadelphia

Broda, Johanna, 1969, *The Mexican Calendar as Compared to Other Mesoamerican Systems*, Acta Ethnologica et Linguistica, 15, Vienna

Broda, Johanna, David Carrasco, and Eduardo Matos Moctezuma, 1987, *The Great Temple of Tenochtitlan: Center and Periphery in the Aztec World*, Berkeley

Burgoa, Francisco de, 1674, *Geográfica descripción*, Mexico

Burkhart, Louise M., 1989, *The Slippery Earth: Nahua-Christian Moral Dialogue in Sixteenth-century Mexico*, Tucson

Campbell, R. Joe, 1985, *A Morphological Dictionary of Classical Nahuatl*, Madison

Carlson, John B., 1983, "The Grolier Codex: A Preliminary Report on the Content and Authenticity of a Thirteenth-Century Maya Venus Almanac," in A. F. Aveni and G. Brotherston, eds., *Calendars in Mesoamerica and Peru: Native Computations of Time*, Oxford, 27–57

——, 1990, *Star Wars and Maya Merchants at Cacaxtla*, Center for Archaeoastronomy Occasional Pub. 7, College Park, Md.

Carmack, Robert, 1981, *The Quiche Mayas of Utatlan*, Norman, Okla

Carrasco, David, 1990. *Religions of Mesoamerica*, New York

——, ed., 1991, *To Change Place: Aztec Ceremonial Landscapes*, Niwot, Colo

Carrasco, Pedro, and Broda, Johanna, eds., 1978, *Economía política e ideología en el México prehispánico*, Mexico City

Caso, Alfonso, 1942, "El paraiso terrenal en Teotihuacan," *Cuadernos Americanos*, 6, 127–36

——, 1967, *Los calendarios prehispánicos*, Mexico City

——, 1969, *El tesoro de Monte Albán*, Mexico City

——, and Ignacio Bernal, 1952, *Urnas de Oaxaca*, INAH Memorias 2

Charnay, Désiré, 1885, *Les anciennes villes du Nouveau Monde*, Paris

Chimalpahin Cuauhtlehuanitzin, Domingo, 1965, *Relaciones originales de Chalco Amaquemecan*, Mexico City

Clarkson, Persis, B., 1978, "Classic Maya Pictorial Ceramics: A Survey of Content and Theme," in R. Sidrys, ed., *Papers on the Economy and Architecture of the Ancient Maya*, Los Angeles, 86–141

Clendinnen, Inga, 1990 "Ways to the Sacred: Reconstructing 'Religion' in Sixteenth-Century Mexico," *History and Anthropology*, 5, 105–141

——, 1991, *Aztecs: An Interpretation*, Cambridge and New York

Codex Aubin (Codex of 1576), 1903, Mexico City

Codex Aubin: Historia de la nación mexicana, 1963, ed. C. E. Dibble, Madrid

Codex Bodley, 1960, ed. A. Caso, Mexico City

Codex Borbonicus, 1974, ed. K. Nowotny, Graz

Codex Borgia, 1976, ed. K. Nowotny, Graz

Codex Boturini, 1944, Mexico City

Codex Colombino, 1966, ed. A. Caso and M. E. Smith, Mexico City

Codex Cospi, 1968, ed. K. Nowotny, Graz

Codex Féjerváry-Mayer, 1971, ed. C. Burland, Graz

Codex Ixtlilxochitl, 1976, ed. J. de Durand-Forest, Graz

Codex Laud, 1966, ed. C. Burland, Graz

Codex Magliabechiano, 1970, ed. F. Anders and Jacqueline de Durand-Forest, Graz

Codex Mendoza, 1938, ed. and commentary by James Cooper Clark, London

Codex Mendoza, 1992, ed. Frances Berdan and Patricia Rieff Anawalt, Los Angeles

Codex Nuttall, A Picture Manuscript from Ancient Mexico, 1975, New York

Codex Rios (Vaticanus A), 1900, Rome

Codex Selden, 1964, ed. A. Caso and M. E. Smith, Mexico City

Codex Vaticanus Nr. 3773 (Vaticanus B), 1902, ed. E. Seler, Berlin

Codex Vaticanus B, 1972, ed. F. Anders, Graz

Codex Vindobonensis, 1974, ed. O. Adelhofer, Graz

Códice Borgia, 1963, ed. and commentary by Eduard Seler, 3 vols, Mexico City

Codice Chimalpopoca: anales de Cuauhtitlan y

leyenda de los soles, 1945, trans. and ed. Primo Feliciano Velázquez, Mexico City

Coe, Michael D., 1968, *America's First Civilization: Discovering the Olmec*, New York

——, 1973, *The Maya Scribe and His World*, New York

——, 1975, *Classic Maya Pottery at Dumbarton Oaks*, Washington, D.C.

——, 1977, "Supernatural Patrons of Maya Scribes and Artists," *Social Process in Maya Prehistory*, ed. N. Hammond, New York, 327–47

——, 1978, *Lords of the Underworld*, Princeton

——, 1982, *Old Gods and Young Heroes*, Jerusalem

——, 1984, *Mexico*, 3rd edn, London and New York

——, 1987, *The Maya*, 4th edn, London and New York

——, 1990, "The Hero Twins: Myth and Image," in J. Kerr, ed., *Maya Vase Book I*, New York 161–84

——, 1992, *Breaking the Maya Code*, London and New York

——, and Diehl, Richard, 1980, *In the Land of the Olmec*, 2 vols, Austin

Coggins, Clemency Chase, 1975, Painting and Drawing Styles at Tikal: An Historical and Iconographic Reconstruction, Ph.D. Diss. Harvard

——, and Orrin Shane III, eds., 1984, *Cenote of Sacrifice: Maya Treasures from the Sacred Well at Chichén Itzá*, Austin

Corpus of Maya Hieroglyphic Inscriptions, 1975–, Drawings and maps by Ian Graham, Eric Von Euw, Peter Mathews. Vols. 1–6, Peabody Museum, Harvard Univ.

Cortés, Hernan, 1986, *Letters from Mexico*, trans. and ed. Anthony Pagden, New Haven

Cortez, Constance, 1986, The Principal Bird Deity in Preclassic and Early Classic Maya Art, M.A. thesis, The Univ. of Texas

Couch, N. C. C., 1985, *The Festival Cycle of the Aztec Codex Borbonicus*, Oxford

Covarrubias, Miguel, 1957, *Indian Art of Mexico and Central America*, New York

Cresson, F. M., 1938, "Maya and Mexican Sweat Houses," *American Anthropologist*, N.S. 40, 88–102

Dänzel, Theodor-Wilhelm, 1922–23, *Mexiko*, 3 vols, Germany

Davies, Nigel, 1977 *The Toltecs Until the Fall of Tula*, Norman

de la Fuente, Beatriz, and Gutiérrez Solana, Nelly, 1980, *Escultura huasteca en piedra: catálogo*, Mexico City

Del Rio, Antonio, 1822, *Description of the ruins of an ancient city discovered near Palenque*, London

Díaz del Castillo, Bernal, 1956, *The Discovery and Conquest of Mexico*, trans. A. P. Maudslay, New York

Drucker, Philip, Heizer, Robert, and Squier, R. J., 1955, *Excavations at La Venta, Tabasco*, BAEB 170

Dupaix, Capitaine, 1834, "Relation des trois expeditions pour la recherche des antiquités du pays," *Antiquités Mexicaines*, 2 vols, Paris

Duran, Diego, 1964, *The Aztecs*, trans. F. Horcasitas and D. Heyden, New York

——, 1971, *Book of the Gods and Rites and The Ancient Calendar*, trans. D. Heyden and F. Horcasitas, Norman

Earle, Duncan M., and Snow, Dean, 1985, "The Origin of the 260-day Calendar: the Gestation Hypothesis Reconsidered in Light of its Use Among the Quiche-Maya," in *Fifth PRT*, 241–44

Easby, Elizabeth and John Scott, 1970, *Before Cortés: Sculpture of Middle America*, New York

Edmonson, Munroe, 1971, *The Book of Counsel: The Popol Vuh of the Quiche Maya of Guatemala*, MARI 35

——, 1982, *The Ancient Future of the Itzá: the Chilam Balam of Tizimin*, Austin

——, 1986, *Heaven-born Merida and its Destiny*, Austin

Emmerich, Andre, 1965, *Sweat of the Sun and Tears of the Moon*, New York

Essays in pre-Columbian Art and Architecture (with essays by S. K. Lothrop et al), 1964, Cambridge, Mass

Estrada, Alvaro, 1981, *María Sabina: Her Life and Chants*, trans. and comm. by Henry Munn, Santa Barbara

Fash, William L., 1991, *Scribes, Warriors, and Kings*, London and New York

Flannery, Kent V., and Joyce Marcus, 1983, *The Cloud People: Divergent Evolution of the Zapotec and Mixtec Civilizations*, New York

Förstemann, Ernst Wilhelm, 1880, *Die Mayahandschrift der Königlichen Offenlichen Bibliothek zu Dresden*, Leipzig

——, 1901, "Der Mayagott des Jahresschlusses," *Globus* 80, 189–92

Foster, Michael S., and Phil C. Weigand, eds., 1985, *The Archaeology of West and Northwest Mesoamerica*, Boulder

Fought, John, 1972, *Chorti (Mayan) Texts*, Philadelphia

Furst, Jill, 1978, *Codex Vindobonensis Mexicanus I, A Commentary*, Albany

Furst, Peter, 1965, "West Mexican Tomb Sculpture as Evidence for Shamanism in Prehispanic Mesoamerica," *Antropológica* 15

——, ed., 1972, *Flesh of the Gods: the Ritual Use of Hallucinogens*, London

——, and Coe, Michael, 1977, "Ritual Enemas," *Natural History*, February, 88–91

Galarza, Joaquin, 1974, *Codex mexicains, catalogue*, Bibliothèque nationale de Paris, Paris

Galindo y Villa, Jesus, 1922, *El Museo Nacional de Arqueología Historia y Etnografía: Breve reseña*, Mexico City

Gallagher, Jacki, 1983, *Companions of the Dead*, Los Angeles

Gallenkamp, Charles, and Regina Elise Johnson, eds., 1985, *Maya: Treasures of an Ancient Civilization*, New York

Gamio, Manuel, 1922, *La población del Valle de Teotihuacan*, Mexico City

Gann, Thomas, 1900, "Mounds in Northern Honduras," BAE, 19th *Annual Report*

García Icazbalceta, Joaquín, 1886–92, *Nueva colección de documentos para la historia de México*, Mexico City

García Payón, José, 1946, "Los monumentos arqueológicos de Malinalco," *RMEA*, 8, 5–64

Garibay, K., Angel María, 1964, *Poesía nahuatl*, Mexico City

———, 1979, *Teogonía e historia de los mexicanos: tres opúsculos del siglo XVI*, Mexico City

Girard, Rafael, 1966, *Los Mayas*, Mexico City

Glass, John, B., 1975, "A Survey of Native Middle American Pictorial Manuscripts," *HMAI*, 14, 3–81

Goldstein, Marilyn M., ed., 1988, *Ceremonial Sculpture of Ancient Veracruz*, Brooklyn

Gordon, George B., and J. Alden Mason, 1925–28, *Examples of Maya Pottery in the Museum and Other Collections*, 3 vols, Philadelphia

Gossen, Gary, 1974, "A Chamula Solar Calendar Board from Chiapas, Mexico," in ed. N. Hammond, *Mesoamerican Archaeology: New Approaches*, 217–53

———, ed., 1986, *Symbol and Meaning Beyond the Closed Community*, Albany

Graham, Mark Miller, n.d., "In Place of a World that Never Was: Toward an Iconography of Rulership in the Classic Art of West Mexico," paper delivered at the February 1990 College Art Association Annual Meeting

Graulich, Michel, 1981, "The Metaphor of the Day in Ancient Mexican Myth and Ritual," *Current Anthropology*, 22, 45–60

Grove, David, 1970, *The Olmec Paintings of Oxtotitlan Cave*, DOS 6

———, 1984, *Chalcatzingo*, London and New York

———, 1987, *Ancient Chalcatzingo*, Austin

Guzmán Monroy, Virginia, 1978, *Localización de codices, lienzos y mapas del México prehispánico y colonial*, Mexico City

Hamy, E-T., 1897, *Galérie americaine du musée d'ethnographie du Trocadero*, 2 vols, Paris

Handbook of Middle American Indians (HMAI), 1965–, ed. Robert Wauchope, 16 vols, 4 supplements, Austin

Hanks, William, and Rice, Don, eds., 1989, *Word and Image in Maya Culture*, Salt Lake City

Hellmuth, Nicholas M., 1987, *Mönster und Menschen in der Maya-Kunst*, Graz

Heyden, Doris, 1975, "An Interpretation of the Cave Underneath the Pyramid of the Sun in Teotihuacan, Mexico," *American Antiquity*, 40:1, 131–47

Historia de los mexicanos por sus pinturas, 1965, in A. M. Garibay, ed., *Teogonía e historia de los mexicanos*, Mexico City, 21–90

Historia Tolteca-Chichimeca, 1976, ed. P. Kirchoff, L. O. Güemes and L. Reyes García, Mexico City

Histoyre du méchique, 1905, ed. E. de Jonghe, *Journal de la Société des Americanistes*, N.S., 1–42

Houston, Stephen D,, 1989, *Maya Glyphs*, London

———, 1992, "A Name Glyph for Classic Maya Dwarfs," in J. Kerr ed., *The Maya Vase Book*, vol. 3, New York, 526–31

———, **and Stuart, David**, 1989, *The way Glyph: Evidence for "Co-essences" among the Classic Maya*, RRAMW 29

Humboldt, Alexander Von, 1810, *Vues des cordillères et monuments des peuples indigènes de l'Amérique*, Paris

Hvidtfeldt, Arild, 1958, *Teotl and Ixiptlatli: Some Central Conceptions in Ancient Mexican Religion*, Copenhagen

Hunt, Eva, 1977, *The Transformation of the Hummingbird*, Ithaca

Ichon, Alain, 1973, *La religión de los Totonacos de la sierra*, Mexico City

Iconography of Middle American Sculpture (essays by I. Bernal et al.), 1973, New York

Ixtlilxochitl, Fernando de Alva, 1982, *Obras Históricas*, 2 vols, Mexico City

Jansen, Maarten, van der Loo, P., and Manning, R., eds., 1988, *Continuity and Identity in Native America: Essays in Honor of Benedikt Hartmann*, Leiden

Jiménez Moreno, Wigberto, 1941, "Tula y los toltecas según las fuentes," *RMEA*, 5, 79–83

Jones, Christopher, and Linton Satterthwaite Jr., 1982, *The Monuments and Inscriptions of Tikal: The Carved Monuments*, TR 33a

Jones, Tom, 1985, "The Xoc, the Sharke, and the Sea Dogs: An Historical Encounter," in *Fifth PRT*, 1983, San Francisco, 211–22

———, 1991, "Jaws II: Return of the *Xoc*," in *Sixth PRT*, 1986, Norman, Okla, 246–54

Joralemon, P. David, 1971, *A Study of Olmec Iconography*, DOS 7

———, 1974, "Ritual Blood-Sacrifice Among the Ancient Maya, Part I," *First PRT*, vol 2, 59–74

———, 1976, "The Olmec Dragon: A Study in Precolumbian Iconography," in H. B. Nicholson, ed., *The Origins of Religious Art and Iconography in Preclassic Mesoamerica*, Los Angeles, 27–72

Josserand, J. Kathryn, and Dakin, Karen, eds., 1988, *Smoke and Mist: Mesoamerican Studies in Memory of Thelma D. Sullivan*, 2 vols, Oxford

Justeson, John S., and Lyle Campbell, eds., 1984, *Phoneticism in Mayan Hieroglyphic Writing*, IMS 9

Kampen, Michael, 1972, *The Sculptures of El Tajín, Veracruz, Mexico*, Gainesville

Karttunen, Frances, 1983, *An Analytical Dictionary of Nahuatl*, Austin

Keen, Benjamin, 1971, *The Aztec Image*, New Brunswick

Kelley, David H., 1962, "Glyphic Evidence for a Dynastic Sequence at Quirigua, Guatemala," *American Antiquity*, 27, 323–35

———, 1976, *Deciphering the Maya Script*, Austin

Kendall, Jonathan, 1991, "The Thirteen Volatiles: Representation and Symbolism," senior essay, Yale Univ.

Kerr, Justin, 1989–92, *The Maya Vase Book*, 3 vols, New York

Kidder, Alfred V., Jennings, Jesse D. and Shook, Edwin M., 1946, *Excavations at Kaminaljuyú*,

Guatemala, CIW Pub. 561

Kingsborough, Lord, 1831–48, *Antiquities of Mexico*, 9 vols, London

Klein, Cecilia F., 1976, *The Face of the Earth: Frontality in Two-Dimensional Mesoamerican Art*, New York

——, 1976, "The Identity of the Central Deity on the Aztec Calendar Stone," *Art Bulletin*, 58,1–12

——, 1980, "Who was Tlaloc?" *Journal of Latin American Lore*, 6, 155–204

Klor de Alva, J. Jorge, 1981, "Martín Ocelotl: Clandestine Cult Leader," in D. G. Sweet and G. B. Nash, eds, *Struggle and Survival in Colonial America*, Berkeley, 128–41

——, **Nicholson, H. B., and Quiñones Keber, Eloise**, eds, 1988, *The Work of Bernardino de Sahagún*, Albany

Knorosov, Yuri, 1967, *The Writing of the Maya Indians*, trans. and ed. T. Proskouriakoff and S. Coe, Harvard Univ. Russian Trans. Series 4

Kowalski, Jeff Karl, 1989, *The Mythological Identity of the Figure on the La Esperanza ("Chinkultic") Ball Court Marker*, RRAMW 27

Kubler, George, 1967, *The Iconography of the Art of Teotihuacan*, DOS 4

——, 1969, *Studies in Classic Maya Iconography*, Memoirs of the Connecticut Academy of Arts and Sciences 18

——, 1977, *Aspects of Classic Maya Rulership on Two Inscribed Vessels*, DOS 18

——, 1990, *The Aesthetic Appreciation of American Art*, New Haven

LaFaye, Jacques, 1974, *Quetzalcoatl et Guadalupe*, Paris

Landa, Diego de, 1941, *Landa's Relación de las cosas de Yucatán*, ed. A. M. Tozzer, PMP 18

——, 1937 (reprinted 1978), *Yucatan Before and After the Conquest*, ed. and trans. W. Gates, Baltimore

Laughlin, Robert M., 1975, *The Great Tzotzil Dictionary of San Lorenzo Zinacantan*, Smithsonian Contributions to Anthropology No. 19

Lee, Thomas, 1985, *Los códices mayas*, Tuxtla Gutiérrez

Lehmann, Walter, and Gerdt Kutscher, 1981, *Geschichte der Azteken: Codex Aubin und verwandte Dokumente*, Berlin

Leon-Portilla, Miguel, 1963, *Aztec Thought and Culture*, Norman

——, 1987, *Mexico-Tenochtitlan: su espacio y tiempo sagrados*, Mexico City

——, 1992, *The Aztec Image of Self and Society*, Norman

Leon y Gama, Antonio de, 1792, *Descripción histórica y cronológica de las dos piedras*, Mexico City

Levenson, Jay A., ed., 1991, *Circa 1492*, New Haven and London

Leyenaar, Ted J. J., 1978, *Ulama: The Perpetuation in Mexico of the Pre-Spanish Ball Game Ullamaliztli*, trans. Inez Seeger, Leiden

——, **and Parsons, Lee**, 1988, *Ulama; The Ballgame of the Mayas and Aztecs, 2000 B.C.–A.D. 2000*, Leiden

Leyenda de los soles, trans. and ed. F. Paso y Troncoso, Florence, 1903

Lincoln, Charles E., 1990, *Ethnicity and Social Organization at Chichén Itzá, Yucatán, Mexico*, Ph.D. Diss, Harvard University

Linné, Sigvald, 1934, *Archaeological Researches at Teotihuacan, Mexico*, Ethnological Museum of Sweden Publication No. 1, N.S.

Litvak King, J., and Noemí Castillo Tejero, eds., 1972, *Religión en mesoamerica*, Mexico City

Lombardo de Ruíz, Sonia, et al., 1986, *Cacaxtla: el lugar donde muere la lluvia en la tierra*, Mexico City

López Austin, Alfredo, 1985, *Educación mexica: antología de documentos sahaguntinos*, Mexico City

——, 1988, *The Human Body and Ideology: Concepts of the Ancient Nahuas*, 2 vols, trans. T. and B. Ortiz de Montellano, Salt Lake

Lothrop, Samuel K., 1924, *Tulum: An Archaeological Study of the East Coast of Yucatán*, CIW Pub. 335

——, 1952, *Metals from the Cenote of Sacrifice, Chichen Itza, Yucatan*, PMM 10:2

Lounsbury, Floyd, 1973, "On the Derivation and Reading of the 'Ben-Ich' Prefix," in E. P. Benson, ed., *Mesoamerican Writing Systems*, ed., Washington, D.C., 99–143

——, 1982, "Astronomical Knowledge and its Uses at Bonampak, Mexico," in A. F. Aveni, ed., *Archaeoastronomy in the New World*, New York, 143–68

McVicker, Don, 1985, "The 'Mayanized' Mexicans," *American Antiquity*, 50, 82–101

Maler, Teobert, 1901–03, *Researches in the Central Portion of the Usumasintla Valley*, PMM 2

Manuscrit Tovar, 1972, ed. Jacques LaFaye, Graz

Marcus, Joyce, 1974, "The Iconography of Power Among the Classic Maya", *World Archaeology*, 6:1, 83–94

——, 1980, "Zapotec Writing," *Scientific American*, 242:2 50–64

Marquina, Ignacio, 1951, *Arquitectura prehispánica*, Mexico City

Martinez Donjuan, Guadalupe, 1985, "El sitio olmeca de Teopantecuanitlán en Guerrero," *Anales de Antropología*, 22, 215–26

Matos Moctezuma, Eduardo, 1988, *The Great Temple of the Aztecs: Treasures of Tenochtitlan*, trans. D. Heyden, New York

Matrícula de Huexotzinco, 1974, ed. Hanns J. Prem, Graz

Maudslay, Alfred P., 1899–1902, *Biologia Centrali-Americana: Archaeology*, 5 vols, London

Mayer, Karl Herbert, 1980, *Maya Monuments: Sculptures of Unknown Provenance in the United States*, trans. S. L. Brizee, Ramona, Calif

——, 1991, *Maya Monuments: Sculptures of Unknown Provenance*, Suppl. 3, Berlin

Mendelson, E. Michael, 1959, "Maximon: An Iconographical Introduction," *Man*, 59, 57–60

Merwin, Raymond E. and George C. Vaillant, 1932, *The Ruins of Holmul, Guatemala*, PMM 11:2

Mesa Redonda de la Sociedad Mexicana de Antropología XI (Teotihuacan), 1972, 2 vols, Mexico City

Miller, Arthur, 1973, *The Mural Painting of Teotihuacan*, Washington, D.C.

——, 1982, *On the Edge of the Sea: Mural Painting at Tancah-Tulum, Quintana Roo, Mexico*, Washington, D.C.

Miller, Mary Ellen, 1986, *The Murals of Bonampak*, Princeton

——, 1989, "The History of the Study of Maya Vase Painting," in Justin Kerr, ed., *The Maya Vase Book*, Vol. 1, New York, pp. 128–45

——, and Stephen D. Houston, 1987, "The Classic Maya Ballgame and Its Architectural Setting," *RES*, 14, 47–65

Miller, Virginia, 1991, *The Frieze of the Palace of the Stuccoes, Acanceh, Yucatán, Mexico*, DOS 31

Millon, René, 1974, *Urbanization at Teotihuacan, Mexico*, 2 vols, Austin

Moholy-Nagy, Hattula, 1963, "Shells and Other Marine Material from Tikal," *ECM*, 3, 65–83

Monaghan, John, 1990, "Sacrifice, Death and the Origins of Agriculture in the Vienna Codex," *American Antiquity*, 55, 559–69

Morgan, Lewis Henry, 1877, *Ancient Society*, New York and London

Morley, Sylvanus G., 1920, *Inscriptions at Copán*, CIW Pub. 219

——, 1937–38, *Inscriptions of Petén*, 5 vols, CIW Pub. 437

——, 1946, *The Ancient Maya*, Palo Alto, Calif

——, George W. Brainerd, and revised by Robert Sharer, 1983 *The Ancient Maya*, 4th ed., Palo Alto, Calif

Morris, Earl H., Jean Charlot, and Ann Axtell Morris, 1931, *The Temple of the Warriors at Chichen Itzá, Yucatán*, 2 vols, CIW Pub. 406

Nagao, Debra, 1985, "The Planting of Sustenance: Symbolism of the Two-Horned God in Offerings from the Templo Mayor," *RES*, 10, 5–27

Nicholson, H. B., 1971, "Religion in Pre-Hispanic Central Mexico," *HMAI*, 10:1, 396–446

——, ed., 1976, *Origins of Religious Art and Iconography in Preclassic Mesoamerica*, Los Angeles

——, with Eloise Quiñones Keber, 1983, *Art of Aztec Mexico: Treasures of Tenochtitlan*, Washington, D.C.

Norman, Garth, 1973, *Izapa Sculpture, Part I: Album*, Papers of the New World Archaeological Foundation 30

Nuttall, Zelia, 1908, "A Penitential Rite of the Ancient Mexicans," *PMM*, 7, 439–65

Olmos, Andrés de, 1985, *Arte de la lengua mexicana y vocabulario*, ed. Thelma Sullivan and René Acuña, Mexico City

Ortiz de Montellano, Bernard R, 1978, "Aztec Cannibalism: An Ecological Necessity?" *Science*, 200, 611–17

Paddock, John, ed., 1966, *Ancient Oaxaca*, Palo Alto

Parsons, Elsie Clews, 1939, *Pueblo Indian Religion*, 2 vols, Chicago

Parsons, Lee A., 1967–69, *Bilbao, Guatemala: An Archaeological Study of the Pacific Coast Cotzumalhuapa Region*, 2 vols, Milwaukee

——, 1986, *The Origins of Maya Art: Monumental Stone Sculpture of Kaminaljuyú, Guatemala, and the Southern Pacific Coast*, DOS 28

Pasztory, Esther, 1974, *The Iconography of the Teotihuacan Tlaloc*, DOS 15

——, 1976, *The Murals of Tepantitla, Teotihuacan*, New York

——, ed, 1978, *Middle Classic Mesoamerica: AD 400–700*, New York

——, 1983, *Aztec Art*, New York

Paxton, Merideth D., 1986, Codex Dresden: Stylistic and Iconographic Analysis of a Maya Manuscript, Ph.D. diss., Univ. of New Mexico

Paz, Octavio, et al, 1990, *Mexico: Splendors of Thirty Centuries*, New York

Pendergast, David M., 1969, *Altun Ha, British Honduras (Belize): the Sun God's Tomb*, Royal Ontario Museum Occ. Paper 19

Pohl, John, 1984, The Earth Lords: Politics and Symbolism of the Mixtec Codices, Ph.D. thesis, UCLA

——, and Byland, Bruce, 1990, "Mixtec Landscape Perception and Archaeological Settlement Patterns, *Ancient Mesoamerica* 1:1, 113–31

Pohorilenko, Anatole, 1990, Structure and periodization of the Olmec Representational System, Ph.D. diss., Tulane

Porter, James, 1989 "Olmec Colossal Heads as Recarved Thrones," *RES*, 17/18, 22–29

Prescott, William, 1843, *The Conquest of Mexico*, 3 vols, New York

Proskouriakoff, Tatiana, 1946, *An Album of Maya Architecture*, CIW Pub. 558

——, 1950, *Classic Maya Sculpture*, CIW Pub. 593

——, 1960, "Historical Implications of a Pattern of Dates at Piedras Negras," *American Antiquity*, 25, 454–75

——, 1963, "Historical Data in the Inscriptions of Yaxchilan, Part I," *Estudios de Cultura Maya*, 3, 149–67

——, 1964, "Historical Data in the Inscriptions of Yaxchilan, Part II," *Estudios de Cultura Maya*, 4, 178–201

Puleston, Dennis, 1976, "The People of the Cayman/Crocodile: Riparian Agriculture and the Origins of Aquatic Motifs in Ancient Maya Iconography," in F.-A. de Montequin, ed., *Aspects of Ancient Maya Civilization*, Saint Paul

Quirarte, Jacinto, 1979, "Representation of Place, Location, and Direction," in *Third PRT*, 99–110

Reilly, F. Kent, 1990, "The Shaman in Transformation Pose: A Study of the Theme of Rulership in Olmec Art," *Record of The Art Museum of Princeton University*, 48:2, 4–21

Relación de Michoacán, 1970, trans. and ed. Eugene Craine and Reginald Reindorp, Norman, Okla

Riese, Berthold, 1984, "Kriegsberichte der klassichen Maya," *Baessler-Archiv, Beiträge zur Völkerkunde*, 30:2, 225–321

Ringle, William M., 1988, *Of Mice and Monkeys: The Value and Meaning of T1016, the God C Hieroglyph*, RRAMW 18

Robelo, Cecilio A., [reprinted] 1980, *Diccionario de mitología nahuatl*, 2 vols, Mexico City

Robertson, Donald, 1959, *Mexican Manuscript*

Painting of the Early Colonial Period: The Metropolitan Schools, New Haven

Robertson, Merle Greene, 1983–92, *The Sculpture of Palenque*, 4 vols, Princeton

Robicsek, Francis, 1978, *The Smoking Gods: Tobacco in Maya Art, History and Religion*, Norman, Okla

——, and Hales, Donald, 1981, *The Maya Book of the Dead: the Ceramic Codex*, Norman, Okla

—— and ——, 1982 *Maya Ceramics from the Late Classic Period: the November Collection*, Charlottesville

Rosny, Leon de, 1864, "Les documents écrits de l'antiquité américaine," *Mémoires de la Société d'Ethnographie*, N.S. 1:1, 57–100

Roys, Ralph L., 1933, *The Book of Chilam Balam of Chumayel*, CIW Pub. 438

——, 1965, *The Ritual of the Bacabs*, Norman, Okla

Ruíz de Alarcón, Hernando, 1982, *Aztec Sorcerers in 17th Century Mexico: the Treatise on Superstitions*, ed. and trans. Michael Coe and Gordon Whittaker, IMS Pub. 7

Ruz Lhuiller, Alberto, 1973, *El templo de las inscripciones, Palenque*, Mexico City

Sahagún, Bernardino de, 1905–09, *Historia de las cosas de Nueva España*, trans. F. Paso y Troncoso, Madrid

——, 1950–82, *The Florentine Codex: A General History of the Things of New Spain*, trans. and ed. A. J. O. Anderson and C. E. Dibble, Santa Fe

——, 1964, *Códices matritenses de la historia general de las cosas de la nueva España de Fr. Bernadino de Sahagún*, Madrid

——, 1979, *Códice florentino*, 3 vols, Mexico City

Sandstrom, Alan, 1991, *Corn is our Blood*, Norman, Okla

Saville, Marshall H., 1920, *The Goldsmith's Art in Ancient Mexico*, MAI Notes and Monographs 7

——, 1922, *Turquoise Mosaic Art in Ancient Mexico*, MAI Contribution 6

——, 1925, *The Wood-carver's Art in Ancient Mexico*, MAI Contribution 9

——, 1929, "Votive Axes from Eastern Mexico," MAI Notes and Monographs 6, 266–99; 335–42

——, 1933, "Reports on the Maya Indians of Yucatan by Santiago Méndez, Antonio García y Cubas, Pedro Sánchez de Aguilar and Francisco Hernández," MAI Notes and Monographs 9: 133–226

Scarborough, Vernon L., and Wilcox, David R., eds, 1991, *The Mesoamerican Ballgame*, Tucson

Schele, Linda, 1987, "Architectural Development and Political History at Palenque," in E. P. Benson, ed., *City-States of the Maya: Art and Architecture*, Denver, 110–37

, and Freidel, David, 1990, *A Forest of Kings: The Untold Story of the Ancient Maya*, New York

, and Miller, Jeffrey H., 1983, *The Mirror, the Rabbit and the Bundle*, DOS 25

, and Mary Ellen Miller, 1986, *The Blood of Kings: Ritual and Dynasty in Maya Art*, Fort Worth (London 1992)

Schellhas, Paul, 1904, Representations of Deities in the Maya Manuscripts, *PMP* 4:1

Scholes, France, and Roys, Ralph, 1948, *The Maya Chontal Indians of Acalan-Tixchel*, CIW Pub. 560

Schöndube, Otto, and Galván, L. Javier, 1978, "Salvage Archaeology at el Grillo-Tabachines, Zapopán, Jalisco, Mexico," in C. Riley and B. C. Hedrick, eds, *Across the Chichimec Sea: Papers in Honor of J. Charles Kelley*, 144–64

Scott, John, 1980, *The Danzantes of Monte Albán*, 2 vols, *DOS 22*

Séjourné, Laurette, 1956, *Burning Water: Thought and Religion in Ancient Mexico*, New York

——, 1959, *Un palacio de la ciudad de los dioses: exploraciones en 1955–58*, Mexico City

——, 1966, *El lenguaje de las formas en Teotihuacan*, Mexico City

Seler, Eduard, 1902–23, *Gesammelte Abhandlungen*, Berlin

Siméon, Rémi, 1977, *Diccionario de la lengua Nahuatl o Mexicano*, Mexico City

Sisson, Edward B., 1983, "Recent Work on the Borgia Group Codices," *Current Anthropology*, 24, 653–56

Smith, Robert E., 1955, *Ceramic Sequence at Uaxactun, Guatemala*, 2 vols, MARI Pub. 20

Solís Olguín, Felipe, 1976, *Museo de Santa Cecilia Acatitlan: Catálogo de la escultura mexica*, Mexico City

——, 1981, *Escultura del Castillo de Teayo, Veracruz, Mexico: Catálogo*, Mexico City

——, 1991, *Tesoros artísticos del Museo Nacional de Antropología*, Mexico City

Sosa, John Robert, 1985, The Maya Sky, the Maya World: A Symbolic Analysis of Yucatan Maya Cosmology, Ph.D. diss, SUNY Albany

Soustelle, Jacques, 1964, *The Daily Life of the Aztecs on the Eve of the Spanish Conquest*, trans. P. O'Brien, London

Spinden, Herbert J., 1913, *A Study of Maya Art*, *PMM* 6

Spranz, Bodo, 1973, *Los dioses en los códices mexicanos del grupo Borgia: una investigación iconográfica*, Mexico City

Stenzel, Werner, 1976, "The Military and Religious Orders of Ancient Mexico," *42nd ICA*, 7, 179–87

Stephens, John Lloyd, 1841, *Incidents of Travel in Central America, Chiapas, and Yucatan*, 2 vols, New York

——, 1843, *Incidents of Travel in Yucatan*, 2 vols, New York

Stern, Theodore, 1948, *The Rubber-Ball Games of the Americas*, New York

Stevenson, Robert, 1968, *Music in Aztec and Inca Territory*, Berkeley

Stirling, Matthew, 1943, *Stone Monuments of Southern Mexico*, BAEB 138

Stone, Andrea, 1989, "Disconnection, Foreign Insignia, and Political Expansion: Teotihuacan and the Warrior Stelae of Piedras Negras, in J. Berlo and R. Diehl, eds, *Mesoamerica After the Decline of Teotihuacan*, Washington, D.C., 153–72

Stresser-Péan, Guy, 1971, "Ancient Sources on the Huasteca," *HMAI* 11:2, 582–602

Stuart, David, 1984, "Blood Symbolism in Maya Iconography, *RES*, 7/8, 6–20

——, 1987, *Ten Phonetic Syllables*, *RRAMW* 14

——, 1988, "The Río Azul Cacao Pot: Epigraphic Observations on the Function of a Maya Ceramic Vessel, *Antiquity*, 62, 153–57

Stuart, George, 1992, "Quest for Decipherment: A Historical and Biographical Survey of Maya Hieroglyphic Investigation," in E. Danien and R. Sharer, eds, *New Theories on the Ancient Maya*, Philadephia, 1–63

Sullivan, Thelma, 1963, "Nahuatl Proverbs, Conundrums and Metaphors Collected by Sahagún," *ECN*, 4, 93–177

——, 1982, "Tlazolteotl-Ixcuina: The Great Spinner and Weaver," in E. Boone ed., *The Art and Iconography of Late Post-Classic Central Mexico*, Washington, D.C.

Summer Institute of Linguistics, 1974, *Bibliography of the Summer Institute of Linguistics, 1935–72*, ed. Alan C. Wares, Huntington Beach, Calif.

——, 1985, *Bibliografía del Instituto Linguistico de Verano en el Mexico, 1935–1984*, ed. Maria De Boe de Harris and Margarita H. de Daly, Mexico City

Taggart, James, 1983, *Nahuat Myth and Social Structure*, Austin

Taube, Karl A., 1983, "The Teotihuacan Spider Woman," *Journal of Latin American Lore* 9:2, 107–89

——, 1985, "The Classic Maya Maize God: A Reappraisal," *Fifth PRT*, 1983, San Francisco, 171–81

——, 1986, "The Teotihuacan Cave of Origin: The Iconography and Architecture of Emergence Mythology in Mesoamerica and the American Southwest," *RES*, 12, 51–86

——, 1992, *The Major Gods of Ancient Yucatan*, DOS 32

——, **and Bade, Bonnie L.** 1991, *An Appearance of Xiuhtecuhtli in the Dresden Venus Pages*, *RRAMW* 35

Tedlock, Barbara, 1982, *Time and the Highland Maya*, Albuquerque

Tedlock, Dennis, 1985, *Popol Vuh: The Definitive Edition of the Mayan Book of the Dawn of Life and the Glories of Gods and Kings*, New York

Tezozómoc, F. Alvarado, 1944, *Crónica mexicana escrita hacia el año de 1598*, Mexico City

——, 1949, *Crónica mexicáyotl*, Mexico City

Thompson, J. Eric S., 1930, *Ethnology of the Mayas of Southern and Central British Honduras*, Field Mus. of Nat. Hist. Anthro. Series 18:2

——, 1961, "A Blood-drawing Ceremony Painted on a Maya Vase," *ECM*, 1, 13–20

——, 1962, *A Catalog of Maya Hieroglyphs*, Norman, Okla

——, 1970, *Maya History and Religion*, Norman, Okla

——, 1971, *Maya Hieroglyphic Writing*, 3rd edition, Norman, Okla

——, 1972, *A Commentary on the Dresden Codex*, Philadelphia

Torquemada, Juan de, 1975–83, *Monarquía indiana*, ed. M. Leon-Portilla, 7 vols, Mexico City

Tovar Calendar, 1951, ed. G. Kubler and C. Gibson, New Haven

Townsend, Richard, F., 1979, *State and Cosmos in the Art of Tenochtitlan*, DOS 20

——, 1992, *The Aztecs*, London and New York

Tozzer, A. M., 1907, *A Comparative Study of the Mayas and the Lacandones*, London

——, 1957, *Chichen Itzá and its Cenote of Sacrifice*, 2 vols, *PMM* 12

Trejo, Silvia, 1989, *Escultura huaxteca de Río Tamuín*, Mexico City

Troike, Nancy P. 1978, "Fundamental Changes in the Interpretations of the Mixtec Codices," *American Antiquity*, 43:4, 553–68

Umberger, Emily, 1981, Aztec Sculptures, Hieroglyphs, and History, Ph.D. diss, Columbia Univ.

——, 1984, "El trono de Moctezuma," *ECN*, 17, 63–87

Urcid, Javier, 1992, Zapotec Hieroglyphic Writing, Ph.D. diss, Yale Univ.

Vaillant, George C., 1927, The Chronological Significance of Maya Ceramics, Ph.D. diss. Harvard Univ.

Villacorta, J. A., and C. A. Villacorta, 1930, *Códices Maya*, Guatemala City

Villela F., Samuel, 1989, "Cacahuazqui: nuevo testamonio rupestre olmeca en el oriente de Guerrero, *Arqueología*, 2, 37–48

Vogt, Evon Z., 1968, *Zinacantan: A Maya Community in the Highlands of Chiapas*, New York

——, 1976, *Tortillas for the Gods: A Symbolic Analysis of Zinacanteco Rituals*, Cambridge, Mass

Von Winning, Hasso, 1974, *The Shaft Tomb Figures of West Mexico*, Los Angeles

——, 1987, *La Iconografía de Teotihuacan*, 2 vols, Mexico City

——, **and Olga Hammer**, 1972, *Anecdotal Sculpture of West Mexico*, Los Angeles

Waldeck, Frédérick de, 1838, *Voyage pittoresque et archéologique dans la province d'Yucatan pendant les années 1834 et 1836*, Paris

Ward, Fred, 1987, "Jade: Stone of Heaven," *National Geographic Magazine*, 172:3, 282–315

Wauchope, Robert, 1962, *Lost Tribes and Sunken Continents*, London

Wilkerson, S. Jeffrey K., 1980, "Man's Eighty Centuries in Veracruz," *National Geographic Magazine*, 158:2, 203–31

Willey, Gordon R., and Jeremy A. Sabloff, 1980, *A History of American Archaeology*, San Francisco

Winfield Capitaine, Fernando, 1988, *La Estela 1 de La Mojarra, Veracruz, Mexico*, RRAMW 16

Zimmermann, Günter, 1956, *Die Hieroglyphen der Maya-Handschriften*, Hamburg

Sources of Illustrations

Unless otherwise credited, all line drawings are by Karl Taube
a = above c = center b = below
l = left r = right

Frontispiece Museo Nacional de Antropología, Mexico; **page 8a** Courtesy Peabody Museum, Harvard University; **8b** Photo J. A. Sabloff; **12–13** Drawing Hanni Bailey; **16** Photo Mary Miller; **19** Photo © René Millon; **21a** Photo J. A. Sabloff; **21bl** Courtesy University Museum, Philadelphia; **21br** Drawing P. P. Pratt after Ruz; **22** Drawing David Kiphuth, after photo by M. D. Coe; **23** Drawing P. P. Pratt; **25** Reconstruction painting Ignacio Marquina, Instituto Nacional de Antropología e Historia, Mexico; **27** Courtesy Frank Hole; **29** Drawing F. Pratt, after Carlo Gay, *Xochipala: the beginning of Olmec Art*, 1972; **31** After Matos Moctezuma, *Great Temple of the Aztecs*, 1988; **34** After W. J. More and S. M. Higuera, *Códice de Yanhuitlan*, 1940; **41c** Akademische Druck-u. Verlagsanstalt; **43a** After Matos Moctezuma, *Great Temple*, 1988; **43c** Sketch by Karl Weiditz, 1528; **45ca** Museo Nacional de Antropología, Mexico; **45cb** Drawing Linda Schele; **47a** From M. D. Coe, *Mexico*, 1984; **47cb** Akademische Druck-u. Verlagsanstalt; **51a** After J. E. S. Thompson; **51b** Akademische Druck-u. Verlagsanstalt; **53a** Courtesy University Museum, Philadelphia; **53b** From M. D. Coe, *Breaking the Maya Code*, 1992; **55a** Archivo General de la Nación, Mexico; **55b** Photo J. A. Sabloff; **57a** From M. D. Coe, *The Maya*, 1987; **59a** Courtesy American Museum of Natural History; **61a** Photo M. D. Coe; **61c** Theodor-Wilhelm Dänzel, *Mexiko I*, 1923; **61b** Bibliothèque Nationale, Paris; **63a** *Vaticanus No. 3773*, 1902–1903; **65a** After Matos Moctezuma, *Great Temple*, 1988; **65c** Photo Irmgard Groth-Kimball; **65b** Courtesy American Museum of Natural History; **67c** Photo Irmgard Groth-Kimball; **69a** Drawing David Kiphuth, from Coe, *Mexico*, 1984; **71a** Akademische Druck-u. Verlagsanstalt; **73a** Archivo General de la Nación, Mexico; **73c** Courtesty Carter Brown Memorial Library, Brown University, Providence, Rhode Island; **73b** After Hellmuth 1987; **75c** Photo Salvador Guilliem, courtesy Great Temple Project; **77a** After A. Kidder, *Artifacts of Uaxactun, Guatemala*, Carnegie Institution of Washington, Publication 576, 1947; **79a** Courtesy Merseyside County Museums; **79b** Akademische Druck-u. Verlagsan-stalt; **81a, 81c** Photo Irmgard Groth-Kimball; **81b** Vatican Library, Rome; **83c** Photo Salvador Guilliem, courtesy Great Temple Project; **85c** Photo Irmgard Groth-Kimball; **87a** Akademische Druck-u. Verlagsanstalt; **87ca, 87b** Theodor-Wilhelm Dänzel, *Mexiko I*, 1923; **89a** Photo Irmgard Groth-Kimball; **89b** Trustees of the British Museum; **91a** Archivo General de la Nación, Mexico; **91ca** After Miguel Covarrubias, *Indian Art of Mexico and Central Mexico*, 1957: fig. 72; **93a** Akademische Druck-u. Verlagsanstalt; **93b** Photo Salvador Guilliem, courtesy Great Temple Project; **95b** After Matos Moctezuma, *Great Temple*, 1988; **97b** Archivo General de la Nación, Mexico; **99b** From Alfred Tozzer, *A Comparative Study of the Maya and the Lacondones*, 1907; **101c** Akademische Druck-u. Verlagsanstalt; **103a** Photo Salvador Guilliem, courtesy Great Temple Project; **103c** After Henderson 1981: pp. 154–155, fig. 50; **105b** Drawing Linda Schele; **107a** Drawing Linda Schele; **109a** Archivo General de la Nación, Mexico; **111a** Drawing Linda Schele; **113a** From Sahagún, *Historia de las Cosas de Nueva España*, 1905; **115b** *Vaticanus No. 3773*, 1902–1903; **117c** Photo Irmgard Groth-Kimball; **119c** Drawing Linda Schele; **119b** From Codex Magliabechiano, facsimile edition (1904); **123a** Archivo General de la Nación, Mexico; **123b** After Warwick Bray, *Everyday Life of the Aztecs*, 1968, fig. 12 (drawing Eva Wilson); **125cb** After M. D. Coe, *Breaking the Maya Code*, 1992; **127a** After M. D. Coe and Richard Diehl, *In the Land of the Olmec*, 1980 (drawing Felipe Dávalos); **127ca, 127cb** After Peter David Joralemon, *A Study of Olmec Iconography*, 1971; **127b** From Dresden Codex; **129c, 129b** Drawings Linda Schele; **131ar** After Nicholas Hellmuth 1987, drawing S. Reisinger; **131c** After Miguel Covarrubias, *Indian Art of Mexico and Central Mexico*, 1957: fig. 72; **133a** Photo Irmgard Groth-Kimball; **133c** From Codex Magliabechiano, facsimile edition (1904); **133b** From William L. Fash, *Scribes, Warriors and Kings*, 1991: 164 (drawing Barbara Fash); **137a** Bodleian Library, Oxford; **139a** From Eduard Seler, *Gesammelte Abhandlungen zur Amerikanischen Sprach-und Altertumskunde*, 1902–1923; **139b** From Codex Magliabechiano, facsimile edition (1904); **141a** Archivo General de la Nación, Mexico; **141c** Theodor-Wilhelm Dänzel, *Mexiko I*, 1923; **143c** Archivo General de la Nación, Mexico; **145a** Drawing Ian Graham, courtesy Peabody Museum of Archaeology and Ethnology, Harvard University; **147** Drawing Paul Schellhas, courtesy Peabody Museum of Archaeology and Ethnology, Harvard University; **149a** Drawing Stephen Houston, from S. Houston 1989; **149b** Photo Salvador Guilliem, courtesy Great Temple Project; **151a, 151c** Photos Trustees of the British Museum; **151b** Drawing Linda Schele; **153b** Vatican Library, Rome; **155c** Photo courtesy Matthew Stirling and the National Geographic Society; **155b** Photo Irmgard Groth-Kimball; **157b** Photo A. P. Maudslay, courtesy American Museum of Natural History; **159a** After M. D. Coe and Richard Diehl, *In the Land of the Olmec*, 1980 (drawing Felipe Dávalos); **159c** From Codex Borgia; **159b** From Codex Magliabechiano, facsimile edition (1904); **161c** Akademische Druck-u. Verlagsanstalt; **161b** Bibliothèque Nationale, Paris; **165c** Akademische Druck-u. Verlagsanstalt; **165b** Museo Nacional de Antropología, Mexico; **167a** Theodor-Wilhelm Dänzel, *Mexico I*, 1923; **167c** Bodleian Library, Oxford; **167b** Photo Salvador Guilliem, courtesy Great Temple Project; **169a** From Richard F. Townsend, *The Aztecs*, 1992 (drawing Annick Peterson); **171a** Akademische Druck-u. Verlagsanstalt; **171b** Photo Alberto Ruz L; **173a** From Codex Borgia; **173b** Drawing Linda Schele; **177a** Akademische Druck-u. Verlagsanstalt; **177ca** From Matos Moctezuma, *Great Temple*, 1988; **177cb** Drawing David Stuart; **178** Akademische Druck-u. Verlagsanstalt; **181a** From Dresden Codex; **185c** Drawing Ian Graham, from Coe, *The Maya*, 1987; **186b** After Miguel Covarrubias, "El arte 'Olmeca' o de La Venta, *Cuadernos Americanos*, 1946; **187c** Courtesy Merseyside County Museums; **187b** After M. D. Coe, *Breaking the Maya Code*, 1992; **189al** Archivo General de la Nación, Mexico; **189ar** Photo Irmgard Groth-Kimball; **189b** Archivo General de la Nación, Mexico; **191a** Museo Nacional de Antropología, Mexico; **191ca** Akademische Druck-u. Verlagsanstalt; **191cb** *Vaticanus No. 3773*, 1902–3; **193b** After Miguel Covarrubias, *Indian Art of Mexico and Central Mexico*, 1957: fig. 72.